ProActive
Hospitality & Catering

City & Guilds

Professional Cookery

Level 2 Diploma

Series Editor: **Pam Rabone**

Holly Bamunuge · **Trevor Eeles** · **Mark Furr**
Shyam Patiar · **Dereick Rushton** · **Sue J Wood**

working together

Heinemann is an imprint of Pearson Education Limited, a company incorporated in England and Wales, having its registered office at Edinburgh Gate, Harlow, Essex,CM20 2JE.
Registered company number: 872828

Heinemann is the registered trademark of Pearson Education Limited

© City & Guilds and Harcourt Education Ltd 2007

First published 2007

12 11 10 09
10 9 8 7 6 5 4 3 2

British Library aloguing in Publication Data is available from the British Library on request.

ISBN: 978 0 435464 10 3

Designed and typeset by Kamae Design, Oxford
Original illustrations © Harcourt Education Limited and City & Guilds, 2006
Illustrated by Asa Andersson, Ron Dixon, Steiner Lund, Mark Turner and Kamae Design
Printed in the UK by Bath Colour
Cover photo: © City & Guilds
Printed in China (CTPS/02)

Acknowledgements
Harcourt Education Ltd would like to thank Phil Dobson, Leighton Anderson, Adam Pickett, Richard Brocklesby, Rod Burton, Colin Cooper, David Hunter, Ian Monger, Tony Perry and Anthony Wright of the Birmingham College of Food, Tourism and Creative Studies, Iain Baillie, Ben Ross, Gerry Shurman and Rob Zahra of South Downs College; and Andreas Hein of Farnborough College for their invaluable help in the development and trialling of this course.

The authors and publishers would like to thank the following individuals and organisations for permission to reproduce photographs:
Anthony Collins / Alamy – page 159, Black Star / Alamy – page 3, Camelot Theme Park – page 17, Center Parcs – pages 15 and 149, Daniel Templeton / Alamy – page 25, David Crausby / Alamy – page 22, David Gordon / Alamy – page 17, David Marsden/Anthony Blake Photo Library – page 480, Food Features – pages 240 and 405, foodfolio / Alamy – pages 442 and 531, G. TOMSICH / SCIENCE PHOTO LIBRARY – page 278, George Hunter/Superstock – page 498, Graham Kirk / Anthony Blake Photo Library – page 310, Hilary Moore / Anthony Blake Photo Library – page 375, Hoberman Collection UK / Alamy – page 2, isifa Image Service s.r.o. / Alamy – page 267, Joff Lee / Anthony Blake Photo Library – pages 311 and 383, JupiterMedia / Alamy – page 552, LOOK Die Bildagentur der Fotografen GmbH / Alamy – page 8, Lourens Smak / Alamy – page 151, Maximilian Stock Ltd / Anthony Blake Photo Library – page 466, Meat and Livestock Marketing Services – pages 317, 318, 321 and 323, Peter Jordan / Alamy – page 149, Philip Wilkins / Anthony Blake Photo Library – page 441, Profimedia.CZ s.r.o. / Alamy – page 250, Roddy Paine/FoodAndDrink – pages 300 and 312, SHOUT / Alamy – page 18, Sian Irvine / Anthony Blake Photo Library – page 352, Studio Adna / Anthony Blake Photo Library – page 466, Tim Hill / Anthony Blake Photo Library – pages 350 and 477, WoodyStock / Alamy – page 45

The authors and publishers are grateful to those who have given permission to reproduce material. Every effort has been made to contact copyright holders of material reproduced in this book. Any omissions will be rectified in subsequent printings if notice is given to the publishers.
Nash, C. (1998) *Food Safety: First Principles*, Chartered Institue of Environmental Health Reproduced by permission of CIEH – pages 42 and 48; Wimpy International Ltd. – pages 16 and 146; Aramark UK – pages 27 and 30; Center Parcs – pages 15, 29 and 162; Camelot Theme Park – pages 17 and 18; British Hospitality Association – pages 11, 12 and 15; Accor – page 114; Holroyd Howe – page 26; *Caterer and Hotelkeeper* magazine; Springboard UK.

Crown copyright material is reproduced with the permission of the Controller of HMSO and the Queen's Printer for Scotland.

Websites
There are links to relevant websites in this book. In order to ensure that the links are up to date, that the links work, and that the sites are not inadvertently linked to sites that could be considered offensive, we have made the links available on the Heinemann website at www.heinemann.co.uk/hotlinks. When you access the site the express code is 4103P.

Contents

Introduction

This book has been written to support the practical skills and knowledge required for the City & Guilds Level 2 Diploma in Professional Cookery. The aims of the Diploma are:

○ To provide a broad understanding of the hospitality and catering sector and the vocational skills required.

○ To provide bite-sized chunks of learning.

○ To combat fear of failure by ensuring that all achievement is recognised.

○ To encourage progression by enabling candidates to build a qualification based on their own needs.

○ To provide a highly-valued qualification.

The Diploma consists of 14 units that are assessed in different ways (see pages iv–v and Figure 1). It is possible to take individual units (see page vii) but in order to achieve the full Diploma you have to:

○ complete all of the units

○ take a number of practical tests.

Methods of assessment

Your tutor will prepare you so that you are ready to take an assessment. The Diploma is assessed in several different ways.

Unit number	Unit title	GLH	Assessment
201	Investigate the catering and hospitality industry	20	Theory assignment
202	Food safety in catering	9	Online multiple-choice test
203	Health and safety in catering and hospitality	10	Theory assignment
204	Healthier foods and special diets	10	Theory assignment
205	Kitchen operations, costs and menu planning	40	Theory assignment
206	Applying workplace skills	21	Theory assignment
207	Prepare and cook stocks, soups and sauces	40	Practical test and short-answer questions
208	Prepare and cook fruit and vegetables	40	Practical test and short-answer questions
209	Prepare and cook meat and offal	60	Practical test and short-answer questions
210	Prepare and cook poultry	40	Practical test and short-answer questions

211	Prepare and cook fish and shellfish	40	Practical test and short-answer questions
212	Prepare and cook rice, pasta, grains and egg dishes	20	Practical test and short-answer questions
213	Prepare and cook desserts and puddings	50	Practical test and short-answer questions
214	Prepare and cook bakery products	50	Practical test and short-answer questions
	Total	**450**	

Figure 1: Assessment methods and Guided Learning Hours (GLH) for each unit. GLH are a guide to the likely delivery time of each unit.

Practical tests: This key part of the qualification will be tested in a variety of ways with varying durations. Some practicals will be graded pass, credit or distinction. You are required to achieve a minimum of a pass across all practicals in order to achieve the qualification. Part of the practical assessment will take the form of a synoptic test; this means it covers a number of different units. You should be told what you will be expected to cook three weeks before the test. You should prepare – and keep – a time plan, your recipes and an equipment list. Your tutor should also give you the grading criteria so you are clear about what you need to do to achieve a pass, credit or distinction. You may like to take a photograph of the food you have cooked. The synoptic tests are important because they demonstrate that you can manage your time and resources as well as cook.

Theory assignments: These are paper-based research and report type activities. You will be given the assignment and should read this against the grading criteria so that you are clear about what you need to produce to get the highest grade possible. Always read the assignment carefully. It is your chance to show what you have learned.

The assignments are divided into tasks. You need to complete them all successfully. The tasks may cover the key skills requirements so you may be asked to produce a variety of types of evidence, e.g. to write and deliver a presentation and then answer questions, or to produce a report.

Your centre will give you a time period within which you must complete each assignment. They may be completed away from the centre, in your own time and at your own pace.

You can ask your tutor for some feedback about how your grade could be improved before the final submission of your work. Once the assignment has been formally submitted the grade awarded will stand.

Short-answer questions: These are used in the practical units to check your underpinning knowledge. They will be taken under supervised conditions and are closed-book tests.

On-line multiple choice test: Each question will normally have one correct answer and three incorrect answers. The test will be taken under supervised conditions.

Grades

The Diploma is graded at:

- pass
- credit
- distinction.

Grades for synoptic practical tests: Once the practical test has been marked your tutor should provide you with written and oral feedback. This will allow you to see if there are areas of your performance that require improvement so you can work towards improving your grades. If you do not fulfil the Pass criteria for the practical test you can re-sit it but you will only be able to gain a Pass or Fail.

Grades for theory assignments: To achieve a particular grade in your theory assignments you must achieve all the points for that grade. For example, if a candidate met all the Pass criteria but only one of the Credit criteria, they would receive a Pass grade. To gain a Distinction all the criteria must be met for every grade.

Task	Pass	Credit	Distinction
	The candidate needs to have	**The candidate needs to achieve everything at pass grade and**	**The candidate needs to achieve everything at pass and credit grade and**
A	demonstrated understanding of the requirements and produced the minimum evidence required provided evidence which demonstrates knowledge relevant to the task	demonstrated sound understanding of the tasks and provided clear and relevant evidence shown the use of a range of relevant sources/resources presented the task well and in an organised and logical sequence demonstrated evidence of analysing research information	demonstrated excellent understanding of the tasks with evidence of analysis and evaluation critically evaluated a wide range of sources/resources which are clearly referenced provided evidence which demonstrates a good breadth and depth of knowledge that has been used to good effect in the task presented the task to a high level provided evidence of creative and original thoughts completed the task with minimal assistance

Figure 2: Grading descriptors for a theory assignment

Unit route overview

In order to develop your skills in specific areas the qualification is split into units which can be taught and assessed separately. The unit route is a particularly good way of building skills and allows flexibility in how the content of the unit is delivered. So, it is possible to cover a 20-hour unit over two and half days or over five weeks.

Once the content has been taught your tutor will arrange a 'Practical observation' to assess your skills. Your tutor will tell you what dishes you need to prepare. You need to successfully complete all the dishes. The observation will not cover everything you have learnt in that unit. Each Practical observation has a time limit although in some observations a specified amount of extra time can be added.

Once all the dishes have been completed a marking sheet will be filled in. However, you will still be expected to work in a safe, hygienic and organised manner throughout the practical observation.

Once you have achieved all of the units, if you want to achieve the full qualification, you will need to take a set number of practical tests, called **synoptic tests**, to prove that you can organise your workflow to produce a number of dishes in a set time while working in a safe, hygienic, efficient and organised way. These tests are more demanding than the practical observations because you have to produce a number of dishes in a set time period. In order to be successful you will need to plan your time well and practise the dishes before the test. You will be graded at Pass, Credit or Distinction. Your tutor will explain how you can achieve the grades before the tests.

Definition

Synoptic tests: these tests cover different parts of the qualification at the same time. They are important because they demonstrate that you can manage your time and resources as well as cook.

Did you know?

A quality assurance person, someone working within your centre, will check some aspects of your work. This is to make sure that the allocation of grades is fair. A City & Guilds representative, called an external verifier, will then check that the quality assurance meets national standards.

Key features

Look out for the following special features as you work through the book.

All important technical words are defined to help you develop your underpinning knowledge.

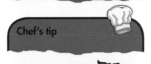

Interesting and useful culinary facts.

Useful practical ideas and good advice – nearly as good as having a real chef to help you!

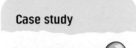

Ideas for healthy alternative ingredients and methods.

These short real-life case studies tell you about the experiences of other people working in the catering industry.

Important points to promote good practice in the kitchen and reminders about safe working practices.

These independent research activities help you explore new areas and extend your knowledge.

When you see this feature you will know that there is a related video clip for you to watch. The ProActive Catering e-learning site can be accessed at http://www.proactive-online.co.uk

This feature helps you understand what you need to do to get the higher grades.

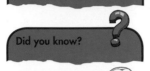

Short practical activities for you to try in the classroom. Sometimes they may provide evidence for your portfolio.

At the end of each chapter there is a set of questions to check your knowledge. These are a useful way of revising the underpinning knowledge for a unit ready for assessment.

E-learning

The ProActive Catering e-learning site can be accessed at http://www.proactive-online.co.uk. If your centre has a licence then you will be given a login and password.

There are various types of electronic resources available on the site for independent learning:

- Video clips clearly demonstrate skills, e.g. how to cut a chicken for sauté.
- Interactive tutorials teach you about a specific topic, e.g. food safety. At the end of the tutorial there is a short multiple-choice test which checks your understanding.
- You can print off recipes, menus and worksheets as directed by your assessor.

Investigating the catering and hospitality industry

1

This chapter covers the following outcomes from Diploma unit 201: Investigating the catering and hospitality industry

- Outcome 201:1 Demonstrate knowledge of the hospitality and catering industry
- Outcome 202:2 Demonstrate knowledge of national and international employment opportunities available in the hospitality and catering industry

Working through this chapter could also provide evidence for the following Key Skills:

C2.1, C2.2a, C2.2b, C2.3, N2.1, N2.2a, N2.2c, N2.3, ICT2.1, ICT2.2, ICT2.3, LP2.1, LP2.2, LP2.3

In this chapter you will learn how to:

Identify the structure, scope and size of the hospitality and catering industry and the key influences on its development

Explain the main features of establishments within each sector and their importance to the national economy

Describe the main job roles and responsibilities in a catering establishment and the difference in roles and conditions in the different sectors

Identify the legal requirements to work within the law

Identify sources of information about the industry nationally and internationally

Describe the functions of different professional associations

The hospitality and catering industry

It is a great time to join the hospitality and catering industry. Over the last few years it has become increasingly vibrant, exciting and forward-thinking. The importance of the industry is set to increase, helped by London hosting the Olympic Games in 2012. The eyes of the world will be on the UK, looking at the standards we set for catering and hospitality for the event, and beyond.

Structure of the UK hospitality and catering industry

The structure of hospitality and catering reflects the different organisations that make up the industry, and how they relate to each other.

The hospitality and catering industry can be divided into:
o the commercial sector, and
o the public service sector.

Commercial sector

The commercial sector covers businesses where accommodation and/or catering are the main source of income, e.g. hotels and restaurants. Those working in the commercial sector provide food, drink and accommodation to UK residents and overseas visitors.

Did you know?
There are about 1.64 million people employed in hospitality and catering in the UK. This is about 6 per cent of the total working population in the UK.

Did you know?
The commercial sector is sometimes known as the profit sector.

Figure 1.1 Fine dining restaurant at the Ritz hotel, Piccadilly, London

Public service sector

In the public service sector accommodation and/or catering are not the main business interest but these services are still needed for customers, staff and visitors. It covers hospitality and catering occupations in non-hospitality industries, e.g. hospitals, residential homes, schools and colleges and the workplace. These services may not be paid for directly by the customer or the customer may pay only part of the cost if the services are **subsidised**.

Hospitality and catering services may be:

○ owned or managed 'in house', e.g. school meals may be managed by the local council, or

○ contracted out to another organisation that provides hospitality (often called a contract caterer).

See Figure 1.3 for more information.

At one time the public service sector was mainly welfare catering, e.g. in hospitals. Contract catering for industry falls within the public service sector but in terms of conditions of service and skills needed by employees it often has more in common with the commercial sector; see page 2.

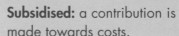

Definition
Subsidised: a contribution is made towards costs.

Did you know?
The Public Service Sector is sometimes known as the Not for Profit Sector or the Cost Sector.

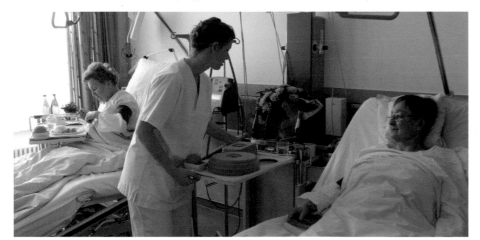

Figure 1.2: Food being served in a hospital

Operations

The hospitality and catering industry provides three main operations:

○ catering

○ accommodation

○ hospitality.

Top marks!
When researching, try to collect different information from different sources, e.g. websites, professional magazines, local guides and advertisements. Find out about national and international companies.

Catering

Catering operations involve preparing, distributing, finishing and serving food and drink. Commercial establishments (such as fast food outlets, cafés, restaurants, motorway service areas, pubs and bars) and public sector establishments (such as school canteens) are all types of catering operation. Catering operations are very diverse and range from a small café run by the owner to a company with a **chain** of restaurants employing hundreds of staff to a specialist caterer contracted to provide food and drink at a football game.

> **Definition**
>
> **Chain:** when there are a lot of establishments that operate under a particular name, e.g. McDonald's operates a chain of fast food restaurants.

Accommodation

Accommodation operations are about providing somewhere for people to stay. It includes **serviced accommodation** like guesthouses, and **self-catering accommodation** like caravans and chalets. Some accommodation-only functions are similar to those in a catering establishment, e.g. taking reservations and receiving customers. Providing accommodation involves other areas of operation, however, that are different to those of a catering establishment.

> **Definition**
>
> **Serviced accommodation:** some catering is provided, e.g. bed and breakfast.
> **Self-catering accommodation:** customers cater for themselves.

Hospitality

Hospitality operations provide accommodation, catering and service, e.g. an hotel. These aspects may be divided between departments in a large hotel. In a small family hotel just one or two people are likely to run the whole operation.

See Figure 1.3 for more information.

Types of establishment	Descriptions/examples
Commercial sector	
Hotels	○ Provide food, drink and accommodation ○ Range from low cost with restricted catering to expensive 5-star hotels with full restaurant service, a range of places to eat and 24-hour room-service menu ○ May accommodate conferences ○ Include: independent, owner-run hotels; large chains, e.g. Hilton and Intercontinental; independent consortium, e.g. Best Western; boutique hotels; country house hotels ○ Demand and number/type of staff varies according to quality, reputation and location

Lodges	o Provide basic, low-cost accommodation with tea and coffee making facilities
	o Usually near motorways
	o Minimal staffing, with evening shift usually finishing by 11pm
	o High demand with low-cost leisure travellers and people travelling on business
	o Standard, modern designs
	o Often next to restaurants, e.g. Whitbread's Premier Travel Inn is always next to one of their Brewers Fayre or Beefeater restaurants.
Guest houses	o Provide accommodation with a limited range of catering
	o Limited hours of service
	o Low-cost
	o Improving quality has increased popularity
	o Run by one person or just a few staff.
Restaurants	o Provide food and drink
	o Includes independents and chains
	o Can be conventional, speciality, themed, e.g. La Tasca tapas bars and restaurants or ethnic, e.g. Chinese food
	o Seated dining ranging from those offering quick service to fine dining
	o Prices, staffing, opening hours, demand and design vary according to brand, style, quality, location and menu offered.
Traditional cafés	o Provide food and drink
	o Independent
	o Full fried breakfast-style menu with non-alcoholic drinks
	o Low-cost in basic surroundings
	o Minimum staffing
	o Opening hours to suit local hours, often daytime only.
Chain café outlets	o More sophisticated international café style, e.g. Café Rouge
	o Offer interesting meals and alcoholic drinks
	o Opening hours are daytime or day and evening
	o Staffing, prices and demand vary according to location, quality and reputation.
Fast food outlets	o Limited choice standard menu
	o Food to eat in and/or take away
	o Low cost
	o Little or no waiting
	o Some, e.g. local fish and chip shops, open only at lunchtime and in the evening
	o Chain outlets, e.g. McDonald's, often have long hours or 24-hour opening
	o Mainly low-skilled staff
	o Located in areas of high demand, e.g. shopping centres
	o Often counter service with multiple till points

Travel and leisure outlets: trains, airlines, coaches	o Standards of catering can depend on type of seat booked, e.g. standard, business or first class o Catering provided at terminals, motorway service stations and on board o Often contract caterers o On airlines, tray service is by airline staff, serving pre-prepared food o Usually only self-service drinks on board a coach, except for executive coaches o Train service varies from refreshments brought round on trolley or purchased in the buffet car, to good-quality meals in the dining car and fine dining on the Orient Express o Demand varies according to length of journey, standard of catering and whether it is included in the cost of travel o Hours are linked to departure and travelling times, often 24-hour opening o Prices and staffing vary.
Travel and leisure outlets: cruises	o Provide accommodation and extensive catering in a wide range of establishments o Very high standards o Opening hours are linked to stopovers, sailing times and type of establishment o Demand is high as food is normally included in the cost of the cruise and passengers have no alternatives while at sea o Large numbers of staff at all levels in kitchen, restaurants, bars, coffee bars, etc. o Staff often employed through an agency o Employ a mix of nationalities.
Tourism and recreation outlets: museums, historic buildings, theme parks, visitor attractions	o Catering should be part of the 'visitor experience' o Frequently fast-food outlets or quick service restaurants o Some have well-known brands o Staffing according to the outlet types o Much use of Catering Assistants to serve prepared or partly prepared food o Large theme parks like Disney have fine dining restaurants o Prices may be slightly more than outside the attraction o Opening hours match those of the attraction o High demand at peak times.
Retail store outlets	o Food courts o Frequently fast-food outlets or quick service restaurants o Some have well-known brands o Staffing according to the outlet types o Much use of Catering Assistants to serve prepared or partly prepared food o Little or no waiting o Opening hours in line with store or shopping centre o Department stores like Harvey Nicholls or Harrods offer a range of high-quality eating establishments.

Event and outside catering	o One-off events or functions o Catering matched to the needs of the event or function o Range from burger vans at a flower show to VIP catering for corporate clients at a racecourse to a wedding at a private house o Contract caterers, sometimes with extra staff o Mobile equipment.
Public service sector	
Employee catering – staff restaurants, cafeterias, directors' dining rooms, catering for business meetings, special events, etc.	o Often contracted out to specialist catering companies (also called Food service management) o Opening hours, menus, design, etc. match the needs of the individual site o Often the business subsidises costs to provide good-quality low-cost meals o Demand is high, particularly at remote sites o Some employers are removing subsidies to reduce costs, which brings employee catering nearer to the commercial sector o Excellent conditions for many contract catering staff who cater for employees, reflected in job titles, pay, etc.
NHS hospitals	o Usually a tray service at set times o Patients do not pay directly o Often subsidised, but a low budget per head o Charged staff meals and catering for visitors normally provided o Usually open to match main working and visiting hours o Some or all of these services are often contracted out o High volume as patients rely on catering provided.
Private hospitals	o Meals paid for by patients or their medical insurance o May be in-house or contracted out o Staff meals may be subsidised o Greater flexibility in meal times and better quality meals.
Residential homes	o Catering and other services may be provided by the individual home, a direct service from the local authority, or contracted out o Some subsidisation o In homes for old people and children this is often the only food residents will have access to o Usually set times for meals and refreshments, although drinks may be provided on request during the night o Private residential homes may include catering in the overall charge or make separate charges.

School meals and college canteens	o Catering may be controlled by the individual school, a direct service from the local authority, or contracted out
	o Local authority has a duty to provide a paid meal in school where parents request it
	o Now emphasis on healthier menus, and government guidelines on nutrition
	o Opening hours usually just fit in with school lunchtimes
	o Some schools and college canteens provide breakfast, lunch and refreshments and provide for evening and weekend courses
	o Emphasis on quick service
	o Low/reasonable cost
	o Some subsidies.
Prison services	o Catering may be run by the Prison Service or contracted out
	o Usually set meal times
	o Low budgets for food costs
	o Minimum staffing supplemented by food being prepared by inmates
	o High demand as no alternatives
	o Separate, higher standard catering for prison staff
	o Some innovative schemes, e.g. where inmates are given training and achieve qualifications.

Figure 1.3 Summary of main types of establishment and their characteristics showing the type of operation and the sector to which they belong.

Figure 1.4 A very specialised type of operation: a buffet on a cruise ship

Scope of the catering and hospitality industry

In every town you will find many different types of hospitality and catering establishment. The scope of their operations will vary a great deal.

Regional, national, international, multinational, global operations

Many of today's multinational hospitality and catering companies began with just one person opening an establishment which became popular in the local area. Figure 1.5 shows the development stages of a business.

> **Definition**
>
> **Local:** operates within a small, defined area
> **Regional:** operates within the surrounding local area
> **National:** operates throughout one country
> **International:** operates in more than one country
> **Multinational:** this type of business has a significant proportion of operations abroad
> **Global:** this type of business operates on a worldwide scale.

Business type	Description	Area of operation	Examples
Sole trader	○ A sole trader is self-employed and can start trading immediately, subject to any specific licences ○ A sole trader is responsible for all the liabilities of their business, e.g. debts.	Local	Sandwich bar Café Bed and breakfast
Ordinary partnership	○ A partnership of two or more people has no legal status. It is just a means of linking two or more self-employed people in a simple business structure ○ Partners are personally liable for any debts incurred.	Local/regional	Bistro Take-away Guest house
Private limited company	○ Most small businesses (except sole traders and partnerships) set up as private limited companies ○ The term 'limited' means the company's finances are separate from the personal finances of the owners ○ Shareholders in limited liability companies are not responsible for company debts ○ The company must be registered at Companies House, produce and file annual accounts and returns, pay corporation tax if due.	Regional/national	Restaurant – single/multiple/chain Hotel – single/multiple/chain Contract caterer
Public limited company (PLC)	○ Designed for wider share ownership and can raise much more capital ○ Subject to more controls ○ The company can offer shares to the public, and may also apply to be listed on the Stock Exchange, so that shares can be bought and sold more easily ○ The original owners may have less control of the business, or lose control completely.	Regional/ national/ international/ multinational/ global	Large chain of themed restaurants Chain of branded hotels

Figure 1.5 Business development stages

Case study — Pizza Express

Gondola Holdings is one of the fastest growing casual dining groups in the UK and Ireland. It owns the Ask, Zizzi and Pizza Express brands. It employs over 11,000 staff and served 30 million meals in 2005/06. Visit the Pizza Express website. A link has been made available at www.heinemann.co.uk/hotlinks. Just follow the links and enter the express code 4103P. When did Pizza Express start? How did it develop? How many restaurants are there now? In which countries?

Investigate!

Choose a multinational or international hospitality or catering business or brand that interests you. Produce a short fact sheet about the stages in its development and operations. Include brief details about its history and development and present-day operations, e.g. sector, business type, the countries in which it operates, number and range of establishments, staffing. Discuss your findings in a group.

Definition

Enterprise: business. An enterprise is often a small or family business.

Other business types

SMEs

There are lots of SMEs (small, micro and medium-sized **enterprises**) in hospitality and catering. SMEs tend to be more flexible than large companies. Their owners often have new ideas, creativity and a 'can-do' attitude. They need support that is specifically for small businesses, e.g. in the European Economic Area SMEs can apply for special grants and loans. Within the UK there is also lots of help for small or family hospitality and catering businesses, e.g. the UK Environmental Agency's website for SMEs contains guidance for guest houses, small hotels, camping and caravan sites, restaurants, pubs and bars, mobile catering, etc. about meeting environmental legislation. A link has been made available at www.heinemann.co.uk/hotlinks. Just follow the links and enter the express code 4103P.

Franchises

If you have ever bought something to eat or drink at a Wimpy Bar or from Domino's Pizza, then you were a customer in a franchised catering establishment. A franchise is where a company (the

Did you know?

KFC started as a small restaurant at a Kentucky roadside service station. There are now outlets across North and South America, Europe, Asia and Australia. KFC is part of the American based company YUM! Brands Inc, which is one of the largest fast food operators in the world.

franchisor) lets its brand name be used in return for payment. There are strict policies and procedures which must be followed to make sure the brand is protected. Franchising is often used as a way of rapidly expanding a brand.

Size and importance of the hospitality and catering industry

Workforce

As over 80 per cent of the population of the UK lives in England, the vast majority of hospitality and catering employees work in England, followed by Scotland, then Wales and then Northern Ireland. Hospitality and catering employers and staff make important contributions to national insurance and corporation tax and income tax. Figure 1.6 shows that there was an increase in the number of people employed in hospitality and catering between 2000 and 2004, which was followed by a drop in the number of people employed in 2005.

Did you know?
One in ten people worldwide now work in the hospitality industry. In the UK, 1.64 million people work in hospitality and catering. Forecasts suggest that by the London Olympics in 2012 an extra 846,000 employees will be needed.

Type of establishment	2000	2004	2005
Hotels	245,000	247,071	238,400
Restaurants	446,300	518,738	513,700
Pubs, clubs and bars	383,100	368,394	333,900
Food and service management	167,000	179,589	178,300
Hospitality services	336,300	402,062	379,900
Other (includes travel and tourism services, gambling, holiday parks, youth hostels and attractions)	255,000	233,261	241,400
Total	**1,832,650**	**1,968,753**	**1,885,600**

Figure 1.6 The number of people that work in each type of establishment from 2000 to 2005. Note that individual sums may not add up to totals for statistical reasons.

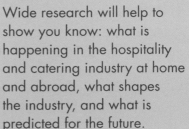

Top marks!
Wide research will help to show you know: what is happening in the hospitality and catering industry at home and abroad, what shapes the industry, and what is predicted for the future.

Number of establishments and total turnover

Look at Figure 1.7. You will see that the number of hotels declined between 2003 and 2005. This is a result of the closure of small hotels and guest houses. The remaining hotels are larger so the number of meals served and the income from food and drink sales has increased. The number of pubs also declined. However, the number of restaurants increased by almost 2 per cent and the number of quick-service establishments also increased. Notice that, in terms of total numbers, the commercial sector is much larger than the public service sector.

Hospitality, catering, leisure, travel and tourism establishments in the UK are estimated to generate over £135 billion a year in sales turnover. Tourism and leisure contribute around 4 per cent to the UK's **GDP**.

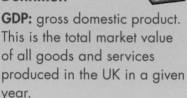

Definition

GDP: gross domestic product. This is the total market value of all goods and services produced in the UK in a given year.

Type of establishment	2003	2004	2005
Hotels	47,725	47,389	47,009
Restaurants	25,954	26,208	26,416
Quick service	29,459	29,496	29,645
Pubs	51,352	51,267	51,046
Leisure	18,869	18,995	19,121
Total commercial sector	**173,369**	**173,355**	**173,237**
Business and industry	20,875	20,839	20,625
Health care	30,926	31,048	31,384
Education	34,663	34,630	34,663
Ministry of Defence	3,078	3,076	3,073
Total public service sector	**89,542**	**89,593**	**89,745**
TOTAL	**262,910**	**262,948**	**262,982**

Figure 1.7 Estimated number of establishments in all hospitality and catering sectors

Try this!

Produce a bar chart to show the number of people working within hospitality and catering in the UK in the last five years.

Produce a pie chart to show numbers of commercial establishments and public service sector establishments in 2005.

Factors affecting the hospitality and catering industry

Inflation

Inflation influences how much spare money customers have to spend on eating out. Low **rates of inflation** have for many years helped keep costs down, which in turn has kept the price of eating out down. Inflation rates began to rise in 2006, which makes it more expensive to borrow money and increases the cost of goods, staff wages, etc. It is therefore likely that selling prices will begin to rise slightly.

Tourism

Tourism is important to the success of many economies around the world. Spending by overseas visitors and UK residents on holiday in the UK is very important to the commercial sector. Almost 30 million tourists visited the UK in 2005 and spent nearly £14,250 million.

In 2005 UK residents took nearly 139 million trips within the UK and spent £22,667 million. The pie chart below shows how this money was spent:

Figure 1.9: How UK residents spent money on UK holidays

> **Definition**
>
> **Inflation:** increase in average prices. If prices rise there is a fall in the value of money, as people have to spend more money to buy the same items.
> **Rate of inflation:** a measure of how much prices rise (or fall), usually given as a percentage by comparing prices at two points in time.

Figure 1.8: Tourism is very important to the UK economy

> **Try this!**
> With a partner discuss why tourism has a big influence on the hospitality and catering industry.

Hospitality and catering establishments
Commercial sector

Hotels and other hospitality providers

Investigate!

Visit the website for the trafalgar hotel in London. A link has been made available at www.heinemann.co.uk/hotlinks. Just follow the links and enter the express code 4103P.

How many guest rooms does it have? What are they like? What is Rockwell Upper? What are the bar's opening hours? What type of food is served at the hotel and at what times? Make an information poster about the hotel.

Case study — Accor international hotel group

In 2006 Accor was the fifth largest hotel operator in the UK with 93 hotels (13,529 rooms). In June 2006 Accor had 480,036 rooms in 140 countries and employed 168,500 staff.

The group began in France in 1967 with the Novotel hotel chain concept, followed by Ibis in 1974 and Formule 1 in 1985. Accor has successfully developed its hotel portfolio to cover all budgets from luxury to low-cost hotels. Accor also owns Wagons-Lits onboard train services, Eurest food service management and the Relais Autoroute motorway restaurants among others.

Accor has lots of employee benefits, e.g. good salaries, annual profit-sharing, a savings plan and stock options, staff training, intern and apprenticeship programmes. Three-quarters of hotel managers got their jobs through internal promotions. Staff can move from country to country if they have the language skills.

A link has been made available to their website at www.heinemann.co.uk/hotlinks. Just follow the links and enter the express code 4103P.

Investigate!

Find a website that is promoting a large, city centre hotel and another that is promoting a small, rural hotel. Compare the two establishments.

Investigate!

Find a website that is promoting a business hotel with conference and exhibition facilities. Now find one that is promoting a hotel aimed at the family holiday market. Compare the two establishments.

Investigate!

Center Parcs is part of the commercial sector and operates holiday villages in the UK, Denmark, Holland, France, Germany and Belgium. About 90 per cent of their staff are employed from the local area, so they are a major contributor to the local economy. Download the Student Information Pack from the website. A link has been made available at www.heinemann.co.uk/hotlinks. Just follow the links and enter the express code 4103P.

Prepare a short talk about Center Parcs. Talk about the accommodation available, the restaurants, staffing and other points that interest you.

Try this!

Worksheet 56

In two minutes, write down as many establishments as you can think of that provide accommodation in your local area. Now categorise them into:

- *commercial sector/public services sector*
- *hotels/guest houses/lodges/residential homes*
- *budget hotels/mid-class hotels/high-quality hotels*
- *restaurant on site, no restaurant*
- *local/regional/national/international.*

Restaurants

The table below shows the top ten restaurant groups in 2006. There are many familiar brand names, but note that the ownership of the brands can change rapidly.

Owner	No. of outlets	Selected brands
Mitchells & Butlers	799	Harvester, All Bar One, Toby
Spirit Group	510	Chef & Brewer, Two for One, Miller's
Gondola	505	Pizza Express, Ask, Zizzi
Restaurant Group	279	Frankie & Benny's, Garfunkel's
Wimpy	250	Wimpy
People's Restaurant Group	235	Little Chef (sold late 2006 – operating problems)
Tragus	162	Café Rouge, Bella Italia
Whitbread	157	TGI Friday's
Greene King	90	Hungry Horse
Nando's	133	Nando's

Figure 1.10: The top ten restaurant groups in 2006

Case study – Wimpy

The Wimpy brand was created in Chicago in the 1930s. It can now be found in many countries. Wimpy has been in operation in the UK since the mid-1950s and has been franchising for over 40 years. Wimpy International Ltd is one of the largest independent chain restaurants in the UK.

Wimpy now has over 270 franchised restaurants and units. Opening hours vary, depending on location, e.g. 24-hour opening in a motorway service station or opening for just a few hours on match days in a football stadium. Staffing varies according to the opening hours and the anticipated number of customers.

There are three types of Wimpy outlet in the UK. What are they? What type of locations are they suitable for? What type of menu do they offer? What support and benefits do franchisees receive?

A link to their website has been made available at www.heinemann.co.uk/hotlinks. Just follow the links and enter the express code 4103P.

Did you know?

'Wimpy' is named after the burger-eating character J. Wellington Wimpy from the cartoon strip *Popeye*.

Did you know?

The British Franchise Association represents franchise companies and promotes good standards. A link to their website has been made available at www.heinemann.co.uk/hotlinks. Just follow the links and enter the express code 4103P.

Travel and leisure

Case study – RoadChef

People who travel by road need to stop from time to time for refreshments, a comfort break and a rest. The RoadChef Coach Support Team help people in the coach travel industry plan routes and pre-book into RoadChef motorway service areas, so the service station is prepared for the coach's arrival.

How many sites do RoadChef have? How many have a Costa Coffee outlet? How many have a Premier Travel Inn? What other services do they offer? What benefits do they offer employees?

A link to their website has been made available at www.heinemann.co.uk/hotlinks. Just follow the links and enter the express code 4103P.

Figure 1.11: Coaches at a RoadChef

Case study — Wagons–Lits

Wagons–Lits trains (part of the Accor Group) have an on-board attendant. They work from a small galley and look after passengers on French Railways' overnight sleepers, making sure everything is clean and in order, and distributing water, breakfasts and other products. Prior experience in a hotel is helpful and the position can lead on to Sleeping Car Attendant and possibly to On-board Services Manager, or back into hotel reception work.

Figure 1.12: Food being served by an on-board train attendant on the Gatwick Express

Try this!

Think of a recent journey you have made. Describe the catering available, e.g. type of food and drink, amount of choice, how it was served, name of brand/catering company.

Tourism and recreation outlets

Case study — Camelot theme park

Camelot is a theme park in Lancashire. There are around 350,000 visitors per year, mainly families and school children. The aim is to serve food quickly as customers want to make the most of their time at Camelot. There is a range of fast food catering units to suit different customers and different locations. They include:

- Wimpy outlets, 2
- Fish and chip shops, 2
- Coffee shop, 2
- Pasta unit, 1
- Ice cream parlour, 4
- Rollover hot dogs, 3
- Hot drinks and snacks units, 2

Groups can book a buffet lunch with the Catering Manager. The Park Manager holds a licence so that alcoholic drinks can be served if requested in advance.

Camelot is open for around 145 days each year. The park opens at 10 a.m. but closes at different times according to the season. The catering outlets have different opening hours to the park based on their location and customer demand. The approach has to be flexible to meet the needs of customers, operate effectively and control costs. Savings are made by reducing opening hours and/or reducing staffing when demand is low.

Except for the Catering Manager, most staff are seasonal and part-time. Students often take on these types of jobs. Camelot's main competitors for staff are the retail trade and local catering outlets. In a typical year the park will employ:

- 70 Catering Assistants
- 6 Team Leaders
- 3 Supervisors
- 1 person in the stores.

Staffing costs use over 25 per cent of Camelot's income. The budgeted income in a recent operating year was £4.5m, with wages of £1.125m. That means, for every £1 the park takes in sales, 25p goes on paying wages and salaries.

Staff receive full training, a free uniform and are given a pass to the park for them and their family. They work on rotas. There are two staff parties each year. In January or February Catering Assistants who have done well will be asked to come back and work for the next season; they often get a promotion and Camelot's policy is to promote from within.

A link to their website has been made available at www.heinemann. co.uk/hotlinks. Just follow the links and enter the express code 4103P.

Catering Manager
in charge of all catering operations

↑

Catering Supervisor
supervises several units

↑

Catering Team Leader
looks after one unit

↑

Catering Assistant
prepares food and drink, serves customers, cleans

Figure 1.13: Progression route at Camelot

Public services sector

School meals

The main purpose of a school or college is education, but hungry and thirsty students, staff and visitors need suitable on-site catering facilities.

Figure 1.14: Food being served in a primary school

Case study – Hertfordshire Catering

Hertfordshire Catering provides school meals for Hertfordshire Education Authority. They serve 36,000 primary school meals a day and provide catering services to 44 secondary and middle schools. The team of 1,600 staff aim to provide high-quality, tempting and nutritious meals within a fixed budget. The current Head of Catering has extensive experience of the school meals service as a Cook Manager, Area Manager and Business Development Manager. The service sent out 90,000 menu leaflets to parents across the county to launch the new primary menu, which included a nutritional analysis.

Investigate!

Research a commercial hotel restaurant, themed restaurant, quick service restaurant or fast-food outlet. Find out the opening hours, types of menu, price ranges, number of staff, type of uniforms worn, how the food is served, what it looks like and whether it has a popular brand name. What does it have in common with your college canteen? How is it different? Prepare a short talk.

Top marks!

Remember to keep a note of all your sources of information, plus copies where appropriate. They can then be checked by you or by someone reading your assignment.

Professional bodies

Professional bodies work within the UK and internationally to promote their members' interests.

Institute of Hospitality (formerly the Hotel and Catering International Management Association)

This is a worldwide professional body for managers and potential managers in the hospitality, catering, leisure and tourism industries. Its purpose is to:

- help members keep up to date with industry issues and developments
- raise standards within the industries, in general and through special schemes like Hospitality Assured, the industry standard for service and business excellence
- help the industries to meet new challenges, e.g. Hospitable Climates, a scheme that shows participating members how to improve energy efficiency
- set recognised educational standards and offer accreditation or endorsement to UK and international study programmes
- provide access to a wide range of services, e.g. discounted and free entry to conferences and seminars, free legal helpline, BIH library and information service.

Try this!

Links to the Institute of Hospitality and BHA websites have been made available at www.heinemann.co.uk/ hotlinks. Just follow the links and enter the express code 4103P.

British Hospitality Association (BHA)

The BHA, incorporating the Restaurant Association, is the UK's national trade association for the hotel, food service and leisure industry. It has been representing the hotel, restaurant and catering industry for 90 years. The BHA's main role is to unite the industry and make its views known to governments across the UK and in Europe. It also aims to lead the industry towards better practices, e.g. Best Practice Forum.

Other major professional bodies

British Institute of Innkeeping: This is the licensed trade's professional body, and promotes good practice within the industry by offering a comprehensive system of training and qualifications for both new and experienced members.

Craft Guild of Chefs: This is the leading chefs' association in the UK, representing members worldwide. Activities include training and demonstrations.

Hospital Caterers' Association: This association exists to promote and improve catering standards and to protect the interests of catering staff within healthcare establishments in the UK. Every year it hosts a national conference as well as seminars, study days and equipment demonstrations.

International Travel Catering Association: This is a forum and representative body for all companies involved in the airline, sea and rail catering industry, plus suppliers of products and equipment.

International Hotel and Restaurant Association: This is a networking and lobbying body for the hotel and restaurant industry around the world. It organises conferences, exhibitions, forums and social events.

Local Authority Caterers' Association: LACA is the professional body representing catering managers in all sectors of local authorities. It organises an annual conference plus events such as National School Meals Week.

National Association of Care Catering: This body promotes good catering standards in care homes, social service environments and meals-on-wheels services.

Top marks!

When you finish a piece of work, check that you have covered everything and given sufficient detail. Giving lots of relevant, current examples helps to show that you have a wide and up-to-date knowledge of the hospitality and catering industry.

Top marks!

Professional bodies like the BHA play an important role within the hospitality and catering industry and will help you to understand it. Professional bodies are an excellent source of information, often summarising information from other key players.

Key influences

Many influences affect the range and style of what the hospitality and catering industry offers.

Media

The past ten years have seen an increased interest in:
- cooking
- different cookery methods
- different types of cuisine
- working in hospitality and catering.

Famous chefs, helped by the media, have raised interest in food and drink, and concerns about unhealthy eating practices. This has prompted many establishments, including hospitals, schools and airline caterers to introduce healthy eating options and to source their ingredients locally.

Social trends

Changes in society have led to:
- fewer families sitting down to eat together
- people having less time to cook
- people not wanting to wait more than a few minutes for food to be cooked and served
- people having more money to spend on eating out and takeaways.

As a result, there is a major demand for fast-food and quick service catering establishments in shopping centres, leisure attractions, airports, stations and other places where customers want food to be served quickly in clean premises and at value for money prices.

Re-generation plans for city centres include leisure facilites, e.g. hotels, restaurants, wine bars, pubs and coffee shops. These often appeal to young people with money to spend. There are a growing number of luxury and/or specialist establishments for customers who are 'cash rich and time poor'.

Globalisation

As a result of globalisation it is now possible to go almost anywhere in the world and see the same branded restaurants, e.g. McDonald's. If you compare cities in the UK you will see that many of them have the same restaurant and coffee shop brands.

Definition
Globalisation: indicates that companies are expanding their operation internationally.

Tourism, culture and fashion

The increase in overseas holidays by UK residents since the 1960s and the influence of ethnic communities has created an interest in other cuisines. The UK now offers a wide range of restaurants where exciting national and ethnic dishes are served, and the increase in competition has improved standards. The presentation of food is better and theatre cooking has been introduced.

Clean, uncluttered furnishings and designs are currently fashionable in restaurants, with out-dated premises being refurbished. Boutique hotels and sushi bars are recent exciting developments.

Figure 1.15: The sushi bar at Harvey Nicholls, Manchester

Legislation and regulation

Regulations and legislation have a tremendous effect on the industry, e.g. nutrition guidelines for school meals. Stricter food hygiene, health and safety and environmental regulations improve standards, but increase costs. The introduction of minimum wage levels in 1999, plus increased rights for part-time staff, significantly increased labour costs throughout the UK, particularly in hospitality and catering.

The ban on smoking in the workplace, which was introduced in July 2007, will affect how premises are designed.

Test yourself!

1 Are these statements true or false?
   a The Public Service Sector is sometimes called the Cost Sector.
   b Hotels and guesthouses are part of the Public Service Sector.

2 Complete the sentence.
   A _____ caterer for employees at an industrial site needs to plan _____ that are suitable for the client.

3 How many people are employed in hospitality, catering, tourism, travel and leisure within the UK?

4 Describe three influences on today's hospitality and catering industry and the impact of each.

5 Draw a chart or table of the structure of the hospitality and catering industry.

Job opportunities in catering and hospitality

The most important people in catering and hospitality are the customers, but without the staff there would be no customers.

Main job roles in catering

Many different types of people choose to work in the industry and there is something to attract almost everyone. By exploring some of the job roles in catering you will be able to see what it is like to work in the industry and the range of career choices available to you.

Level	Role and approximate salary range	Description
Operational ○ members of staff who carry out the day-to-day work ○ may be skilled, semi-skilled or trainees ○ helped by on- and off-the-job training.	Commis Chef/ Assistant Cook/ Trainee £8,000–£16,000	This starting position involves food preparation, basic cooking, and presenting food under supervision. The term 'Commis Chef' is mainly used in a traditional kitchen for fine dining while 'Assistant Cook' is used in the public service sector.
	Cook £9,000–£12,000	A cook helps to prepare, cook and present food. In a very large commercial kitchen there might be cooks to help out in each section. The term 'cook' is often used in public service catering.
	Wine Waiter £12,000	Responsible for serving wine. Able to recommend wines to suit the food the customers have ordered, the occasion and the customer's budget.
	Waiter £8,000–£15,000	Responsible for serving food and drinks. Works closely with the kitchen to make sure that food is served swiftly and appropriately.
Supervisory ○ direct and oversee the operational staff ○ usually started as operational staff and been promoted as their skills developed.	Chef de Partie £14,000–26,000	Runs a section in a large traditional kitchen. In smaller, more modern kitchens may be responsible for preparing, cooking and presenting a range of dishes. Usually in charge of Commis or Trainee Chef(s).
	Head Waiter £13,000–£22,000	Assists the Restaurant Manager and supervises the restaurant staff. Often greets customers and takes orders. If there is no Wine Waiter, will take and serve the wine order.
	Bar Manager £15,000–£27,000	Manages the daily running of the bar(s) and the cellar, orders stock and liaises with suppliers. Oversees the bar staff.

Management	Head Cook/Catering Manager/Cook Manager £19,000+	Number 1 in a public services sector kitchen.
o in charge o make the main decisions o have the most responsibility o will often have worked their way up from an operator, to supervisor, to manager.	Head Chef/Executive Chef £22,000–£50,000+	Number 1 in a commercial kitchen. Manages staff, plans menus, works out the costings, orders stock, plans staff rotas and training, makes sure the kitchen and staff work within the law, ensures standards. (In a large business the Executive Chef will be a separate role above that of Head Chef and in charge of several outlets.)
	Restaurant Manager £16,000–£50,000+	Responsible for running the restaurant, particularly supervising the service and the restaurant staff. Responsible for hiring staff, encouraging food/drink sales, ensuring profitability, customer service. Liaises with Head Chef and customers.
	Catering Manager (£13,000–£35,000+)	A catering expert managing a team, responsible for food production to agreed budgets, menu planning and training. Usually in charge of food production and food service for an establishment. In the public service sector may work in-house for a contract caterer. Often responsible for several catering services or outlets.

Figure 1.16: The main job roles in catering

The owner and manager of a small catering establishment will, in addition to their business responsibilities, probably welcome customers, take orders, serve the wine, work out the bills, cash up, and so on. They are likely to select staff because they are reliable and able to multi-task.

Differences in staff roles and conditions

Kitchen and restaurant staff

Traditionally the kitchen brigade worked behind the scenes and was unlikely to come into direct contact with customers. These days some catering establishments have brought the cooking equipment into the restaurant so the chef can be seen by the customers and may sometimes interact with them. In some Pizza Express restaurants, for example, children are given a chef's hat to wear and can choose their pizza toppings with the help of the chef and the waiters. Similarly, a chef working at a carvery within the restaurant area or a kitchen assistant who also serves at a self-service counter will also meet customers face to face.

Staff who work in the restaurant, e.g. waiters and bar staff, are seen by customers as they are responsible for meeting, greeting and serving them.

Uniforms

Uniforms are normally worn by both kitchen and waiting staff and are often provided by management. The commercial sector and industrial contract caterers for employees tend to have more money to spend on uniforms than the public service sector. Uniforms are designed to be fit for purpose (see Chapter 2 for more information). In some kitchens chefs at different levels wear different styles of uniform. There is more attention to style than there used to be.

Uniforms for waiting staff reflect the type of establishment. They range from the smart formal outfits worn in hotels to casual trousers and polo tops with a black apron worn in contemporary seated restaurants to the overalls worn in a residential home. Managers usually wear formal suits.

Figure 1.17: A waiter in a bistro

Progression

Many top chefs started as kitchen porters, doing the washing-up, cleaning, preparing vegetables and washing salads. This provides good first-hand experience and on and off the job training, with opportunities to study for qualifications such as a Food Hygiene Certificate, NVQ or VRQ.

Another way to progress is to continue on to Higher Education and gain experience through part-time work or work experience placements.

Advanced Business Studies course. P/T job at local hotel. → University course in Hotel and Restaurant Management, with work placement at top hotel resort in the, USA. → Graduate Trainee, e.g. with Aramark UK's one year programme which includes, varied training around the UK, then a permanent post.

Promoted to General Catering Manager at a major industrial contractor in the UK. ← Promotion to Assistant Manager at industrial contractor in the UK.

Figure 1.18 A possible progression route

Management roles

Head Chef in a traditional hotel kitchen

The Head Chef is in charge of the kitchen but still has hands-on involvement in creating and cooking the food. When the Head Chef is absent, the Sous-Chef (Under-Chef) will take charge of the kitchen.

The duties of the Head Chef include:

- Planning, choosing and writing menus
- Running the kitchen, in line with company policies and procedures
- Implementing food safety, health and safety and other practices to meet the requirements of relevant legislation
- Managing the staff
- Liaising with the Restaurant Manager and Heads of other hotel departments as required
- Cooking (depending on the size of the kitchen and number of staff)
- Costing, ordering stock and storing food
- Managing gross profits
- Staff rotas, recruitment and training
- Making sure that what goes on the plate is of the highest quality.

Head Cook in a residential care and nursing home

> **Head Cook needed** to manage a small brigade, catering for 90 residents plus staff, 3 meals a day, 7 days a week. Overtime is paid at T½ if Sunday is worked.
>
> Applicants must be currently residing in the UK and have authorisation to work in the UK.
>
> **Salary: £19,000.**
>
> *Hours: Rota based on 37.5 hours a week, 5 out of 7 days, 10.30am–6.30pm, 6.30am–2.30pm or 11am–7pm.*

Figure 1.19 Job advertisement for a Head Cook to work for a contract caterer providing the catering for a residential care and nursing home in the South East

Rotas are common within hospitality and catering where operations may be seven days a week, and cover long hours, e.g. industrial catering for workers on an oil rig, 24-hour hotel room service, high-demand fast-food outlets or hospital catering for staff.

> **Try this!** Worksheet 57
>
> What do you think might be the likely progression routes for:
>
> 1 A school leaver to Head Cook in a residential home
> 2 A kitchen assistant to Catering Manager in a hospital
> 3 A waiter to Restaurant Manager

Case study — James Blackwell

James Blackwell is a Head Chef at Holroyd Howe, a contract caterer. James says:

'I started as an apprentice working for the Moat House hotel group for one year and then moved on as Commis and Junior Chef de Partie in a one-rosette restaurant. After a further two years I worked in a cocktail bar and restaurant where I was promoted to Chef de Partie. I then moved to Chef de Partie with a golf and country club and worked my way up to Sous-Chef, running the hospitality kitchen and members' restaurant. After three years' experience in hospitality, I moved to work for Holroyd Howe as Sous-Chef in a large private business university. After one year I was promoted to Head Chef and now oversee all food operations in student restaurants, hospitality and private directors' dining. I have been in my current role for three years.'

James describes a typical day at work. 'First I open up the building and meet with my Sous-Chef to give out plans for the day. Then I work on main courses and hand over to the Sous-Chef so I can work on menu planning and costing. Part of my mid-morning will be for client meetings and future planning before I return to the kitchen to oversee lunch service and hospitality. Early afternoon is used for training and developing new ideas within my site and for the company. Two afternoons per week are used for junior training and development. After lunch service is finished I meet again with my Sous-Chef to plan for the evening service and any directors'/hospitality dining. Late afternoon is used for finalising menus and working on current and financial projects in conjunction with my General Manager. Final checks and meetings with evening teams are done and then I meet with all Heads of Departments to debrief on the day's business and the following day.'

Try this!

Worksheet 57

1 Produce a flow chart to show James's career progression.
2 If you have a part-time job or a work placement in hospitality and catering, describe your duties on a typical day.

Catering Manager

We are seeking a Catering Manager for a healthcare contract in SE London.

You will be responsible for overseeing the catering at this hospital including patient feeding, a staff/visitor restaurant and a coffee shop. You will manage a team of 15. You will preferably have experience of working in a healthcare contract as a Catering Manager. You need to be a good communicator, with an eye for quality, able to give direction and support to all catering staff. You will need to identify areas where the service can be improved and implement initiatives. Financial ability is important as you will need to work within your budget and control costs. Salary: £25,000–£26,000 depending on experience. Excellent benefits.

Figure 1.20 Job description for a Catering Manager in healthcare. Note the variety of hospital catering and outlets for which the Catering Manager is responsible

Restaurant Manager

The benefits of a Restaurant Manager will depend on the type of establishment, sales turnover, whether it is independently owned or part of a chain.

RESTAURANT MANAGER

JOB DESCRIPTION

Job Purpose

To be responsible for the smooth and successful day-to-day running of the restaurant, ensuring satisfied customers and that all financial targets are achieved

Key Responsibilities
• Be the host and communicate with guests
• Organise the restaurant team: their tasks, schedules and information meetings
• Manage the staff: recruitment, training, evaluation and promotion
• Monitor customer service levels
• Ensure the quality of service and service provision
• Maximise restaurant occupancy
• Ensure on-going profitability and have knowledge of financial matters
• Increase restaurant sales.

Qualifications
• 2 years' further education in hotel/food and beverage studies to BTS/HND standard or similar
• Significant experience of restaurant management.

Figure 1.21 Job description for a Restaurant Manager

Case study — Stella Martin

Stella Martin is the Restaurant Manager for a major chain of fast-food restaurants. Stella says, 'I'm responsible for all aspects of running the restaurant, including building sales, training my team, maintaining product quality standards and ensuring the restaurant is profitable. I work with people from a cross-section of society. It's a fun atmosphere and you get through the busy times by everyone working as a team. Restaurant Managers at my company earn £18,000–£24,000, depending on the volume of the site and the location. There's a staff discount scheme, a pension scheme and training and development. I get free meals when I'm on duty, and we get 20 days' holiday, which increases with service.

Try this! | Worksheet 58

Look at the job descriptions, advertisements and case studies. Choose either the roles of Head Chef and Head Cook or Restaurant Manager and Catering Manager. Describe the similarities and differences between their duties, responsibilities and conditions.

Supervisory roles in the kitchen

Chef de Partie

CHEF DE PARTIE JOB DESCRIPTION

Hours: 160 hours per 4-week period. Shifts as per rota. Average 5 days per week

Job purpose

To prepare, cook and present service menu items to agreed standards. To deputise for the senior Chef de Partie in their absence and supervise the unit chefs to maintain the smooth running of the kitchen.

Minimum educational/vocational qualifications:

NVQ 2 in Professional Cookery or equivalent

Intermediate Food Hygiene

1:1 Trainer (either formal qualification or by experience)

Good standard of spoken and written English

Minimum previous work experience

3 years' experience as Chef de Partie in a small establishment or in a more junior position within a large brigade with supervisory and training responsibility.

Responsibilities

Produce a high standard of work to meet company standards and guest satisfaction.

Manage the cost of sales through effective use of the ordering system, stock control, portion control and minimising of food wastage.

Deputise for the Senior Chef de Partie in their absence.

Provide general supervision and coaching to junior staff.

Assist with the production of rotas, sickness and holiday management to ensure optimum staffing.

Work closely with team to create and maintain a good working environment

Work with Senior Chef to create new menu ideas, ensuring that accurate costing and specifications are considered.

Figure 1.22 Part of the job description for a Chef de Partie at Center Parcs

Case study — Mark Symmers

On leaving school Mark started a Youth Training Scheme working in a local hotel and attending college. He then had various chef positions in small restaurants, a hospital and in contract catering sites. He now works as a chef for the UK part of the international contract catering company Aramark.

The order of a typical day is:

- stock take/open kitchen diary
- enter details from invoices in diary, including temperature control readings
- cook hot food, etc. for breakfast
- freshbake for the day, e.g. breakfast scones
- make soups
- prepare and make the special dishes for that day's menu
- have a break
- prepare and cook vegetables for menu
- support hospitality with buffets
- help on servery
- do more paperwork and go through checklists
- clean down
- place orders
- prepare for the next day.

Bar Manager

Experienced Hotel Bar Manager required. Reporting to the Food and Beverage Manager you will be responsible for all Bar Operations within the Hotel and a team made up of a Food and Beverage Supervisor and Bar Assistants.
Job Type: Permanent. **Location:** Midlands.

Main Duties will include:

- To deliver food and beverage service of high standard and in accordance with departmental standards and procedures
- To develop departmental standards and procedures to promote salesmanship, beverage creativity and profit
- To communicate to your superior any difficulties, guest comments and other relevant information
- To deliver daily briefings and attend other meetings as scheduled
- Cellar management
- Stock order
- Financial management control

Who we are looking for: Someone with a Personal License. A minimum of 2 years' experience in Bar Supervision or Management. A confident team motivator with an eye for detail.

About the employer: The employer is a high-quality national hotel group with large conference capabilities. Many opportunities for career progression. Salary: £17,500, free uniform, 20 days' holiday, other benefits

Figure 1.23 Advertisement for a hotel Bar Manager in a large city in the Midlands

Head Waiter

Job Title	Head Waiter
Salary	£16,000–£17,000 per annum
Type	Permanent
Location	Club la Playa, Valencia, Spain
Job Details	Luxury 4* hotel with superb leisure facilities is looking for a Head Waiter. The chosen individual will be enthusiastic and friendly with previous experience as a supervisor and an eye for detail. You will be responsible for the smooth running of your section in a restaurant, training new staff, maintaining high standards of service and reporting to managers. If you are looking for a great career opportunity and an ambitious role, please apply by sending your CV.

Figure 1.24: Job summary for a Head Waiter for a high-quality 4-star hotel in Spain

Try this!

Produce a short talk to give at a careers evening about one of the supervisory jobs described. Include a comparison of that job with a job of the same title in another establishment.

Operational roles

Commis Chef

Case study — Sarah Pettit

Sarah is a chef at a low cost, 2-star hotel in Bristol. She says: 'I am part of the Food and Beverage team in a hotel that is part of a multi-national chain. Although I am a chef, I sometimes work in the bar or the restaurant. This is good because I get to learn about what it takes to run a hotel. The money is OK and it's important to work hard. Once I've worked at the hotel for over a year I'll get a staff discount card that I can used at other hotels in the same chain. My ambition is to work in a 4- or 5-star hotel. I'd like to be the Head Chef of a big hotel.'

This flexible, multi-skilled approach is becoming more and more common in hospitality and catering. It helps to reduce labour costs and also makes work more varied.

Cook

> Cooking for 30 children and staff a day catering for lunch and tea. This nursery is seeking an experienced cook, preferably who has worked in a similar environment. Knowledge of allergies would be an advantage.
>
> Satisfactory disclosure from the Criminal Records Bureau will be required. All candidates need to be currently living in the UK and provide proof of identity, eligibility to work in the UK and any relevant qualifications.
>
> **Salary: £6.15 per hour. Hours 9.30–4.30 p.m. Monday to Friday.**

Figure 1.25 Advertisement for a School Cook for a contract caterer at a nursery school in the South East

A cook in a large secondary school is likely to earn slightly more, probably around £12,500 a year.

The background of staff working with children or vulnerable people must be checked by the Criminal Records Bureau to try to ensure these customers' safety and security.

Waiting staff

Job Description	Hotel wine waiter/waitress

Duties
- Be able to recommend a wine or wines to guests to suit the food they have ordered, the occasion and their budget.
- Ensure the wine is served at the correct temperature, in the correct glasses and with suitable ceremony. Some wines may have to be decanted.
- You may have a role in recommending what wines are included on the wine list.
- Be in charge of selling and serving liqueurs, brandies and other drinks for after the meal, and cigars.
- Liaise closely with other restaurant staff so you are on hand to take drink orders and serve guests at the appropriate time.
- Be responsible for briefing restaurant colleagues on the wine list, so that they promote particular wines and can advise customers.
- Pass the wine check to the restaurant cashier.
- Be knowledgeable about the laws relating to the service of alcohol.

Relevant qualifications
NVQ/SVQ; National Traineeship; Modern Apprenticeship or similar

Progression
You could continue to specialise, and increase your knowledge of wines, or move into a management position in the restaurant or hotel.

Figure 1.26 Job description for a hotel Wine Waiter/Waitress

Working in the UK

Rates of pay normally reflect:

- the level of responsibility of the job
- the number of staff managed or supervised
- the range and difficulty of duties
- the location, e.g. in the London area an extra 'London weighting allowance' is often added to basic rates
- whether unsociable hours need to be worked
- how many hours need to be worked
- the sector, type and size of the establishment
- how successful the establishment is
- the amount of money available for salaries, benefits, etc.
- how the market is doing.

Hourly rates are often advertised for lower-level jobs, particularly within the public service sector. These should be at or above national minimum wage rates. An annual salary is normally advertised for higher level roles within both sectors, and will relate to the hours worked. Large organisations normally have set pay scales, which are looked at each year, and a clear career progression route. Benefits such as free uniforms, staff meals, a pension scheme, a profit-sharing scheme, staff and family discounts add value to pay. When job seeking, it is sensible to compare extras as well as rates of pay. Part-time employees should receive the same treatment as full-time employees.

Waiting staff often rely on tips to increase their income, although these should be declared for tax purposes. Some restaurants pool tips, and then share them between all of the staff. Some restaurants add a service charge to the bill but staff do not always benefit directly from this.

Physical working conditions vary tremendously. They relate partly to how well designed an establishment's kitchen and restaurant are and partly to the attitude of the management. Often large companies set minimum standards which are over and above legal requirements. Many smaller organisations also maintain high standards. Good working conditions are very important in hospitality and catering and are often stressed in job advertisements.

> **Try this!**
> Which of the operational roles described above would you most like to do? Explain what appeals to you about it and why you feel you could be good at it.

Legal requirements and qualifications

In the UK there are laws covering maternity and paternity rights, equal opportunities, working time, paid holidays, national minimum wage, disability and age discrimination, etc. They are designed to protect employees. Hospitality and catering employers and employees also have to take into account the following:

- **The Licensing Act**: People can work in a bar from 16 years of age. To manage a licensed premises, a person must be over 18, hold a Level 2 National Certificate for Personal Licence Holders, apply to their local authority licensing office and have a criminal record check.
- **Employment Equality Age Regulations**: It is against the law to discriminate on the grounds of age unless this is a requirement of other regulations.
- **Criminal Records Bureau check**: Employees and volunteers who work with children or vulnerable adults, e.g. in a school, may be asked to apply for a Criminal Records Bureau check.
- **Work permits**: People who are British, Swiss or from a country in the European Economic Area do not need permission to work in the UK. Special arrangements apply to workers from Romania and Bulgaria. People from other countries need a work permit.
- **Food Hygiene Regulations**: The level of training a food handler needs depends on their job. See Chapter 2 for more information.
- **Health and Safety and Food Hygiene legislation**: This is important for both employers and employees. All staff have a duty to take reasonable care and to notify management if they are ill. Proof of vaccinations or a health check may be required. See Chapter 3 and the Food Standards Agency website for more information. A hotlink has been made available. Access the Heinemann website at wwww.heinemann.co.uk/hotlinks. Enter the express code 4103P.

Working abroad

UK qualifications and/or work experience are useful when looking for a job abroad. A person who works for an international organisation, e.g. a major hotel chain, may be able to apply to work for that chain in another country. A reputable employment agency can advise on the requirements of a particular country. Some organisations provide accommodation for staff. Membership of a professional body like the Institute of Hospitality (formerly the HCIMA) can help a person to stand out.

Case study — Mark Furr

During 22 years of Army Service, I have served in military units worldwide and undertaken a variety of exciting roles within food service.

I trained as a military chef and provided high quality cuisine for Royalty and VIPs as well as providing large volume catering at home and on overseas deployments.

As the principal catering authority to the Commanding Officer of a Logistics Regiment I was responsible for the management and provision of all food service. This involved detailed planning and the co-ordination of complex feeding on overseas operations and routine feeding in-barracks, plus fine dining within military messes. I managed 50 catering staff and supervised multi-activity contracts. I managed a £750,000 annual food budget and ensured rigid compliance with Defence food safety management systems and food safety legislation.

I have reached the pinnacle as a Warrant Officer Class One Chef Instructor and Quality Assurance Co-ordinator. I am currently the Chief Internal Verifier for the Defence Food Services School.

Army chefs give a catering demonstration

If you want to work in another country you will need to have good job-based and interpersonal skills and at least a basic command of the language. You will need to abide by the laws in that country. There are fewer restrictions for EU nationals wanting to work within the EU. For countries outside the EU a work permit and/or a visa may be required and possibly health checks.

Case study — Jayne Johnston

I spend my winters in France working as a cook for a catered ski chalet company. My duties include menu planning, buying and storing food and drink. I prepare and serve breakfast and a three-course evening meal as well as bake cakes for afternoon tea. In addition, I clean the chalet and eat with the guests.

I earn €100 a week with one full day off, free food and accommodation, a ski pass and insurance plus travel to and from the resort.

My catering qualification and restaurant experience helped me to get the job. You also need to be able to work independently, enjoy company, drive — and love skiing!

Sources of information

There are lots of sources which can inform you about job opportunities in the UK and abroad:

- specialist hospitality and catering careers magazines and websites
- trade magazines, e.g. *Caterer and Hotelkeeper*
- research published by organisations such as *People1st*
- company publications, e.g. annual report, publicity materials and websites
- job centres
- staff recruitment agencies
- local, regional and national newspapers
- information from professional bodies
- libraries, tourist information centres and guide books.

Investigate!

Choose a job role you feel would be suitable for you on finishing your studies. Then choose a job role you feel would be suitable for three years after that. Identify which sector and types of establishments appeal to you. Explain your choices.

Investigate!

Find out about three jobs at either operational, supervisory or management level. One should be in the commercial sector, one in the public service sector and one in non-welfare contract catering. Write a short summary for a trade magazine, comparing the three jobs and the sectors. Look at job titles, levels of authority and responsibility, qualifications needed, progression opportunities, working conditions, uniforms, pay, working hours, legal requirements and benefits.

Test yourself!

1 A waiter is promoted to Head Waiter. To what job role are they most likely to progress next? Explain your answer.

2 What do the initials BHA stand for? Describe the function of the BHA.

3 Are these statements true or false?
   a A Commis Chef's work permit is about to expire. He should discuss the situation with his manager.
   b A Commis Chef strains her back while at the gym. She must report the injury to her manager.

4 Why were regulations introduced covering minimum wages?

Practice assignment tasks

Background information

Imagine you are just about to complete your Diploma in Professional Cookery. You need to consider which part of the industry you would like to work in. You need to think about the structure, scope, size, types of establishment and key influences in the sector.

Task 1

Produce a brief report to:

- Give a description of the term 'hospitality and catering'.
- Summarise the structure of the sector and give examples of different types of operations.
- Include a table with examples of a range of establishments, explaining the features of each.

Task 2

In preparation for an interview produce a PowerPoint presentation to show you understand the:

- key influences in the hospitality and catering sector
- importance of the sector to employment rates and GDP.

Task 3

Using a range of resource material/sources of information (which you must list in the notes) identify a job in a specific sector and briefly describe:

- The main job roles in the chosen environment.
- The key features of each job.
- Legal requirements that may apply in the chosen job role.

Food safety

2

This chapter covers the following outcomes from Diploma unit 202: Food safety in catering

- Outcome 202:1 Behave as responsible individuals within food safety procedures
- Outcome 202:2 Keep him/herself clean and hygienic
- Outcome 202:3 Keep the working area clean and hygienic
- Outcome 202:4 Receive and store food safely
- Outcome 202:5 Prepare, cook and serve food safely.

Working through this chapter could also provide evidence for the following Key Skills:

C2.1a, C2.2, C2.2b, C2.2b, C2.3, N2.1, N2.2a, N2.3, N2.2c, ICT2.1, ICT2.2, ICT2.3, LP2.1, LP2.2, LP2.3

In this chapter you will learn how to:

Identify the causes of food poisoning and ways to avoid it

Identify allergens, food intolerances and contaminants

Recognise good and bad practices in personal hygiene

Report and handle illnesses and infections

Identify correct cleaning procedures and practices

Maintain surfaces and manage waste management

Identify types of pest and signs of infestation and describe correct pest management and control methods

Describe and carry out methods of food storage and stock control

Manage temperature control

Identify food safety procedures.

Food poisoning

What is food poisoning?

If food is not prepared, stored or cooked correctly it becomes a **hazard** and those who consume it may become very ill or even die. This is why there are many laws and regulations controlling the provision of food. In the catering industry this puts a great responsibility on all employees whose job involves food preparation.

Food poisoning is caused by eating food contaminated with harmful **micro-organisms** (e.g. **bacteria**). These micro-organisms need food and water to survive. They have to multiply to a dangerous level to make a person ill. Food poisoning symptoms are usually fairly mild and short-lived.

A food-borne disease is passed on by the micro-organisms causing the illness being present in food or water. Food-borne diseases cause severe illnesses which can kill. Bacteria or viruses causing food-borne diseases such as typhoid and hepatitis can make a person very ill even when present in small numbers. Bacteria causing food-borne diseases do not become harmful only after multiplying in the food; they are very dangerous by themselves. Some of the symptoms of food poisoning and a food-borne disease are very similar.

Symptoms of food poisoning

The main symptoms are:
- abdominal pain
- diarrhoea
- vomiting (being sick)
- fever.

Other symptoms that may occur are:
- abdominal cramp
- difficulty in breathing
- nausea (feeling sick)
- flu-like symptoms
- rashes
- convulsions (fits).

Definition
Hazard: something which could be dangerous.

Did you know?
Shigella bacteria cause **dysentery**. The bacteria are highly infectious and just a few can cause illness. Shigella bacteria do not multiply in food. The bacteria get onto the hands of food handlers from toilet seats, tap handles and nail brushes in washrooms and toilets. If the food handler does not wash their hands thoroughly the bacteria are transferred onto any food they touch. If an outbreak of dysentery occurs all the toilet and washroom areas must be thoroughly disinfected and the nail brushes sterilised. All staff must receive training in the importance of correct personal hygiene procedures.

Definition
Bacterium: a single bacteria, which is a single-celled organism.
Dysentery: a food-borne disease causing mild to severe diarrhoea and fever. It can be fatal.
Micro-organism: a very small life form which cannot be seen without a microscope.
Organism: any living animal or plant.

The time between consuming the food and experiencing the symptoms can be as little as one hour or as long as 70 days!

If you are suffering from food poisoning, the doctor will want to know what your symptoms are and how much time passed from the consumption of any suspect food to the symptoms appearing. This information often gives the first indication of the type of bacteria responsible for the outbreak. To find out the exact cause of food poisoning a **faeces** sample will have to be taken and sent to a laboratory for analysis.

People at risk from food poisoning

The majority of people who suffer food poisoning will have some very unpleasant symptoms for a few days and will feel rather weak and uncomfortable. They should make a full recovery within one to two weeks. Unfortunately, some sectors of the population may have a more severe reaction to the condition and need hospital treatment. Some people may even die from severe symptoms. Those most at risk are:
- babies and young children
- pregnant women and nursing mothers
- the elderly and infirm
- those already suffering from an illness or medical condition.

Some of those most at risk from food poisoning may be found:
- in hospitals
- in children's and old people's homes
- attending medical centres.

Any confirmed outbreak of a food-related illness causes severe problems for a business. Reports in newspapers and on the television and radio will stop many people from visiting a restaurant or take-away outlet. Many catering firms who have had an outbreak of food poisoning have had to close down, so the staff lost their jobs.

Causes of food poisoning

The most common cause is consuming a large number of the types of bacteria which cause illness. Other possible causes include:
- chemicals
- viruses which are present in some types of food, e.g. shellfish
- moulds
- physical contaminants.

Figure 2.1 The symptoms of food poisoning can be very unpleasant

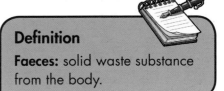

Definition
Faeces: solid waste substance from the body.

Micro-organisms

Bacteria

Bacteria are **micro-organisms**. They cannot be seen with the naked eye and cannot be tasted or smelt if they are on food.

Bacteria multiply by splitting into two. They can do this every 20 minutes. This means that after a few hours one bacterium can have multiplied to over one million. When there are about one million **pathogenic** bacteria per gram of a portion of food eaten food poisoning can occur.

Definition

Pathogen: an organism that causes disease.

Did you know?

Certain types of bacteria are very useful to us. We use some types of bacteria to:

o grow crops
o digest food
o treat sewage
o create medicines
o manufacture cleaning products
o make food, e.g. yoghurt and cheese.

Figure 2.2 Bacteria can multiply very quickly

The types of bacteria that cause food poisoning are called pathogenic bacteria. The table below shows common types of pathogenic bacteria.

Pathogenic bacteria	Where they come from
Salmonella	Raw meat and poultry, eggs and milk, pets, insects, sewage
Staphylococcus aureus	Human body (skin, nose, mouth, cuts, boils), milk
Clostridium perfringens	Human and animal **excrement**, soil, dust, insects, raw meat
Clostridium botulinum	Soil, raw meat, raw, smoked and canned fish
Bacillus cereus	Cereals (especially rice), soil, dust

Figure 2.3 Types of pathogenic bacteria

MORE TAKEN ILL IN E. COLI OUTBREAK

CAMPYLOBACTER BUG ON THE RISE

FOOD POISONING SHUTS SCHOOL

Girl, 5, struck down by E. coli

Figure 2.4 Food-borne diseases are widely reported

Definition

Excrement: solid waste matter passed out through the bowel.

Food-borne diseases are caused by micro-organisms which are found in food and water but do not depend upon them to survive. This makes them different to bacteria. Only a small number of these micro-organisms are needed to cause illness.

The table below shows where food-borne diseases come from.

Micro-organism	Where they come from
Campylobacter	Raw meat and poultry, milk, animals
E. coli 0157	Human and animal gut, sewage, water, raw meat
Listeria	Soft cheese, **unpasteurised** milk products, salad, pâté
Shigella dysenteriae (Bacillary dysentery)	Water, milk, salad, vegetables
Salmonella typhi and paratyphi Typhoid/paratyphoid	Food or water contaminated by human faeces or sewage

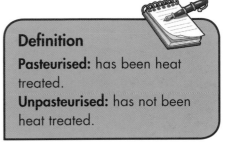

Definition
Pasteurised: has been heat treated.
Unpasteurised: has not been heat treated.

Figure 2.5 Sources of food-borne diseases

Spores

Some bacteria can form **spores**. A spore is a form of protective coating in which the bacteria can survive being cooked, dried and treated with cleaning chemicals. They cannot multiply when in this state, but when the conditions become more suitable, they start multiplying again.

Figure 2.6 Some bacteria can form protective **spores**

Conditions for bacterial growth

Bacteria multiply when they have ideal conditions to grow. These are:
○ **Food**: Bacteria multiply on food, particularly protein-based food, e.g. meat, fish and dairy items.
○ **Moisture**: Bacteria thrive in moisture, but cannot survive in food preserved by drying, salting or adding sugar.
○ **Warmth**: Bacteria prefer body temperature but they are also happy at room temperature. In the fridge or freezer they do not die but become **dormant**, so they do not multiply. High temperatures of over 70°C for more than three minutes will kill most bacteria.

Definition
Spores: cells produced by bacteria and fungi.
Dormant: not active or growing.

- **Time**: In the best conditions the fastest time in which a bacterium can multiply is ten minutes. The average time for most bacteria is 20 minutes.
- **Oxygen**: Some bacteria need oxygen to multiply, and others prefer no oxygen. There are also types of bacteria that multiply regardless of whether there is oxygen or not.

High-risk foods

As the tables on page 00 show, there are several types of food that can harbour the dangerous bacteria that can cause food poisoning. These are known as high-risk foods for these reasons:

- They are mainly ready-to-eat foods which will not be cooked further (cooking can make food safe to eat).
- They involve mixing and processing several ingredients. This increases the preparation time at room temperature. Time and temperature are needed by bacteria to multiply.
- Some dishes involve breaking down and mixing surface tissue with internal muscle. This happens with minced meat, poultry and fish. Few bacteria are found within the muscle and when this is cooked in a large piece, e.g. chicken breast, the bacteria on the outside surface are killed quickly. If the meat is minced, the outside surfaces – which contain more bacteria – are mixed in with the muscle areas.
- Some ingredients are sourced from high-risk areas, e.g. seafood from contaminated water.

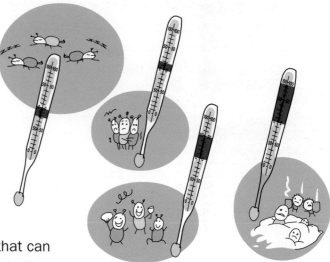

Figure 2.7 The effect of temperature on bacteria

The most common high-risk food categories:

- Cooked meats and poultry, plus pâtés and spreads made from these ingredients.
- Meat stews, gravy and meat-stock-based soups and sauces.
- Milk, cream and eggs – particularly items that involve raw or lightly cooked ingredients. Artificial creams and custards are included here.
- Shellfish and seafood including prawns, mussels, oysters both raw and cooked.
- Cooked rice that is not used immediately.

Try this!
Produce a booklet for staff training that details:
- *a table of the main micro-organisms*
- *types of non-bacterial food poisoning*
- *conditions for growth*

Did you know?

Procedures for handling food safely have existed for centuries. Some religious laws mirror basic food hygiene rules.

o Many people from other parts of the world eat with their hands. In these countries you should only eat with your right hand. This is because when going to the toilet, you should wash your bottom with your left hand.

o Jewish people separate the preparation and consumption of milk and meat products. Sometimes these items are prepared in different kitchens so that no equipment comes in contact with the wrong food type.

Figure 2.8 Eating with your right hand

Viruses

A virus is a germ which causes disease. Viruses are even smaller than bacteria. Viruses multiply once eaten so only a few of these tiny micro-organisms are needed to cause illness. The most common food that can cause viral poisoning is shellfish which may have been grown in contaminated water and not been correctly cleaned before consumption. Viruses can be also passed from person to person via poor personal hygiene, e.g. not washing your hands after using the toilet.

Moulds

Moulds are multi-cellular organisms which will grow on food of all types – sweet, salty, acid or alkaline. They grow fastest at a temperature of 20–30°C, but can also grow slowly at temperatures as low as –10°C. Mould spores survive in the air, so even if they are destroyed by cooking it is virtually impossible to prevent them existing on food. Some moulds produce toxins which cause food poisoning symptoms and also may cause cancer. Moulds present on cereals, nuts, herbs, spices and milk can produce toxins in this way. Other moulds produce chemicals which are toxic to bacteria and help to destroy them, such as that used in penicillin.

Did you know?

Some moulds are very useful to us. Particular moulds are produced to ripen cheese, e.g. Danish Blue, Roquefort and Camembert.

Figure 2.9 Mould

45

Non-bacterial
Chemicals

Poisoning from chemicals is rare in the UK but it does happen occasionally. Some chemicals can get into food accidentally and can cause poisoning. These are examples:

o **Cleaning chemicals** can cause poisoning if surfaces and equipment have not been rinsed properly. When the surfaces and equipment are used, the chemical residue can contaminate food.

o **Pesticides** may be present from harvesting crops which have recently been sprayed with chemicals. In this case, poisoning can occur if the food is not peeled or washed properly.

o **Metallic poisoning** can occur if food is poorly stored (e.g. leaving food in unlined tin cans in the fridge), or if food is cooked in unlined copper or aluminium pans, particularly acidic foods, e.g. fruit.

Toxins

Toxins forming in poorly stored oily fish, e.g. tuna, sardines and salmon, can cause severe illness. Shellfish, e.g. mussels, may become poisonous if they have fed on toxic **plankton**. This particular plankton only occurs at certain times of year in specific areas and so fishing is restricted during this season.

Incorrect cooking methods

Some food is poisonous if it is not cooked correctly. Red kidney beans can make people ill if they have not been boiled for at least ten minutes. (Tinned red kidney beans are safe as they have been thoroughly cooked as part of the canning process.)

Other food safety risks
Physical contaminants

Any item which is discovered in food when it is not supposed to be is a foreign body. Foreign bodies found in food include:

o pieces of glass, plastic and metal
o mouse and rat droppings
o gemstones and settings of jewellery
o blue and natural-coloured plasters
o strands of hair
o flies, caterpillars and other insects

> **Definition**
> **Plankton:** a layer of tiny plants and animals living just below the surface of the sea.
> **Toxin:** a poison produced by bacteria.

Figure 2.10 Metallic poisoning can occur from poor storage

○ pen tops, drawing pins, paper clips

○ screws, nuts and bolts.

If such an item is found in food it is extremely unpleasant and upsetting for the consumer and embarrassing and inconvenient for the business. It is very probable that the presence of the foreign body breaks the law – either the Food Safety Act 1990 or HACCP procedures, see pages 83–86. If this happens, the catering organisation will have to look very carefully into its food safety system to find out where it failed.

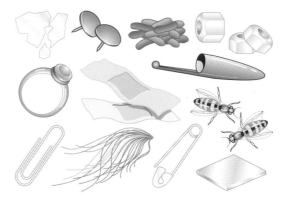

Figure 2.11 Foreign bodies that have been found in food

Allergies

An allergy is an intolerance some people have to certain substances, some of which may be types of food. An increasing number of people now suffer from mild allergic reactions to a range of food including:

○ wheat products (such as bread and biscuits)

○ dairy products (such as milk and cheese)

○ gluten (the elastic protein which is found in wheat flour).

Some symptoms of an allergic reaction can be very similar to that of a food-borne illness. It is important that they are not confused. An allergic reaction will only concern one person and usually occurs within a very short time of consumption. An incidence of food poisoning can affect a large number of people at the same time.

Symptoms of food allergies include:

○ vomiting

○ difficulty in breathing

○ diarrhoea

○ collapse

○ headache

○ rash.

The most dramatic reactions tend to occur in response to peanuts and shellfish.

Some allergic reactions are very severe, come on very quickly and can be fatal. This is why it is extremely important to inform customers of the precise ingredients in any dish they ask about.

Prevention of food poisoning

To try to prevent food poisoning:

o handle food hygienically (see page 49, Personal cleanliness and hygiene)
o prepare food carefully
o store food in the correct manner
o keep all food preparation areas clean
o avoid cross-contamination (see pages 71–72, Controlling food safety hazards)
o cook all food thoroughly.

Remember!

Always:
o keep yourself and your workplace clean at all times
o wear suitable, clean, washable protective clothing
o protect food from contamination at all times
o minimise the time that high-risk foods are left at room temperature
o keep hot food really hot at 63°C or above
o keep cold food in the fridge at below 5°C
o tell your supervisor your symptoms if you are ill
o take responsibility for working safely and hygienically
o follow all instructions and rules at work
o report all potential hazards.

Test yourself!

1 Which of the following is not a pathogenic bacterium?
   a Penicillin
   b Salmonella
   c Staphylococcus aureus
   d Bacillus cereus.

2 Which of the following describes the conditions necessary for most bacteria to reproduce?
   a Warmth, oxygen, food, moisture
   b Cool, oxygen, food, moisture
   c Warmth, carbon dioxide, food, dryness
   d Cool, carbon dioxide, food, dryness.

3 Which of the following is not a symptom of food poisoning?
   a Rash
   b Nausea
   c Sneezing
   d Abdominal pain.

4 Which Regulation concerns the safe system of food production?
   a COSHH
   b RIDDOR
   c HASAWA
   d HACCP.

5 Which of the following statements is true?
   a All pathogens cause illness
   b All moulds cause illness
   c All bacteria cause illness
   d All foreign bodies cause illness.

Personal hygiene

A high standard of personal hygiene is a requirement under the Food Safety (General Food Hygiene) Regulations 1995. Everyone who works in a job that requires them to handle food must:

○ be in good health
○ have hygienic personal habits
○ wear the correct, clean, protective clothing
○ be aware of the potential danger of poor hygiene practice.

Personal hygiene is very important when working in a catering environment. You need to be pleasant to work with (no body odour!) and feel comfortable in the kitchen. Make sure you wash your hair – if it feels sticky and heavy it will not be pleasant to work in a hot kitchen. Clean your teeth regularly – your colleagues will not want to work near you if you have bad breath! Keep your hands and nails clean and in good condition when working directly with food.

Figure 2.12 Would you want to eat at this chef's restaurant?

General health

It is important to remember that working in a catering kitchen can involve:

○ standing up for long periods of time
○ working in a hot, noisy atmosphere
○ having to concentrate and multi-task for long periods of time
○ starting work early in the morning
○ finishing work late at night.

Bearing these points in mind make sure you:

○ have sufficient sleep and relaxation during your time off
○ eat regular, balanced meals – this is essential as it is too easy to 'pick' which is not good for your digestion in the long term
○ drink plenty of water during your shift at work, otherwise your concentration may be affected
○ remember that healthy eating applies to staff just as much as to customers, see Chapter 4.

Clothing

Your uniform should fit correctly and be comfortable to wear. If your shoes are too tight and make your feet hurt, for example, you will not be able to concentrate properly. This could cause an accident if you are using dangerous equipment, e.g. knives or mixers.

It is important to wear the correct clothing in the kitchen, not only for health and safety but also to create a professional image. Customers, visitors and other members of staff are impressed by kitchen staff who are dressed in a clean, smart uniform. Kitchens may have 'house rules' regarding correct dress but it will be a version of the traditional chef's whites.

Top marks!
Make sure your uniform is always pressed.

Hat This should be close-fitting and clean. It should be made of an absorbent material and washable or disposable. A hair net should be worn underneath if your hair reaches below the collar.

Necktie This should be made of cotton, correctly tied and clean.

Jacket This should be made of an absorbent, thick but cool material (usually cotton mix). It should be double-breasted, so it can be fastened either way to give a double layer of material across the chest, and long-sleeved for protection.

Apron This should be made of white cotton with long strings to tie in front. It may be bibbed. It should cover you from the waist to below the knee for protection, but should not be any longer as this would be a safety risk.

Trousers These should be cotton mix and loose-fitting for comfort. They should not be too long as this is a safety risk.

Shoes These should be comfortable, strong, and solid with protected toes. Clogs may be acceptable, trainers are not. Footwear must have non-slip soles and non-absorbent uppers. Socks (or tights) must be worn.

Figure 2.13 The correct clothing

It is important to remember the following aspects of good clothing practice:

○ Clean, comfortable underwear is just as important as a clean uniform.

○ Do not enter the kitchen in outdoor clothing; it will be contaminated.

○ Do not wear your kitchen uniform outdoors for the same reason.

○ Press studs or Velcro fastenings are more hygienic and easier to use than buttons.

○ Change your uniform as soon as it gets dirty. This is usually every day for aprons and jackets. Trousers should be changed two or more times a week.

○ If you are working for several hours in a cold area your supervisor may provide you with a body warmer to wear under a white coat.

You may need to wear gloves while at work. Types of gloves include:

○ thin rubber or latex gloves for fine work with high-risk foods

○ non-latex or vinyl gloves if the food handler has an allergic condition

○ chain metal gloves to give protection from sharp knives

○ thick, warm gloves to handle frozen items when taking stock from the freezer

○ thick insulating gloves or a cloth to handle very hot items straight from the oven.

The advantages of wearing disposable gloves to work include:

○ Using a fresh pair of gloves to handle food is more hygienic than using washed hands.

○ Cross-contamination is reduced if a new pair of gloves is used for different food preparation processes.

○ Strong smells cannot be transferred from one type of food to another.

○ They give the wearer protection from damage by constant dampness, extreme cold and heat and rough surfaces, e.g. when peeling chestnuts.

○ It is much more hygienic to cover a cut, burn or other condition (e.g. a boil) with a dressing and then to wear gloves too.

○ Wearing gloves when preparing or serving food gives customers a more hygienic impression.

Did you know?

The most hygienic way of putting on your kitchen uniform is to put your hat on first to stop loose hairs falling onto your whites. When taking off your uniform, your hat should be removed last.

Figure 2.14 The correct order to put on your kitchen uniform

Try this!
Produce a presentation that outlines the training requirements of food handlers. Include recommendations for training staff in the following areas:

○ *personal hygiene and presentation*

○ *good hygiene practice*

○ *reportable illnesses*

○ *suitable dressings for wounds with an explanation of the risk of infection.*

However, wearing gloves has some disadvantages including:

○ It can be difficult to grip certain items, e.g. fresh fish.
○ Failing to use clean gloves can cause cross-contamination. It can take longer to complete a task.
○ Having to keep changing gloves can be fiddly and time-consuming.
○ Providing frequent changes of gloves is expensive.
○ It can be easy to forget to use a fresh pair of gloves.

Figure 2.15 Latex gloves for fine work, rubber gloves for handling wet food and chain mail for butchery

Personal habits

Hair: Wash your hair regularly and keep it under a hat. Longer hair should be tied back securely or contained in a net. This reduces the danger of flakes of skin or strands of hair falling into food. Beards and moustaches should also be covered. Do not touch your hair while working. When you have your hair cut, make sure you wash it again before you go to work.

Ears: Do not put your fingers into your ears while working in a kitchen. Earwax and bacteria can be transferred to food and work surfaces and equipment this way.

Nose: The pathogenic bacteria staphylococcus aureus, see page 00, is found in many adult noses and mouths. Sneezes and coughs can spread this bacteria over a wide area. This means that work surfaces, food and equipment can be contaminated very easily. A disposable handkerchief should always be used to catch a sneeze or blow your nose. Always wash your hands thoroughly after using a tissue. Nose picking is an extremely unhygienic activity as is wiping your nose on your sleeve, and neither should ever be carried out in a kitchen (or elsewhere!)

Mouth: Tasting food is essential but you must use a clean spoon each time. A spoon used for one taste should not be put back into the food for any reason without being thoroughly washed first. Spitting is extremely unhygienic – never do this. It is not acceptable to eat sweets or chew gum in the kitchen. Do not lick your finger and then use it to open bags, pick up small, light items or separate sheets of paper. All these activities can spread bacteria easily.

Neck: Do not wear strong perfume or aftershaves, deodorant or cosmetics as they can taint food.

Remember!
Do not touch any part of any glassware, crockery or cutlery that may make contact with anyone's mouth. You would not like to drink out of a cup that someone's fingers had touched around the rim, would you?

Underarms: Daily bathing or showering removes the bacteria that cause body odour. Perspiration smells can be avoided by using a non-perfumed deodorant.

Hands: The most common method of contaminating food is by having dirty hands. Do not use your fingers for tasting. Keep your nails short and clean. Do not use nail varnish. Watches and rings (other than a plain wedding ring) are not allowed as bacteria can live in the food particles caught under them. Gemstones in jewellery may fall out and become foreign bodies in food. It is impractical to wear a watch because of the frequent use of water in the kitchen.

Keep your hair clean and tied back, wear a hat.

Do not touch your ears, do not wear earrings other than sleepers (maybe!)

Taste food with a clean spoon each time.

Use a tissue to blow your nose and wash your hands afterwards.

Wash your underarms regularly, apply unscented deodorant.

Do not wear strong perfume, cosmetics or jewellery.

Cover cuts, burns and sores with a blue plaster dressing.

Keep your nails short and clean, wash your hands frequently.

Change your underwear regularly.

Keep your feet clean and dry, wear clean, cotton socks.

Figure 2.16 Rules for good personal hygiene

Hand washing

Hand washing is one of the most important hygiene activities that all food handlers must carry out. Bacteria are transferred from dirty hands onto food all too frequently.

How to wash your hands properly:

1 Wet your hands with a non-hand-operated warm-water spray or fill the wash hand basin with hand-hot water and wet your hands.

2 Use a non-perfumed antibacterial liquid soap or gel to provide a good lather over the top and palms of your hands, between your fingers, around your wrists and lower forearms.

3 Only use a nailbrush to clean under your fingernails if it is disinfected regularly or is disposable.

4 Rinse your hands thoroughly with clean water.

5 Dry your hands well, preferably with disposable paper towels; hot-air dryers take longer and roller towels must be clean to be safe.

Wounds, illness and infection

Working in a kitchen with hot items, knives and dangerous equipment means it is likely that you will suffer a slight injury occasionally.

From a hygiene point of view it is essential that all wounds are covered. This is to:
○ prevent blood and bacteria from the injury contaminating any food
○ prevent bacteria from raw food infecting the wound.

Using a coloured waterproof dressing (blue plaster) keeps the injury clean and protects it. Blue is the best colour for a dressing in food areas as it is easily spotted if it falls off. Very few foods are blue!

Spots, blisters and boils are unpleasant skin conditions which can cause problems in food-handling areas because they will be infected with the pathogenic bacteria staphylococcus aureus (see page 42). If you have blemishes on your hands, work in suitable gloves (see pages 51–52). If they are on your face you must be very careful to avoid touching them with your hands while working. In severe cases your supervisor may give you non-food-handling tasks to carry out until the condition has cleared up.

Did you know?
There are three items used in hand washing which can contaminate hands rather than clean them! They are:
○ a dirty bar of soap used by many different people
○ a non-disposable nail brush which is not disinfected very regularly
○ a roller towel which is not changed very regularly.

Remember!
Always wash your hands:
○ when entering the kitchen
○ after using the toilet
○ between each task
○ between handling raw and cooked food
○ after touching your face or hair
○ after coughing, sneezing or blowing your nose into a handkerchief
○ after any cleaning activity
○ after eating, drinking or smoking during a break
○ after dealing with food waste or rubbish.

Remember!
Always tell your supervisor straightaway if you are wearing a waterproof blue plaster dressing and it goes missing in food!

If you are ill and suffer any symptoms that could be from a food-borne illness you must let your supervisor know as soon as possible. The symptoms concerned include:

- diarrhoea
- vomiting
- nausea
- discharges from ear, eye and nose.
- colds and sore throats
- skin infections (e.g. eczema).

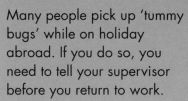

Remember!
Many people pick up 'tummy bugs' while on holiday abroad. If you do so, you need to tell your supervisor before you return to work.

You should not work as a food handler while you display any of these symptoms. It is likely you will have to seek medical help if you suffer severe bouts of these illnesses. You may need clearance from your doctor before you can resume work as a food handler.

Your supervisor also needs to know about any similar symptoms suffered by the people with whom you live. This is because you may be a carrier of an infection without displaying any symptoms of the illness. If you are carrier it means you can transmit the infection to others.

Certain illnesses legally need to be reported to the local health authority. Many of them are identified by the symptoms listed above. Your supervisor or doctor should arrange for this to be done if necessary.

Test yourself!

1 How often should you have a bath or shower during a working week?

2 How many occasions are there when you should wash your hands before resuming work?

3 What is a 'carrier' of a food-borne disease?

4 When changing ready to start work, which item of kitchen uniform should you put on first?

5 State three advantages of wearing gloves to handle food.

6 Describe the correct procedure to follow when tasting food.

Cleaning

Cleaning is an essential process of removing dirt. It is vital to the safe operation of food businesses. Cleaning staff are employed in many establishments but it is the responsibility of all employees to make sure:

○ all equipment and work areas remain clean

○ the environment they work in is clean and safe.

Regular cleaning is vital in an area where food is handled for the following reasons:

○ To reduce the danger of contamination of food from:
  – bacteria, by removing particles of food upon which they can feed
  – pests
  – foreign bodies.

○ To create a good impression for:
  – customers
  – other staff and visitors
  – inspectors.

○ To reduce the risk of:
  – accidents
  – equipment breakdown.

Methods of cleaning

A high standard of cleanliness is essential to keep the risk of food safety hazards low. Cleaning can reduce the risk of food safety hazards because it:

○ removes food particles upon which bacteria can feed

○ reduces the risk of contamination of food which is being prepared or stored

○ reduces the danger of pests, e.g. insects, rats and mice, coming into the kitchen

○ helps to prevent accidents by providing a clean work area

○ encourages safe working methods

○ helps keep the area pleasant to work in.

Cleaning has to be carried out in all areas of the kitchen. These include:

○ **surfaces**: floors and worktops

○ **equipment**: manual or electrical machinery

○ **utensils**: hand-held kitchen tools.

The COSHH Regulations (see page 98) cover cleaning because there are several potential hazards which could occur. These include:

o Using dirty cloths to clean, which spreads bacterial contamination.
o Using the same cleaning equipment to clean raw food preparation areas as well as those for preparing cooked food and causing cross-contamination (see pages 71–72).
o When cleaning has been carried out very poorly and contamination remains.
o When there is no separate cleaning equipment for cleaning toilet and changing room areas and the kitchen so cross-contamination is likely.
o Using cleaning chemicals incorrectly, leaving a residue over food preparation areas, which will cause chemical contamination (see Chemical contaminants on page 46).
o Storing chemicals in food containers, which could result in contamination.
o Pest infestation (see pages 64–67).

Cleaning products

o **Water** is the most effective cleaning agent. It can be used hot or cold and also under pressure. When used in the form of steam it can also disinfect. Water leaves no residue and is very environmentally friendly. It is also used for rinsing.
o **Soap** is made from fat and caustic soda. Soap can leave a scum on surfaces, so it is not suitable for kitchen cleaning. Disinfectants are sometimes added to soap for hand washing.
o **Detergents** are chemicals manufactured from petroleum. They break dirt up into fine particles and coat them so they are easy to remove. Detergents can be in the form of powder, liquid, foam or gel. They usually need mixing with water before use.
o **Disinfectants** are chemicals that will reduce the numbers of micro-organisms to a safe level if left in contact with the surface for a sufficient amount of time. It is better to apply the chemicals with a spray rather than a cloth. Their efficiency is affected if the surface that is being treated is not clean.
o **Sanitiser** is a mixture of detergent and disinfectant chemicals. It is often used in sprays for hard surface cleaning. It needs to be left in contact with the surface to be cleaned for a sufficient amount of time to be effective. Always read the manufacturer's instructions.

- **Bactericides** are substances which have been specifically formulated to kill bacteria.
- A **steriliser** is a piece of equipment that usually uses extremely hot water or steam to kill all the micro-organisms on a surface. Alternatively, sterilisers may use strong chemical disinfectants or bactericides. It is difficult to successfully sterilise equipment in a normal catering situation.

What to disinfect	Example	When to disinfect
Food contact surfaces	Chopping boards, containers, mixers	Before and after each use
Hand contact surfaces	Refrigerator handles, taps, switches	At least once per shift
Contamination hazards	Cloths and mops, waste bins and lids	At least once per shift, cloths and mops after each main use

Figure 2.17 Disinfection frequency table

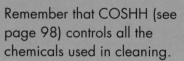

Remember!
Remember that COSHH (see page 98) controls all the chemicals used in cleaning.

When using any type of cleaning chemical:
- Always follow the manufacturer's instructions correctly.
- Store chemicals in their original containers, away from food and in clean, cool, dry conditions.
- Never decant a chemical into a different container which is not labelled correctly.
- Always wear any recommended protective equipment when preparing and using the product.
- Never mix chemicals.
- Always dispose of chemicals safely. Check the instructions before you pour any chemical down a drain.

Cleaning equipment

To clean effectively you need suitable equipment. This is likely to include:
- small equipment, e.g. cloths, brushes, mops and buckets
- large equipment, e.g. dishwashers, jet washers, wet and dry vacuum cleaners.

Small equipment should be colour-coded so that it is only used in the correct areas and for the correct job. Red equipment could be used in raw food preparation areas, and yellow in cooked food preparation areas for example. A blue set of equipment could be reserved for cleaning changing-room areas and this should be stored separately.

Cloths frequently spread more bacteria than they clean away. All reusable cloths should be changed every few hours in a shift as they will contain constantly increasing numbers of bacteria at room temperature. Reusable cloths should be washed and disinfected thoroughly before being dried ready to use again. It is more expensive but much more hygienic to use disposable cloths. These are available in a range of colours to help with coding and controlling where they are used. Disposable cloths should be thrown away as soon as they are dirty.

Energy used in cleaning

Cleaning is an expensive process. As well as specialist chemicals and equipment it also requires energy. The energy used does not only involve plugging a machine to an electrical socket! Effective cleaning usually involves two or more of these energy sources:

○ **Physical energy**: carried out by people using pressure and movement on surfaces (also known as elbow grease!)
○ **Kinetic energy**: produced by machines using their weight in conjunction with movement, e.g. a floor cleaner.
○ **Agitation**: provided by liquids being constantly moved against a surface, e.g. in a washing machine or when cleaning tubes or pipes.
○ **Thermal energy**: using high and low temperatures combined with pressure to remove dirt, e.g. in a steam pressure cleaner or when freezing a skirt to remove chewing gum.
○ **Chemical**: Using a chemical reaction between two substances to loosen and remove dirt, e.g. washing powder and water.

Figure 2.18 Colour-coded kitchen equipment

 Investigate!   Worksheet 5

Some materials will be damaged by usual cleaning methods and therefore need special attention. Find out how the following materials should be cleaned:
○ cast iron
○ copper
○ aluminium.

 Remember!
Never use a cloth that has been used on a floor or in a toilet area to wipe a work surface.

Six stages of cleaning

The main stages of thorough cleaning apply to each area. Before starting to clean, switch off and unplug electrical machinery and dismantle any items as required.

1 **Pre-clean** to remove any loose dirt and heavy soiling, e.g. soak a saucepan, sweep the floor or wipe down a mixer.
2 **Main clean** by washing the item with hot water and detergent. Use a suitable cloth or brush to remove grease and dirt.
3 **Rinse** with hot water only to remove the detergent and any remaining dirt particles.
4 **Disinfect** with extremely hot water (82°C) or steam in a controlled area, e.g. in a dishwasher. Where this process is not safe or practical use a chemical disinfectant. Apply it to the appropriate surface and leave it for the length of time stated on the instructions.
5 **Final rinse** to remove all cleaning chemical residue.
6 **Dry** – air drying is the most hygienic, otherwise use paper towels or clean, dry cloths.

When cleaning is finished, put the equipment back together correctly and safely. Put it in the right place ready for use.

Figure 2.19 Cleaning a slicing machine

Cleaning schedules

A cleaning schedule forms part of the HACCP procedures and may be used together with checklists to ensure a thorough job is done.

A cleaning schedule is a written plan that tells everyone in the kitchen:
○ what items and surfaces are to be cleaned
○ where they are to be cleaned
○ who is to carry out these tasks
○ how often the cleaning is to be carried out
○ when the cleaning should be done
○ how long it should take to clean correctly
○ what chemicals and equipment are needed to clean it
○ what safety precautions should be taken when cleaning, e.g. wearing goggles and gloves, putting out warning signs
○ the method of cleaning that should be used.

Frequently used items and work areas may have to be cleaned after each task in preparation for the next. It is the responsibility of all food handlers to carry out this clean-as-you-go system correctly. It is particularly important when you are preparing raw foods. You must disinfect the work area thoroughly once you have cleaned it, to prevent cross-contamination.

Remember!
A cleaning schedule forms part of the HACCP procedures and may be used together with check lists to ensure a thorough job is done.

Investigate!   Worksheet 6

How frequently are the following cleaning tasks carried out at your workplace?
○ **Cleaning the ovens**
○ **Washing down the walls**
○ **Cleaning out the refrigerators**
○ **Cleaning the bin area.**

Cleaning schedule and checklist

Area/item of	Frequency	Responsiblity	Cleaning materials	H&S precautions	Method of cleaning	Checked by
Walls	Daily	Kitchen porter & 2nd chef	Detergent & cloth	Ladder to be used to reach areas above shoulder height	1) Pre-clean 2) Clean, apply detergent with hand-held spray, leave for 2 mins 3) Rinse 4) Air dry	
Floors	Daily	Kitchen porter	Detergent & mop & bucket	Hazard notices to be put out in entrances to the area being cleaned	1) Pre-clean 2) Clean, apply detergent with mop 3) Rinse 4) Air dry	
Work surface	Daily	Chefs	Sanitiser & cloth	None required	1) Pre-clean 2) Apply sanitiser with trigger spray, leave for 2 mins 3) Wipe over 4) Air dry	
Oven	Weekly	Kitchen porter	Oven cleaner	Rubber gloves, overall, mask & goggles	1) Ensure oven is turned off & cool 2) Pre-clean 3) Clean, apply oven cleaner, leave for 30 mins 4) Rinse 4) Air dry	
Fridges	Weekly	Kitchen porter & 2nd chef	Hot water & detergent	None required	1) Pre-clean 2) Clean, apply detergent with hand-held spray, leave for 2 mins 3) Rinse 4) Air dry	
Bins	Weekly	Kitchen porter & 2nd chef	Hot water & detergent	Gloves	1) Pre-clean 2) Clean, apply detergent with hand-held spray, leave for 2 mins 3) Rinse 4) Air dry	
Windows	Monthly	Kitchen porter	Hot water & detergent	Ladder to be used to reach areas above shoulder height	1) Pre-clean 2) Rinse 3) Air dry	
Ceiling	Monthly	Kitchen porter	Detergent & cloth	Ladder	1) Pre-clean 2) Clean, apply detergent with hand-held spray, leave for 2 mins 3) Rinse 4) Air dry	
Freezer	Monthly	Kitchen porter & 2nd chef	Hot water & detergent	Gloves	1) Pre-clean 2) Clean, apply detergent with hand-held spray, leave for 2 mins 3) Rinse 4) Air dry	

Figure 2.20 Example cleaning schedule and checklist

Hygienic work surfaces and equipment

It is very difficult to maintain good standards of work and hygiene in a food production area if the working area and equipment are unsuitable. All equipment and work surfaces should be specifically produced and designed for catering kitchens.

All surfaces that come into contact with food should be:
○ easy to maintain, clean and disinfect
○ made from a safe, **non-toxic** material that is **inert** and will not react with any food or chemical
○ smooth and **impervious** to water, i.e. waterproof
○ designed to avoid any joins or seams where food particles could lodge
○ resistant to corrosion, e.g. rusting or pitting
○ strong enough to support heavy weights and heat resistant so hot pans can be put on it.

Stainless steel has all these qualities. It is the most commonly used material in modern catering kitchens.

For reasons of health and safety and to follow the HACCP procedures, it is important to act when you notice any damage to surfaces or equipment in the kitchen.

Definition

Non-toxic: not poisonous or harmful.

Inert: has no reaction with any other substance.

Impervious: does not allow water to pass through it.

Waste management

Every catering establishment wants to manage waste carefully for several reasons:
○ All food thrown away represents lost income to the business.
○ All businesses have to pay to have their waste removed, so large amounts of waste can increase this cost.
○ Reducing the amount of waste produced helps the environment.
○ Waste can attract pests which can be a food safety hazard.

Figure 2.21 Kitchen waste bins should be emptied regularly

In every kitchen there should be sufficient waste bins provided at suitable points. The bins should:

○ have tight-fitting lids
○ be lined with a polythene disposable sack (if appropriate)
○ not be overfilled
○ be emptied regularly
○ be cleaned regularly
○ not smell
○ not be left in the kitchen overnight.

The bagged waste from kitchen bins should be transferred to a large lidded bin in the outside refuse area as soon as necessary. The bags should be tied securely to prevent any spillages. This will help to reduce the hazard of pest infestation. The outside refuse area should be kept clean for the same reason.

Recycling waste

Many establishments are now trying to recycle as much material as possible. Food waste may be kept apart as it can be collected separately. Individual bins should be provided for paper, cardboard, glass and plastic to allow recycling systems to be used. In large businesses this type of waste may be crushed by compactor machines to take up less space before binning. Waste oil may be collected separately from the main rubbish collection as it can be recycled. Eventually it may be used as fuel for cars.

Figure 2.22 A well-organised outside bin area

> **Remember!**
> Some waste can be dangerous, e.g.
> o broken glass can cause injury
> o fat and oil can leak out of containers and make floors slippery.

> **Remember!**
> Waste oil should **never** be poured down drains. It should be put in a suitable container (often the drum in which it was delivered).

Figure 2.23 Used oil can be poured into a suitable container ready for recycling

Pest control

Pests are responsible for the majority of closures of food establishments by the Environmental Health Officer. Pests are also responsible for large amounts of food being wasted by infestation or contamination. Staff and customers become very upset if they find any type of pest on the premises. Under the HACCP procedures a catering business is expected to have effective pest control methods in place.

Pests live in or near catering premises because they provide:

o **food** in store rooms, waste areas, poorly cleaned production areas
o **moisture** from dripping taps, outside drains, **condensation** droplets
o **warmth** from heating systems and equipment motors, e.g. refrigerators
o **shelter** in undisturbed areas, e.g. the back of store cupboards, behind large equipment.

By removing as many of these conditions as possible, pests may be put off living in the area and look elsewhere.

> **Definition**
> **Condensation:** a coating of tiny drops formed on a surface by steam or vapour.

Signs of infestation

How can you tell if there is a pest infestation in your workplace? Look for:

o dead bodies of insects, rodents and birds
o droppings, smear marks
o eggs, larvae, pupae cases, feathers, nesting material
o paw or claw prints
o unusual smells
o scratching, pecking or gnawing sounds
o gnawed pipes, fittings or boxes
o torn or damaged sacks or packaging
o food spillages.

Pests cause hazards in the following ways:

o Bacterial contamination from pathogenic bacteria found:
  – on the surface of the pest's skin
  – in pest droppings.
o Physical contamination from fur, eggs, droppings, urine, saliva, dead bodies, nest material.

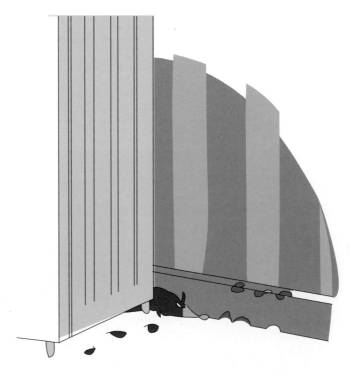

Figure 2.24 Evidence of infestation

- ○ Chemical contamination from using strong chemicals to kill the pests which then gets into food.
- ○ Cross-contamination which occurs when a pest transfers pathogenic bacteria from one area to another, e.g. a fly landing on raw meat and then moving on to a cooked chicken.

Types of pests

Insects

Flies are one of the most common insect pests. They are usually found in places which have not been cleaned thoroughly and where rubbish is allowed to gather. A female housefly can lay up to 600 eggs in her life. An egg takes about two weeks to go through the maggot stage and become a fully grown fly.

Cockroaches are one of the oldest types of insects, said to date from prehistoric times. They do not usually fly and only come out when it is dark. Their eggs take around two months to hatch. They can live for up to a year. Cockroaches can be detected by their droppings or their unpleasant smell.

Weevils are very tiny insects that live in dry goods, e.g. flour, cereals and nuts. They can only be seen with the naked eye if they are moving. It is possible to spot an infestation if there is tunnelling or speckling in the commodity.

Ants are attracted by sweet items which have not been stored securely. They usually nest outdoors, and follow set paths to food sources.

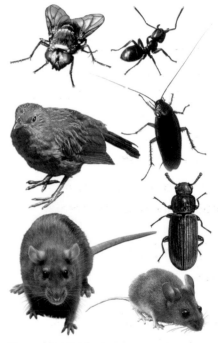

Figure 2.25 Kitchen pests

Rodents

Rats commonly get into buildings through drains or holes but they also burrow under walls. Rats are a particular hazard as they can transmit Weil's disease, and a worm-type parasite as well as food poisoning bacteria. They also bite. The Norway rat is the most common in the UK. It usually lives outside.

House mice are the main problem in buildings. They can climb very well and cause considerable damage by gnawing to keep their teeth short. Like rats, their teeth grow throughout their lives and unless they wear them down, their teeth will pierce through their heads! Mice dribble urine nearly all the time and leave droppings at frequent intervals. They breed very quickly – a pair of mice can have 2,000 offspring in one year!

Did you know?

This is what happens when a fly lands on your food: flies can't eat solid food so to soften it up they vomit on it. Then they stamp the vomit in until it's a liquid, usually including several bacteria for good measure. When it's good and runny they suck it all back in again, probably dropping some excrement at the same time. And then, when they've finished eating, it's your turn.

Birds

Pigeons, starlings and seagulls can be a problem in outside waste areas where bins are allowed to overflow and are not kept covered. Once in the area, birds may then get into a building through doors and windows and will often try to nest in roof spaces. As well as contaminating food with feathers and droppings, birds can block gutters with nests and spread insect infestation.

Pets

Domestic pets, e.g. cats and dogs, are classed as pests and should not be allowed to enter catering premises.

Preventing pest infestation

It is almost impossible to prevent pests entering a building. It is possible, however, to discourage them from staying! There are some ways of preventing pests:

- Regular thorough cleaning of areas, e.g. changing rooms and food stores, particularly in corners where pests may be able to hide unnoticed.
- Clearing up any spillages thoroughly and promptly.
- Not allowing waste to build up and keeping bins covered at all times.
- Keeping doors and windows closed, using self-closing doors or using insect screens across openings.
- Using bristle strips and kick plates on doors that are ill-fitting to prevent gnawing damage and rodent access.
- Moving cupboards and equipment as far as possible to clean behind and under them regularly (see Safe lifting techniques on page 00).
- Removing any unused equipment and materials from the area.
- Ensuring food storage containers are properly closed when not in use.
- Checking all deliveries – of all items, not just food – for signs of infestation.
- Storing and rotating stock correctly.

Pest control management

Most businesses use specialist pest control companies to monitor and control pest infestation in their premises. They agree a contract which specifies the number of visits per year by a pest control specialist.

The pest control contractor will inspect premises looking for evidence of infestation by any type of pest. They will then deal with any pests they discover. Finally, they will complete a report describing what action they have taken. A copy of the report is left on the premises.

A pest control contractor may:
- lay bait and set baited traps
- use sticky boards
- install electric ultraviolet insect killers
- spray an insecticide chemical over an area.

The contractor will leave instructions regarding the treatments used. It is important not to touch or move any items that have been left to catch pests. Any sprayed areas must be left untouched for the instructed period of time.

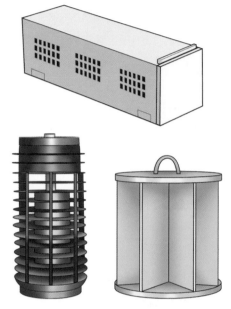

Figure 2.26 Pest control equipment

Test yourself!

1 What is the most important reason for cleaning?
   a To make a good impression on customers
   b To keep the work area pleasant
   c To reduce the danger of contamination
   d To prolong the life of equipment.

2 Which is the correct order for the cleaning process?
   a Pre-clean, clean, rinse, disinfect, rinse, dry
   b Pre-clean, rinse, clean, disinfect, rinse, dry
   c Pre-clean, disinfect, rinse, clean, rinse, dry
   d Pre-clean, rinse, clean, rinse, disinfect, dry.

3 Which cleaning agent kills bacteria?
   a Detergent
   b Disinfectant
   c Soap
   d Warm water.

4 Where might you find an infestation of weevils?
   a Flour
   b Fish
   c Fruit
   d Fennel.

5 Which part of the refrigerator should be cleaned very carefully?
   a Door seals   b Shelves   c Walls   d Floor.

Food storage and stock control

A considerable range of ingredients is used in the average catering kitchen. If you were to list all the food items used in your workplace it could run into hundreds! Some of these commodities can be stored for very long periods of time before use, e.g. dried fruit. Other food items will only remain safe to prepare and eat for a very short time, e.g. fresh mussels need to be used within a couple of hours of delivery if they cannot be stored in a refrigerator.

Correct delivery and storage of all foods is required under the HACCP procedures and appropriate records should be kept.

Receiving stock

Food items are delivered to a catering business in one of three temperature ranges:
o ambient/room temperature for fresh, dried or tinned items
o chilled/refrigerator temperature for high-risk fresh or processed foods
o frozen/freezer temperature for high-risk items that are in longer term storage.

Figure 2.27 Accepting a delivery of food items

Checking a food delivery

If you receive a food delivery at your workplace you need to check the following.

The **vehicle** delivering the items:
o Is it suitable?
o Is it clean inside?
o Is it refrigerated for the delivery of chilled items?

The **temperature** of the delivered items:
o Are chilled items below 5°C?
o Is frozen produce kept below −10°C?
o Use a temperature probe to check if necessary. If the temperature is too high reject the goods.

The **packaging**:
o Is it clean and undamaged?
o Is there any sign of mould or other spoilage?
o Are any containers dented, bulging or leaking?

- Are the items labelled with:
  - the name of the company?
  - description of the food?
  - product code?
  - ingredient list?
  - use by date?
  - weight?
- Is the 'best before' or 'use by date' still several days in the future?
- Do the items delivered match the delivery note provided in terms of:
  - amounts of each item? (e.g. 1 x 25kg bag)
  - specification of each item? (e.g. King Edward potatoes)

If you have to reject a delivery make sure:

- The delivery person has agreed to return the item to the supplier.
- The item being returned is recorded on either the delivery note or a separate return slip.
- The delivery person signs the delivery note or return slip, as you may do if requested.
- You give your copy of the delivery note or return slip to your supervisor as soon as possible. You need to make sure that your employer does not pay for goods that have been rejected and returned.

Stock rotation

It is very important to use ingredients in the same order that they have been delivered. This is because:

- food loses quality the longer it is kept
- food will have to be wasted if it is not used by the 'best before date'
- food thrown away is money wasted for the business.

Storage systems must ensure that stock is used in the correct rotation. When putting food away it is very important that:

- older stock of the same item is moved to the front so that it is used first
- new stock is never mixed up with old stock on shelves or in containers.

Did you know?

One way of remembering stock rotation is to think 'FIFO'. **F**irst **I**n **F**irst **O**ut – food that is put into storage first should be used first.

Try this! Worksheet 59

Produce a flow diagram of the key stages of food receipt and storage to include:

- *key checks that need to be made on receipt of goods*
- *stock rotation systems*
- *food types and storage conditions*
- *temperature for food storage*

Storing stock

A delivery must be put into the appropriate storage as soon as possible after arrival.

Frozen and **chilled** items must be put away first. Prompt storage is necessary because:

○ frozen items must not be left in warm conditions where they could start defrosting

○ chilled items must not be allowed to warm to an unsafe temperature at which bacteria could grow. This is especially important with ready-to-eat items, e.g. salads.

Packaged items should have storage instructions included on the label. These should be followed exactly.

Fresh items must be put into cool storage to preserve their quality ready for preparation.

Dry goods should be taken to the stores area where they should be entered on to the stock record to prevent theft.

Your employer may have a system for date coding all items delivered. A date sticker may have to be attached to the items as they are put away. As you put new stock away, move the old stock to a position where it will be used first. This is called stock rotation. See page 69 for more information. Handle all items carefully. Do not attempt to lift heavy items on your own (see page 103).

Some items may need to be removed from the original external packaging before storage, e.g. if a cardboard box is breaking or there is not enough space to store an item in its full packaging. Care must be taken to transfer any important information, e.g. use by dates, onto the replacement container. Your workplace should have a system for this.

Some businesses ensure stock rotation of short life items by marking the item with a coloured sticker to indicate the day of delivery. This encourages the use of food in the correct order.

Did you know?

In many countries it is now the law to label food with a date after which it is not assured of being safe to eat. It is an offence to change this date without re-treating or processing the food appropriately. Highly perishable foods (those that spoil quickly) must be marked with a 'use by' date. Less perishable items (which are preserved in some way) are marked with a 'best before' date. These dates indicate that the food will be in its best condition before this date. If consumed after this date it may have deteriorated in quality but it will not be a health risk.

Figure 2.28 Date code deliveries

Try this!

Imagine you have been asked to put away a delivery of fresh, whole chickens. The box they have been delivered in is very weak and flimsy. Describe exactly what you would do to make sure the chickens were stored safely.

What is cross-contamination?

Bacteria cannot move by themselves and so are only able to contaminate food by being transferred onto it by something or someone else. This is known as cross-contamination and is one of the main factors in outbreaks of food poisoning.

Types of cross-contamination

There are three main types of cross-contamination:
- **Direct**: when contaminated food comes into direct contact with another food item and bacteria are transferred from one item to the other.
- **Indirect**: when contaminated food comes into contact with a surface which then comes into contact with another food item, which then becomes contaminated.
- **Drip**: when a contaminated item (usually raw meat or poultry) is stored above other food and the juices from the contaminated item drip down and contaminate the food underneath.

Illness will result if the newly contaminated food item is not cooked thoroughly before service.

The most common type is indirect cross-contamination. The main sources are:
- hands of staff working in food production areas
- cloths and equipment used by staff in these areas
- infestation of pests in the kitchen (see pages 64–67)
- poor storage of food.

Hands: if hands are not washed thoroughly in between one job and another then cross-contamination can occur very easily (see Personal hygiene on page 49). There is a particular risk in the following situations:
- If raw food is prepared, followed by cooked food.
- If food preparation is resumed directly after a visit to the toilet or a smoking break.

Cloths and equipment: if cloths are not changed or cleaned regularly then cross-contamination can occur. Cloths can carry large amounts of bacteria and have been known to spread more over a surface than were present in the first place!

Equipment: this must be cleaned thoroughly after each use and checked for cleanliness before being used again. Some pieces of equipment may only be used for specific types of foods or in certain areas of the kitchen. Large catering operations may have completely separate preparation areas for certain food, e.g. a meat kitchen, a vegetable kitchen and so on. Most establishments have a separate pastry area.

Infestation of pests: cross-contamination can occur by an insect or animal touching the surface of a raw food product and then one that has been cooked, thus transferring bacteria from one to the other. Pests can also transfer bacteria by leaving fur or droppings on food. (Further information on pests can be found on pages 64–67.)

Poor storage of food: this can result in cross-contamination. If food is not put into suitably sized containers and covered, spillages may result. This could involve amounts of one item falling into another. Apart from being very messy and wasteful, this can become a food safety hazard, e.g. if an uncooked chicken defrosting on the top shelf of a refrigerator drips liquid onto an uncovered trifle on the shelf below, it is highly likely that salmonella bacteria will be transferred from the chicken to the trifle.

Methods of preventing cross–contamination

Cross-contamination can be prevented by breaking the chain of raw items getting into direct or indirect contact with other foods. To do this effectively, the workflow and storage systems of a kitchen must be looked at carefully to identify where there are weaknesses which may allow cross-contamination to take place.

Ways in which cross-contamination can be prevented:
- Use colour-coded systems for food types or store them in separate areas, e.g. a separate refrigerator for raw meat.
- Have separate preparation areas for raw and cooked items.
- Colour code equipment so that it is only used for either raw or cooked food preparation.
- Store food at the correct temperature, package it correctly, label it fully and use it in order.
- Organise the work area to prevent raw and cooked produce coming into contact by having a linear work flow.
- Ensure all staff wash their hands thoroughly at the appropriate times (see page 54).

Figure 2.29 Flies cause cross-contamination

Remember!

Chopping boards may be colour coded to reduce the risk of cross-contamination. The following code is commonly used in the industry:
o red – raw meat
o brown – vegetables
o blue – raw fish
o white – bakery, dairy
o yellow – cooked meat
o green – salad, fruit

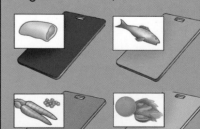

Figure 2.30 Colour-coded chopping boards

○ Use disposable cloths for one purpose only. Sometimes these are colour coded.

Storing food

All the methods of storing food are intended to keep the food safe from contamination and to reduce the speed at which spoilage occurs. When storing food, it must be kept covered, cool (refrigerated in most cases) and dry.

There are three main areas where food is stored in the kitchen:

○ dry stores

○ refrigerator

○ freezer.

These may be free-standing or walk-in units.

Follow these general food storage rules:

○ Always protect food from contamination by keeping it in suitable containers.

○ Store all food items off the floor on shelves or pallets.

○ Do not overload shelves.

○ Leave space between items for air to circulate.

○ Keep storage areas clean, dry and free from debris at all times.

○ Rotate stock correctly (see page 69).

○ Tell your supervisor about any signs of pest infestation (see page 64).

Figure 2.31 A well-organised dry stores area

Dry storage

○ The store should be cool and well-ventilated.

○ Flours and cereals may be stored in wheeled bins to protect them from pests. The bin must be fully emptied and cleaned before new stock is added.

○ Shelves should not be overfilled and old stock must always be put in front of new.

○ Move items from flimsy bags or unsuitable containers, make sure the description label with the 'use by' date is transferred.

○ Cleaning products should not be stored with food; they should be in a separate area.

Did you know?

A blown tin has both ends bulging as the contents have spoiled and gases have been produced in the process. The contents of these tins are not safe to eat and must be discarded. Be careful! The pressure built up inside the tin from the gases may cause the tin to explode.

Keep the following items in the dry store:
○ Dry foods, e.g. flour, sugar and dried herbs.
○ Canned and bottled items (unless the label specifies they need to be refrigerated).

Fruit and vegetable storage

○ Fresh fruit and vegetables should be stored in a cool, dry place.
○ Root vegetables store best in a dark area.
○ Loose soil around fresh vegetables should not be taken into the kitchen.
○ Fresh fruit and vegetables are often stored in a refrigerator if there is space, in a safe position.

Temperature and conditions for food storage

High-risk foods and those which will spoil quickly need to be stored in a refrigerator. This is because most pathogenic and food spoilage bacteria multiply very slowly or not at all between 0°C and 5°C – the temperature of a refrigerator.

All industrial refrigerators should defrost automatically. If ice is allowed to build up inside the unit it will reduce its efficiency.

Refrigerators

When separate refrigerators are not available for raw and high-risk foods then these items have to be positioned carefully in one unit. Raw food should **always** be stored below other food so that no blood or juices can drip down and contaminate items on the lower shelf.

Take care with strong-smelling foods (e.g. strong cheese and fish), as they can taint more delicate items (e.g. milk and eggs) and make them taste very strange. All items in a refrigerator should be covered, e.g. in a container with a fitted lid or covered with waxed paper, cling film, greaseproof paper or foil. Do not put food directly in front of the cooling unit if possible as this can affect how efficiently the refrigerator operates.

The following food should be refrigerated:
○ raw meat, poultry, fish and seafood
○ cooked meat, poultry, fish and seafood
○ meat, poultry and fish products, e.g. pies and pâtés
○ the contents of any opened cans in suitable containers
○ milk, cream, cheese and eggs, and any products containing them (e.g. a flan)

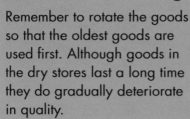

Remember!
Remember to rotate the goods so that the oldest goods are used first. Although goods in the dry stores last a long time they do gradually deteriorate in quality.

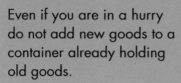

Remember!
Even if you are in a hurry do not add new goods to a container already holding old goods.

Did you know?
Opened cans of food should never be left in a refrigerator. As well as the danger of a cut from the sharp, exposed lid of the tin, if the juices inside the tin are acid (e.g. as with tinned fruit) they can react with the lining of the tin once exposed to the oxygen in air. This reaction can taint the food and give it a metallic flavour which is unacceptable. Some tins now have a plastic coating on the inside to stop this. It is still best to change the container of opened tinned items to be stored in the fridge.

- prepared salads
- fruit juice
- spreads and sauces
- any other item labelled for refrigeration.

Try this!
What problems can you identify with this refrigerator?

Remember!

Never put hot food into a refrigerator.
Never leave the refrigerator door open longer than necessary.
Both practices will cause the temperature inside the refrigerator to rise.

Did you know?

Unwrapped food in the freezer may suffer from 'freezer burn', i.e. the surface will be damaged as if it has been burnt. When thawed, the quality of the surface of the food will be poor and it may not be usable.

Freezers

Food is frozen to make it last longer without spoiling. It also keeps it safely, as pathogenic bacteria cannot multiply in temperatures below −18°C. However as soon as the temperature rises bacteria may start reproducing. Food that has been allowed to thaw should not be refrozen. This is in case the number of bacteria present have been able to reach a dangerous level and cause food poisoning. If a thawed item has been cooked it may be refrozen. This is because the cooking process will have killed any pathogenic bacteria present.

Storing foods inside a freezer

When loading a freezer with frozen food remember to:
- make sure all items are well wrapped
- label items clearly and include the date
- stack items close together to maintain the temperature
- place raw food below high-risk foods
- put stock with the shortest shelf life at the front.

Storage conditions required by different foods

An alternative way of stopping spoilage is to preserve the food. There are several methods of preservation that can delay the process or prevent it altogether. These include:
- **Heat treatment** by cooking, canning, bottling, sterilising, pasteurising and ultra-heat treatment (UHT). The amount of heat

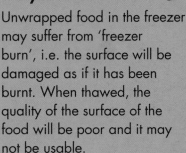

Remember!

If a fridge or freezer breaks down:
- call the service engineer to come and repair it
- do not open the door if at all possible.
Most freezers are fitted with alarms that will sound if there is a malfunction.

Remember!

If food has been cooked, cooled and reheated it should never be cooled and reheated a second time. It should always be thrown away.

and the length of heat treatment will increase the storage time. UHT products will keep for several months, canned goods will keep for several years.

○ **Low temperatures** used in the chilling or freezing of food.
○ **Dehydration**, i.e. the drying of fish, meat, fruit, vegetables, soups, stocks and beverages. This process excludes water. Dehydrated items stored in airtight containers will last a considerable period of time.
○ **Chemical preservation** by salting, pickling and curing (using sodium nitrate and nitrite salts). This method also alters the flavour of the item. It is often combined with the canning or bottling processes.
○ **Vacuum packing**, also known as 'sous vide', is used mainly for meat, fish and poultry. This process removes oxygen from around the food and greatly extends the shelf life. The items should remain in chilled storage.
○ **Smoking**, used particularly for fish, poultry and meat including ham and sausages. This process imparts a strong flavour to the food. Smoked items last longer than non-smoked items but still have to be kept in the refrigerator.
○ **Irradiation**, is a process that kills pathogenic bacteria and spoilage organisms. It works by subjecting the food to a low amount of radiation. It does not kill spores and toxins.

Thawing and defrosting food

Some food can be cooked straight after being removed from the freezer. If this is the case there will be appropriate instructions on the packet. Otherwise the item must be allowed to thaw before cooking. This is especially important with raw meat and poultry.

The rules for thawing food:
○ Always keep thawing raw meat items well away from other food.
○ Thaw items in a cool room, thawing cabinet or in the bottom of a refrigerator.
○ Always thaw items on a tray where juices can collect safely.
○ Once the item is thawed keep it in the refrigerator and cook it within 24 hours.
○ If using a microwave oven to defrost an item be aware of cool spots where it may remain frozen.
○ Never refreeze an item that has been thawed.

Did you know?

Some ingredients in dishes do not freeze well. Sauces which are to be frozen should not be made with wheat flour because once defrosted they will separate if not used within a few weeks. Sauce recipes should be adapted to use modified starch instead.

Did you know?

Some tinned foods have been opened after hundreds of years and the contents have still been edible (although not very nice to eat!)

Figure 2.32 Fruit that is canned or frozen lasts much longer than fresh fruit

Figure 2.33 Is your Christmas turkey safe?

Food storage and temperature control documentation

Under the HACCP procedures it is important to record readings and actions taken while preparing food. These procedures provide protection for the catering business and its employees in the event of a food safety issue.

The Environmental Health Officer visits all catering businesses regularly to check that food is being prepared according to the Regulations. The Officer will expect to see evidence of how food safety is being maintained. They will expect to see records of a variety of monitoring procedures, including:

o temperature records of all refrigerators and freezers
o pest control reports
o probe temperature records of reheated foods and those held at hot temperatures
o cleaning checklists and schedules
o delivery monitoring forms recording temperature of foods at time of delivery.

If there was an outbreak of food poisoning in a restaurant, the manager should be able to prove that all the food safety procedures have been carried out correctly. This process is known as showing '**due diligence**'. The Environmental Health Officer may decide that the blame for the outbreak is not with the restaurant and investigate other possible causes, e.g. the food suppliers.

Did you know?

Be careful with Christmas dinner! Thawing large frozen turkeys has to be carried out very carefully to avoid outbreaks of food poisoning. A 9kg turkey will take several days to thaw. Great care has to be taken to make sure the inside of the bird is defrosted. If not it will not cook to a safe temperature and bacteria will continue to reproduce.

Definition

Due diligence: that every possible precaution has been taken by the business to avoid a food safety problem.

Test yourself!

1 What is the maximum acceptable temperature for a chilled food delivery?
   a 3°C
   b 5°C
   c 7°C
   d 9°C.

2 What is the correct order in which the following delivered goods should be put away?
   a Frozen, chilled, fresh, tinned
   b Chilled, fresh, tinned, frozen
   c Fresh, tinned, frozen, chilled
   d Tinned, frozen, chilled, fresh.

3 What does FIFO stand for?

4 What is the term describing damaged unwrapped frozen food?

5 Define the term 'cross-contamination'.

Temperature control

Cooking and reheating food

There are many different methods of cookery. No matter which method is used, it is important to cook food thoroughly. The choice of method should suit the food to be cooked, e.g. you cannot grill an egg. The time and temperature at which the food is cooked must ensure that all the harmful bacteria that may be present are destroyed. This must be achieved without spoiling the quality of the item that is to be served to the customer. Overcooked food may be very safe but may also be **inedible**!

To make cooking as safe as possible, remember these points:

○ Heat items as quickly as possible to reduce the time spent in the temperature danger zone when bacteria will reproduce quickly.

○ Cut large joints of meat and poultry into smaller portions where possible to ensure even cooking all the way through.

○ Cook stuffings separately (they often do not reach the required temperature quickly enough and have caused many outbreaks of food poisoning in the past).

○ Stir stews and casseroles regularly during cooking to keep the temperature even throughout the pan.

> **Definition**
> **Inedible:** unable to be eaten.

> **Remember!**
> All food must be heated to at least 75°C and that temperature held for at least two minutes to make it safe. In Scotland food must be heated to at least 82°C for at least two minutes. No food should be reheated more than once.

Chilling or freezing food

If food has been cooked and is not for immediate consumption it should be cooled as quickly as possible. Ideally this should be carried out in a blast chiller (see page 75). Large production kitchens may operate a large cook-chill operation producing hundreds of chilled meals every day. Some cook-chill systems also use the 'sous vide' method for preservation of food in vacuum-packs (see page 228). This type of production involves specialist equipment. See Refrigerated storage on page 74.

Cooling cooked food is a very high-risk procedure. Unlike cooking, when high temperatures will be achieved to kill bacteria, if there are bacteria alive in the food they will reproduce as it cools.

Harmful bacteria may be present in cooked food as a result of spores not being destroyed in the cooking process. They may also have been transferred onto the cooked food from another source, e.g. dirty

Figure 2.34 A blast chiller

equipment. Bacteria will then remain in the food either reproducing at room temperature or dormant in the refrigerator or freezer.

Many catering premises now use blast chillers to reduce the temperature of cooked food as quickly as possible to make it safe.

Cooked food must not be cooled in a refrigerator or freezer where other food is being stored. If a hot item is put into this environment to cool down quickly it will raise the temperature of the surrounding air. This will result in the other chilled food becoming warm. Bacteria may then start reproducing in the food being stored. The warmth may also cause frozen food to start defrosting. Condensation may then occur and drip liquid onto food and contaminate it.

When cooling cooked food remember:
○ The smaller the size of the food item, the more quickly it will cool.
○ Shallow, flat containers have a greater surface area to allow faster cooling.
○ The greater the difference in temperature, the faster cooling will take place.

If food is to be frozen rapidly, specialist equipment is needed to carry out this procedure safely. Blast freezers cool food down to −20°C in 90 minutes.

If freezing food you must remember to:
○ reduce the temperature as quickly as possible
○ keep the thickness of the food to be frozen as even and thin as possible
○ wrap the food thoroughly
○ label the food clearly.

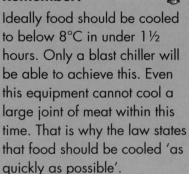

Remember!
Ideally food should be cooled to below 8°C in under 1½ hours. Only a blast chiller will be able to achieve this. Even this equipment cannot cool a large joint of meat within this time. That is why the law states that food should be cooled 'as quickly as possible'.

Remember!
Frequent opening and closing of the door of a refrigerator will cause the temperature inside to keep rising and falling.

Figure 2.35 A shallow, flat container allows faster cooling

Try this!
If an item is frozen in a standard freezer it will take much longer to freeze and the ice crystals that form within the item will be much larger. This will cause the texture of the item to be poor. Freeze a strawberry in a domestic freezer and then let it thaw! What happens to the strawberry?

Holding hot and cold food for service

Hot food

Hot cupboards and counter service equipment are designed to store food for a few hours at a safe hot temperature. The heating elements in this equipment are not sufficiently powerful to raise the temperature of the food quickly. This could mean that pathogenic bacteria could survive and reproduce to a dangerous level during the slow heating process.

The following rules apply when using hot holding equipment:
○ Always preheat the equipment before use.
○ Do not use the equipment to reheat food.
○ Check the equipment regularly if hot water is used; if it needs topping up use hot water (not cold).
○ If heated lights are used, keep the food fully in the lit areas.

When hot food is out on display and cannot be kept above 63°C it can only be put out for one continuous period of up to two hours. After this period of time the food must be thrown away. This is because it will have been at a temperature at which bacteria can multiply rapidly for too long and may no longer be safe to eat.

Figure 2.36 A bain-marie, one type of hot holding equipment

Cold food

Food which is to be held for service at room temperature has to be treated very carefully. This is because the temperature at which it has to be kept is ideal for bacteria to multiply rapidly. However, if the food were held at a lower temperature it could be unpleasant to eat. Imagine eating a sandwich which has been taken straight out of a refrigerator!

Cold food in a display cabinet or vending machine must be kept at below 8°C and ideally at below 5°C. Where this is not possible, cold food can be put out on display at room temperature for only one continuous period of up to four hours. After this time it must be thrown away. The length of time the food is left out must be recorded so it is never left out for too long. Different establishments use different systems to record this information. It is very convenient when the meal service time lasts four hours as the food put out at the beginning and left unsold can be thrown away when service finishes.

Did you know?

To ensure that all heat-resistant spores are destroyed by cooking, a temperature of 75°C must be reached for two minutes. In Scotland it must reach 82°C. Such intense heat may damage the quality of the food. It is also possible to destroy spores by heating food at a lower temperature for a longer period of time.

How to use a temperature probe

Some food may reach the required temperature on the outside but still be a very different temperature in the middle. This is where a temperature probe is needed to check that the internal temperature has reached the necessary level.

A temperature probe is a type of thermometer on a long stick that is used to take the core temperature from the middle of food. It is particularly useful when:

○ reheating a tray of cottage pie ready to serve on a counter
○ testing to see if the inside of a whole chicken is cooked
○ measuring the temperature of a joint of meat which is being roasted in the oven.
○ checking to see if a hot item has cooled down sufficiently to be put in the refrigerator.

Temperature probes are usually digital and can be battery operated. It is important to keep them very clean. They should always be sterilised before and after each use, otherwise they could transfer dangerous bacteria from one food to another.

Temperature probes need to be checked regularly to make sure they are working correctly. If they are not accurate they should not be used until they have been repaired or replaced.

Figure 2.37 Use a temperature probe to measure the temperature of a joint of meat

Test yourself!

Complete the following statements:

1 The transfer of bacteria from raw to cooked food is called _____ _____ .

2 The person authorised to enter food premises to inspect them for food safety is called an _____ _____ _____ .

3 The main law controlling the hygienic supply, preparation and service of food is called the _____ _____ _____ .

4 To make it safe, all raw food should be heated to _____ °C for _____ minutes.

5 To find out if food being heated is the correct temperature all the way through a _____ _____ needs to be used.

6 The _____ of bacteria may survive high temperatures.

Food safety procedures

To ensure that all food served to the public is safe, there is a range of laws and regulations which need to be followed by all catering businesses. Each catering organisation has to produce a policy document giving details of the standards it is setting and the training it undertakes to give all the catering staff. A detailed set of records has to be kept on a day-to-day basis in a catering kitchen to prove that the correct procedures are being followed. In this way customers should be confident they will not be made ill by eating food produced by the establishment. Environmental Health Officers regularly inspect all the hygiene, health and safety aspects of businesses to make sure the standards are met.

Key requirements of food safety legislation

Food safety laws require all catering businesses to ensure:

○ All their food production and service staff practice a high standard of personal hygiene, see page 49.
○ All their staff have regular training in all hygiene, health and safety matters relating to their workplace, see Chapter 3.
○ All their staff comply with the rules and regulations of their organisation, particularly regarding the preparation and service of food.
○ All their staff obey the requirements of the food safety legislation which relates to them. This should be explained clearly to staff by their employer and training records should be kept.

It is very important that all required records, e.g. temperature records, are accurately kept. They may be needed as evidence if there is a food safety incident. If an organisation is investigated but can show that it has kept all the records correctly and has high food safety standards it may be given a lower penalty if it is prosecuted, or not prosecuted at all. This defence is called 'due diligence' (see page 77).

Did you know?
The Basic Food Hygiene test makes sure food handlers know the main principles of food safety. Some food handlers take the Intermediate Food Hygiene examination. Supervisors may take the Advanced Food Hygiene qualification.

Case study – A due diligence defence

A customer complained that he had been made ill by eating mussels at a seafood restaurant. The Environmental Health Officer visited the restaurant and inspected the way in which the mussels had been prepared and stored, both before and after cooking. The Officer checked the refrigerator temperature and the delivery temperature records and the quality checks that had been carried out. The Food Hygiene Certificates of the staff were presented to indicate that they were all trained in hygienic work practices. The Environmental Health Officer also studied the kitchen layout and the workflow system to try and find out if cross–contamination could have occurred during the preparation and service of the mussels. As the Officer was satisfied that every possible precaution had been taken the restaurant was able to offer the defence of due diligence and was not prosecuted for making the customer ill.

Definition
Documented: making a detailed record of information.

HACCP practices and procedures

In every business that produces, serves or sells food it is vital that there is an organised system to reduce all risk of food safety hazards.

The HACCP procedures require there to be a **documented** system highlighting all areas where special attention should be paid to food safety. The system should cover all food used on the premises and follow the route from the delivery of the raw materials through to the consumption, service or sale of the items.

Did you know?
The HACCP procedures were first developed in the 1960s to ensure that astronauts going up in space had food to eat that was absolutely safe.

Step	Hazard	Action
1 Purchase	High-risk (ready-to-eat) foods contaminated with food-poisoning bacteria or toxins.	Buy from reputable supplier only. Specify maximum temperature at delivery.
2 Receipt of food	High-risk (ready-to-eat) foods contaminated with food-poisoning bacteria or toxins.	Check it looks, smells and feels right. Check the temperature is right.
3 Storage	Growth of food poisoning bacteria, toxins on high-risk (ready-to-eat) foods. Further contamination.	High-risk foods stored at safe temperature. Store them wrapped. Label high-risk food with the correct 'sell by' date. Rotate stock and use by recommended date.
4 Preparation	Contamination of high-risk (ready-to-eat) foods. Growth of food-poisoning bacteria.	Wash your hands before handling food. Limit any exposure to room temperatures during preparation. Prepare with clean equipment and use this for high-risk (ready-to-eat) food only. Separate cooked foods from any raw foods.

5 Cooking	Survival of food-poisoning bacteria.	Cooked rolled joints, chicken, and re-formed meats e.g. burgers, so that the thickest part reaches at least 75°C. Sear the outside of other, solid meat cuts (e.g. joints of beef, steaks) before cooking.
6 Cooling	Growth of food-poisoning bacteria. Production of poisons by bacteria. Contamination with food-poisoning bacteria.	Cool foods as quickly as possible. Don't leave out at room temperatures to cool, unless the cooling period is short, e.g. place any stews or rice, etc. in shallow trays and cool to chill temperatures quickly.
7 Hot-holding	Growth of food-poisoning bacteria. Production of poisons by bacteria.	Keep food hot, above 63°C.
8 Reheating	Survival of food-poisoning bacteria.	Reheat to above 75°C.
9 Chilled storage	Growth of food-poisoning bacteria.	Keep temperatures at right level. Label high-risk ready-to-eat foods with correct date code.
10 Serving	Growth of disease-causing bacteria. Production of poisons by bacteria. Contamination.	COLD SERVICE FOODS – serve high-risk foods as soon as possible after removing from refrigerated storage to avoid them getting warm. HOT FOODS – serve high-risk foods quickly to avoid them cooling down.

Figure 2.38 Critical control points – Department of Health.

The stages a food safety management system should cover are:
o quality, packaging and temperature of the food at delivery
o packaging, temperature, location and method of storage
o method of preparation
o type and length of storage between preparation and cooking
o method of holding hot food after cooking
o method of cooling and storing after cooking
o method of reheating cooked food
o method of serving.

The HACCP system exists to identify food safety hazards. Once a hazard has been identified then the risk it poses is analysed and a solution to reduce the risk put into place. The system is very logical and methodical and looks in detail at each stage of the food production process in each catering organisation. It can involve a large number of checks to be carried out and records to be kept. Several systems of HACCP have been developed for use in the catering industry:
o Codex HACCP
o Assured safe catering
o Safer food better business.

Try this!
Produce a report that outlines the HACCP practices and procedures required to maintain food safety in a typical kitchen environment. Identify the:
o hazard analysis at all stages of food production
o control points and critical control points
o control limits
o corrective action
o audit and verification documentation
o key safety records
o reporting procedure.

Many small catering businesses will use one of these systems successfully. Larger catering companies may decide to develop their own. A HACCP system must include:

○ an analysis of the possible hazards at all stages of food production
○ identification of the points at which these hazards can be controlled
○ identification of the most important critical points at which the hazards must be controlled
○ the maximum and minimum limits at which the hazard must be controlled
○ the ways in which the hazard can be reduced or removed
○ the records that are needed to show how this process is being carried out.

HACCP monitoring

One of the key procedures in the HACCP system is **monitoring**. To be able to check condition, it has to be measured against a standard that has already been set. For example, if your speed of work was being monitored, it would be measured against an average that had been worked out in advance. This would be obtained by watching and timing a range of people all carrying out the same task.

In a catering kitchen there are many types of monitoring that take place:

○ The Head Chef monitors the standard and amount of work produced by the kitchen staff.
○ Refrigerator and freezer temperatures are monitored and recorded several times each day.
○ Cleaning is monitored daily by supervisors to make sure standards of hygiene are being maintained.
○ Contractors regularly monitor a range of equipment in the kitchen including:
  – pest control equipment
  – alarm systems
  – fire-fighting equipment
  – microwave ovens and other cooking equipment, e.g. steamers
  – refrigerators and freezers
  – dishwashers
  – extraction systems.
○ Deliveries are checked for quality, temperature, best before dates and correct weight.

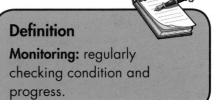

Definition
Monitoring: regularly checking condition and progress.

Fridge temperatures					
Week commencing: _____					

	Time	Signed	Time	Signed	Time	Signed
MON						
	Temp		Temp		Temp	
TUE	Time	Signed	Time	Signed	Time	Signed
	Temp		Temp		Temp	
WED	Time	Signed	Time	Signed	Time	Signed
	Temp		Temp		Temp	
THURS	Time	Signed	Time	Signed	Time	Signed
	Temp		Temp		Temp	
FRI	Time	Signed	Time	Signed	Time	Signed
	Temp		Temp		Temp	
SAT	Time	Signed	Time	Signed	Time	Signed
	Temp		Temp		Temp	
SUN	Time	Signed	Time	Signed	Time	Signed
	Temp		Temp		Temp	

Comments

_____
_____
_____

Figure 2.39 Temperature control record sheet

- Rotation of stock is monitored frequently to make sure the oldest products are used first.
- The amount of wasted food thrown away may be checked very regularly in some kitchens.
- The presentation standard of the food produced is monitored, often by checking against prepared photographs.

The process of monitoring can take several forms, including:

- completing a checklist
- recording specific information on a chart
- filling in particular sections on a schedule
- carrying out spot checks
- questioning staff and contractors
- observing work practices and work areas
- taking samples – of food or **swabs** of work surfaces and equipment
- weighing items.

> **Definition**
>
> **Swab:** a sterile piece of cotton used to take a sample for chemical analysis.

Figure 2.40 Completing a checklist

Try this! Worksheet 8

Which monitoring processes would you use for the following situations?

- *Keeping the results of refrigerator temperature checks.*
- *Making sure all areas of the staff changing room have been cleaned thoroughly.*
- *Checking that a meat delivery is correct.*
- *Finding out if there is any evidence of mice in the dry stores area.*

Action to take when monitoring reveals a problem

The purpose of monitoring and checking is to spot a potential problem or risk before it becomes a serious hazard. If checking is carried out regularly then any difference in results should show up very quickly.

The action taken depends on the type of problem. Urgent action is necessary if the problem concerns a possible food safety hazard.

The table on the next page shows the type of action that may be necessary to prevent food becoming a hazard.

Problem	Possible action to be taken
Poor standard of work produced by kitchen staff	Retraining and closer supervision by Head Chef.
Refrigerator temperature rises significantly	Check that the refrigerator is not defrosting automatically. If this is not the case: ○ move items to another refrigerator with the correct temperature ○ unplug the refrigerator if possible ○ put an 'out of order' notice on it ○ tell your supervisor as soon as possible.
A mouse is spotted in the corner of the kitchen	○ Tell your supervisor as soon as possible. ○ The pest control contractor will be called out immediately. ○ Kitchen staff will need to look out for evidence of mouse infestation. ○ Make sure that no food crumbs are left around or any food left uncovered in kitchen and stores areas.
Microwave does not heat the food properly	○ Check the portion of food is the correct size for the time allowed. ○ Test the microwave by heating a cup of water. ○ If it does not perform as it should, unplug the equipment so it cannot be used. ○ Put an 'out of order' sign on the machine. ○ Tell your supervisor. ○ An engineer should attend to rectify the problem.
Chilled produce is delivered in a van that is not refrigerated	○ Check the temperature of the delivered items. If over the safe limit of 8°C, refuse the delivery. ○ Tell your supervisor, as this may have been a problem before and the supplier may be changed.
Out-of-date salad items are found at the back of the refrigerator during a stock take	○ Throw the out-of-date items away. ○ Tell your supervisor, as stock figures will be affected.
A large amount of raw vegetable waste is found in the bin	Head Chef to retrain staff in efficient preparation methods.
A large amount of cooked waste is found in the bin	Head Chef will investigate and take action. Possible reasons: ○ portions served too large ○ quality of food poor.
The plated food items do not look like the prepared photographs	Head Chef will investigate and take action. Possible reasons: ○ poor quality food used ○ staff not trained correctly.

Figure 2.41 Action to take when monitoring reveals a problem

The relative importance of different hazards

It is important to be able to identify which situations require urgent action and which problems can be solved a little later on.

All circumstances which put any person in danger should be dealt with immediately. These include any:

o fire or security alert
o accident to any person in the area
o foreign body found in food
o equipment found in a dangerous condition
o floor surface found in a dangerous condition
o food left in an unsafe condition
o food stored in an unsafe condition.

Try this!
Worksheet 9

Put the following incidents in the order you would deal with them if they all happened together. Then state the action you would take in respect of each hazard.

o *A carton of cream is past its 'use by' date in the refrigerator.*
o *There is a pool of water around the door of an upright freezer and the contents are thawing.*
o *A chef cuts their finger and needs a plaster.*
o *A fly falls in a pan of soup on the stove.*
o *A frying pan overheats and catches fire on the stove.*

Figure 2.42 Can you spot all the things that have gone wrong?

Identifying types of food safety hazard

Food safety hazards can come from the most unlikely sources – some of them quite unexpected. When trying to identify possible food safety hazards you need to be very open-minded.

The table below shows the questions you need to ask when trying to identify food safety hazards:

Question	Possible answers
Where could harmful bacteria be found in the workplace?	o Poor cleaning of equipment. o Insect or rodent infestation. o Poor hygiene practices of staff – not washing hands sufficiently, staff being ill and still coming to work.
How is cross-contamination caused?	o By using the same chopping boards for raw and cooked foods. o By storing raw food above cooked food in the refrigerator. o By food handlers not washing their hands thoroughly in between dealing with raw and cooked foods.
What other possible ways are there for food to be contaminated in the workplace?	o Cleaning chemicals getting into food from poor storage or not rinsing properly. o 'Foreign bodies' getting into food from breakages not being cleared away carefully.
Which high-risk foods come into the kitchen in an uncooked state?	o Chicken o Eggs o Meat o Vegetables o Rice. These are high-risk due to the food poisoning bacteria or toxins that may be found in them in their raw state.
Is it possible for harmful bacteria to be able to multiply to a dangerous level?	o Is any food cooked and then left out at room temperature for a long time before being put in the refrigerator? Is there a better procedure that can be used? o Is any high-risk raw food left out for a long time at room temperature? Can this be avoided? o Is there ever a significant delay between cooking food, keeping it hot and it being served? Is there an alternative to this practice?
Is a probe used correctly to ensure thorough cooking and reheating of food?	If no, what happens instead?
Is food ever served before it has been reheated properly?	If yes, why and how can this be avoided next time?

Is frozen food sometimes not defrosted in time?	If yes, what happens?
Does the correct equipment exist in the kitchen for certain processes? Is it used when it should be (e.g. a blast chiller used to chill food quickly)?	If the equipment is not available, what happens?
What happens when demand is unpredictable? How is extra food provided at short notice?	Is there a stock of stand-by items kept in a freezer? How long does it take to get this ready for service?
What happens when food has to travel some distance between preparation and service? Does this happen when the food is hot or cold?	Is specialist equipment provided? If not, how is the food kept free from contamination and at the correct temperature?

Figure 2.43 Identifying food safety hazards

It is very important to report all possible hazards to your supervisor. The situation may result in:

○ a serious safety hazard (food or health and safety)

○ a high level of wastage leading to shortages and inaccurate stock records

○ a repair or service call-out to fix or maintain a piece of equipment or to maintain the hygiene of the premises

○ the identification of a need for staff training.

Try this! Worksheet 7

Look at the table above. Now think about your workplace. Make a similar list that identifies risk areas that exist with present work practices. This is the first stage of the HACCP procedures for creating a food safety management system.

Key elements of a food safety policy

Current food safety legislation recommends that all catering organisations have a food safety policy. This document describes how the business provides training and maintains standards to keep within the food safety laws. A policy will include:

○ standards of personal hygiene required by all food handlers (see page 49)

○ procedures for reporting sickness and accidents within the workplace (see page 119)

- requirements for pest control measures within the building (see page 67)
- minimum acceptable standards of cleaning and disinfection in food production areas (see pages 56–61)
- requirement for all visitors to the production areas to wear suitable protective clothing. This is usually a white coat and hat but sometimes gloves, hairnets and special footwear are also provided.

Records and reporting procedures

Under the HACCP legislation there is a requirement to keep records relating to the hazard analysis and monitoring process. The type and number of records kept will depend on the size and type of catering operation. The most common types of records and reporting systems are:

- training records for the use of dangerous machines, cleaning procedures, hygiene requirements, etc.
- pest control records (see page 67)
- temperature records for freezers, refrigerators, hot and cold holding equipment, cooling food, etc.
- accident report forms (see page 119)
- sickness records of any notifiable illnesses (see page 54)
- customer complaints regarding possible food safety issues
- maintenance record of equipment which could affect food safety.

Test yourself!

1 Which of the following is an example of monitoring food safety?
   a Taking fridge temperatures
   b Writing weekly menus
   c Washing the kitchen floor
   d Calculating food cost.

2 What is the process of collecting information to prove food safety called?
   a Assessing hygiene methods
   b Monitoring bad practice
   c Copying clear records
   d Demonstrating due diligence.

3 Which of the following is not an example of a HACCP record?
   a Staff rota
   b Temperature chart
   c Cleaning schedule
   d Equipment checklist.

4 Complete the table below indicating the conditions and location where you would store the following items and which you would put away first:

Item	Order of storage	Location	Conditions (e.g. temperature)
Fresh fish			
Tinned tomatoes			
Dried basil			
Fresh garlic			
Chilled potato salad			
Frozen peas			

Health and safety

3

This chapter covers the following outcomes from Diploma unit 203: Health and safety in catering and hospitality

- Outcome 203.1 Explain the importance of health and safety in the catering and hospitality industry
- Outcome 203.2 Identify hazards in the catering and hospitality workplace
- Outcome 203.3 Contribute to controlling hazards in the workplace
- Outcome 203.4 Maintain a healthy and safe workplace.

Working through this chapter could also provide evidence for the following Key Skills:

C2.1, C2.2a, C2.2b, C2.3, N2.1, N2.2a, N2.3, N2.2c, ICT2.1, ICT2.2, ICT2.3, LP2.1 LP2.2, LP2.2

In this chapter you will learn how to:

Identify the responsibilities, costs and benefits of health and safety legislation and regulations

Identify the causes of ill health, accidents and injuries in the workplace and ways to avoid them

List the steps and benefits of the risk assessment processes

Identify the methods, reasons and legal requirements for reporting accidents

Recognise safety signs and other sources of information to assist in developing health and safety systems

Outline procedures to be followed when an incident or accident is reported.

The importance of health and safety

It is important that all workers are able to carry out their tasks without causing any accident or injury to themselves or others (e.g. work colleagues or members of the public). Many years ago injuries at work were quite common, but since the Health and Safety at Work Act 1974 was brought in, most people take much greater care to work in a safe manner. This means there are fewer accidents in the workplace.

Figure 3.1 All chefs need to know the laws on health and safety

Under the Health and Safety at Work Act both employers and employees are responsible for keeping the workplace safe. They have a duty to themselves, each other and any visitors, customers and guests. If they fail to carry out this duty they could be personally liable and could be fined or imprisoned!

The Health and Safety at Work Act has had a considerable impact within the catering industry. As well as staff having a responsibility to keep the workplace safe, designers, manufacturers and suppliers of catering equipment, goods and services have also had to consider the impact of their products on the working environment. Local authorities have had to employ and train staff to go out into workplaces to make sure safe procedures are being followed.

Did you know?

During the past ten years over 2,000 workers in the catering industry have had to take more than three days off work to recover from an accident in the workplace. Over 800 of these people suffered a major injury.

Employers' duties

The Health and Safety at Work Act makes sure that employers do not put their staff in dangerous situations where they could hurt themselves or others. Under this Act, employers must:

○ keep all their staff safe while working
○ provide safe equipment, tools and surroundings in which to work
○ train staff how to work, clean, use chemicals and maintain the equipment they use
○ produce a policy document telling everyone how to behave safely
○ provide first-aid equipment and help
○ keep an accident book and use it correctly.

Employees' duties

While at work an employee must:

○ take reasonable care of their own safety and the safety of others
○ work in the manner laid down by the employer, especially regarding safety
○ tell their supervisor if they see anything that they think may be unsafe and could cause an accident.

Powers and actions of enforcement officers

Health and safety laws are enforced by an inspector from the Health and Safety Executive (HSE) or sometimes from the local council. If there has been a serious accident on the premises, an inspector will investigate how it happened. They will ask many questions and watch how people work in the area.

A Health and Safety Inspector has the power to:
○ enter the premises with or without notice
○ talk to employees and safety representatives
○ inspect health and safety records
○ take photographs and samples
○ issue a notice requiring improvements to be made
○ prevent the use of dangerous equipment
○ prosecute either the business or an individual for breaking health and safety law.

> **Did you know?**
>
> The most common dangerous occurrences in the catering industry which break the Health and Safety at Work Act are:
> o missing guards on food slicing machines
> o trailing cables
> o insecure wiring on plugs
> o faulty microwave seals
> o broken or worn steps
> o poor lighting of work areas.

Figure 3.2 An inspector will investigate a serious accident

people over school leaving age (16 years of age) and after full training and supervision. The list includes:

- Worm-type mincing machines
- Rotary knife bowl-type chopping machines
- Dough brakes
- Dough mixers
- Food-mixing machines (when used with various attachments)
- Pie- and tart-making machines
- Vegetable-slicing machines
- Potato-chipping machines
- Circular knife-slicing machines
- Machines with circular saw blades
- Machines with a saw in the form of a continuous blade or strip
- Wrapping and packing machines.

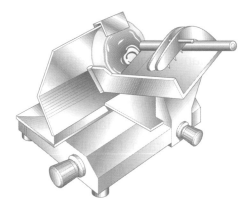

Figure 3.3 A meat slicing machine

COSHH

The COSHH Regulations form part of the Health and Safety at Work Act. They are rules which control substances which are considered hazardous to health. The COSHH Regulations state that:

- chemicals that may be dangerous to people must be clearly identified
- those chemicals must be stored, issued and used safely
- training must be given in the use of these chemicals
- suitable protective clothing must be provided when using the chemicals.

When using any type of chemical:

- always follow the manufacturer's instructions carefully
- never mix one chemical with another
- never move any chemical from its original container into an alternative one which is incorrectly labelled or has no label at all
- never use food containers to store a cleaning chemical
- always store chemicals in the correct place.

Definition

Caustic: a substance that will stick to a surface and burn chemically. It is used for heavy-duty cleaning.

Case study

A pub kept some beer pipe cleaning fluid in an unlabelled, clear glass bottle on the floor. It was placed near the beer pipes ready to use. A new member of staff who was very thirsty opened the bottle and drank from it. The liquid was clear and looked like lemonade but in fact was an extremely strong, caustic chemical. The member of staff suffered extensive burning of mouth, throat and stomach and can no longer eat normally.

Figure 3.4 Never pour a liquid into an unlabelled container

Why have health and safety regulations?

Most accidents are a result of human error. Over 3,000 accidents occur in the hospitality industry each year. The purpose of health and safety regulations is to reduce this figure. When working with other people and dealing with members of the public, it is particularly important to conduct yourself in a safe and hygienic manner. Official rules ensure everyone knows what their responsibilities are.

Common causes of accidents are:
○ lifting and carrying heavy, awkward objects
○ stacking and storing objects carelessly
○ slipping and falling in work areas
○ working in a rush
○ not concentrating when using equipment and machinery.

Effects of an accident in the workplace

When an accident happens at work it is not only the person involved who may be affected. Accidents can lead to:
○ wastage of materials, e.g. if food is burned or glass broken
○ wastage of time, e.g. delays in replacing food or equipment
○ increase in workload for others if an accident victim cannot return to work quickly
○ disruption in workflow if an area of the kitchen cannot be used for some time
○ loss of revenue if a smaller quantity of a dish can be produced
○ an increase in costs if an additional member of staff has to be brought in to cover.

Try this!

Imagine you have been asked to tell a new member of staff about health and safety law and how it operates on catering premises. What is the best way of doing this? Will you be understood clearly? Will the new member of staff remember the important points? You may like to design a booklet or put together a PowerPoint or flipchart presentation.

Top marks!

Always bear in mind the wider impact of what you do as an employee in terms of health and safety.

Benefits of good working practice

It is very important to work in a safe and hygienic way for several reasons:

○ It avoids injuring yourself or others.
○ It is usually quicker and easier.
○ It is more professional.

To reduce the risk of accidents you should follow any guidelines given to you about safe working practices. If health and safety regulations are not met you or your employer could be fined and your workplace may be closed down until safety improvements have been made. The fine for not following health and safety law is unlimited. You could also be sent to prison for an unlimited length of time! This means that a serious health and safety problem, e.g. a major accident, could be very expensive and also give the person responsible a criminal record.

Investigate!
○ **What year was the Health and Safety at Work Act introduced?**
○ **If there is a safety problem at work what is the name of the government organisation which will become involved?**

Investigate!
Which of the prescribed dangerous machines listed on page 98 can be found in your kitchen?

Test yourself!

1 Complete the sentences.
The _____ and _____ at Work Act requires all staff to work safely in the kitchen.
All _____ are responsible for the safety of themselves and others.
Staff can find out more information about these Regulations by asking their _____ and looking at the _____ .

2 What do these initials stand for?
a HACCP
_____

b COSSH
_____

c PPE
_____

3 Name two common dangerous occurrences which break the Health and Safety at Work Act.

4 How old must a person be in order to use a machine listed under the Prescribed Machines Order?

5 Complete the sentence.
The Manual Handling Operations Regulations aim to _____ the number of _____ caused by people moving _____ and _____ shaped items while at _____ .

Hazards in the workplace

What is a hazard? A hazard is anything that can cause harm, e.g. a knife, a slicing machine or a slippery floor.

What is a risk? A risk is the chance of harm being done. A risk usually involves a hazard, e.g. walking across a slippery floor.

Top marks!
Make sure you are clear about the difference between a risk and a hazard.

Types of hazard and how to control them

In a kitchen environment there is a range of hazards which have to be controlled constantly to reduce the risks they pose. The most common hazards are:
- slippery surfaces, particularly floors
- sharp objects such as knives and slicing machine blades
- hot liquids and surfaces such as fryers, stove tops and boiling water
- moving heavy items, e.g. drums of oil and sacks of potatoes
- working very fast because of the pressure of service time
- frequently moving around a poorly laid out kitchen.

Did you know?
To warn others in the kitchen that a hot saucepan had just come out of the oven it was traditional to sprinkle flour on the handle or cover the handle with a cloth.

The risk from these hazards can be reduced by:
- using non-slip flooring
- training staff to use equipment and machinery correctly
- maintaining equipment and machinery
- providing and using appropriate protective clothing and equipment
- providing trolleys and sack trucks and training staff how to move items safely
- adapting work methods to reduce the need to move around the kitchen so much.

Figure 3.5 Use a trolley to move items safely

101

Hazardous work methods

Many accidents are caused by poor work methods. Before starting work consider these points:

○ When a range of tasks has to be completed they should be carried out in order.

○ Finish one task before starting the next.

○ Assemble all the equipment necessary before starting the task.

○ Allow sufficient time and space to carry out the task involved.

○ Follow a logical sequence. The flow of work should move one way e.g. left to right.

○ Make sure there are no spillages on the floor. They will make the floor slippery and could cause an accident.

Figure 3.6 An untidy work area showing hazardous work methods

Figure 3.7 How a work area should be organised for safety

Hazardous work area

Some areas of the kitchen may not be the most appropriate to work in, for example:

○ A larder area might be very cold. It is difficult to prepare food with very cold hands.

○ The kitchen may be very crowded if there are several staff on duty. It is easy to collide with other people in a small space. This could be very dangerous if you are carrying a pot of hot liquid.

○ Floors can get greasy and wet if spillages are not cleared up quickly and thoroughly. Staff walking from the kitchen into a walk-in cold room and out again may make the floors slippery.

Did you know?

If a floor is getting slippery during service, you should throw several generous handfuls of salt over the surface. This is a quick, temporary remedy as the salt absorbs the liquid or grease. The floor can then be cleaned properly when there is time.

Manual handling

It is very easy to hurt yourself if you do not know how to lift and move items safely. It is not just heavy items that can cause problems when moving them about.

- Be very careful moving pots containing hot liquids. Do not have them too full.
- When taking items out of ovens be careful not to burn someone who may be passing by.
- Do not overload trolleys or trucks.
- Always make sure you can see where you are going.
- Stack heavier items at the bottom and lighter items at the top of a pile.
- Do not stack shelves too high.
- Use steps with great care. Have someone hold them at the bottom if possible.

Figure 3.8 Careless handling and lifting can lead to problems

Lifting a heavy object

To lift a heavy object safely needs correct training. A few guidelines follow:

- Keep your muscles relaxed: tense muscles strain easily.
- Plan what is to be carried to where.
- Check the route is clear, doors open, ramps in position, lights on.
- Get help if the object is likely to be heavier than you can easily handle.
- Position your feet carefully at either side of the object to keep your balance.
- Use one hand to support the weight of the item, the other to pull the item towards you. This way your body can take part of the weight. Use your whole hand to lift, not just the tips of your fingers.
- Do not twist to change direction as you are lifting or carrying. Move your feet in plenty of small steps.

Figure 3.9 Lifting a heavy object safely

Try this!

Try lifting a medium-sized, empty box following the guidelines above to avoid straining yourself.

Equipment

Equipment can be manual or electrical. Training must be given in the operation of equipment and the equipment must be checked regularly.

You can be injured by equipment in these ways:

○ **Entrapment**: getting your finger stuck in a mincing machine.
○ **Impact**: dropping a heavy saucepan on your foot.
○ **Contact**: touching a hot pan with your hand.
○ **Ejection**: not fitting a processor lid correctly and it flying off and hitting you during use.
○ **Faulty equipment**: using a mixer with a faulty on/off switch.
○ **Inappropriate use of equipment**: using a knife blade to open a tin.

Types of manual equipment include:

○ knives
○ mandolins.

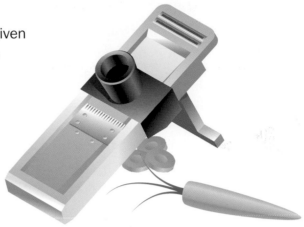

Figure 3.10 A mandolin

Knife care and safety

Poor knife techniques and untidy work methods are often a cause of accidents in the kitchen. Follow the rules below:

○ Store your knives in a specially designed area when not in use, e.g. in a box, case, wallet or on a magnetic rack. Storing loose knives in a drawer can damage the blades and cause injury.
○ When moving knives, transport them in the appropriate box or case. Never leave them loose. This avoids accidents in the workplace. It also stops you getting into trouble with the police when carrying your knives to and from work.
○ When carrying a knife, always point it down and hold it close to your side. Work colleagues can be unintentionally stabbed if this rule is not followed!
○ If passing a knife to a colleague always offer it to them handle first.
○ Never leave a knife on a work surface with the blade upwards.
○ Never leave a knife hanging over the edge of a work surface.
○ Never try to catch a falling knife – let it come to rest on the ground before you pick it up.
○ Never use a knife as a can opener or screwdriver.

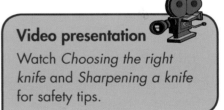

Video presentation
Watch *Choosing the right knife* and *Sharpening a knife* for safety tips.

Figure 3.11 A set of chef's knives. Always take care when handling these.

- Do not use a knife which is blunt or has a greasy, loose or damaged handle. A knife in any of these conditions can easily slip and cause a serious cut.
- It is recommended that you use colour-coded knives to prevent cross-contamination, see Chapter 2.
- Only use a knife on a chopping board which has a damp cloth underneath to prevent slippage.
- When wiping a knife clean after use, wipe from the blade base to the tip with the sharp edge facing away from your body.
- Never leave a knife in a sink. Wash it and remove it immediately.

Electrical equipment

Electrical equipment includes:

- slicing machines
- mixers
- mincers
- blenders.

These are known as **prescribed dangerous machines** and have special regulations relating to their use.

All electrical equipment should be tested regularly by qualified electricians. They will ensure that the cables are not damaged and the correct fuses and circuit breakers are fitted. No item of electrical equipment should be used if it has a damaged flex or is faulty. It should be removed from the work area if possible and have an out of order sign attached to it until it can be checked and repaired by a qualified person.

Rules for operating machinery

- Always follow the manufacturer's instructions.
- Never operate machinery if the safety guards are not in place. Many machines will not work unless correctly and fully assembled. However, some older models may work without the safety equipment being fitted (be very careful with these).
- If the machine will not work properly seek help from your supervisor.
- Ensure that the correct attachments are being used on the equipment for the task to be carried out.
- Never push food against a cutting blade with your hands – use a proper plunger or the handle supplied.

Case study

A student visiting a fast-food restaurant was electrocuted when she accidentally touched a live wire sticking out of a hand dryer which had been vandalised. The dryer had been damaged at least ten days prior to the accident but had not been repaired.

Figure 3.12 Negligence can result in serious consequences in the workplace

Remember!

Take great care when operating machinery. No one under the age of 18 may clean, lubricate or adjust a machine if they will be at risk of injury from a moving part.

- If using a spoon do not let it touch any moving parts. If it does the spoon and the machine will be damaged.
- Do not use faulty machinery. Label it 'out of order' and unplug it or partly dismantle it so it cannot be used. Report the problem to your supervisor so a repair can be arranged.
- Do not overload electrical sockets. This may cause a fire or cause fuses to blow and could affect everybody working in the building.
- Do not operate electrical equipment with wet hands or near sinks or any other source of water. An electric shock could result from this action.
- Keep your hands away from sharp blades. Wait for them to stop rotating after switching the machine off before starting any other activity, e.g. cleaning.
- Make sure the power is disconnected before starting to clean electrical machinery.
- Do not use machinery if the plug or flex is damaged in any way.

Hazardous substances

Any substance that is not in the appropriate place or is not being used correctly may become a hazard. In catering, the types of substances that may become hazardous include:

- Cooking oil, gels or spirits which may:
  - overheat and catch fire
  - get spilt on a floor and make it very slippery.
- Cleaning chemicals which may:
  - be used incorrectly, e.g. not **diluted** sufficiently
  - not be used with the appropriate protective equipment, e.g. goggles and gloves
  - be mixed together and give off dangerous fumes
  - be decanted from a large, labelled container into a smaller, unlabelled container and mistaken for another liquid.

In order to reduce the risks from hazardous substances the following rules must be observed:

- Staff must be trained in the use of these substances.
- The appropriate protective equipment should be worn when using them, e.g. gloves, goggles and masks.
- If necessary, suitable signage should be put out.
- The work method used must always be safe and carried out in a suitable area, e.g. use cleaning chemicals in a well-ventilated area, and refill a fryer with oil only when cold.

Remember!
Before using any type of machinery or equipment the member of staff must be trained in the correct procedures. They must be fully instructed about any danger which may arise and be supervised adequately by someone with knowledge and experience of the machine.

Definition
Dilute: to add extra liquid (usually water) to make the solution weaker.

Did you know?
Using a cleaning chemical, e.g. bleach, in a stronger concentration than necessary does not kill more germs or get the job done more quickly. Instead it:
- wastes the cleaning chemical (which can cost quite a lot of money)
- might damage the surface on which it is being used
- will need more rinsing off after use (which makes the job take longer in the end!)

Fire and explosions

Fire is very dangerous and can easily become life-threatening. It is very important that you know what to do in the event of a fire. Respect fire and treat it with the utmost caution. Explosions are not as common as fires but they can cause serious injury.

Case Study

A waiter refilling flambé lamps turned into a human fireball when the vapour given off from the fuel ignited around him. The flammable liquid had not been stored properly, the waiter had not been trained properly in this procedure and there were no suitable fire extinguishers to use nearby.

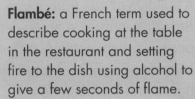

Figure 3.13 Training is essential in preventing disaster

Causes of fire and explosions in the workplace

Fires can quite easily be started in kitchens. There are hot stoves which are left on for long periods of time and hot fat in fryers which can overheat and catch fire. There is a large amount of electrical equipment which can develop a fault and start a fire. Over 28 per cent of fires on catering premises start in the kitchen and are caused by cooking procedures.

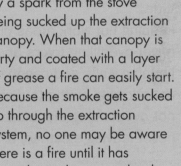

Did you know?

Many fires on catering premises have been started by a spark from the stove being sucked up the extraction canopy. When that canopy is dirty and coated with a layer of grease a fire can easily start. Because the smoke gets sucked up through the extraction system, no one may be aware there is a fire until it has spread to a dangerous level. Some commercial insurance companies will not insure catering premises unless the kitchen canopy is professionally cleaned very regularly.

Figure 3.14 A fire can start when a spark from the stove is sucked into a dirty extraction canopy

How to follow emergency procedures

When there is an emergency it is important that everybody does exactly as they are told and follows the rehearsed procedure. The immediate result of some emergencies is evacuation of the building.

Evacuation procedure

If you have to leave the kitchen as the result of an emergency, remember to do the following:

○ Turn off all the power supplies (gas and electricity). This may mean hitting the red button in a modern kitchen or turning off all the appliances individually.

○ Close all the windows and doors in the area.

○ Never stop to gather personal possessions.

○ Leave the building by the nearest emergency exit (do not use a lift).

○ Assemble in the designated area away from the building.

○ Answer a roll-call of names so that everyone knows you have left the building safely.

External emergency procedure

If there is an emergency, e.g. a bomb alert outside the building, you may have to stop working and take shelter inside. Staff should rehearse for this type of emergency as well as the evacuation procedure. This external emergency procedure should include the following instructions:

○ Turn off all power supplies in the kitchen.

○ Close all the windows and doors in the area.

○ Do not stop to gather personal possessions.

○ Gather in a designated safe area. This is usually in central stairwells or corridors away from windows and as close to the middle of the building as possible.

○ Stay in this area until told to leave by an emergency official.

○ Answer a roll-call of names to make sure no one is missing.

A modern kitchen has a red button that turns off power supplies in an emergency.

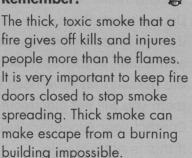

Remember!

The thick, toxic smoke that a fire gives off kills and injures people more than the flames. It is very important to keep fire doors closed to stop smoke spreading. Thick smoke can make escape from a burning building impossible.

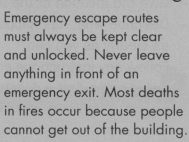

Remember!

Emergency escape routes must always be kept clear and unlocked. Never leave anything in front of an emergency exit. Most deaths in fires occur because people cannot get out of the building.

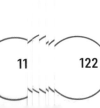

Test yourself!

1 Where can you find out information about Health and Safety?

2 State three health and safety points you should remember when working in a kitchen.

3 Write down five facts you should record when an incident occurs.

Further information

- St John Ambulance
- Health and Safety Executive
- Royal Society for the Prevention of Accidents
- Institute of Hospitality.

You can find out more about these organisations by visiting their websites. Links have been made available at www.heinemann.co.uk/hotlinks – just enter the express code 4103P

Health and safety in catering and hospitality

Task 1 — The importance of health and safety in the catering and hospitality industry

You have been asked to produce a table to be used during staff induction. The table should:
- List the different groups that have responsibilities under current legislation.
- Identify the potential costs of accidents.
- Identify the potential benefits of following health and safety practices.

Task 2 — Control hazards in the workplace

Design a poster or an A4 booklet on one of the following topics:
- Common causes of slips, trips and falls in the workplace and how these can be prevented.
- Safe manual handling – the correct lifting procedure and the main injuries caused when manual handling is not carried out correctly.
- Identify ways that machinery can cause injuries and control measures to reduce these risks.
- Identify the types of hazardous substances in a kitchen. List their common uses and the protection measures employees should take when using them.
- Indicate the main causes of fire and explosions; identify the elements required for a fire to be maintained; state how the exclusion of one of the elements can control a fire.
- Identify the dangers associated with electricity; how to deal with the dangers; and methods to prevent electrical dangers.

Task 3 — Contribute to controlling hazards in the workplace

It is important that you understand how to contribute to the control of hazards:
- Complete a risk assessment sheet for the kitchen in which you work. See Worksheet XX.
- Design an accident report form that contains all the information legally required. Include a notice to employees on why they should complete the accident book.

Task 4 — Maintain health and safety in the workplace

You have been asked to produce an induction booklet. Include the following information:
- The layout of the kitchen including the fire exits, fire fighting equipment, location of changing rooms, first aid box, toilets, rest facilities. Do this in a diagram, in writing, or both.
- List the types of incidents/situations that may occur and give: a brief description; the procedures to follow; and the reporting procedures for each type of incident.
- State the fire evacuation procedure for the organisation.
- Give examples of Personal Protective Equipment and comment on why each item should be used.

Healthier food and special diets

4

This chapter covers the following outcomes from Diploma unit 204: Healthier food and special diets

- Outcome 204.1 Demonstrate knowledge of special diets
- Outcome 204.2 Identify allergies and special diets

Working through this chapter could also provide evidence for the following Key Skills:

C2.1, C2.2a, C2.2b, C2.3, LP2.1, LP2.2, LP2.3, N2.1, N2.2a/b, N2.3, ICT2.1, ICT2.2, ICT2.3, PS2.1, PS2.2, PS2.3

In this chapter you will learn how to:

Identify different categories of nutrients

Identify and explain the sources of information and nutritional values

Explain nutrition principles and their importance

Describe the effects of preparation and cooking on nutrition

List different ways of informing the customer

Explain information on food labels

Identify practices and needs in preparing different meal occasions

List types of special diets

List allergic food items

List the effects of allergies and intolerances

A balanced diet

Everyone is constantly told by the press, doctors and the government that healthy eating is very important. People generally live much longer now that they did fifty or one hundred years ago. On average people also grow taller and weigh more. The amount and variety of food available today is the greatest ever. Many food items are much cheaper than they used to be.

Food provides material that our bodies can convert into heat and energy and can use to grow and repair internal systems.

Food is made up of various amounts of carbohydrate, protein, fat, vitamins, mineral salts and fibre. A balanced diet must contain all of these nutrients in the correct proportions. Lack of any one will affect the body in different ways:

○ Lack of carbohydrate → lower energy levels.
○ Lack of protein → poor growth and healing.
○ Lack of fat → poor health and low energy.
○ Lack of vitamins → poor health.
○ Lack of mineral salts → poor teeth and bones and general health.
○ Lack of fibre → poor digestion.

If we eat more food than our bodies require, the excess amounts will:
○ build up fat which is stored on our bodies
○ increase the weight which we have to carry around
○ create an imbalance of chemicals in our bodies (e.g. too much salt or sugar).

This leads to problems such as:
○ obesity (from the build-up of fat)
○ joint problems (from the increase in weight)
○ diabetes, high blood pressure, thyroid problems (from the increase in sugar and from particular types of fat which are much more common now in the food we eat).

A large number of today's health problems would be avoidable if people were more careful about the type and amount of food they ate. Modern life means that people are always very busy and do not spend enough time preparing food from raw ingredients. Most meals eaten in this country are ready meals. Consequently, people do not eat enough fibre and eat too much sugar and salt, which affects their health. This may result in people not living as long as they could.

Figure 4.1 Eating healthily can lead to a longer life

Figure 4.2 A food pyramid

Heart conditions, strokes, cancers and diabetes can all be caused by poor diet. People who suffer from these serious illnesses often need to take expensive medication and many find their quality of life is affected. If too many people suffer with such conditions our health and welfare systems may not be able to cope in the future.

When they are at home, people have the choice of eating healthily. Some people are not in this position and have to eat meals that have been prepared for them. Examples of people in this situation include residents of:

- hospitals
- prisons
- care homes
- boarding schools
- residential homes
- armed forces barracks.

If you work in a food production operation which caters for one of these sectors you have a particular responsibility to ensure that they have a balanced diet.

Nowadays people eat out more than ever before. This places a duty on caterers to ensure that safe, nutritious, healthy choices appear on restaurant menus. Chefs must be aware of the need to offer a choice of dishes with:

- fewer calories
- less fat
- less sugar
- less salt.

Government guidelines for healthy eating

The government, together with experts from the food industry, regularly carries out investigations into the health of the population. From these investigations it produces a series of reports with recommendations.

A 2005 government report states:

'Good nutrition is vital to good health. Poor nutrition is a recognised cause of ill-health and premature death in England – an estimated one-third of cancers can be attributed to poor diet and nutrition. While there is a high awareness of healthy eating, most people consume less than the recommended amounts of fruit and vegetables but more than the recommended amounts of fat, salt and sugar.'

Did you know?

In the UK 65 per cent of men and 56 per cent of women – 24 million adults – are either overweight or obese. This is a form of 'malnutrition' – meaning 'bad nutrition' – although this term is more often used to describe people who do not have sufficient food to eat.

The government issued the following guidelines for everyone to follow:

○ Increase the amount of fruit and vegetables eaten to at least five portions per day.
○ Increase the amount of fibre consumed.
○ Reduce the amount of salt consumed.
○ Reduce the amount of saturated fat eaten.
○ Reduce the amount of sugar consumed.

The Food Standards Agency has developed a programme called 'The Balance of Good Health' to show people what proportions and types of foods make up a healthy, balanced diet.

This programme divides foods into five different groups. For each group it gives a recommended daily serving. This will vary slightly according to the age, sex and occupation of the person. The groups are as follows:

○ Bread, other cereals and potatoes – one to two servings per day.
○ Fruit and vegetables – five servings per day.
○ Milk and dairy foods – two to three servings per day.
○ Meat, fish and alternatives – one to two servings per day.
○ Foods containing fat and food containing sugar – one small serving per day.

Other sources of information

Other sources of information about nutrition and healthy eating:

○ *The Manual of Nutrition*, which is published by the government and regularly updated
○ The British Nutrition Foundation
○ Department of Health
○ Department of Environment, Food and Rural Affairs (previously Ministry of Agriculture, Food and Fisheries)
○ Food Standards Agency.

Links to these websites have been made available at www. heinemann.co.uk/hotlinks. Just follow the links and enter the express code 4103P.

Remember!

The way you cook food can affect how healthy it is to eat. Chicken breast is a healthy food – but not if it is breadcrumbed and then deep fried!

Remember!

Your customers should:
○ enjoy their food
○ eat a variety of different foods
○ eat the right amount to be a healthy weight
○ eat plenty of foods rich in starch and fibre
○ eat plenty of fruit and vegetables
○ not eat too many foods that contain sugar or salt
○ not eat too many foods that contain a lot of fat.

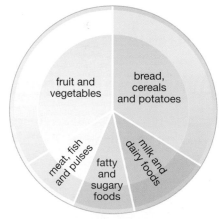

Figure 4.3 The five different food groups

Types and combinations of ingredients that make a healthy dish

Including the following items in a dish will increase its health value:

- Generous amounts of fruit and vegetables which are an excellent source of vitamins, minerals and fibre.
- Moderate amounts of meat, fish and dairy foods.
- Small amounts of fats and oils.
- Wholegrain items such as oats, wheat and other cereals.

Basic nutrition

Nutrition is the study of the various ways in which food can nourish the body. The human body is very complicated. Nutritional scientists are still discovering ways in which the body uses food. New recommendations about diet are issued when new research has been successfully carried out. These may recommend that we eat more of certain types of food, or identify food items which have been found not to be good for health.

The table below shows which types of food are the best sources of the nutrients that are needed for a balanced diet.

Nutrient	Type of food	Why it is needed
Carbohydrates	Potatoes, bread, pasta, rice – as starch Sweet food and drinks – as sugars	To provide energy
Proteins	Meat, fish, nuts, lentils	For growing and repairing tissues
Fats	Meat, fried food, cakes and pastries	For energy and certain vitamins
Vitamins and minerals	Fruit, vegetables and many other types of food	For general health
Fibre	Fruit, vegetables, unrefined cereals	To aid digestion
Water	Pure water is best but 4 pints per day of water-based liquid (such as low-sugar squash) is recommended	To aid digestion and most other body processes

Figure 4.4 Types of food that provide different nutrients and why they are needed

Did you know?

A prolonged lack of certain substances may lead to particular illnesses, e.g.:
- a lack of vitamin C leads to a skin condition called scurvy
- a lack of iron leads to a blood condition called anaemia.

Try this! Worksheet 13

Protein is essential for growth and the repair of the body. List five types of food that are high in proteins and five that are low in proteins. You can repeat this exercise for the other basic nutrients too.

The digestive system

The body is able to make use of the food we eat by a process called digestion. Most food contains more than one nutrient. Food needs to be broken down by the body into individual nutrients ready for use.

The digestive system breaks down the food we eat into a substance from which it can remove the nutrients. It does this in a series of stages:

1   Your teeth physically reduce the size of the food. If you do not chew your food well you can put strain on your oesophagus (the tube from your mouth to your stomach).
2   The food is then mixed with saliva, which breaks down starch into simple sugars. This is why if you leave bread or potatoes in your mouth for a while before swallowing they start to taste sweet.
3   In the stomach the food is mixed with gastric juices. These juices are made up of hydrochloric acid and substances called enzymes. These break down the complex structure of protein and curdle any milk present.
4   In the small intestine:
    ○   any remaining starch is converted to glucose
    ○   proteins are converted into a range of amino acids
    ○   fats are broken down into a watery solution ready to move into the intestines.
5   Most nutrients are absorbed into the bloodstream through the lining of the small intestine. The nutrients can then be carried round the body to where they are needed.
6   Bacteria are naturally found in the large intestine and they help the body to process food.
7   Any indigestible matter – such as fibre – continues through the colon and passes out through the rectum and anus. A meal may take 24 hours or more to completely pass through the digestive system.

We need to look at the nutrients in food in more detail to be able to appreciate their importance when creating healthy dishes.

Figure 4.5 The digestive system

Did you know?

If you unravelled your intestines they would be the length of a double-decker bus!

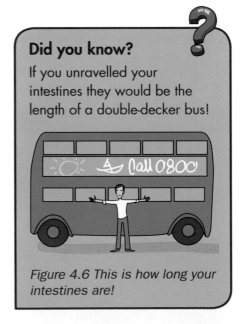

Figure 4.6 This is how long your intestines are!

Did you know?

Some of the acids present in your stomach are as strong as industrial strength cleaner!

Proteins

All proteins are made up from amino acids. There are 22 of them and all are needed by the body to grow and repair itself. When proteins are broken down by the digestive process, the body can manufacture most of these amino acids for itself – but there are a few that it cannot create. These are known as 'essential' amino acids. To ensure the body has all the amino acids it needs it is important to use protein food from both animal and vegetable origins.

These include:

Animal	Vegetable
Meat Game Poultry Fish	Peas Beans Nuts
Eggs Milk Cheese	Wheat products

Figure 4.7 Types of protein

Fats

As well as providing energy, fats also carry certain important vitamins. Both plants and animals contain fats, but they are of different sorts. They include:

Animal fats	Vegetable fats
Butter	Margarine
Cheese	Nuts
Lard	Soya beans
Fish oil	Olive oil

Figure 4.8 Types of fat

Differences between fats are caused by the variety in fatty acids from which they are made. Animal fats are 'saturated' and fish and vegetable fats are 'unsaturated'. Some animal fats also contain vitamins A and D. A manufacturing process called 'hydrogenation' can turn liquid oils into solid fat known as 'trans-fat'. This type of fat can be found in increasing amounts in ready-prepared meals. To be digested successfully all fats have to be broken down into fatty acids and a chemical called 'glycerol'. Animal fats and trans-fats are said to cause a higher amount of cholesterol to be found in the bloodstream.

Carbohydrates

The vast majority of food items in which carbohydrates are found are vegetable. They provide energy for the body. There are two main types of carbohydrates:

○ Sugars are very simple for the body to absorb.
   They include:
   – glucose
   – sucrose
   – maltose
   – fructose
   – lactose.

○ Starch is difficult to digest unless it has been cooked.
   Sources include:
   – all cereals (such as wheat flour)
   – potatoes
   – pulse vegetables such as lentils.

Vitamins

Vitamins are chemical substances which are very important for health. Without the correct balance of vitamins in your body you may not grow properly and will feel generally unwell. If you take in too large an amount of some vitamins you can poison yourself – but it is extremely unusual for this to happen.

The table below gives more information about the main groups of vitamins.

Vitamin	Type of food	Why it is needed
Vitamin A	Dairy products Fish oils Dark green vegetables	Helps growth and resists infection Helps eyesight
Vitamin B group	Yeast (in bread) Meat Cereals	Helps growth and energy levels Helps the nervous system
Vitamin C	Fresh fruit Green vegetables Potatoes	Helps growth and healing of injuries Prevents gum and mouth infections
Vitamin D	Sunlight Dairy produce Oily fish	Prevents brittle bones and teeth

Figure 4.9 What types of food provide vitamins and why they are needed

Minerals

You may be familiar with minerals such as iron, salt and copper and what they can be used for, e.g. manufacturing. But did you know that the human body needs very tiny amounts of 19 minerals to keep it healthy? However, too much of any mineral can be extremely bad for you. For example, most people in Britain eat far too much salt.

The table below gives more information about the most important minerals.

Mineral	Type of food	Why it is needed
Calcium	Dairy products Fish Bread	Helps bones and teeth grow Helps blood clot
Iron	Meat Green vegetables Fish	Helps keeps the blood healthy
Sodium (salt)	Meat Eggs Fish	Helps keep all the fluids in the body balanced

Figure 4.10 What foods provide minerals and why they are needed

Did you know?
Thinking uses up less than one calorie per hour!

Calories

All food has a value in numbers of calories. Calories measure the amount of energy food can produce in the body. If the body does not use this energy it tends to be saved as fat. It is useful to know the number of calories in the food you are eating if you are training for a particular sport when you need to use a lot of energy. It is also helpful when you are trying to keep a balanced diet and control your weight.

Figure 4.11 The more active you are, the more calories you will use

Different activities use up different numbers of calories. For example:
- Sitting watching television – 15 calories per hour.
- Walking moderately fast – 215 calories per hour.
- Climbing up stairs – 1000 calories per hour.

Try this!   Worksheet 14

When you are next out shopping for food, look at the label of the item you are buying. It will usually tell you how many calories the food will provide. See which food has the highest value and which has the lowest. The highest value food is likely to be the most fattening!

133

What makes a balanced diet?

> **Try this!**
>
> Imagine you have been asked to give a presentation about healthy eating to a final year group at your old school. Construct a series of PowerPoint slides or a flip chart showing the important things to remember about a balanced diet. Make sure you use language suitable for school age children.
>
> You may want to include information about:
>
> ○ *How the need for different minerals and vitamins and the number of calories to consume can differ according to age and occupation.*
>
> ○ *How the body uses the various nutrients it receives. Where to find further information from the Government.*
>
> ○ *Tips on healthy methods of preparation and cooking of food.*

Now that you know the main nutrients that are needed by the body you may be able to understand the problems that people can experience from not eating a balanced diet.

If people eat too much **fat** they are in danger of:

○ obesity

○ high blood pressure

○ heart attacks.

If people eat too much **sugar** they may suffer from:

○ tooth decay

○ diabetes

○ obesity.

If too much **salt** is consumed, people may experience:

○ kidney problems

○ high blood pressure.

The government's research has discovered that many people have medical problems brought on by eating too much fat, sugar and salt. This is why it is trying to promote a healthier diet and lifestyle for everyone. A healthier diet would include more starchy food, fruit, vegetables and pulses. Why are these important?

Eating **starchy** foods helps:

○ the digestive system work better

○ provide many of the minerals and vitamins needed for health.

Top marks!

Think about how good health principles and government guidelines can impact on a catering establishment.

Did you know?

Most people eat too much salt – probably around one and a half times more than is good for them. Adults should eat no more than one teaspoonful of salt per day.

Eating more **fruit and vegetables** helps:

o general health improve
o the digestive system work better
o provide many of the minerals and vitamins needed for health.

Eating more **pulses** helps:

o the digestive system work better
o provide a useful alternative to meat and fish
o reduce the amount of fat consumed.

How to interpret food labels

Labels on packaged food now have a great deal of nutrition information. This is to try to help everyone eat a balanced diet. There is also a lot of information about ingredients which is very important for anyone who is allergic to a particular substance (see Allergies, page 47). Look at promotional leaflets and tables of nutritional values for further information.

The law now states that food labels must contain:

o the name of the food – including any method of processing, e.g. dried peanuts, smoked mackerel
o the weight or volume
o a list of ingredients – in order of weight from largest to smallest
o a use-by date for perishable food or best-before date for preserved food
o storage conditions
o preparation instructions – to ensure the food tastes its best and that it will be thoroughly heated to the safe temperature of 75°C
o the name and address of manufacturer, packer or seller – in case further information is required
o a production lot number – in case there is a problem and the product has to be recalled.

Additional information may also be provided, e.g.:

o nutrition information
o cooking instructions
o serving suggestions.

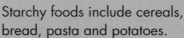

Remember!
Starchy foods include cereals, bread, pasta and potatoes.

Remember!
Pulses include butter beans, kidney beans, lentils, soya beans and chick peas.

Remember!
In Britain, most foods sold loose do not have to display all the information required by the food labelling laws for packaged foods.

Did you know?
A new European Union law will require certain food ingredients to which many people are allergic to be very clearly labelled. The foods include milk, eggs, peanuts, fish, soya, wheat, sesame and sulphur dioxide.

135

Preparing ingredients in a healthy way

If fresh ingredients are prepared a long time before they are used, they lose some of their important vitamins and minerals. The quality also suffers as they may become dried-up and stale. Onions prepared too far in advance will lose their flavour and beetroot will 'bleed'. There is also likely to be more waste from food that cannot be used.

Ways of reducing saturated fat in dishes

○ Use olive oil or sunflower oil instead of butter.
○ Select lean cuts of meat and trim the fat off other cuts.
○ Cut chips as thickly as possible as they absorb less fat.
○ Avoid glazing vegetables.
○ If frying, make sure the oil is hot enough. Otherwise the food will absorb more fat. Food which has been fried needs to be drained on absorbent paper to remove the surplus fat.
○ Use fish such as salmon, trout, mackerel and fresh tuna in place of cod, haddock, plaice and tinned tuna.
○ Use semi-skimmed or skimmed milk in place of the full-fat type.
○ Use a strong cheese so that you can use less of it.
○ Use yoghurt, **quark**, crème fraîche or fromage frais, not cream.

Definition

Quark: A German cheese with the texture and flavour of soured cream.

Ways of reducing sugar in dishes

○ Eat plain fresh fruit as a dessert.
○ Always use tinned fruit in natural unsweetened fruit juice rather than in syrup.
○ Use fresh or unsweetened fruit juices whenever possible.
○ In place of fizzy drinks, try fruit juice with sparkling water.
○ Cut back on the amount of sugar used to make desserts (except meringues and ice cream – which cannot be made with less sugar).
○ Use sugar-free cereals and low-sugar jams where appropriate.
○ If appropriate, use a sugar substitute or honey.

Ways of reducing salt in dishes

○ Add less salt – do not automatically add salt when beginning to cook, only use it to adjust the seasoning at the end.
○ Check the labels of any processed foods you use for flavouring dishes. It is surprising how many already contain salt, e.g. mustard, soy sauce.
○ Do not combine foods high in salt together in one dish such as bacon, beefburgers, sausages, cheese and ham.

Did you know?
The concentration of salt in soy sauce is twice that of seawater!

○ Combine salty foods with fruit or vegetables which contain potassium. This will help to reduce the effect of the salt.

○ Avoid using preserved ingredients that contain high levels of salt such as dried fish, smoked salmon and capers.

Ideas for flavouring dishes using less salt

○ Make your own stock. Ready-made stocks or bouillon are often high in salt.

○ Use lemon juice, lime juice and balsamic vinegar instead of salt.

○ Use lots of fresh herbs and spices.

○ Onions, shallots, leeks and garlic flavour food without using salt.

○ Freshly ground black pepper can be a popular alternative to salt.

Ways of increasing fibre and starch in dishes

○ Use high-fibre, wholemeal or granary bread.

○ Use wholemeal flour instead of white flour.

○ Use wholemeal pasta and brown rice.

○ Include pulses in dishes where appropriate.

○ Offer jacket potatoes.

Presenting healthier dishes

Good presentation will enhance a well-flavoured and healthy dish. Effective presentation techniques are:

○ Use a fresh leaf garnish such as basil or parsley.

○ Make sure sauces are of good colour.

○ Do not overfill the plate as it can look unattractive. Use a larger sized plate if necessary.

○ Do not put a small portion on a large plate, as this can also put off customers.

○ Use plates with a coloured or decorated rim.

○ Arrange items neatly and use a little artistic flair. Try:
  – painting contrasting sauces on the plate using squeezable sauce bottles or templates
  – creating a design using a cocktail stick to draw through contrasting colours
  – using moulds for some ingredients e.g. rings for rice.

○ Make sure the plate and its rim are clean – no drips, stains or marks – when it leaves the kitchen.

Did you know?
Substituting wholemeal flour for white flour is most successful when making savoury dishes. However, pastry can be very heavy if made with all wholemeal flour. A mix of half wholemeal, half white flour produces a better result.

Did you know?
Brown rice will take longer to cook than white rice.

Figure 4.16 Effective presentation techniques

Healthier sauces, dressings, toppings and condiments

As fashions change, so do ingredients and methods of cookery and presentation. With so much talk about healthy eating, many establishments are changing how they prepare their sauces. Traditional sauces use flour, butter and cream, but the following styles of sauces are more healthy and are becoming popular:

- Herb, olive and walnut oils and dressings.
- Sauces made from reductions of stocks and flavourings.
- Yoghurt-based dressings.
- Fruit-based sauces and dressings.

Cooking dishes to maximise nutritional value

Vitamins and minerals can be destroyed by long periods of cooking at high temperatures. To preserve its nutritional value, food needs to be cooked quickly. Do not use cooking methods that add fat.

The types of cookery that are the healthiest to use include grilling, steaming, baking and poaching.

Deep-fried items are popular, and quick and easy to produce, but are very unhealthy. Shallow fry with sunflower oil rather than deep fry with solid fat.

Special diets

Types and features of special diets

Increasing numbers of people are adopting diets that cut out certain types of food or only allow food of particular origin. People may follow these diets for religious, medical or ethical reasons. As a caterer it is essential that you respect such diets and only serve customers appropriate items.

Vegetarian and vegan diets

A vegetarian diet is one of the most common special diets. A vegetarian will not eat any item made from meat or fish. If you use convenience items such as stocks, flavourings and setting agents make sure you avoid those of animal origin.

> **Did you know?**
> Organic food is produced under strict controls restricting the use of chemicals. Food produced in a more intensive way is not subject to these controls. Crops may have substances used on them such as pesticides (used to kill insects). In high-volume meat production, additives which speed up growth in animals may be used.

> **Did you know?**
> Bovril is made from beef extract while Marmite is made from yeast extract.

A vegan will not eat any food of animal origin, including dairy products, honey and eggs. Note that pasta made without eggs, soya products and pulses are suitable to accompany the vegetables, fruits and grains which make up the vegan diet.

Diets for religious reasons

Muslim and Jewish people will not eat pork. They prefer meat to be slaughtered in a particular way which is indicated by the description of 'halal' (Muslim) or 'kosher' (Jewish). Jewish people eat meat dishes separately from milk or dairy items. Hindu people will not eat beef. Some religions do not allow alcohol to be consumed and this means there must not be any alcohol in food or sauces.

Diets for medical reasons

Medical diets are required by people who are unable to eat certain foods or seasonings which may aggravate their condition and make them ill. A medical diet may mean that ingredients and cooking methods must be as low in fat, salt or sugar as possible. A diabetic, for example, must have a high-fibre diet.

Food intolerance

A person who has coeliac disease will be allergic to the gluten found in flour. This means it is not possible to use wheat, rye, barley or oat products. You must also take care when using products such as malted drinks, ready-made sauces and some brands of mustard as these all use grains in their production. If a person with coeliac disease eats a grain-based item they will have an upset stomach. Rice, potato and sago are useful alternatives to grain.

Lactose intolerance means a person cannot digest milk and dairy items properly. They will have an upset digestive system if care is not taken to avoid serving them with milk, cream, cheese or any other dairy-based product.

Did you know?
Common items which may produce allergic reactions:
o soya
o shellfish
o tomatoes
o oranges
o chocolate
o cumin (a spice).

Some allergic reactions can produce violent and life-threatening symptoms. If a person who has a nut allergy comes into contact with nuts they can go into **anaphylactic shock**. This can result in death. It is vitally important to be certain that none of the specific ingredient is served to a customer with such an allergy.

Other allergies are discussed on page 47.

Definition
Anaphylactic shock: a severe allergic reaction to a particular substance, which is often life threatening.

Preparing and serving special diet items

Great care must be taken when preparing and serving items for people who are on special diets. Read food labels very carefully and make sure you understand the terminology. For example, you need to know whether a product contains aspic or gelatine, which are made from animals, if you are cooking for vegetarians.

Adjust menus and recipes appropriately. Arrangements for changes must be made well in advance to make sure the ingredients will be available. The replacement must provide a balanced meal.

Substitute ingredients successfully. The replacement ingredient must produce the same result as the original ingredient. Cornflour or **fecule**, for example, thicken a sauce in the same way as flour.

Definition
Fecule: potato starch

Separate food and equipment when necessary. This is particularly important when serving kosher meals as all the equipment used for preparing and serving meat-based items must be kept separate from that used for dairy food.

Clearly label food which has been specially prepared for a customer. If the dish is served to the wrong person it may not be easy to replace it quickly and easily and a mistake could have fatal results. If there is any doubt about whether a food contains a particular allergen, it must be clearly labelled to say that there is a risk of it containing the allergen.

Communicate effectively with special diet customers. It is always best to have a member of the catering staff speak directly to any customer who requests a special diet or says that they have a food allergy. Both parties can then ask questions to make sure no mistakes are made. Most customers appreciate having the extra attention!

Did you know?
Some catering outlets provide two separate, fully equipped kitchens for Jewish functions so that meat and milk items can be kept apart throughout the event.

STARTER

Smoked Salmon Pâté with Granary Toast

or

Roast Plum Tomato and Basil Soup with Seasoned Crostini

MAIN COURSE

Parma Ham and Mozzarella Stuffed Chicken Breast
with Pesto Potatoes

or

Mushroom Ravioli with Three Cheese and Tarragon Cream Sauce

DESSERT

Lemon Tart with Raspberry Sauce

Figure 4.17 A banqueting menu with a vegetarian alternative

Try this!

Worksheet 61

Choose one special diet from this chapter. Find out as much as you can about the diet. Prepare a chart for someone who is restricted to this special diet. The chart should indicate what types of food can be consumed and suggestions of different ways in which they can be eaten.

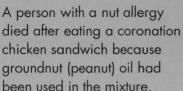

Did you know?

A person with a nut allergy died after eating a coronation chicken sandwich because groundnut (peanut) oil had been used in the mixture.

Top marks!

When choosing two special diets for your assignment, try to make sure their restrictions do not overlap too much. You need to demonstrate your menu planning skills to get higher marks. Think about dishes that you know and find out if there is a diet for which they may be appropriate.

Test yourself!

1 Which of the following are nutrients?
   a Fat
   b Carbohydrate
   c Cellulose
   d Additives
   e Vitamins
   f Minerals.

2 Which of these should we eat more of?
   a Bread
   b Vegetables
   c Fruit
   d Sweets
   e Salt
   f Crisps.

3 Which of these should we eat less of?
   a Bread
   b Vegetables
   c Fruit
   d Sweets
   e Salt
   f Crisps.

4 Complete the following sentences:
   a Fromage frais can be used instead of _____ .

   b Herbs and spices can be used instead of _____ .

   c Honey can be used instead of _____ .

5 What percentage of the population is overweight – males and females?

Practice assignment task

Healthier food and special diets

Task 1

Produce a balanced menu for a three-course meal for one of the following groups:
- vegetarians or vegans
- religious
- medical
- allergies.

Write a brief summary of why the menu addresses the special dietary requirements of the chosen group.

Task 2

Keep a diary for one week covering the meals, drinks and snacks you eat each day.

Identify the nutritional content of a typical day's food and suggest improvements to your diet, e.g. reduced salt, sugar or fat; increased fruit, fibre or water.

Suggest good practice tips for purchasing, preparing and cooking food that will preserve the nutritional content of food and make it healthier.

Task 3

Collect a range of material from different sources about nutritional values of food.

Identify a person's key life stages and describe briefly how the dietary requirements change at each stage. This can be a report or a table.

Choose one life stage and plan a week of healthy meals. Produce a table with the headings: Breakfast / Lunch / Dinner. For each meal type:
- suggest a meal
- give the reason for your choice
- state the nutritional content, e.g. vitamins, minerals, of that meal.

Kitchen operations, costs and menu planning

5

This chapter covers the following outcomes from Diploma unit 205: Kitchen operations, costs and menu planning

- Outcome 205.1 Describe the organisation of a kitchen
- Outcome 205.2 Plan and prepare menus for catering operations
- Outcome 205.3 Demonstrate awareness of basic costs associated with the catering industry
- Outcome 205.4 Apply basic calculations used in catering operations.

Working through this chapter could also provide evidence for the following Key Skills:

N2.1; N2.2a/b/c; N2.3; C2.2a; ICT2 2.1, ICT2.2, ICT2.3

In this chapter you will learn how to:

Explain the importance of kitchen layout and correct workflow

Outline the staffing hierarchy in a traditional kitchen

Explain the importance of the menu, describe menus for different meal occasions and plan menus

Calculate costs and quantities in catering operations

Explain why it is important to monitor and control food costs

Work out selling prices of dishes and menus.

Kitchen organisation

The kitchen is the heart of any catering establishment. A poorly designed, equipped or staffed kitchen is likely to affect the quality of the food produced and therefore the success of the business.

The importance of kitchen layout

A kitchen is a busy place. Kitchen activities include:

- receiving, checking and storing deliveries
- collecting food items from the stores
- preparing food, using sharp knives and other dangerous equipment
- moving around the kitchen to get equipment, going to the sinks, fridges and to the cooking area
- taking the waste to the waste disposal area
- cooking and finishing dishes ready for holding or service
- working with hot liquids, e.g. boiling water and hot fat
- collecting food to serve to customers in the restaurant.

A kitchen's layout should enable all these activities to be carried out efficiently and in line with health and safety and food safety legislation.

Plans for a new catering establishment or for refurbishing an existing one will cover the eating areas, serving areas and the kitchen. A detailed drawing, usually to scale, will show the layout of the kitchen. The drawing will usually identify the location of the main equipment.

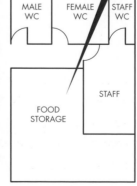

Top marks!

Always read carefully any tasks you are given several times. Make sure you understand what you have to do. As you work on a task keep looking at the details and the grading criteria to make sure that you are on the right track.

The trading area consists of the entrance and the restaurant with 115 covers, with a variety of seating types.

The kitchen is separated into a servery, a theatre-style cooking area and a wash-up area.

The large food storage area is easily accessible from the back door and from the kitchen zone.

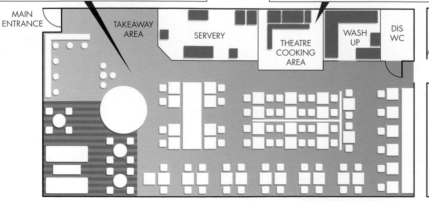

Figure 5.1 Layout plan for a waiter service, seated, Wimpy restaurant

Layout in different catering establishments

Kitchen layouts must be designed to meet the operational needs of individual catering establishments, providing for particular types of customers and target numbers, including the maximum numbers at any one sitting. A small café offering mainly full English breakfasts will need a basic kitchen and a few staff. A pizza restaurant will need a kitchen big enough to house a pizza oven. A fast food outlet will need the kitchen to be designed and equipped to serve a limited range of food to large numbers of customers as quickly as possible. A large fine dining restaurant offering an **à la carte** menu will have a traditional kitchen brigade, with lots of staff allocated to separate areas of a big kitchen.

Importance of good workflow

Designing a good **workflow** means looking at how materials and people move around in the kitchen, and making sensible changes to speed up the production process, without introducing problems or reducing the quality of the end product.

Food safety and health and safety good practice

A professional kitchen must be designed, constructed, and maintained so that it can be operated in line with health and safety and food safety legislation. A poor or outdated kitchen layout can cause workflow problems. The stages of the workflow are closely linked to the control points of food safety management systems (HACCP). It is therefore very important in designing any kitchen layout to identify correct workflows that not only help to improve efficiency, but also ensure that food is produced more safely and hygienically, in line with legislation and regulations. See Chapter 2, Food safety and Chapter 3, Health and safety.

Promoting good workflow

It is important for any catering establishment to have a kitchen which is fit for purpose and which is laid out, equipped and organised in ways which make it possible for the staff to run it efficiently. Time and motion studies in kitchen operations measure workflows, how long it takes to do particular jobs and staff movements. These have helped to produce some basic guidelines

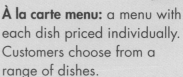

Definition

À la carte menu: a menu with each dish priced individually. Customers choose from a range of dishes.

Definition

Workflow: the stages in the process of food production in a kitchen.

Did you know?

The main causes of injury in catering are:

○ slips, trips and falls on wet or contaminated floors
○ manual handling or back and other injuries
○ exposure to hot or harmful substances, e.g. hot oil, cleaning chemicals
○ being struck by something, e.g. sharp knives or falling objects.

Did you know?

A sensible kitchen layout with correct workflow, plus good training, can help to prevent many of these injuries while at the same time helping to ensure food safety and increase efficiency.

147

which are relevant to most catering operations. It makes good business sense to design a kitchen layout with workflows that help to reduce costs and increase efficiency. Different types of establishment operate different food production systems but there are common features to designing workflows, see Figure 5.2. Workflow patterns can be drawn onto a kitchen layout plan in many different ways, see Figure 5.3.

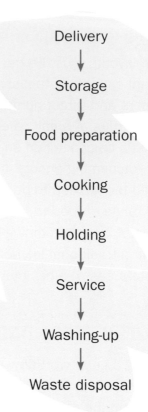

Figure 5.2 The basic stages of kitchen operations, a simple workflow

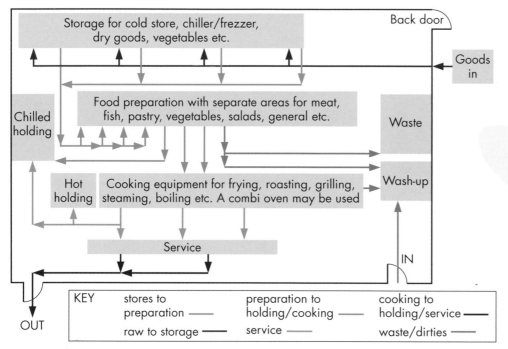

Figure 5.3 A simple kitchen layout, showing the different stages of food production and different types of food separated out and showing basic workflows

Many different processes are used in preparing and cooking food. Some areas of the kitchen are used for specific tasks. For example:

○ vegetable preparation needs a sink for washing and draining
○ meat preparation is kept separate from pastry preparation to avoid cross-contamination
○ plate washing, pot washing and refuse create 'dirty' areas.

Where possible, there should be sufficient space and equipment to keep processes separate. This is particularly important with high-risk or contaminated products, e.g. raw meat and fish should be kept separate from prepared foods.

In smaller establishments where separation by space is not possible, there must be strict controls and procedures to make sure processes are done separately, particularly dirty and clean processes so that utensils and tables are suitably sanitised between processes.

The layout must allow a continuous workflow in one direction to avoid cross-contamination. A well-designed layout will mean that staff do not get in each other's way. This not only ensures food safety but also improves efficiency. Most staff will respond to a well-designed kitchen and good working environment and work better as a result.

Delivery

It is important that goods vehicles have adequate access to the premises, providing direct deliveries to the catering area. Adequate space must be allowed for a goods check-in area before entering the kitchen.

Storage

Where possible, bulk storage should be close to the goods-in area so that there is no need for delivery personnel to enter the kitchen and food preparation area. This helps to reduce the possibility of the kitchen area being contaminated by spreading dirt, infection or pollution. It is also useful if the bulk storage area is near the kitchen. Smaller quantities of the goods can then be taken into the kitchen area as required. There will need to be freezers, refrigerators, cold store and dry store areas so that food is kept at the correct temperature.

Food preparation

A kitchen layout should show good practice by positioning the main food preparation areas between the bulk storage and the cooking areas to ensure the correct workflow.

If there is space, smaller fridges and freezers should be located in the food preparation and/or cooking areas. For example, under the counter refrigerators can be used for prepared garnishes and salad items.

In food preparation it is important to have the right equipment and utensils close to hand. Work surfaces must be made of stainless steel and of the right size for the type of preparation. See Chapter 2, Food safety.

Cooking

Staff safety is of prime importance in the cooking area. For example:
- there should always be a set-down space next to deep-fat fryers
- a sufficient corridor (usually 900–1,200mm) must be left in front of cooking equipment to allow staff to pass safely.

Remember!
The workflow must be:
raw ⟶ finished

Figure 5.4 Food preparation area

Figure 5.5 A chef in charge of a large gas burner range

The equipment shown in Figure 5.5 suits the cuisine of Center Parcs' contemporary Indian restaurant Rajinda Pradesh. The long-handled pans are close together for ease of control but there is plenty of space on and in front of the range. There should not be any through traffic – only staff who are cooking food should be there.

The flow of the cooking area should also suit the style of service, with fast-cook equipment such as fryers, salamanders and griddles nearest to the point of service and bulk cooking kit such as **bratt pans**, convection ovens and boiling pans further away.

Holding

Some food production systems require extensive hot and cold food holding systems. The holding area is usually near to the food service area. Food must be kept at the correct temperature.

Food service area

Whether the operation is waited service or tray-line style, queuing can be kept to a minimum by:

- providing multi pick-up and service points
- having adequate space and equipment for hot and cold holding of prepared food ready for service
- in an à la carte restaurant, allowing sufficient space for plating up and **hot pass**.

Where possible, service points should be located close to the final cooking process to avoid **double handling**.

Wash-up

Nearly always undersized by space planners, the wash-up area is also important. There must also be enough space for storing clean items and for rubbish disposal. These must be separated to avoid cross-contamination.

Location is vital to the efficient management of the space. Ideally the wash-up area should be close to both the restaurant and the service area to avoid double handling.

Definition

Bratt pan: a deep, oblong-shaped cooking pot with a pull-down lid and a tilting feature so that food that has been cooked can be poured into containers through a 'vee' in the top forward edge. A bratt pan is a versatile piece of high production equipment that can also be used for multi-function cooking of one product, e.g. browning off then braising meat.

Figure 5.6 A bratt pan

Definition

Hot pass: where customers' orders are passed from the service staff to the kitchen staff and waiters collect the finished dishes to serve to the customers.

Double handling: handling an item more than once e.g. when a chef hands a finished dish to a member of staff who then takes it to the service point.

Waste disposal

There must be a hygienic waste disposal system. Workflows should include a clear route for dirty dishes away from preparation and service areas. Rubbish must be kept separate and should not pass through other areas to get to the bin. An outside refuse bay must be well away from the kitchen entrance. Rubbish must be kept covered to avoid problems with pests. Many kitchens have a recycling area.

Communication between departments

Good communication is essential for a successful kitchen, e.g. a chef de partie in charge of vegetables needs to be able to talk to and supervise the team members preparing and cooking them. Although high equipment is useful for storage, if it is in the middle of a kitchen it will make it difficult to see across the room.

In any size of kitchen, routine jobs like preparing vegetables can be much more enjoyable and finished more quickly if the kitchen is designed so that staff members are able to work facing each other or alongside each other, rather than with their backs to each other. Good kitchen design can help to improve working relationships and teamwork. For more information see Chapter 6, Applying workplace skills.

Cooking and serving must be co-ordinated so the dishes are ready to serve at the same time and when the customers are ready for each course. The service points need to be:
- easily accessible to restaurant staff, who should not enter the preparation or cooking areas
- designed so that the kitchen staff are able to communicate with the restaurant and vice versa.

Better service to customers

Good kitchen design with correct workflows helps to ensure that the food served to customers will be:
- of the right quality
- hygienically prepared and presented
- served at the correct temperature
- served within the expected timescales.

> **Remember!**
> Correct workflows:
> - help to eliminate hazards and therefore reduce the number of accidents
> - ensure that food is prepared, cooked and served hygienically
> - improve efficiency.

Figure 5.7 Staff members are happier if they can work alongside or opposite each other

Chef's tip

Almost all designs are a compromise. A good design is one that best suits the constraints of space and budget while still providing a good service.

Food production systems

It is important in designing a kitchen to adjust the layout and workflows so they are suitable for the food production system, as well as for the style of the establishment and the area and space allocated. A straight line layout may be suitable for a snack bar or café, but an island layout may be better for the restaurant of a large hotel.

Fast food production system

The kitchens in fast-food establishments should be designed to keep queuing and serving times down to an average of just a few minutes. To achieve this, fast-food establishments typically have a very limited menu, with most of the choices being cooked in a similar way, e.g. a range of battered fish, chips and fried battered sausage. Fast-food production systems try to predict the variety of choices customers will make and are not designed to cater for individual requests.

Fast-food operators tend to purchase prepared or partly prepared foods. These will normally be bought in bulk, so a large storage area may be needed. Using convenience foods changes the requirements of the kitchen, e.g. a butchery area will not be needed. Fast-food production systems need fewer food preparation areas and, usually, less equipment. Space is often very limited, so appropriate workflows are very important. Many fast-food outlets serve food in disposable containers with plastic knives and forks, which reduces the amount of dish and cutlery washing facilities needed, but increases the flows through to the waste disposal area and the recycling area and the size of those areas.

Top marks!

When you have finished a task, check that you have covered everything and given sufficient detail. Giving lots of relevant, current examples helps to show that you have a wide and up-to-date knowledge of catering.

Top marks!

Ask your tutor's advice before deciding how to approach a task to make sure that you are on the right track.

Low-skilled staff are usually trained to do all tasks within the outlet. At peak periods there are likely to be lots of staff each doing just one task. This helps to reduce staff movements and improve the efficiency by allowing uninterrupted workflows. Staff are often rotated around the different tasks to make the work more varied. Kitchens for fast-food systems can be expensive to set up as they may involve special equipment, developed to do just one job.

À la carte menu partie system

This is the food production system used in a traditional kitchen for fine dining, e.g. in restaurants of quality hotels that offer an à la carte **call order menu**. The à la carte menu food production system is designed to make it possible for the kitchen to prepare dishes cooked to order. It also allows the kitchen to meet specific requests from customers.

Staff and functions will usually be separated out. There will tend to be more skilled staff within the kitchen brigade, plus trainees. The layout of a large traditional kitchen will usually be divided up into lots of different sections and the workflows will follow separated stages of food production. Workflows can become quite complicated because of the size of the operation and the number of staff. Flows therefore need to move logically within and between sections.

The kitchen will have to meet the needs of an à la carte menu. There may be frequent menu changes, and this food production system is able to cope with that. Most dishes are prepared from scratch using raw ingredients, e.g. unprepared vegetables and meat which requires butchering. The chef may also make use of prepared and partly prepared foods, but the emphasis will be on fresh ingredients, beautifully cooked and finished. It is not usually necessary to serve customers quickly, although a meal should be completed in an acceptable time, e.g. a lunch or pre-dinner menu should be served more quickly than a dinner menu.

Some catering establishments offer a very extensive menu with less-skilled staff by carrying out much of the preparation prior to service (**mise en place**) throughout the day and keeping the food refrigerated until needed at service time. The kitchen design will need to include plenty of refrigeration and a good finishing kitchen, along with adequate cooking facilities.

Definition

Call order menu: where customers are able to ask for dishes on the menu to be prepared, cooked or finished to meet their own specific tastes.

Did you know?

Airline catering is often done by contract caterers. Large premises are needed for storage, preparation, cooking, blast-chilling and freezing. Meal trays are assembled on conveyor belts, then stacked into aircraft trolleys and kept chilled until the food is re-heated and served on board.

Definition

Mise en place: basic preparation of ingredients prior to service.

Workflows also have to take into account the type of service, e.g. silver service, plated service or customers helping themselves. The decision will influence the amount and type of dishwashing needed. Many hotel restaurants these days also use a mixture of service styles which can:

○ make it easier to prepare food in advance

○ speed up service

○ reduce space, equipment and staff.

A large hotel kitchen may have to produce food for more than one type of restaurant or for a function, e.g. a wedding, and for different types of service.

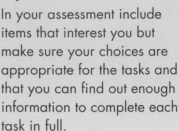

Case study

Read what the Head Chef at London's Commonwealth Club has to say about how changes to layout helped to improve their à la carte menu partie food production system on the Caterer and Hotelkeeper website. A link has been made available at www.heinemann.co.uk/hotlinks. Just follow the links and enter the express code 4103P.

Self-service counter system

In a self-service restaurant or café the customer enters the food service area and goes to the counter at the starting point, often joining a queue, then picks up a tray and follows the counter, selecting their own food on the way. A long counter is needed, with equipment for holding and displaying chilled and hot food. There may be a 'call order' approach with customers waiting at the counter until their chosen dish is ready.

The food production system has to match the needs of the self-service counter system. There is likely to be a mix of prepared and partly prepared food. The range often includes chilled foods and easily held items like hot soup throughout the day, with hot items during peak periods of breakfast and lunch. This will vary though, e.g. a counter service restaurant in an airport is likely to offer hot items all day. These will have to be **replenished** when empty or after being displayed for a certain period of time. Non-disposable crockery and cutlery is usually – but not always – used. This means more flows through to the dishwashing area than a fast food system.

Definition
Replenish: fill up again.

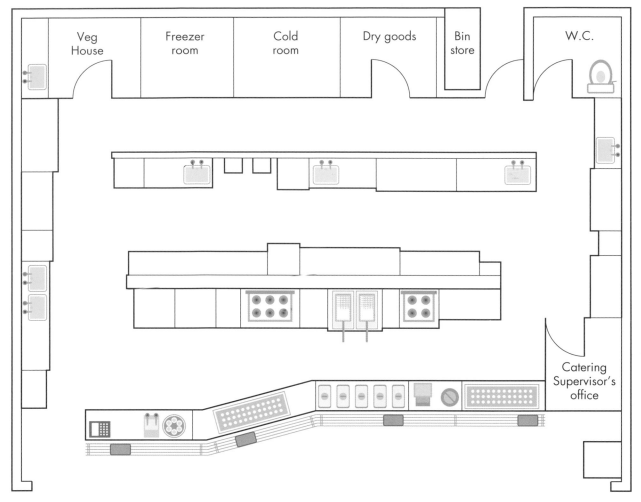

Figure 5.8 Layout of a typical kitchen supporting a self-service counter system within a public service sector establishment

Try this!   Worksheet 62

Describe the workflows in the kitchen in Figure 5.8.

Try this!   Worksheet 62

Draw to scale a kitchen layout plan for a professional kitchen with which you are familiar. Show the workflows.

Staffing in a traditional kitchen

This section looks briefly at the traditional kitchen. For information about job responsibilities see Chapter 1.

Kitchen hierarchy

The hierarchy of a traditional kitchen is:

Head Chef: the person in charge of food preparation in a hotel or restaurant kitchen, sometimes called Chef de Cuisine or Executive Chef. The Head Chef is responsible for managing staff,

Definition

Kitchen hierarchy: the system of organising kitchen staff into a set order of responsibility and authority.

155

implementing food safety and health and safety legislation, menu planning, costing, ordering stock, the staff rota and staff training.

Sous Chef (Second Chef): assists the Head Chef and takes over when they are absent. Responsibilities include supervising staff, supervising food safety and health and safety practices and quality control.

Chef de Partie (Section Team Leader): in charge of a section of the kitchen, e.g. soups.

Commis Chef (Assistant Chef): assistant to a Chef de Partie.

In a very large traditional kitchen, e.g. in a large international hotel, the duties of food production will be divided between several sections. The chefs in each section will have clearly defined duties. See Chapter 6, Applying workplace skills, to see how kitchens are organised in different types of establishment.

Reasons for good working relationships

Good working relationships, communication and co-operation within the kitchen brigade help to create an effective team, which is essential to running an efficient, productive operation. See Chapter 6, Applying workplace skills, for more information about what makes a successful team.

> ### Try this!
> Prepare a short talk about the role of a Head Chef in a catering establishment of your choice. Say what you like/dislike about the role.

Future trends

There have been vast changes in the UK over the last 60 years in what people want to eat, the number of people who can afford to eat out, the range of catering establishments, the type of cuisine and the technology available. Influences are examined in Chapter 1. What might the future hold?

○ Technological advances mean more catering equipment will be designed for speed and ease of use, maintenance and cleaning. There is likely to be an increase in the use of computers for purchasing and stock control and of 'intelligent' kitchen equipment, e.g. ranges that adjust the heat automatically.

- Many local authorities are likely to put proper kitchens back into schools.
- Some establishments in hospitals, prisons and residential homes are likely to continue to buy in frozen and chilled food to reduce the cost of on-site preparation and cooking. If the current criticism of poor-quality, processed food continues, a better balance of fresh and partly prepared food may become more common.
- Fewer families sit down to eat together, so snacking will continue to influence how kitchens are operated to ensure speed of service.
- Food sales are a growth area for pubs so there is expected to be an increase in the large range of good-looking and functional equipment designed specially for use within the bar area.
- Catering establishments will look for equipment, methods and techniques that aid recycling and reduce the use of gas and electricity. This will also save on rising energy costs. Customers are likely to demand more evidence of green policies in food production.
- The trend in the UK and overseas towards making eating places more attractive is likely to continue. One trend is to bring the kitchen into view, e.g. a pizza oven, sushi table and grills for preparing food to order. Theatre-style cooking is likely to continue, as it shows customers some dishes are cooked from fresh ingredients.
- As the cost of property continues to increase, the trend towards smaller kitchens is likely to continue. Equipment is being designed to take up less space.
- Some establishments may choose to employ fewer staff. This will reduce the space and facilities needed in a kitchen and increase the demand for advanced yet simple to operate kitchen equipment.
- The major food manufacturers are likely to continue to make advances in food technology, e.g. ensuring consistency in food, using new techniques to solve manufacturing problems, identifying the most efficient methods of operation and developing new products to attract customers.

Top marks!

Remember to explain your choices and decisions when completing a task. You may know why you have taken a particular approach, but you also need to make it clear to someone reading your work. Explanations will show that you have thought things through and looked at a variety of options. Include relevant factors that influence catering today.

○ Chefs will continue to experiment with new dishes. There is a new trend for combining different cookery methods. For example, chefs are combining meat that has been cooked slowly (e.g. by stewing, braising, slow roasting for prolonged periods of time) with meat that has been cooked quickly (e.g. by grilling). This may result in a dish such as grilled steak served with a braised beef item.

○ The movement and migration of different ethnic groups and the availability of different commodities, herbs, spices, seeds and flavourings will continue to impact on cuisine.

○ The debate over whether cookery is an art or science continues. About 35 years ago experimentation led to the develpment of 'sous vide' cookery. This literally translates from the French as 'under vacuum'. Food is placed in a bag which is sealed under vacuum. The food is then cooked slowly in a water bath. This process results in tender textures and enhances the flavour of the food. A more recent experiment uses a very long slow cookery process where meat or poultry is not sealed at the beginning but instead is coloured at the end. This results in food that is moist and full of flavour.

Test yourself!

1 Which is the correct workflow in a kitchen?
   a Delivery → Storage → Food preparation → Cooking → Holding → Service → Washing-up → Waste disposal
   b Delivery → Storage → Cooking → Food preparation → Holding → Service → Washing-up → Waste disposal

2 True or false? The layout of a kitchen needs to match the chosen food production system and type of service.

3 Which of the following statements are correct?
   a A Chef de Partie takes charge of the kitchen when the Head Chef is absent.
   b A Commis Chef will be supervised by a Chef de Partie.
   c A kitchen operates best when the staff do not talk to each other.

Planning and preparing menus

Why have a menu?

The content of a **menu** creates an image, which reflects the overall style of the catering establishment. Creating a menu is one the most important jobs for a chef. Often the Head Chef of a catering establishment will create the dishes and put the menu together. In a large catering organisation, e.g. a fast-food chain or a contract caterer, there may be one or more Head Chefs, who decide on the menus and provide standard recipes.

Communication with customers

In the past, eating out in the UK was sometimes intimidating as menus were complicated and used unfamiliar words or a foreign language. Fortunately, even a formal dining restaurant now tries to put customers at ease. A good starting point is to provide a menu that customers can understand.

A menu is a way of communicating and is the main means of selling food to customers. A menu needs to attract people to eat at the catering establishment and encourage customers to order as much as possible and/or order particular items, e.g. a daily special. The information on a menu needs to be stated clearly and certain information is required by law, e.g. service charges. Menus are usually set out in courses so they are easy to understand.

A good menu will inform customers about:
- the price and any extras that have to be paid for
- the quality of the dish, e.g. fresh green beans, locally sourced best beef, prime rib of beef, freshly cooked
- an indication of the size of the dish, e.g. 10-inch pizza, 100-gramme rump steak
- how the dish is prepared, e.g. grilled, pan-fried, roast
- which ingredients are used
- an explanation of any foreign or unusual terms
- what the dish is served with, e.g. a side salad or a baked potato
- whether it is suitable for people on special diets, e.g. vegetarian or vegan.

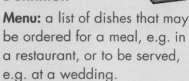

Definition

Menu: a list of dishes that may be ordered for a meal, e.g. in a restaurant, or to be served, e.g. at a wedding.

Figure 5.9: Rick Stein's fish restaurant, Padstow. What information do you think these visitors are looking for?

Chef's tip

It is good practice to identify ingredients to which people may be allergic, e.g. eggs, fish, shellfish and nuts. Many menus include a **disclaimer** which states that it is not possible to guarantee dishes are completely free of such ingredients.

Definition

Disclaimer: a statement that denies responsibility for something.

Style

The trend today is to present a simple, clear menu that helps the customer to make informed choices. The style of the menu will depend on the establishment:

o in a bistro the menu may be written on a blackboard
o in a pub the menu may stand on the counter
o in a pub restaurant there may be a menu on each table plus daily specials on a board.

Using a menu as a planning tool

A menu is an important planning tool. A menu tells:

o the Head Chef what to order
o the kitchen brigade what to prepare and finish for service
o the waiting staff what is available.

The menu plays a major part in:

o working out the cost of the dishes
o deciding on the price to be charged
o working out what staff and other resources will be needed
o deciding on the type of service required.

Some of the most successful menus contain a balance of traditional and modern dishes. A well-planned menu will:

o balance the choice of dishes within courses, e.g. a five-course menu is likely to include lighter, smaller dishes than a three-course menu
o balance the choice of dishes across courses, e.g. a main course dish will be more substantial than a starter
o be well-balanced from a nutritional point of view and include some healthy eating options
o have sufficient choices for the customer
o use a variety of ingredients, flavours, textures, seasonings and colours
o balance expensive ingredients, e.g. foie gras and truffles, with cheaper ingredients, e.g. potatoes
o use a mix of cooking techniques
o offer fewer good-quality dishes rather than lots of lower-quality dishes.

Top marks!

Be realistic. This unit is about the practical aspects of kitchen operations, costs and menu planning. Think about:

o Would your suggestion work?
o If not, why not?
o Have you included enough information?
o Have you explained it properly?
o Have you included a list of sources?
o Is your work in a logical order?
o Could you use graphs or charts to present the information?
o Are your menu items balanced?
o Do the kitchen layouts have a good workflow?

Legal requirements

The following legal points apply to menus:

○ The descriptions of ingredients and cooking terms must be true and accurate. Particular care must be taken when using words such as: *British*, *home-made*, *fresh* and *organic*.

○ The prices must be accurate.

○ Any additional charge, e.g. a service charge, should be included in the menu prices or clearly stated on the menu.

○ Dishes containing genetically modified (GM) soya or maize must be clearly labelled.

Different types of menu

The origins of menus

Originally the menu or bill of fare was not given to diners at the table. Banquets used to be made up of lots of dishes served in two courses. The first course would be put on the table before the diners entered. This is where the term *entrée* comes from. Once eaten, these dishes would be removed and replaced by the second course, which is where the words *removes* and *relevés* come from.

Later, a very large menu or bill of fare was put at the end of the table for everyone to read. In time menus became smaller and several copies were made so that diners could have their own.

Modern menus first appeared during the early nineteenth century in a restaurant in Paris.

Types of menu

There are several types of menu. The main ones are à la carte and table d'hôte.

À la carte menu

This is a menu with each dish priced individually. Customers choose from a range of dishes. The menu is usually divided into courses, e.g. starters, main course and dessert. They may also be divided in other ways, e.g. meat, fish, pasta. Today you will find à la carte style menus in a wide range of catering establishments from fine dining restaurants (where you would expect an à la carte menu partie food production system) to quick service restaurants. Dishes on an à la carte menu should be cooked to order.

Did you know?

The word 'menu' comes from the French *menu de repas* which means 'list of items for a meal'. 'Menu' has been used since the eighteenth century. The first recorded use in English was in 1837.

Did you know?

'Bill of fare' is an old-fashioned English term that means 'list of dishes'.

Did you know?

Other terms sometimes used for a menu are 'bill', 'card', 'carte du jour' and 'carte' but 'menu' is the most common.

Please enjoy a complimentary selection of bread, oils and balsamic vinegar as a small appetiser while you select your meal

Bruschette

Our Bruschette are freshly prepared in the traditional Italian way using toasted rustic bread, garlic and olive oil.

Formaggio di capra
Creamy goats' cheese baked on bruschetta bread, topped with green pesto & served with a sweet tomato chutney £ 4.25

Funghi e pancetta affumicata
An exquisite selection of wild & button mushrooms, bacon & mozzarella cheese, baked & served on bruschetta bread £ 4.25

Antipasti

Risotto ai funghi e asparagi
A creamy mixture of Arborio rice, mushrooms & Parmesan cheese, topped with delicately flavoured asparagus spears £4.45

Selezione di formaggi e salumi
A selection of Italian cured meats, hard & soft cheeses, sun-blushed tomatoes, olives, rustic bread & dipping oil - ideal for sharing £6.75

Zuppa rustica
A traditional Italian vegetable broth served with a chunk of rustic bread £3.40

Gnocchi con pesto
Traditional potato dumplings filled with green pesto, served with a rustic tomato & pesto sauce £4.25

Stuzzicherie

Pizza all'aglio
Freshly baked pizza dough brushed with our garlic & parsley butter £2.85

Pizza all'aglio con formaggio
Freshly baked pizza dough, brushed with our garlic & parsley butter and topped with mozzarella cheese £ 3.00

Insalata mista
A small side salad of rocket leaves, ripe cherry tomatoes, fresh cucumber & spring onions £2.65

Pasta al forno

Lasagne con carne
A traditional Italian dish - sauces of Bolognese & béchamel layered between sheets of pasta, baked with tomatoes & mozzarella £7.45

Lasagne con funghi e porri
Field mushrooms and leeks bound in a béchamel sauce, layered between sheets of pasta and topped with mozzarella cheese £7.45

Specialità di Pasta Ripiena
Choose from green pesto, chilli oil or a rich pomodoro sauce to complement. All are served with Parmesan cheese & cracked black pepper on request

Tortellini spinaci e ricotta
Pasta filled with spinach & ricotta £7.95

Tortellini funghi porcini
Pasta filled with rich porcini mushrooms £7.95

Pizze

As all of our pizze are made freshly to order we are able to offer pizza bases of tomato sauce, bechamel sauce or green pesto. The chef has made the following recommendations; however, please feel free to ask for an alternative

Margherita
Tomato sauce, sliced tomatoes & mozzarella £5.95

Carnivora
Tomato sauce, chorizo, pepperoni, salami, red onion & mozzarella £7.75

Ai quattro formaggi
Green pesto, mozzarella, Parmesan, gorgonzola & goats' cheese £7.95

Pizza con pollo alla Vivaldi
Tomato sauce, sliced breast of chicken, Parma ham & mozzarella cheese £8.45

Verdura al forno e formaggi
Tomato sauce, aubergines, courgettes, mixed peppers, red onions, cherry tomatoes, gorgonzola, ricotta, mozzarella & olives £7.95

Pizza ai gamberoni
Béchamel sauce, topped with marinated anchovies, crayfish tails, and black & green olives, finished with dressed rocket £8.75

Specialità di Pasta

As all of our pasta dishes are made freshly to order. We are able to offer you a choice of penne, spaghetti, fettuccine, coralli or rice and millet pastas. The chef has made the following recommendations; however, please feel free to ask for an alternative.

Fettuccine con carne di manzo
Beef strips sautéed with garlic, basil, red onion & red peppers in a chunky tomato sauce combined with fettuccine pasta £8.45

Napolina
Coralli pasta with a simple tomato sauce, flavoured with basil, Peperonata & finished with mozzarella £7.25

Pasta alla marinara
Coralli pasta bound with a tomato & garlic sauce, mixed fish & shellfish £8.45

Spaghetti con ragù alla Bolognese
The classic Italian sauce served on well seasoned spaghetti £7.25

Giardinara
Rice & millet pasta and Mediterranean vegetables bound in olive oil with fresh herbs £7.95

Specialità

Italian speciality dishes served with rissole potatoes & roasted Mediterranean vegetables

Branzino fritto in casseruola
A succulent pan-fried fillet of seabass served with a luxurious, creamy lobster sauce £11.45

Coscio di anatra
Slow cooked leg of duck, balsamic marinated onions, wild mushrooms & cherry tomatoes £12.45

Peperoni rossi e formaggio di capra
Roasted red peppers and goat's cheese with black olives and sun blushed tomatoes, finished with pesto & a balsamic vinegar reduction £7.95

Insalata della Casa

Insalata nizzarda
A classical salad combining flaked tuna, boiled egg, green beans, potatoes & tomatoes with olives, marinated anchovies & capers £8.25

Insalata di pollo
Fresh salad of chicken breast, goats' cheese, red peppers & black olives served upon rocket & little gem leaves, flavoured with our own Parmesan dressing £8.25

For our tempting selection of desserts & ice creams please ask for a dessert menu

Figure 5.10 Part of an à la carte menu from Luciano's, Center Parcs

Table d'hôte menu

This is a set price menu offering a complete meal of two or more courses at a single price. There may be a choice in one or more courses. Sometimes there is a supplement for more expensive dishes. Table d'hôte menus usually represent good value for money and work out slightly cheaper than ordering the same dishes from the à la carte menu because a set menu is often more efficient. The chef can influence and anticipate demand more easily. It reduces the range of what must be bought in and the chef can order larger quantities which reduces the cost of food items. With a limited menu, much of the preparation can be done in advance which reduces the time taken to cook the dishes, and helps to speed up the turnover of customers.

> Cream of asparagus soup with croutons
>
> Chicken risotto with baby leaf spinach salad

Figure 5.11 A two-course, no choice, table d'hôte menu by an industrial caterer

Starter/Soup	Main course	Dessert
Fish	Fish	Hot pudding
Meat/Poultry	Meat	Cold dessert
Vegetarian	Poultry	Cheese
	Vegetarian	
	Special	
	Side orders	

Figure 5.12 A simple menu grid which can help with basic menu planning

Try this!   Worksheet 63

Choose a type of small catering operation, e.g. a café or bistro and a location. Use Figure 5.12 to help you put together a lunchtime table d'hôte menu. Make sure that the menu is well-balanced and in line with the style of the catering establishment, customer types and requirements, location, opening hours and price range. It should also meet all legal requirements.

Top marks!

Check your work to make sure that you have used the correct terms. Look up meanings or ask your tutor if you are not sure.

Did you know?

Do you know the meaning of these terms from a classic menu sequence? The full menu consists of 14 courses.

Hors d'oeuvres: a French term for a cold dish served at the beginning of a meal consisting of items such as pâté, hard-boiled eggs with mayonnaise, salad or several items brought together as mixed hors-d'oeuvres.

Potage: the French word for soup. Served after the hors d'oeuvres. Now often included as one of the starters on simpler menus.

Farinaceous dishes: starchy dishes including all pasta and rice dishes.

Entrée: if served as part of a classic menu, these are small, garnished dishes served without vegetables, e.g. tournedos, filled vol-au-vents. If served as a main course the dishes may be meat, fish, poultry or other and will be served with vegetables.

Relevé: Roasted items are served with a green salad.

Fromage: the French word for cheese. Served towards the end of a meal, normally includes a selection of cheeses with accompaniments such as biscuits or grapes.

Different meal occasions

Different meal occasions require different approaches to the menu. Here are four of the main UK meal occasions.

Breakfast

Breakfast menus in the UK tend to be either Continental or Full English Breakfast (or equivalents in Scotland, Wales and Northern Ireland). There may be an à la carte menu to choose from or a table d'hôte menu. Service ranges from counter (e.g. in a small café), self-service counter (e.g. in an industrial restaurant), selection from a chilled and/or hot buffet (e.g. conference hotel) and full table service (e.g. in a good-quality hotel). Fish dishes may be included on an English breakfast menu. The most common dish is kippers, or haddock and poached eggs, while smoked salmon and scrambled eggs is a popular modern choice.

Did you know?

Kedgeree is a fish dish traditionally made using smoked haddock mixed with rice and eggs. It is either flavoured with curry sauce or served with a curry sauce. It originated in India and was developed by British colonials living in India during the 19th century who brought it back to Victorian England where it became popular as a breakfast dish.

Try this!

Find a breakfast menu for an establishment of your choice. What do you think is good or bad about this breakfast menu? Are there enough courses? Is the choice wide enough? Is it suitable for the establishment?

Lunch and dinner menus

Lunch menus in the UK tend to be shorter and lighter than dinner menus, as most diners have more time in the evening. The exception is Sunday lunch, for which most catering establishments will have a special menu. Menus for both lunch and dinner may be à la carte or a set price table d'hôte menu of one or more courses, with or without a choice of dishes.

Afternoon tea

Afternoon tea is a particularly British occasion. It may be a no-choice item on a larger menu, see Figure 5.12. An establishment that specialises in afternoon tea may offer a wide choice from an à la carte menu, e.g. sandwiches, cakes, hot buttered tea cakes, pancakes, pastries, gateaux and ice creams. There may also be a range of different types of tea.

Did you know?

The best afternoon tea is said to be at the Ritz, London, where the manager has had to offer tea in more than one of the restaurants to cope with demand from UK residents and overseas tourists, and introduce sittings throughout the day. There is still a waiting list!

Afternoon Tea: £4.50

Two scones with strawberry jam and cream

Pot of tea for one

Figure 5.13 An afternoon tea menu item

Different types of organisation

The type of catering operation and the types of customer that use it help to decide what goes onto the menu and the prices charged. The location of a restaurant will also affect the menu. A city centre location may require a menu that can be served quickly. In the middle of the countryside heartier, more leisurely food may be preferred. If there is a regional speciality, e.g. Lancashire hot pot, customers are likely to look for it on the menu. When designing a menu it is important to look at what nearby establishments are offering in terms of style, price and quality. A similar menu will be in direct competition, so something a little different might be better.

Hotels

Hotels provide breakfast menus for guests booking bed and breakfast, dinner menus for half-board guests and lunch menus for full-board guests. Many hotels also provide a room service menu and a breakfast menu for guests wanting to eat breakfast in their room. There may also be a snack bar in the leisure complex.

Try this!　　Worksheet 63

Design a breakfast menu that can be easily prepared and delivered on a room-service basis.

Restaurants

Each restaurant will develop a menu that suits the:

- style of the establishment
- customers
- location
- facilities and the staffing.

Restaurants serving ethnic cuisine, e.g. Chinese, Indian or Greek food normally offer more than one type of menu. There may be an à la carte style menu, see Figure 5.14, and a range of set price menus with inclusive prices based on the number of people the meal is for, see Figure 5.15. Some restaurants also offer a takeaway at a slightly lower cost. A popular trend is to offer a set price hot and/or cold buffet, where customers serve themselves from a selection of dishes.

À la carte menu selections

Starters
2. Crispy Seaweed　　　　　£2.00

Mains
14. Chicken Chow Mein　　　£4.15
56. Beef Chop Suey　　　　　£4.50

Accompaniments
72. Special Fried Rice　　　£2.50
99. Prawn Crackers　　　　£1.00

Desserts
110. Lychees　　　　　　　£1.50

Figure 5.14 Part of an à la carte menu from a Chinese restaurant. Note the use of numbers for each dish

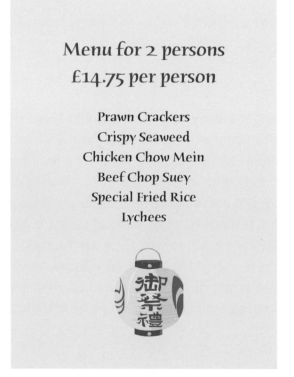

Menu for 2 persons
£14.75 per person

Prawn Crackers
Crispy Seaweed
Chicken Chow Mein
Beef Chop Suey
Special Fried Rice
Lychees

Figure 5.15 Part of a set menu from a Chinese restaurant

Investigate!

Find the menus for different types of restaurants, e.g. a fast–food outlet, a bistro, a fine dining restaurant. Make a list of common design and content features, and then make a list of differences. Compare your lists with a partner.

Hospitals

Hospitals have different types of catering operations and menus:

- NHS patients will often be given a card with a set menu without any prices giving the choices for breakfast, lunch and dinner. The menu card is often given to them the day before and they mark their choices on it. Patients with particular dietary requirements will normally be catered for.
- Private hospital patients will be given an à la carte or a table d'hôte menu for each meal occasion. It will usually show the prices as the patient will be charged.
- Visitors and staff are likely to go to a self-service counter restaurant. The limited menu of hot and cold food is suitable for people in a hurry.

Industrial catering

Menus for people at work will vary. The lunchtime menu is the most important as it needs to be served to a large number of people in a short period of time. Some industrial caterers also provide breakfast menus, limited evening service and snacks. There may also be a fine dining room for directors and business visitors offering a set or an à la carte call order menu. For example, Aramark UK at their Slough estates restaurant offer a daily counter service, plus fine dining for directors' meetings and buffets for special evening events.

Case study — Baxter and Platts

Read about industrial contract caterer, Baxter and Platts, fine dining restaurant in an article on the Caterer and Hotelkeeper website. A link has been made available at www.heinemann.co.uk/hotlinks. Just follow the links and enter the express code 4103P.

School meals

There are now government guidelines on healthy eating for school children in different age groups. Usually there is a counter service offering a limited choice of main courses and desserts which often include salad and fruit. The menu will normally have to cater for different ethnic and religious groups and for special dietary needs, e.g. vegetarians and children with food allergies.

Other factors to consider
Type of customer

It is important to find out what customers like and want. What people want to eat and the surroundings they want to eat in will change according to:

o The time of day or meal occasion, e.g. breakfast, lunch, dinner, coffee break, brunch, afternoon tea, supper, late night snack.
o How hungry they are.
o How much time they have, e.g. enough time to eat a three-course set lunch or just a sandwich.
o How much money they have to spend on a meal.
o The purpose of the meal, e.g. a business lunch, a quick bite before an evening out or lunch during a visit to a museum.
o Their style, taste and how influenced they are by fashion.
o Where they come from, e.g. the local area or region or international visitors.
o Whether they have special dietary needs because of age, health, allergies, religion, etc.

Chef's tip

If a dish is not selling, a restaurant must find out why it is unpopular, e.g. too strong a flavour or too expensive, and make the necessary changes, or take it off the menu.

Chef's tip

A catering establishment may need to vary the content of a menu and how it is presented in order to encourage repeat custom or to try and attract new customers.

Try this!

What types of customers are likely to be attracted by:

o *a children's menu in a fast-food establishment, e.g. McDonald's, in a shopping centre*
o *a carvery 'Early bird' menu such as that offered in Harvester restaurants*
o *an à la carte menu in a smart restaurant in a town centre?*

Investigate!

Imagine you work in a restaurant that always offers a main course vegetarian dish and a healthy option dish. You have been asked to add a gluten–free dish but do not want to increase the number of dishes on the menu. Find a dish that is vegetarian, gluten–free and a healthy option.

Definition

Gluten-free: made without using any wheat, barley, oats, rye. For advice on gluten-free ingredients visit the Coeliac Society UK website: www.coeliac.co.uk

Price being charged

The prices catering establishments charge for food are to some extent based on the cost of the food. The prices to be charged need to represent value for money for the customer. It is important to be able to predict what a customer is likely to buy and how much they are likely to spend. This is called customer spend per head. For example, a customer eating lunch in a fast-food restaurant may be prepared to spend £3.50 on a meal while a customer eating lunch in a smart restaurant is likely to be prepared to spend £10 or more on a two-course set lunch. See page 172, Food costs in catering, for more information.

Try this!

Worksheet 64

Look at Figure 5.16.

1 Add up the cost of each dish. This gives you the total food cost. What is it?

2 Divide the total food cost by the number of dishes. This is the average food cost. What is it?

Menu items	Cost per dish
Cream of asparagus soup with croutons	£1.20
Onion tart served on a bed of green salad	£0.80
Mozzarella and tomato salad with basil	£1.40
Chicken risotto with baby leaf spinach salad	£2.75
Lancashire hot pot with boiled potatoes, fresh carrots and green beans	£2.50
Chilli fried prawns with angel hair pasta	£2.90

Figure 5.16 A table d'hote menu developed by a contract caterer for a business lunch in the directors' meeting room at an industrial site

Availability of food commodities

Catering establishments can now source almost any food product from around the world, at most times of the year. Seasonal ingredients are usually easy to get hold of and reasonable in price. Out of season ingredients, however, are likely to be more expensive, more difficult to source and may not be as fresh or of the required quality.

Seasons affect customers' expectations and they will prefer comfort food in the winter and lighter dishes in the summer, e.g. a chilled soup or a salad will be welcome in the summer but not in the winter.

Investigate!   Worksheet 63

Choose a month of the year. Find out what food products are in season in the UK in that month. Create a table d'hôte lunch menu (or adjust the one you created earlier) so that it uses mainly fresh food that is in season during that month. Include at least one healthy option dish. Use Figure 5.12 to help you.

Availability of equipment and space

A menu should only include dishes that the kitchen is capable of producing. This applies whether the kitchen cooks everything from scratch or uses prepared or partly prepared food products.

If the menu cannot be produced because of lack of equipment or space, then either the menu must be changed or the kitchen re-designed and the correct equipment bought.

Availability of staff

The menu needs to take into account the number, availability and skills of the kitchen brigade and service staff. There is no point including complicated dishes that take ages to prepare and cook if there are not enough staff in the kitchen brigade or they lack ability or experience.

Try this!   Worksheet 63

Create a special festive table d'hôte menu, e.g. for Christmas, Diwali, Burns Night or Valentine's Day. Use Figure 5.12 to help you.

Top marks!

Think of examples of good practice, e.g. balanced menus, healthy eating options, dishes for customers with particular needs, and make sure you follow the relevant laws, procedures and practices that are so important to protect the health and safety of staff and customers. This will help to show your understanding of the kitchen as a workplace and the factors that influence how well it operates.

Chef's tip

Offer fewer dishes of a good standard rather than an extensive list of dishes of average or poor quality.

Test yourself!

1 List five things you must remember when planning a menu.

2 What are the advantages of planning a menu that offers seasonal foods?

3 Write down two features of an à la carte menu.

4 Define a table d'hôte menu.

5 What are the differences between a lunch menu and a dinner menu? Why?

6 A good menu will inform customers about many things. Give four of them.

Controlling food cost

The purpose of a catering business is to make a **profit** or to at least **break even**. Most want to make a profit. Some are **subsidised**.

In order to make a profit a business can control two things:
- Cost of sales (buy cheaper food, hire fewer people, move to smaller premises etc).
- Sales income (put prices up or sell more food).

Managers must get the correct balance between costs and income in order to make a profit. Most set targets for what **profit margin** they want to achieve. Costs and selling prices are calculated in order to achieve these targets.

Calculating sales income

Nat and Becky own and manage the Ruby Café in Newcastle. It is a lively, modern establishment, popular with local office workers and shoppers. The café is open from 8am to 5pm Monday to Saturday. The Ruby Cafe serves breakfast from 8am to 11.30am; lunch from 11.30am to 2.30pm; and afternoon tea from 2.30pm to 5pm.

Nat and Becky took £3,200 last week at their café. This is their **sales income** for the week.

To work out the sales income, multiply the selling price by the number of portions sold.

Figure 5.17 Nat and Becky's sales income for the week is £3,200.

> **Definitions**
> **Profit:** the sales income that is left after costs have been deducted.
> **Break even:** the amount of sales income is equal to the cost of making the sales.
> **Subsidised:** a contribution is made towards food costs in order to keep the selling price down.
> **Profit margin:** the difference between costs and sales income, usually expressed as a percentage of sales income.
> **Sales income:** money that is received from customers in payment for food.

Haddock, chips and salad is a popular dish at the Ruby Café. The price of one portion of this dish is £5.50.

If 34 portions of haddock, chips and salad are sold at lunchtime what is the sales income?

selling price × number of portions sold = sales income

$$5.5 \quad \times \quad 34 \quad = \quad 187$$

The sales income is £187.00

Nat and Becky keep detailed records of all their sales income. The sales income for one course is the total income from all the sales of that course during a given period of time.

On Monday, the Ruby Café sold: | What was the total sales income from starters on Monday?

9 starters at £4.00
10 starters at £3.00
12 starters at £2.50

9 × 4   = 36
10 × 3   = 30
12 × 2.5 = 30
Total   = 96

Monday's total sales income from starters was £96.00

The sales income for a particular menu is the total income from all the sales of that menu during a given period of time. This period of time is called a sitting.

At lunchtime on Monday the Ruby Café sold: | What was the total sales income from the lunch menu on Monday?

9 starters at £4.00
10 starters at £3.00
12 starters at £2.50

9 × 4   = 36
10 × 3   = 30
12 × 2.5 = 30

14 main courses at £5.00
6 main courses at £5.50
11 main courses at £6.00

14 × 5   = 70
6 × 5.5 = 33
10 × 6   = 60

16 desserts at £2.50
6 desserts at £3.00

16 × 2.5 = 40
6 × 3   = 18
Total   = 317

The total sales income from the lunch menu on Monday was £317.00

The sales income for a particular day is the total income from all the sales that day.

> On Monday the Ruby Café's sales income was:
>
> £153 from the breakfast menu
> £317 from the lunchtime menu
> £70 from the afternoon tea menu
>
> What was the total sales income on Monday?
>
>   153
>   + 317
>   + 70
>   = 540
>
> The total sales income on Monday was £540.00.

Try this!
Open spreadsheet **sales income.xls** and complete it.

Definition

Food cost: the cost of purchasing the food which is sold in a catering business.
Gross profit: the money that is left when food costs have been deducted from the sales income.

Nat and Becky also need to work out their sales income over longer periods of time. The sales income for a week is the total of all the sales income for each day that the café is open during a particular week.

> The Ruby Café is open for 6 days a week. Nat and Becky worked out the sales income for each day last week:
> Monday, £540.00
> Tuesday £600.00
> Wednesday £650.00
> Thursday £460.00
> Friday £590.00
> Saturday £360.00.
>
> What was the total sales income last week?
>
>   540
>   + 600
>   + 650
>   + 460
>   + 590
>   + 360
>   = 3,200
>
> The Ruby Café's total sales income last week was £3,200

Calculating food cost and gross profit

Nat and Becky are saving for an automatic fryer for the café but not all their sales income can go towards this. For a start they must pay for all the food that they bought in order to make the dishes that they sold in their café. This week they spent £1,280 on food for the café. This is their **food cost** for the week.

To work out **gross profit**, take away food cost from the sales income.

Figure 5.18 Food cost is £1,280 and the gross profit is £1,920.

What is the gross profit for the week?

 sales income – food cost = gross profit
   3,200   –   1,280   =   1,920

The gross profit for the week is £1,920

Chef's tip

Portion sizes depend to some extent on the type of customers and the prices being charged. The Ruby Café's customers are mainly office workers and shoppers who will not have much time to spend on a meal at lunchtime. They are likely to be happy with a small piece of haddock rather than a large one, or a 5oz rather than an 8oz steak but they will still expect value for money. If the Ruby Café's main customers were manual workers, larger portions would be expected.

Portion sizes may vary between different menus in the same establishment. In a restaurant, a portion of lamb served as part of a three-course dinner menu costing £25 is likely to be smaller than a portion of lamb on the à la carte menu, which alone may cost £25. If the Ruby Café were open in the evening, it might be necessary to introduce a dinner menu and serve slightly larger portions at a higher price.

Calculating food cost and gross profit as percentages

To help them plan for the future success of their business, Nat and Becky need know what **proportion** of their sales income is spent on food. To do this they need to show the food cost as a **percentage** of the total sales income.

Definition

Proportion: the relationship in terms of size or value between different parts of a whole. Proportions are often shown as percentages.

Percentage: a proportion or rate per hundred. For example, 30 per cent means 30 parts out of a total of 100 parts. This is written as 30%.

40%   Food cost £1260

60%   Gross profit £1920

Figure 5.19 Imagine that Nat and Becky took their sales income of £3200 and divided it equally into 100 bags. Each bag would be 1 percent of the total sales income. Now it is easy to see what proportion of the total is spent on food

To work out the food cost as a percentage of sales income:
- first divide the food cost by the sales income
- then multiply the answer by 100 to change it to a percentage.

> What is the food cost as a percentage of sales income?
>
> food cost ÷ sales income × 100 = food cost as a percentage of sales income
>
> 1,280 ÷ 3,200 × 100 = 40 (remember this is a percentage)
>
> The food cost as a percentage of sales income is 40 per cent

To work out the gross profit as a percentage of sales income:
- first divide the gross profit by the sales income
- then multiply the answer by 100 to change it to a percentage.

> What is the gross profit as a percentage of sales income?
>
> gross profit ÷ sales income × 100 = gross profit as a percentage of sales income
>
> 1,920 ÷ 3,200 × 100 = 60 (remember this is a percentage)
>
> The gross profit as a percentage of sales income is 60 per cent

Chef's tip

Notice that the percentage food cost and the percentage gross profit add up to 100%. If you know one of them, you can take it away from 100 to find the other.

Try this!

Worksheet 65

Work out the gross profit and the percentage gross profit for the following dishes:

Dish	Food cost per portion	Sales income per portion
Smoked salmon	£1.72	£8.25
Sirloin steak	£3.63	£14.50
Raspberries	£1.35	£4.55

Many businesses use spreadsheets to take the hard work out of these calculations. They are quite tricky to set up, but once they are created, they can save a lot of time.

Try this!

Open spreadsheets **food cost.xls** and **gross profit.xls** and complete them.

Setting targets

To be successful, a restaurant needs to make a gross profit on food sales of about 65–70 per cent. This means that food costs need to be kept to around 30–35 per cent. Most businesses will have a target gross profit percentage which they aim to achieve. This in turn means that they have a target food cost percentage.

For example, if the target gross profit percentage is 65 per cent then the target food cost percentage will be 35 per cent because the two percentages together must always add up to 100 per cent.

Calculating the selling price needed to achieve a target gross profit

If a business is buying food as efficiently as possible, the only other thing that can be changed in order to improve profits is the selling price of the food. You can calculate what selling price you need to charge in order to make your target gross profit. In order to do this you need to know:

○ the food cost in £
○ the target food cost as a percentage of sales income.

To work out the selling price:
○ first divide the food cost by the food cost as a percentage of sales income
○ then multiply the answer by 100 to get the selling price.

> Nat and Becky decide to set a target for the Ruby Café of keeping food cost to 35 per cent of the sales income. They need to work out the selling price for each dish on the menu.
>
> The food cost for one portion of lasagne, salad and garlic bread is £2.80.
>
> What should the selling price of one portion of this dish be to meet the target of keeping food cost to 35% of sales income?
>
> food cost ÷ food cost as a percentage x 100 = selling price
>   of sales income
>   2.80   ÷   35   x 100 = 8
>
> With a target of keeping food cost to 35 percent of sales income, the selling price of this dish needs to be at least £8.00.

This calculation can be done for individual dishes but also for courses, or whole menus, using average prices.

Try this!
Do you think Nat and Becky's café will be successful if they carry on as they are?

Try this!
Open spreadsheet **calc selling price for set gross profit.xls** and complete it.

Top marks!
When doing calculations, always include your workings to show how you reached the answer, e.g. if you produce a drawing to scale, show how you worked out the measurements. If you are working out costs and selling prices of a portion or a dish, show your workings.

Try this!

1 A caterer must keep food cost to 35 per cent of the sales income.
  The dish costs £3.45.
  What selling price should be charged?

2 A caterer must make a food gross profit of 65 per cent on the sales income from a banquet menu.
  The menu consists of one starter, one main course and one dessert.
  The total food cost is £10.45.
  a What should food cost as a percentage of sales be?
  b What selling price should be charged?

Monitoring food cost

Food cost makes up a quite a large proportion of the costs of operating a catering establishment. It is important to monitor and review costs and change procedures when necessary. Introducing sensible procedures for purchasing food, storing and producing food, may make it possible to reduce costs or at least keep them under control. A business can quickly be ruined by a bad pricing policy. If the menu is under-priced money will be lost each time an under-priced dish is sold.

Sourcing and purchasing good quality food commodities

Food commodities include items such as grain, meat and fish that are used in food production. Price lists are available from all food suppliers. Sometimes, the cheapest price is not the best price. It is important to look for:

○ good quality food that is appropriate for the establishment
○ a reliable supplier with excellent food safety practices.

Locally sourced food should be fresher because the food can be delivered regularly in small batches and is often cheaper because transport costs are lower. A note of the source and quality can be included in menu descriptions.

Control of food commodities

Before placing an order with suppliers the chef needs to work out what will be needed for a given operating period (e.g. daily, weekly or monthly) taking into account the next delivery date. Stock that sits on the shelf ties up money. It is important to follow procedures for purchasing, checking deliveries against orders and stock rotation. See Chapter 2, Food safety, for more information.

Accurate weighing, measuring and portion control

Recipes help chefs to produce food to consistent standards and in consistent quantities. They allow greater control over the costs of dishes and the size of portions. Recipes also help to identify the food that has to be ordered and the quantities needed. Purchasing and portion control must be linked as the kitchen staff need to know how many portions to make from the ingredients.

Providing the correct equipment for weighing and measuring during food preparation, cooking and serving up also helps kitchen staff to follow recipes accurately and serve the correct portion size. Providing appropriately sized scoops, ladles, pie dishes, etc. makes it easier to control portions. Many catering establishments buy commodities that are already divided into portions. They may be more expensive but can save on labour costs as they require less preparation.

Preparation, cooking losses and wastage control

Some wastage is inevitable in a kitchen. Food buyers often work out the average wastage and order slightly more. Controlling orders and wastage are key factors in keeping food cost down. If £50 of food is wasted a day, it adds up to £250 a week and £12,500 a year.

Chefs need to use every part of an ingredient, e.g. a chicken can be made into a variety of dishes by using the breasts in a main course, the legs in a terrine and the wing tips and carcass for stock. Skilled staff reduce losses due to spoiling during preparation and cooking as the cost of food increases if a member of the kitchen team ruins an expensive fresh salmon during preparation.

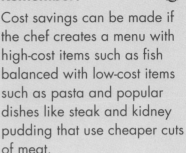

Remember!

Cost savings can be made if the chef creates a menu with high-cost items such as fish balanced with low-cost items such as pasta and popular dishes like steak and kidney pudding that use cheaper cuts of meat.

Did you know?

A computerised Food and beverage management system can help to control costs and increase efficiency and security by automating stock control, ordering, purchasing and requisition. It will streamline reporting on usage, costs and kitchen performance. It can be linked to other systems, e.g. Squirrel point of sale touchscreen terminals to create a fully-integrated system.

The Wiltons fine dining restaurant in London uses such a system to record table bookings, input food and wine orders and send them to the kitchen or bar, print bills and produce restaurant accounts and reports.

Buying good-quality commodities reduces wastage during preparation and cooking. For example:

o a chef pays £20 for ten low-quality 12oz beef steaks
o he has to trim 2oz of unwanted fat from each steak before cooking
o he is left with ten x 10oz steaks, still costing £20.

Low-quality cuts also tend to reduce more during cooking. It is better to buy slightly more expensive better-quality steaks as there will be less wastage and the restaurant can charge more.

Other costs

In addition to food cost, a catering establishment will have to monitor and control other elements of cost.

Labour costs

These are the costs of staff salaries. They are divided into **direct** and **indirect labour costs**. Labour costs can be reduced by:

o cutting hours
o employing fewer staff
o changing food production methods (this could affect quality and customer service)
o improving productivity.

Overhead costs

Overheads include rent, council tax, water rates, services such as gas, electricity and telephone, maintenance and repairs, advertising and sundry expenses. Overheads can also be controlled, e.g. by turning off cooking equipment when not in use.

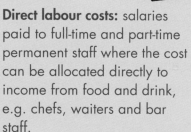

Definition

Direct labour costs: salaries paid to full-time and part-time permanent staff where the cost can be allocated directly to income from food and drink, e.g. chefs, waiters and bar staff.

Indirect labour costs: salaries paid to staff such as managers, office staff and maintenance staff who work for all departments. A proportion of indirect labour costs should be charged to all departments.

Try this!
Open spreadsheet **labour and overhead costs per portion.xls** and complete it.

Calculating the total cost of food sales

In order to get a true picture of how much a business is costing to run, a proportion of these additional costs is often included when calculating the cost of individual menus or dishes.

Food cost   Labour cost   Overhead cost

Figure 5.20 What do you think the fourth pile might be?

To do this:
- first work out the number of individual portions served in a typical week
- then divide that by the labour costs and by the overhead costs
- this will give you the average cost per portion.

Weekly labour costs are £960. The overhead costs are £640.

Nat and Becky need to allocate a proportion of these costs to individual portions. In a typical week the Ruby Café cooks 40 dishes. Each dish provides a different number of individual portions. By keeping records of their business, Nat and Becky know roughly how many portions of each dish they sell in a typical week. They add up all the portions of all the dishes, and work out that that they cook about 400 individual portions in a typical week.

a   What is the average labour cost that should be allocated to one portion?

labour costs ÷ individual portions = average labour cost per portion
     960   ÷   400   = 2.40

Labour costs of £2.40 should be allocated to one portion.

b   What is the average overhead cost that should be allocated to one portion?

overhead costs ÷ individual portions = average overhead cost per portion
     640   ÷   400   = 1.60

Overhead costs of £1.60 should be allocated to one portion.

The same method can be used to work out the average labour and overhead costs to be allocated to a dish or to a particular menu.

Now Nat and Becky can calculate the full cost of producing one portion of any particular dish, using the average labour and overhead costs which they have decided should be allocated to each portion of a dish.

> At the Ruby Café the food cost for one portion of lasagne, salad and garlic bread is £2.80. The labour cost per portion is £2.40. The overhead cost per portion is £1.60.
>
> What is the total cost of one portion of this dish?
>
> food cost + labour cost + overhead cost = total cost of a dish
>   2.80   +   2.40   +   1.60   = 6.80
>
> The total cost of one portion of this dish is £6.80

Net profit

A business which is making a good **net profit** is likely to be successful. It is making enough money to cover all its costs and have some left over. This could be used to improve or expand the business.

Definition

Net profit: the money that is left when food cost, labour costs and overhead costs have been deducted from the sales income.

Figure 5.21 Why are Nat and Becky looking so happy?

Calculating net profit

To work out the gross profit, take away the food cost from the sales income.

To work out the net profit, take away the labour costs and overhead costs from the gross profit.

At the Ruby Café the food cost for one portion of lasagne, salad and garlic bread is £2.80.

The labour costs are £2.40. The overhead costs are £1.60. The selling price of the dish is £7.50.

a   What is the gross profit on this dish?

Sales income – food cost = gross profit
    7.50   –   2.80   = 4.70

The gross profit on the dish is £4.70

a   What is the net profit on this dish?

gross profit – labour costs – overhead cost = net profit
    4.70   –   2.40   –   1.60   = 0.70

The net profit on the dish is £0.70

At the Ruby Café the food cost for a week is £1,280; labour costs are £960; and overhead costs are £640. Sales income is £3,200.

a What is the gross profit on total food sales income that week?

sales income – food costs = gross profit
   3,200   –   1,280   = 1,920

The gross profit that week is £1,920.00

b   What is the net profit on food sales that week?

gross profit – labour cost – overhead cost = net profit
   1,920   –   960   –   640   = 320

The net profit that week is £320.00

Net profit as a percentage of sales income

Net profit is usually shown as a percentage of sales income.

15%	Net profit
35%	Food cost
30%	Labour cost
20%	Overhead cost

Figure 5.22 If Nat and Becky took their sales income and divided it equally into 100 bags, each bag would be 1 per cent of the total sales income. Now it is easy to see the net profit as a percentage of sales income.

To work out net profit as a percentage of sales income:

○ first divide net profit by the sales income

○ then multiply the answer by 100 to change it to a percentage.

What is the net profit as a percentage of food sales income that week at the Ruby Café?

net profit ÷ sales income × 100 = net profit as a percentage

320 ÷ 3200 × 100 = 10

That week the net profit as a percentage was 10 per cent.

Nat and Becky increase the selling prices of all the dishes at the Ruby Café. The next week the total weekly sales income increases from £3,200 to £3,380. Total food costs for the week are still £1,280, labour costs are still £960 and overhead costs are still £640.

a What is the gross profit on food sales that week?

🖩 sales income – food cost = gross profit
  3,380   – 1,280 = 2,100

The gross profit that week is £2,100.

b What is the net profit on food sales that week?

🖩 gross profit – labour cost – overhead cost = net profit
   2,100   –   960   –   640   = 500

The net profit that week is £500.

c What is the net profit as a percentage of sales income?

🖩 net profit ÷ sales income × 100 = net profit as a percentage
   500   ÷   3,380   × 100 = 14.79 (Remember! the answer
                                    is a percentage)

That week the net profit as a percentage of sales income was
14.79 per cent

Try this!
Open and complete the
spreadsheet file **net profit.xls**.

Try this!   Worksheet 67

The costs for one portion of a dish from the main course on the à la
carte menu of Shangri-La restaurant are: food cost £8.00; labour costs
£4.00, overheads £3.50.

1 What is the total cost of one portion of this dish?
2 The sales income (selling price) of the dish is £16.75.
   What is the net profit as a percentage of the sales income?

Calculating the selling price needed to achieve a target net profit

Most catering businesses will have a target that is expressed as
a net profit percentage, e.g. a 10 per cent net profit on food sales
income.

It is necessary to calculate selling prices that will achieve this
target. To do this you need to know the total costs which are made
up of:

○ food cost
○ overhead costs
○ labour costs.

Chef's tip

If the target net profit
percentage is 10 per cent, then
the target total cost percentage
will be 90 per cent. The two
percentages must always add
up to 100 per cent.

To work out the selling price needed to achieve a target net profit:

○ first divide the total costs by the total costs as a percentage of sales

○ then multiply the answer by 100.

> Nat and Becky set themselves a target of achieving a 15 per cent net profit on sales income.
>
> At the Ruby Café the food cost for one portion of rump steak, chips and peas is £3.20. The labour cost is £2.40. The overhead costs are £1.60. The total cost of one portion of this dish is £7.20.
>
> First, they need to work out the target total costs.
>
> 100 − 15 = 85 (remember the answer is a percentage)
>
> The target for the Ruby Café is to achieve a net profit of 15 per cent of sales income. The target total costs must therefore be 85 per cent of sales income.
>
> Nat and Becky must then work out the total cost of one portion of the dish.
>
> food cost + labour cost + overhead cost = total cost of one portion
>   3.2   +   2.4   +   1.6   = 7.2
>
> The total cost of one portion of this dish is £7.20
>
> Now they are ready to calculate the selling price they need to charge.
>
> total costs ÷ total costs as a percentage of sales × 100 = selling price
>   7.2   ÷   85   × 100 = 8
>
> The minimum selling price for one portion of this dish to achieve a 15 per cent net profit on food sales income is £8.47 (rounded up to £8.50 on the menu)

Remember!

The percentage total costs and the percentage net profit add up to 100%. If you know one of them, you can calculate the other by taking away the one you know from 100.

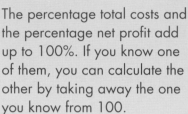 100% − 15% = 85%

Remember!

Setting prices involves making decisions about how much customers will be prepared to spend and what the competition is charging. If customers stay away because they feel a restaurant is overcharging, it may be necessary for the establishment to reduce its profit targets.

Try this!

Open and complete the spreadsheet **calc selling price for set net profit.xls**.

Try this!   Worksheet 68

Develop a simple à la carte menu for a catering establishment of your choice. Include the selling prices. What is your target food cost percentage and target gross profit percentage for each dish?

Test yourself!

1 One portion of fish and chips costs £5.50. If 34 portions of fish and chips are sold at lunchtime what is the sales income?

2 The food cost of a sandwich is 75p. The sales income (selling price) is £1.30.
   a What is the gross profit on food sales?
   b What is the gross profit on food sales as a percentage of the sales income?

3 A restaurant within a leisure attraction has a target to keep food cost to 35 per cent of the sales income.
   The food cost of a hamburger, chips and salad is 49p.
   What selling price should be charged?

4 The food cost for a dish is £2.50. The labour cost is £1.75. The overhead costs are 99p.
   What is the total cost of this dish?

5 The total price of a starter, main course and dessert in an industrial self-service canteen is £4.25. The food cost for this meal is £2.30.
   What is the gross profit as a percentage of sales income?

6 The food cost for a dish is £2.50
   The labour cost is £1.75
   The overhead costs are 99p.
   The selling price of the dish is £6.20.
   a What is the gross profit on this dish?
   b What is the net profit?

Practice assignment task

Background information

You decide to enter a local competition run by a bank to promote new businesses nationally. The winner will receive a £3,000 interest free loan to help them start their own business and free banking for three years.

Task

In order to enter the competition you need to produce a summary of your business proposal. This should include:

○ The name of the business.
○ The type of business.
○ Its place (niche) within the local market.
○ An overview of the large equipment that will be required in the kitchen.
○ The staff structure.
○ The number of covers for the restaurant.
○ A three-course dinner menu with prices.
○ The food costs of three menu items.
○ The labour costs and overhead costs.

Applying workplace skills

6

This chapter covers part of the following outcomes from Diploma unit 206: Applying workplace skills

- Outcome 206.1 Maintain personal presentation
- Outcome 206.2 Applying workplace skills
- Outcome 206.3 Prepare for a job application
- Outcome 206.4 Produce a plan to develop skills

Working through this chapter could also provide evidence for the following Key Skills:

C2.1, C2.2a, C2.2b, C2.3, N2.1, N2.2a/b, ICT2.1, ICT2.2, ICT2.3, LP2.1, LP2.2, LP2.3, PS2.1, PS2.2, PS2.3, WO2.1, WO2.2, WO2.3

In this chapter you will learn how to:

Explain what personal presentation is, the reasons for maintaining it and the effect this has on the organisation

Explain the skills required to maintain a work area and to work effectively with customers and colleagues

Describe how to identify and solve customer and colleague complaints

List the key stages in working to meet team targets

Write a professional curriculum vitae and covering letter

Prepare for and evaluate an interview

Create a development plan and identify the importance of feedback

Personal presentation

Working in food production is a very responsible job and a good chef is well-respected by everyone. A person who is well-presented in the kitchen creates a professional and efficient impression and has every chance to do well at their job.

Professional appearance

To look professional make sure your:

○ uniform is clean and ironed carefully

○ apron is worn correctly

○ hat fits well

○ trousers are clean and the right length

○ shoes are clean.

Good personal grooming is very important as it creates a positive first impression and makes you look professional. People with good personal grooming:

○ have clean, neat and tidy hair

○ wear a beard net (if they are male and have a beard)

○ do not wear any make-up or jewellery

○ have clean, short and well-kept nails

○ have an upright posture

○ have a happy nature and a genuine smile.

Professional behaviour

It is important to create a good impression by demonstrating a professional and mature attitude in the kitchen. This is particularly important as a high standard of hygiene, health and safety is required in a catering kitchen. A professional attitude can be maintained by:

○ Always being well turned out.

○ Behaving in a mature, responsible manner.

○ Taking pride in your appearance and your work.

○ Ensuring that you are on time for work every day.

○ Working efficiently and productively using good time management.

○ Communicating with others politely and effectively.

○ Being reliable and dependable in your standard of work.

○ Using your initiative to help yourself and others.

Top marks!

Remember that you will be graded on the standard of your appearance. Try to ensure that every time you turn up for work in the kitchen you are on time, alert and keen. Make sure that your uniform is clean and in good condition plenty of time before your shift starts so you have time to replace buttons or iron a creased apron, etc.

Try this!

Produce a collage showing an appropriately dressed member of a kitchen brigade. There is a wide range of jacket and trouser styles available. Do not forget to source appropriate shoes, hat and necktie!

- Maintaining standards of speed, accuracy and quality of work.
- Being organised and methodical in your work area.

Why have a professional attitude?

A professional attitude in the kitchen:

- Gives the whole kitchen brigade a professional image.
- Develops your confidence and pride in your position at work.
- Enables you to carry out correct health, safety and hygiene procedures.
- Helps customers and staff to be happy and satisfied.
- Improves the reputation of the establishment.
- Helps boost the profits of the business.

Which skills help to develop a professional approach in the workplace?

The skills which help to develop a professional approach are:

- Organising your materials, equipment and working area.
- Planning the order of tasks and assembling the necessary equipment in advance.
- Deciding in advance how busy the service is likely to be and how many portions of a dish will need preparing.
- Playing your part to ensure that the various sections of the kitchen all work at the necessary speed to be ready together, on time.
- Wasting as little as possible of any ingredients.
- Developing higher levels of skill and speed in the tasks required.
- Cleaning as you go so your work area can be kept tidy, safe and hygienic.

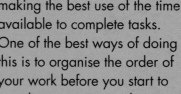

Did you know?

Time management is about making the best use of the time available to complete tasks. One of the best ways of doing this is to organise the order of your work before you start to avoid wasting time or having to repeat jobs during your working day if at all possible.

Case study

Raj and Bertie both left college together and started work as trainee chefs in the same local restaurant. Raj was always on time for his shift and his uniform was clean and well-pressed every day. Bertie usually arrived just as his shift started and often put on the stained, dirty uniform he had worked in the day before. Raj was a careful, methodical worker who always turned out a good standard of food for his section. Sometimes Bertie would produce outstanding dishes, but at other times he would be totally disorganised and the food he prepared would have to be thrown away.

When the Head Chef had to cut back staff to save wages, who do you think was kept in the brigade — Raj or Bertie? What do you think influenced the Head Chef's decision?

Figure 6.1 Who is the best employee?

Communication skills

Being able to work well as a team is only possible if you communicate well. This does not just mean talking to each other. Communication can take different forms, including:

○ talking face to face
○ speaking on the phone
○ sending an email
○ sending a text message
○ writing a message or letter
○ body language.

Most communication in the kitchen involves speaking and body language. However, sometimes there is a need to write things down – food orders, stock requisitions, messages for other members of staff.

Try this!
Design an information poster for staff in the kitchen who do not speak English as their first language. The poster could show how to arrange a work area tidily, how to wash and care for knives, or how a set of dishes should be presented.

Try this!   Worksheet 69
Consider the targets that are set during the service of a meal at a function. Consider how those targets can be met. List the skills that are needed to achieve them.

Talking face to face

Talking face to face is the most effective method of communication, as both people can see the expressions on each other's faces as well as hear what they are saying. This helps them understand better.

Most people do not listen carefully to what is being said to them. This is where many problems occur. The best way to find out if someone has understood what you have said is to ask them a question about it. Alternatively, you could ask them to repeat back what you have said to them. If you have been telling them how to do something, you could ask them to do it for you.

The catering and hospitality industry is international. You may have to communicate with someone who does not speak the same language as yourself. To ensure they understand what you are trying to say to them you may need to:

o show them what you mean
o draw a picture to help you explain
o get someone who speaks both languages to help you.

Using the phone at work

Speaking on the phone is something that we are all used to at home. At work communication must be precise and accurate. The phone is used at work because you can receive an instant response to a question from someone who is not in the same area.

When speaking on the phone you must remember:

o to speak clearly
o not to speak too quickly
o to announce yourself and your position when you answer
o to smile as you speak (it does make a difference!)
o to write down any important information you are given
o to repeat back to the caller any important information to ensure it is accurate.
   This is particularly important with telephone numbers and prices of commodities, for example.

Always keep a record of:

o the name of the caller
o the time of the call
o the date of the call
o the contact number to return the call.

Figure 6.2 Listen carefully and be precise

Try this!
Design a telephone message pad to record important information that must be passed on to someone else. Make sure that all the essential details can be written down. How can you ensure that the message reaches the correct person in time?

193

Body language

Body language is the way people communicate with each other without using words; instead they use gestures. It is done subconsciously – without you noticing. You must be aware of the effect body language can have. If you are trying to hide your feelings from someone, be very careful – body language never lies!

Body language differs from culture to culture. If you are working with people from other parts of the world you need to be aware of this. Examples of this include:

o Japanese people greet each other by bowing very low.
o Indian people may move their heads from side to side when they mean 'yes'.

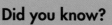

Did you know?

Out of what we communicate to each other:
o 70 per cent is transmitted by body language
o 20 per cent by tone of voice
o 10 per cent by the words that we use!

Try this!

Look at the faces on the right. What feeling or mood do they represent? Note that the only features that change are the eyebrows and mouth which shows how expressive they are!

Now look at the stick people illustrated on the right. What are they saying? You can be quite sure of their meaning but remember no words are being spoken.

Investigate!

Find out how to say 'hello', 'How are you?', 'please' and 'thank you' in at least three different languages. If you work or study with others for who English is not their first language, make sure you can greet them in their own language.

Communicating with customers

You may think that you will never have to communicate directly with customers because you work in a kitchen. However, you are communicating with them all the time through the standard of the work that you produce. Customers can be impressed by the work of the staff in the kitchen by the:

○ quality of the food produced
○ size of the portion
○ taste and seasoning of the items
○ attractive presentation of the food
○ temperature of the dish.

Occasionally, a member of the kitchen brigade may have to speak directly to a customer. The ingredients in a dish may have to be explained or the customer may not be happy with a dish and the chef may be asked to speak to the person.

When speaking to customers it is important to:

○ Empathise with how they are feeling (i.e. try to put yourself in their position).
○ Explain yourself as clearly as possible. Customers may not understand kitchen expressions.
○ Apologise on behalf of all the kitchen staff if the customer is not happy with the food produced.
○ Ask the customer what they would like done to put the matter right. This may mean re-serving a dish, providing an alternative or preparing a dish individually because a customer is allergic to a particular ingredient.

When dealing with customers it is very important to know the:

○ ingredients of dishes
○ methods of cookery involved
○ way the dishes are served
○ customer service policy of your employer.

Top marks!

As you become more experienced, make a note of ways you could prevent potential customer complaints arising in the first place. Why is this important?

Remember!

If a customer is not happy then they will go elsewhere and may not return to your establishment. They will also tell their friends and colleagues about their experience.

Did you know?

One way of remembering how to deal with a customer complaint is:
Listen
Empathise
Act
Revisit to check customer happy
Never be rude!

Organising your work area

To be able to work efficiently you must be organised. Part of being organised is planning ahead to make sure you have everything you need for a job before you start. You also need to position the items you are going to use sensibly on your work area. Remember:

○ Leave yourself sufficient space to carry out the task.

○ Avoid cluttering your work space with any equipment you are not going to use.

○ Use any shelves that may be above or below your work area. Do not overload shelves or position anything on them that might fall off easily.

○ Include waste bowls or trays on your list of equipment. They should be big enough to hold trimmings and peelings without overflowing. They should not be so big that they take up too much space on the worktop and cramp the work area.

○ If working with high-risk foods, avoid any risk of contaminating any of the items (see page 46, Controlling food safety hazards).

○ Make sure you can work in a safe manner so you do not endanger either yourself or others (see Chapter 3, Health and safety).

Figure 6.3 In which area could you work more efficiently?

Using your work time effectively

When working in a kitchen you must have very precise time management. Every chef in a kitchen may have up to three deadlines every day – breakfast, lunch and dinner. Customers will not accept any excuse if their food is not ready – they will go elsewhere to eat, and probably not come back to your outlet again.

Especially when starting work in a new section of the kitchen, or at a new premises, you need to be very well-organised. To be able to manage your time effectively you must:

○ plan out your time to schedule the order of your work

○ assemble all the equipment you will need before you start the job

○ fill in 'gap' times when items are cooking or resting, with other tasks

○ clear and clean as you go – include time for this on your work plan

○ include a break in your plan at a suitable time.

Try this!

Write a time plan for a busy day at work. Allow yourself a realistic amount of time to complete the tasks. Schedule a break and time in between tasks for cleaning down.

Did your plan work? Did you find that it helped you become more organised? Did you find that you completed more jobs than usual in the time because you took the trouble to plan it out first?

Time	Job/Activity	Equipment needed

Figure 6.4 A time planning sheet

Try this!

At work on a fairly quiet day, test how organised you are!

While you carry out one of your routine preparation jobs, make a note of how many times you have to leave your workplace to fetch items you have forgotten. Time yourself from when you start to get ready until the task is finished.

The next time you have the same job to do, take a few minutes to write out all the supplies and equipment you will need, then get them ready. Time yourself from the start of assembling the equipment to the end of the job and see if you have saved any time — you should have!

When to ask for help

Sometimes, particularly when starting a new job, you may not be sure what to do. Being uncertain about a task can result from:

○ not being shown how to do it
○ being unsure of the standard expected
○ forgetting how to carry out a task
○ being uncertain if you have sufficient time to carry out a task properly
○ not knowing how to operate equipment necessary to complete the task.

You need to ask for help whenever necessary, particularly at the start of a new job. If you do not, you could:

○ waste materials and time carrying out the task incorrectly
○ injure yourself or someone else
○ produce a sub-standard item
○ irritate other members of your team who then have to rectify your mistake.

Case study

Paula had just started to work in the pastry department of a large kitchen. The Pastry Chef asked her to make four dozen bread rolls for lunch service. Paula followed the standard recipe the chef had given her. The recipe made eight dozen rolls so Paula had to reduce the ingredients by half. She thought she had done this correctly and was surprised when the mixture seemed very slow to prove. Instead of asking the chef for advice she carried on. When the rolls came out of the oven they were far too small and extremely hard. They could not be used. The Pastry Chef had to stop what he was doing and make some replacement rolls. He was very cross that Paula had not asked for help as soon as she realised something was wrong.

Figure 6.5 The Pastry Chef was very cross

You need to ask for help when:

○ you are asked to do something you have not done before
○ you are still uncertain about a task you have not carried out very often
○ you cannot find something and have had a thorough look for it
○ you have not understood or remembered instructions you have received.

Case study

Phil had to make 500 savoury tartlets for a cocktail party that afternoon. He was very proud of the tartlets he could make — the Head Chef said they were some of the best he had tasted. He was running short of time to finish them, but working as fast as he could. Mike decided to help him and started to prepare the filling. He did not ask Phil for his recipe. He put together the ingredients quickly without measuring them as he did not think there was time to bother with being precise. As a result there was not enough filling for all the tartlet cases. Phil had to make some more filling with the remaining ingredients, but there were not the correct amounts to make the proper recipe. The Head Chef commented that the tartlets were not as good as usual. Phil was very cross with Mike for interfering and spoiling the high quality of his work. Mike could not understand why Phil was so cross — he thought Phil should have been grateful for the help!

Figure 6.6 Why was Phil cross with Mike?

Test yourself!

1 You have been following a recipe to make bread rolls for the first time. The instructions state that the mixture must be 'proved'. You do not understand this term. Should you:

  a ask for help?

  b miss that section of the recipe out?

  c throw the mixture away?

  d leave the kitchen in search of a textbook?

2 When preparing several different dishes for lunch service do you:

  a start with the first one on the list and work your way through to the last?

  b start with the most difficult and leave the easiest until last?

  c pick the one you enjoy making most to do first and leave the others until later?

  d decide in advance which is going to take the longest and start with that dish, working out a time plan to include the others?

3 You find that you have had to go back to the stores several times for ingredients and equipment for your current task. You could save time and energy by:

  a assembling all the ingredients and equipment together at the start

  b leaving that task until the end of the day next time

  c asking someone else to collect the items you had forgotten

  d requesting your work area to be moved nearer to the stores.

4 Complete these guidelines for recording a message:

  ○ _____ as clearly as possible – _____ if necessary.

  ○ Double-check any _____ and _____ as you write them down.

  ○ _____ the message with your _____ and the _____ and _____ you wrote it.

  ○ _____ the message in a _____ _____ where you are sure it will be _____ by the appropriate person as soon as possible.

Working with others

Effective teamwork is vital in the hospitality industry. A good standard of service and production cannot be provided by individuals working alone. A successful meal service depends upon all the staff in the kitchen and restaurant working together to ensure:

○ correct timing
○ smooth service
○ high standard of production
○ food served at the correct temperature.

The perfect team will consist of members who:

○ are committed to the task in hand
○ work together towards a common aim
○ are well-organised
○ communicate openly.

The benefits of working as a team mean that:

○ a higher output of work can be achieved for less effort
○ people are usually happier working in a group
○ responsibility for work and decisions is shared
○ team members are loyal to each other
○ the workforce is more creative.

Case study

Pat was the manager of a school meals kitchen. Each member of staff was responsible for producing one of the dishes on the menu every day. Her staff often complained about their colleagues' speed of work. They had to wait for each other on many occasions when using the same pieces of equipment such as mixers and ovens. Some staff worked more quickly than others and did not want to be held up. Some staff criticised the quality and flavour of the dishes that others had made.

Figure 6.7 Staff complaining

Pat decided to restructure the organisation of the kitchen. She put her staff to work in teams, each responsible for a group of dishes. She also moved the teams around so that they did not make the same dishes all the time. This meant that the staff had to work together and help each other much more. They organised their use of the equipment better and they stopped criticising each other's dishes. They started to share the recipes they used and found they had more time to get their jobs done.

Figure 6.8 Staff working in a team

Working as a team member also has advantages, such as :

o feeling more valued at work
o being able to learn from others
o being able to show others what you can do
o greater job satisfaction
o having the support of others
o benefitting from any team 'perks' – such as a productivity bonus.

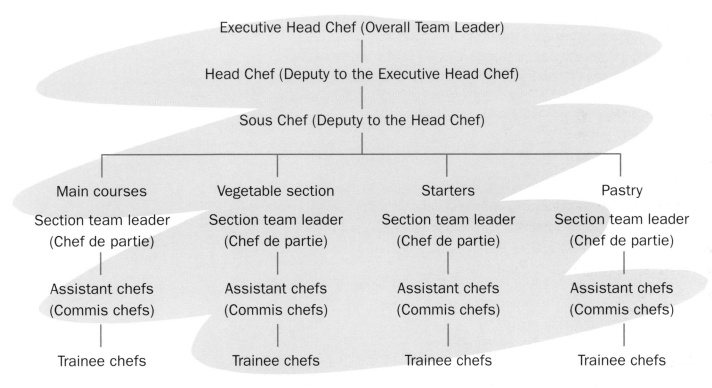

Executive Head Chef (Overall Team Leader)

Head Chef (Deputy to the Executive Head Chef)

Sous Chef (Deputy to the Head Chef)

Main courses	Vegetable section	Starters	Pastry
Section team leader (Chef de partie)	Section team leader (Chef de partie)	Section team leader (Chef de partie)	Section team leader (Chef de partie)
Assistant chefs (Commis chefs)	Assistant chefs (Commis chefs)	Assistant chefs (Commis chefs)	Assistant chefs (Commis chefs)
Trainee chefs	Trainee chefs	Trainee chefs	Trainee chefs

Figure 6.9 A large team in the kitchen of a conference centre

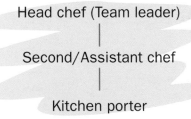

Head chef (Team leader)

Second/Assistant chef

Kitchen porter

Figure 6.10 A small team in the kitchen of a 40-seater restaurant

Investigate!

Find out about the staff organisation in a fast-food kitchen and draw a chart showing the levels of authority, then do the same for a traditional hotel restaurant. Look at the differences. Why do you think the two kitchens have such different staffing patterns?

Try this!

Draw a diagram of the organisation of your kitchen. Compare it with diagrams of people who work in other types of kitchen. The charts are likely to be quite different because:

○ *some kitchens, such as a small fast-food takeaway, will be very small and employ only a few staff*

○ *some kitchens, such as an international exhibition centre with conference and banqueting facilities, will be very large and employ many staff.*

In your diagram, is there one team or several small teams?

Think about if and when any informal teams are used in your workplace.

What are they used for? Are you involved in any informal teams outside the workplace?

Investigate!

Look on the internet or in the catering press for jobs in catering kitchens.

Try to find advertisements for a range of different positions. How many of them include the need to be able to work well in a team?

All teams must have a leader. The success of a team depends very much on this person. The leader of a team should:

○ set a good example

○ be respected by all the team members

○ be consistent in decisions made

○ encourage, motivate and support team members.

How do team members work together effectively?

To be able to work well with others a variety of skills are needed:

○ To co-operate with other team members.

○ To communicate effectively with other team members.

○ To watch and anticipate the needs of customers and staff.

○ The ability to deal with problems and complaints from customers and staff.

Top marks!

A good team member is reliable. Try to make sure that you consistently put into practice the things you have learned about good teamwork and communication.

Case study

Sheila had worked in the kitchen for nearly five years. She was proud of the section she ran and had a team of four staff to help her. At the start of every shift she gathered her staff together to brief them on the tasks that had to be completed that day. She made sure that they all understood what they had to do. If she saw any of them struggle with their workload she would make sure they had help so they could finish their tasks on time. If a member of her team had a problem she would always notice they were not happy and find out why. Sometimes she asked one of her staff to help out one of the other sections if they were short of staff.

Sheila ran her team well. Which of the skills listed above did she use to achieve this?

A good team member will:
- always be reliable and on time for work
- be organised, work cleanly and methodically
- complete all tasks required within a reasonable time
- help other people to complete their work if necessary
- share information and learn from other team members
- communicate clearly with others.

Try this!
Think of your team leader at work. Do they do a good job? Can you identify what they do to make the team work well together?

Case study

Jim used to work alone in a small sandwich bar. He was often lonely and struggled to keep pace with demand at lunchtimes when it was busy. He had to start work really early in the morning to make sure everything was ready. If he wanted a break he had to work even harder to make up for the lost time.

Jim moved to work at a larger sandwich shop. He was much happier straight away. There were other people to talk to while he worked and he enjoyed having a laugh and a joke with them. If he wanted a break, others would cover his job so he did not fall behind. He liked being able to help the others if they needed it. As a team, far more sandwiches were being produced than if each of them worked separately. The group liked to try to invent a different sandwich filling each week. Jim enjoyed the challenge of thinking of new combinations of ingredients. The customers liked several of the new sandwiches and sales rose. The owner of the business was very pleased and gave the whole team a bonus payment.

Figure 6.11 Jim was unhappy working alone

Figure 6.12 Jim enjoyed being part of a team

If a team is working effectively it will:
○ complete the required work on time and to a good standard
○ be able to learn new skills and techniques easily
○ communicate well within the team
○ motivate the team members to work harder and be successful
○ work to and achieve a common aim.

The working day is much less tiring and stressful for everyone if teams work together well.

Identifying and solving problems and complaints

Working in a team, you will be encouraged to help each other. Help is invaluable and your team members will always appreciate support. But remember that help should only be given if:
○ the assistance has been asked for, or offered. People can get upset if others start to take over uninvited, thinking they are helping.
○ by helping, the problem will be solved, not made worse. Too many cooks can spoil the broth!
○ by helping with one problem, another is not created, e.g. by stopping to help, you cannot finish your own preparations on time.

To be able to work together as a team it is important that members:
○ each carry out a fair share of the workload
○ all work to the same standard
○ show consideration to each other
○ communicate effectively with one another.
 In a kitchen there is no choice about how much preparation work has to be completed before service – it all has to be done, otherwise the meal service will be affected.

The reason someone may not be pulling their weight in a team at work could be:
○ they are new at the job and cannot work at the necessary speed yet
○ they are not feeling well
○ they have personal problems which are affecting their performance at work
○ they are tired
○ they are lazy
○ they are not keen or interested in their job.

Figure 6.13 Should these chefs be at work?

New staff members are usually given a period of induction and training when they start a new job. They are not often given a full workload to complete. If they are struggling, the team leader should notice this and assign another team member to help them until they can cope.

Staff who are not feeling well should not come to work. They should contact their employer as soon as possible. This is particularly the case with those employees whose jobs involve handling food. Their illness could be transmitted through the food to other staff or customers (see Wounds, illness and infection on page 54).

Sometimes staff come to work because they do not want to let their other team members down. If this is the case, the team leader should either send them home or transfer them to duties not involving food handling until they feel better.

Many people have to deal with personal problems outside work. Sometimes this can affect their work. If this is the case the poorly performing person should be encouraged to see their team leader or someone else with whom they can talk about their problem. If nothing is done to help, the person could end up losing their job – which would be an additional problem for them.

Working in food production is tiring (see Personal cleanliness and hygiene, page 49). If employees do not look after themselves properly they will not be able to continue to do their job well. This can cause them to be persistently late or careless and slow in their tasks. After a while the rest of their team will not tolerate this.

Case study

Tom started a new job in a busy restaurant kitchen. He worked in the vegetable section with two other chefs. Tom found the work quite hard. He was very tired when he got home, but he still enjoyed going out with his friends later. Most nights he went out and did not come back until after midnight. After a few days he started being late for work. At first the two other chefs helped him catch up with his preparation so that he was ready for service. Tom liked the help. It meant it did not really matter if he was late. After a while the two other chefs stopped helping Tom. Then Tom could not finish his vegetable preparation in time for service. He got into trouble with the Head Chef and received a formal warning for being persistently late for work.

Why did the two other chefs help Tom at first? Why did they stop helping him?

Being reliable and considerate to your other team members is very important.

There are also people who do not pull their weight at work because they are not really interested in the job they do. This situation may result in staff:

o being noisy
o being thoughtless
o being inconsiderate
o being annoying
o being careless
o taking shortcuts
o producing work of a poor standard.

Figure 6.14 The wrong way to deal with a problem

Occasionally members of a team do not get on together or with the team leader for a variety of reasons. These may include:

o a personality clash
o members of the team having different standards and principles
o individuals not accepting criticism very well.

How can you tell if there is a problem in a group of people working together?

o People will not talk to each other.
o Secretive conversations take place away from other people.
o It is difficult to work together in a team.
o People do not help each other.
o Members of the team look miserable and will not work closely together.

Figure 6.15 The right way to deal with a problem

How can problems in a group be solved?

o The members of the team must be persuaded to talk to each other.
o Problems must be discussed so a solution can be reached.
o Ask someone who is not directly involved to control the discussion.

It may take some time for frictions in a team to settle down. As long as all the team members are considerate and motivated this should eventually happen. A positive attitude is required from everyone concerned.

Remember!

Never:
o be rude or swear at anyone
o be malicious or spiteful
o take people for granted
o let your standards slip.

Always:
o show respect for others
o be enthusiastic
o be helpful
o listen carefully to others.

Try this!

Beverley had been working in the kitchen for ten years. She enjoyed her job and knew she was very good at it. She maintained high standards and expected other people to do the same. Beverley did not tolerate fools gladly and she could be very impatient.

Rob started working in the kitchen. It was his first full-time job after completing his college catering course. He did very well at college and won a prize for achievement. He knew he could be very good at his job, and expected to be promoted very soon.

Rob did not agree with some of Beverley's work practices. He told her some of the things she was doing were wrong. This infuriated Beverley. She started to resent Rob and felt that she was being made to look foolish in front of the rest of the staff.

One day the Head Chef asked Rob to make a red wine sauce. Rob left the sauce on the stove to cook and went to the stores to fetch some more ingredients. The sauce started to burn. Despite the smell of burning, no one removed the saucepan from the stove. When Rob returned he found the burnt sauce. He was not sure what to do and asked Beverley. Beverley took delight in telling Rob in a loud voice that he had ruined the sauce and should have known better than to leave a pan unattended. She reminded him that there was no more red wine left and told him he would just have to make do. Rob swore at Beverley and stormed out of the kitchen.

What approach did Rob have that upset Beverley?
What approach did Beverley have that upset Rob?
If you were the Head Chef, how would you put this situation right?

Dealing with customer complaints

Not every customer is going to be happy with the food and service they receive. Sometimes things can go wrong such as:

- equipment breaking down
- stocks running out
- staff not turning up for work
- a large number of customers arriving together unexpectedly
- an accident happening at work
- mistakes being made by staff
- new staff working more slowly.

No matter what the problem, there is no excuse for the customer receiving poor service. If a customer has a complaint you need to know how to handle the situation correctly.

Top marks!

Whatever you are doing, try to always have in mind the effect your behaviour is having on others. Is it helping to produce a good experience for the customer?

How to find out if a customer is unhappy

○ Check the customer is happy with the service and food during their meal.

○ When clearing a plate where the customer has left a large proportion of the food, ask if there was something wrong with the product.

○ Watch how the customer behaves during their meal. Do they keep looking around for attention? Do they play with their food on the plate and then push it to the side? Do they shake their head?

○ Read comments on a customer comment card once the customer has finished the meal.

Top marks!

After you have handled a customer's complaint make a note of what the problem was and what you could do to help avoid the same problem arising again.

Customer complaints procedure

Apologise to the customer.

↓

Ask the customer what has happened. Give them time to explain and do not interrupt them.

↓

Listen very carefully to what they say and empathise with them (i.e. put yourself in their position and think how you would feel about what has happened).

↓

Ask the customer what they would like done.

↓

If the customer's suggestion is reasonable and within your responsibilities, agree to carry out the actions. For example, offering to replace the item, providing an alternative or calling the supervisor to authorise a free meal.

↓

If it is not possible, very tactfully discuss the situation with the customer and try to find a suitable alternative that you can provide. If this is not possible, pass the customer on to your supervisor, explaining what has already happened.

↓

Whatever action has been agreed, make sure it happens!

↓

Check with the customer that they are happy with the result.

Case study

Gemma was serving in the restaurant during a busy lunchtime service. Two members of restaurant staff had not turned up for work and everyone was trying to cover their duties as well as their own. A customer had ordered the vegetarian dish of the day. Gemma took the order but forgot to take it to the kitchen straight away. She had been asked to serve some drinks to another table that had been waiting a long time for them.

When the order arrived in the kitchen the dish of the day had run out. The replacement being offered was not suitable for vegetarians. Gemma knew the customer would not be happy as they had asked her about the menu and had found out exactly what was in the dish of the day before ordering it. It was now twenty minutes since the customer had ordered the meal. Gemma did not know what to do.

What would you advise Gemma to do? What would you do if you were Gemma's supervisor?

Test yourself!

1 List four benefits of working in a team.

2 Give an example of how working in a team can be better than working individually.

3 Complete the sentences.

a Sometimes, members of a team may not _____ _____ _____ because they have personal problems at home.

b Never:
  ○ be rude or _____ at anyone
  ○ be malicious or _____
  ○ take _____ for granted
  ○ let your standards _____.

c Always:
  ○ show _____ for others
  ○ be _____
  ○ be _____
  ○ _____ carefully to others.

Applying for a job

Jobs in the catering industry are advertised in a range of places:

- the local jobcentre
- local newspapers
- trade magazines
- specialist recruitment agencies
- online via any of the above.

Full time Commis Chef – Immediate Start

Location: Central London, United Kingdom

Salary: £13,000–£14,000 per year

Benefits: Meals on duty, uniform supplied

We are looking for a commis chef for a recently opened restaurant which has already had some fantastic reviews.

If you are looking to join a company that is food orientated and want to work in a good team environment and learn new skills, please send your CV in the first instance to:

Ms M Brown, Head Chef, The Plaza Restaurant, Park Lane, London WC12 6RQ

Figure 6.16 Sample job advertisement

Writing a CV

When applying for a job you need to be able to tell your prospective employer certain information about yourself. All potential employers will want to know the same basic information to decide if they want interview you. You can impress employers by having these details prepared already on a document called a Curriculum Vitae (CV).

Curriculum Vitae

Lesley White
18 Orton Close, Haverford, Westham W45 6PQ
Tel: 01234 567 89   Date of Birth: 30.2.88

<u>Education and qualifications</u>
2005–2007   Portsmouth Hospitality College
              NVQ Levels 1 and 2 in Professional Cookery
1999–2005   Secondary School Porth Heath
              6 GCSE subjects at Grade C and above including:
              Mathematics   Grade B
              English   Grade B
              Science   Grade C

<u>Additional qualifications</u>
December 2005   Basic Food Hygiene Certificate
December 2005   Basic Health and Safety Certificate
July 2004   Duke of Edinburgh Bronze Award

<u>Part-time employment</u>
2005–2007 Kitchen assistant The Grill Room, Portsmouth
2003–2005 Washer-up   The Crown Hotel, Porth Heath

<u>Interests and achievements</u>
Member of college football team
3rd place in Level Two Live Cookery Competition at Portsmouth Hospitality
College, July 2007

<u>Referees</u>
Mr M Blake   Mrs H Black
Head Chef   Course Tutor Level 2
The Grill Room   Professional Cookery Dept
Portsmouth   Portsmouth Hospitality College
P56 7TY   P89 5EF
Tel: 0123 456 7890   Tel: 0123 654 9876
Email: m.blake@thegrillroom.co.uk Email: h.black@portsmouthhospcat.ac.uk

Remember!
Your CV should:
o never be longer than two
  sides of A4 paper
o be typed
o be clearly laid out
o be factual
o use bullet points rather than
  long sentences
o be quick and easy to read
o only include relevant
  information that will help
  your application
o be spelled correctly.

Figure 6.17 Sample CV

Your CV should contain:
o **Personal details**: your full name and if you wish your date of
  birth and nationality.
o **Contact details**: a full address, home and mobile telephone
  numbers and an email address if applicable.
o **Qualifications**: school GCSE pass grades and any higher
  qualifications, any catering qualifications, e.g. NVQ Level 1 in
  Professional Cookery and Basic Hygiene Certificate.

Sending a covering letter

When sending a CV either by post or email you need to include a covering letter. This must be clear, correctly laid out and easy to read.

Remember!
Your covering letter should:
o never be longer than one page
o use paragraphs and follow the correct layout
o point out any strengths you have that are being asked for, e.g. enthusiasm and interest in food
o be spelled correctly
o not have any crossings out
o be very neatly written or typed.

Your address

18 Orton Close
Haverford
Westham
W45 6PQ

Name of person applying to with their full job title and address

Mr M Brown
Head Chef
Plaza Restaurant
Park Lane
London
WC12 6RQ

20 September 2007

Date the letter is written

Always include title and surname

Dear Mr Brown

Vacancy for Commis Chef

Title of job applying for

I am interested in applying for the position of Commis Chef which I saw advertised in the latest copy of Caterer and Hotelkeeper. I have read the reviews of your restaurant in Restaurant and the Evening Standard and am very keen to learn more about the cuisine you serve. Please find enclosed a copy of my CV as requested which I hope you will find of interest.

Say which position you are applying for and, if appropriate, where it is. State where you saw the advertisement, or how you found out about the vacancy.

I enjoy working as a member of a team and would like to improve my craft skills to the highest level that I can. I am keen to work hard and am very reliable and punctual.

Point out your strengths which may not be evident from your CV. Make sure you sound enthusiastic in your letter.

Add a closing paragraph.

I do hope you will consider my application for this position. I look forward to hearing from you.

Yours sincerely

Sign your name and then print it clearly underneath

Lesley White

Lesley White

If you have used the person's name at the beginning, end with yours sincerely. If you have put Dear Sir end with yours faithfully.

Figure 6.18 Sample covering letter

The interview process

If an employer is interested in your application and thinks you may have the skills and experience they are looking for they may ask you to come in for an interview. For a chef's position you may also be asked to work in the kitchen for a shift. Interviews are held to allow:

○ both the applicant and the employer to meet each other
○ both parties to ask questions about the job
○ both parties to be impressed by the other
○ the applicant a test shift in the kitchen to see if they have the necessary skills.

Preparing for an interview

If you take the trouble to prepare for an interview it will show on the day. First, find out the best way of getting to the location and how long it is likely to take. Assume there will be delays and allow half as long again to get there, e.g. if the journey should take 30 minutes allow at least 45 minutes.

Decide what you are going to wear several days in advance. Make sure your clothes are clean, ironed and not in need of repair e.g. buttons missing or damaged hem. Find any certificates or information you have been asked to take with you. If it is a trial shift you may need to take your set of knives and uniform with you. Check all your equipment is clean and in good order.

Read over the information about the job. This may be only the advertisement but you may have been sent a job description or information about the company. You need to be familiar with these to ask and answer questions.

Find out about the business. Look on the internet or in the catering press. Find out some facts about the organisation that you find interesting and will be able to remember, e.g. some special dishes on the menu or special promotions they have had recently. If you can, use this information to ask or answer questions.

Think of some questions to ask at the interview and write them down in a small notebook. Take the notebook with you and do not be afraid to look at it if you are asked whether you have any questions. You are showing the employer that you have come prepared.

> **Try this!** Worksheet 70
>
> Prepare your CV and ask a friend, family member or your tutor to check it for you. Collect a range of job advertisements from the catering press that appeal to you. Keep them in a scrapbook to remind you of what to look for when the time comes for you to apply for a full-time job for real!

How to impress an interviewer

Follow these simple tips to impress the person interviewing you:

○ Arrive in plenty of time so you are not hot and flustered.

○ Make sure you look as smart and professional as you can. Check you have clean shoes, tidy hair and ironed clothes.

○ Use positive body language, e.g. walk tall, look at your interviewer and smile, try not to sit with your arms folded, and have your hands relaxed in your lap.

○ Have a firm handshake – not limp and not superman style!

○ Listen carefully to what is being said to you and ask if you do not understand or did not hear properly.

○ Speak clearly and not too quickly.

After the interview

Take some time to reflect after an interview.

○ Think about what you did well during the interview so that you can make sure you do it again if necessary.

○ Consider what did not go so well and how you can stop that happening in the future.

○ Remember any questions you found difficult and make sure you know the answers for next time.

○ If you are successful make sure you know when and where you start work.

○ If you are not successful this time do not be too upset, get ready to try again.

> ### Top marks!
> Try to imagine the effect of your appearance or behaviour on an interviewer. What they want is someone who can work effectively in their team and produce good quality work. If you look scruffy or are not polite they will not think of you as that person.

Test yourself!

1 List three places where jobs may be advertised.

2 What is a CV?

3 Give three tips for writing a good CV.

4 What is a covering letter?

5 Why should a covering letter be written?

> ### Try this!
> Ask your Careers Advisor or a family friend to give you a mock interview. Use details of the type of job you hope to apply for one day. Dress appropriately and have your copy of your CV with you. Be prepared to answer questions about yourself and the job you would like to do.

Your personal development plan

As you become settled in your job, you may wish to improve your skills and abilities. This may help you to get promoted in your workplace. It may also enable you to move employment and get a better-paid and more challenging job in the future.

The ways that you can develop your skills and abilities include:
○ attending college on a part-time or full-time basis
○ going on short training courses from your workplace
○ working alongside very skilled craftspeople.

If you improve your own skills and abilities this will also help your team. The advantages include:
○ productivity for the whole team may improve
○ you can share your skills with your team mates
○ everyone may become more motivated and creative as a result
○ the reputation of the whole team will be improved.

What is a learning plan?

A learning plan is a useful way of organising your development. As you progress in your job you may improve your skills and abilities on a formal basis – such as a college course. You may also learn different skills in your everyday work.

A learning plan can help you in two ways:
○ It can help you to plan out a career path.
○ It can help you organise any formal learning you are undertaking.

Planning out a career path

If you are ambitious and want to own your own catering business or manage a large kitchen, you will need a high level of technical knowledge as well as good business and management skills.
To obtain these skills you may need to study several courses. A learning plan will help you map these out so that you take the right courses in the most suitable order – either full-time or part-time. You need to match these courses with appropriate jobs at the right level to help you develop your skills.

It is useful to have the help of a Careers Advisor when using a learning plan in this way.

Investigate!

Find out where your local Careers Advisor is based and how to get there. Look for jobs you are interested in on the internet, in the catering press and in the local newspaper.

Research the company advertising the position to find out how big it is. Does it have branches all around the country? Abroad? Does it run a training programme?

Try this!

Worksheet 71

When you are preparing to apply for a job you have to consider the skills you have developed and can use well. You then have to consider if there are any other skills you need for your ideal job. How are you going to get these skills? Prepare a table to show:

○ *the skills you have now*

○ *the skills you would like to have in the future*

○ *ways of learning the skills that you need*

○ *the dates that you managed to achieve these skills*

○ *if the skills you gained were as useful to you as you had hoped.*

This exercise can only be completed over a long period of time as you need to be able to acquire new skills and find out their value to you before you can finish this task. You need to keep the table with your CV and refer to it each time you look at new jobs you may like to do!

Top marks!

When preparing your personal development plan look at the qualifications you hope to obtain and the skills required by the job to make sure they complement each other.

Formal learning

If you are already studying a course a formal learning plan can be very useful. It will:

○ help you order the reading and coursework that you need to complete

○ allow you to set realistic targets to achieve these stages in your studying

○ help to train you in time management

○ help you to keep your learning on track so that you can achieve your ambition.

What you need to set up a formal learning plan

You will need a diary and a notebook, in which you can record:

○ your long-term aims – what you want to achieve finally

○ your short-term aims – the achievements you need to fulfil your long-term aims o the formal short-term aims that you may have set for you by your workplace or college, e.g. passing your Intermediate Food Hygiene examination, or completing a project on different types of poultry.

In the diary, set yourself some realistic target dates such as:
o the date you have to take your Food Hygiene examination
o the date by which you should start revising for the examination
o the date you should hand in your project
o a series of dates by which you should have various sections of your project researched, prepared and produced.

By planning your learning in this way, you are giving yourself the best chance of fulfilling all your ambitions. You are also demonstrating to your employer and others that you can be organised, conscientious, focused and reliable. By completing the learning experiences, you acquire knowledge and skills which can be used to help you later in life.

> **Definition**
> **Appraisal:** an assessment of performance providing feedback.

The importance of feedback

Feedback is defined as 'information provided about the quality or success of something'. In the workplace, feedback usually takes the form of:
o customer opinion about the quality of a meal (often from a customer service questionnaire)
o the result of an **appraisal** of an employee by a supervisor or manager.

Feedback will often result in a change or reward, for example:
o A negative customer comment about a dish may mean it is removed from the menu.
o A positive appraisal may mean an employee is considered for promotion.

Figure 6.19 Feedback may be the result of an appraisal

Test yourself!

1 Name three ways in which you could improve your work performance and further your career.

2 What could happen if you had a bad appraisal interview with your manager?

3 What do you need to set up a formal learning plan?

Practice assignment tasks

Applying workplace skills

Task 1

Prepare a PowerPoint presentation on why it is important to maintain personal presentation and good interpersonal skills when working within the hospitality and catering industry, specifically within the kitchen environment.

Task 2

Work in pairs and prepare a role-play on how to deal with a customer who has complained about the quality of their meal and the service in your restaurant. One of you will be the customer and the other the member of staff.

Prepare notes for a presentation and a brief report explaining:

- the skills required to deal effectively with and to solve customer complaints
- ways in which customers' feelings can be interpreted
- solutions that can be offered to solve the problem
- key stages to improving teamwork.

Task 3

Write a report on the process of applying for jobs. Answer the following:

- Why is it important to prepare your application well?
- What information should be included in a CV?
- Why is it important to include a covering letter?
- What can you do to prepare before an interview?
- Why is it important to evaluate the interview afterwards?

Cooking, preserving and flavouring

7

In this chapter you will learn about:

- Boiling
- Steaming
- Blanching
- Poaching
- Stewing and braising
- Frying
- Grilling
- Roasting and baking
- Combination cooking
- Microwaving
- Preserving
- Flavouring.

These methods relate to the following units from the Diploma:

Unit 207.1: Prepare and cook stocks
Unit 207.2: Prepare and cook soups
Unit 207.3: Prepare and cook sauces
Unit 208.2: Cook fruit and vegetables
Unit 209.2: Cook meat and offal
Unit 210.2: Cook poultry
Unit 211.2: Cook fish and shellfish
Unit 212.1: Prepare and cook rice
Unit 212.2: Prepare and cook pasta
Unit 212.3: Prepare and cook grains
Unit 212.4: Prepare and cook eggs
Unit 213.2: Cook and finish hot and cold desserts and puddings
Unit 214.2: Cook and finish paste, biscuit, cake and sponge products
Unit 214.4: Cook and finish fermented dough products

Cooking methods

Various cooking methods are discussed in this chapter. It gives you important information about the processes and safety issues.

Boiling

Boiling is a wet cooking method which requires food to be **immersed** in a liquid, e.g. water or stock, and cooked by a direct heat source, e.g. gas or electricity, on top of a stove, hob or cooking range. The food is cooked at 100°C as this is the temperature at which water boils. The liquid should be bubbling and moving rapidly. Not all food is suitable for boiling as the cooking action can break delicate food down making it limp and unsuitable for service. For example, courgettes have a high water content and disintegrate if boiled.

Boiling can lower the nutritional value of the food, as some vitamins, e.g. vitamins B and C, dissolve in water and so are absorbed into the hot liquid during boiling.

Boiling has different results depending on whether the food is added to cold liquid which is then heated to boiling point, or whether it is added to liquid that is already boiling.

If food is added to cold liquid before boiling, the natural flavours and goodness are extracted. This process is used to make stocks. It softens hard food, e.g. root vegetables, and prevents damage to items which would lose their shape if placed in rapidly boiling liquid. If food, e.g. small cuts of fish, is plunged into hot liquid, the flavour of the food is sealed in. This method also sets the protein and colour in foods, e.g. green vegetables, and can reduce overall cooking times.

The equipment required to boil food is:

- A pan large enough to hold the food and enough liquid to cover it. The pan can be a saucepan or a large industrial boiler or stock pot.
- Spiders or perforated spoons to remove the food from the liquid. If a large amount is cooked a colander (large strainer) can be used.

Remember!
Safety first! When handling hot equipment:
o wear protective clothing
o have a dry oven cloth to hand to hold hot equipment
o have ready utensils, e.g. tongs, palette knife or a slice to agitate and move the items being cooked.

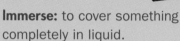

Definition
Immerse: to cover something completely in liquid.

Simmering

Simmering is similar to boiling, but the liquid is kept at a constant temperature just below boiling point. When a liquid is simmering, the surface of the liquid quivers with a gentle bubbling action. The cooking action is quite slow and is appropriate for dishes or food types that require a longer cooking period. When cooking foods such as meat, cheaper cuts of meat would be suitable for this method.

Video presentation
Watch *Prepare fish stock (2) boil, skim, simmer and strain* to see the difference between boiling and simmering. Also watch *Prepare velouté sauce (2) mix, boil, simmer.*

Steaming

Steaming uses a moist heat to cook. Modern equipment can provide atmospheric pressure (normal steam from boiling water) or forced steam using a high-pressure steamer which cooks the product more quickly.

A steaming vessel can be a specially designed piece of industrial equipment or a simple saucepan with a fitted lid containing a trivet to raise the food above the water. Because the lid of a steaming vessel fits tightly, the steam cannot escape and pressure builds up inside the vessel. The pressure can be regulated by letting out more or less of the steam. The higher the pressure the quicker the item will cook. In Oriental and Asian cookery, a covered wicker basket is used for steaming food.

Other equipment needed to steam food includes:

o utensils, e.g. spoons and tongs, to handle the food
o cloths to protect you from heat
o containers to place steamed food into.

Steaming is considered to be an extremely healthy method of cooking, as the nutrients within the product are preserved far better than in other cooking methods. Steaming will not colour the food. This method is often used when cooking for people on diets or people who are unwell, because it ensures maximum nutritional content.

Figure 7.1 Different types of steamer

Remember!
Steam can be extremely dangerous. It can cause severe scalds if you do not use equipment correctly.

Blanching

Blanching is the process in which raw food is immersed in boiling water for a short time, then removed and refreshed in iced water or under cold running water. Blanching is carried out for a variety of reasons:

○ To make it easier to remove the skins of vegetables, fruit and nuts.
○ To make ingredients firmer.
○ To purify ingredients by killing the enzymes that cause the quality of food to deteriorate. Food that has been blanched, e.g. garden peas, can then be stored fresh or frozen for later use.
○ To remove the salt or bitterness from ingredients.
○ To reduce the volume of ingredients.

You can blanch chips in hot oil before frying them.

Video presentation
Watch the techniques used in *Blanch a tomato to remove the skin* and *Blanch meat bones*.

Poaching

Poaching, a wet cooking method, means to simmer slowly and gently in liquid. The amount of liquid used depends on the dish to be cooked. A whole chicken will require more liquid than a breast, but generally the minimum amount of liquid is used.

Video presentation
Poach a salmon fillet teaches you how to do this like an expert.

The liquid used to poach food is usually boiled first. When the food is added the liquid is not brought back to the boil, but is kept just below boiling point. The cooking liquid may affect the food being poached, e.g. it may add flavour to a food (stock) or its boiling point may be lower (milk). Liquids commonly used in poaching are water, wine, stock and milk. Fish, vegetables, eggs and some offal are examples of food suitable for poaching.

The equipment used to poach poultry is usually a heavy-based pan with a lid. The heat source can be an open flame, a solid or electric hob or oven. If food is poached in the oven (e.g. fish), this is known as 'oven poaching'. It is a speedy and gentle method of poaching. Overcooking food during oven poaching could lead to the food drying out.

When poaching, the food may be only half-covered by liquid. It is a good idea to cover the food, e.g. with a lid or buttered paper. This will keep the moisture in and prevent the food drying out.

Once cooked, poached food must be well drained. Excess liquid could alter the consistency of a sauce added to poached food and spoil it.

Stewing and braising

Stewing and braising are wet methods of cooking in a pot on top of the stove or in the oven. This is a slow cooking method, which allows food to be cooked gently until it is soft and ready for service. In stewed or braised dishes the food and liquid is served together as a dish.

Use a large, heavy-based saucepan or dish, with a minimum amount of liquid covering the food. Bring the liquid to the boil and simmer it slowly. Take care not to burn the base of the pan, as this will spoil the flavour of the dish. Always ensure there is enough liquid in the pan to prevent burning.

Remember!

Food that is stewed or braised will be hot and dangerous. Use protective clothing and equipment to prevent accidents from spilling hot liquid and burning yourself.

Frying

Frying means cooking in hot fat, e.g. oil or butter. There are four types of frying:

1 shallow frying
2 sauté
3 stir-frying
4 deep-frying.

Shallow, sauté and stir–frying

Shallow, sauté and stir-frying are all versions of a similar frying process. Food is cooked with a small amount of butter or oil. Cooking this way colours the food and makes it more appealing. Stir-frying is usually associated with Asian food dishes. It is a quick cooking method using a wok and hot oil. The food is cut into small, evenly-sized pieces and tossed in hot oil in the wok for a short period of time.

The equipment required for shallow or stir-frying is:
- a sturdy pan with steep sides
- a cloth to protect you from high temperatures
- utensils, e.g. tongs, palette knives, spoons, to move and agitate the food
- a range or hob to provide the heat source. To achieve even cooking you will need to regulate the heat under the pan; gas hobs make it particularly easy to do this.

Remember!

Hot oil can inflict serious injury. For safety reasons:
o make sure the food you are frying is free from water and excess liquid, which may cause the oil to spit and possibly burn you when cooking
o place the food into a hot frying pan away from your body to avoid splashing yourself with hot oil.

Video presentation

Watch the video *Stir-fry beef* to find out more about this cooking method. Watch *Deep-fry goujons* to learn how to do this safely.

Smoking

This method is used to preserve food such as fish and meat. Food is heated gently over a fire to dry it out. Aromatic hydrocarbons (e.g. chicory wood chips) are burned to give the food a strong smoky flavour. This specialist process is carried out in a smoke house. See page 324.

Salting

This is one of the oldest methods of preservation, adopted hundreds of years ago as a means of preserving food for the winter. Salt draws out the moisture from the food and its acidity means that bacteria cannot grow. This is a cheap and easy way to preserve food. The disadvantage of this method is that it makes the food extremely salty. Food items need to be reconstituted in water to draw out the salt.

Healthy eating
Too much salt is bad for you so you need to consider this when serving food preserved in salt. It will also dominate the flavour of a dish.

Flavouring

Various flavourings can be added to complement dishes. Flavourings which can be used, depending on dish requirements:
- vegetables
- fruit
- nuts
- pastes, e.g. curry
- purée, e.g. tomato
- wines and spirits
- vinegars
- oils
- herbs and spices
- yoghurt
- soy sauce
- oyster sauce
- lemon juice
- other prepared sauces.

Definition
Seasoning: the addition of ingredients, e.g. salt, pepper and certain spices and herbs, to give a particular flavour to a dish or type of food.

Seasoning

Adjusting the quantity of the **seasoning** will affect the flavour but you must be careful. Too much of some seasonings, e.g. salt, can make the dish inedible. The overall seasoning of the dish should be adjusted after cooking when all the flavours have combined.

Marinating

Marinating is another technique used to flavour food. It involves combining a cooked or uncooked liquid or paste with the main ingredient. The liquid or paste is called a marinade. It contains ingredients which change and improve the flavour of the food.

Some marinades are cooked and then cooled before being combined with the main ingredient. Most marinades are cold and can be created very quickly to flavour the food. Some marinades are used after the main ingredient has been removed to create a sauce to accompany the dish.

Suitable ingredients to use in marinades:
○ wines and spirits
○ vinegars
○ oils
○ herbs and spices
○ yoghurt
○ soy sauce
○ oyster sauce
○ lemon juice
○ sauces, e.g. barbeque sauce.

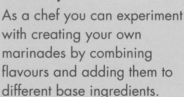

Chef's tip

As a chef you can experiment with creating your own marinades by combining flavours and adding them to different base ingredients.

Test yourself!

1 Are these cooking methods wet or dry?
Put a W next to the wet cookery methods
and a D next to the dry cookery methods.
   a Simmering _____
   b Braising _____
   c Baking _____
   d Stewing _____
   e Grilling. _____

2 What is the recommended standby
temperature for a deep-fat fryer?
   a 90°C
   b 92°C
   c 93°C
   d 95°C.

3 There are four types of frying. What are
they?

4 What is the difference between roasting
and baking?

5 Why must you not use food in damaged
cans?

Stocks, soups and sauces

8

This chapter covers the following outcomes from Diploma
unit 207: Prepare and cook stocks, soups and sauces:

○ Outcome 207:1 Prepare and cook stocks
○ Outcome 207:2 Prepare and cook soups
○ Outcome 207:3 Prepare and cook sauces

**Working through this chapter could also provide evidence for the following
Key Skills:**

C2.1, C2.2, C2.2b, C2.3, ICT2.1, ICT2.2, ICT2.3, PS2.1, PS2.2, PS2.3, LP2.1, LP2.2, LP2.3

In this chapter you will learn how to:

Identify the ingredients, quantities and equipment required in the preparation and cooking
of different stocks, soups and hot sauces
Prepare, cook, finish and serve stocks, soups and hot sauces
List quality points to look for
Indicate the uses of stocks and sauces
Indicate the temperature for the cooking, holding, service,
chilling and storage of stocks, soups and sauces

You will learn to cook basic stocks, soups and hot sauces, including:

○ white beef stock
○ white fish stock
○ clear soup (consommé)
○ purée of lentil soup
○ cream of cauliflower soup
○ béchamel sauce
○ velouté sauce
○ tomato sauce.

Basic stocks

A stock is a broth that is used as a braising liquid, a sauce base or as liquid for soup. A good stock should have a delicate flavour and a high proportion of natural gelatine. A gelatinous stock gives richness and body to a preparation without masking the flavours of the basic ingredients.

Stock is made by slowly simmering bones and/or vegetables with **aromatic** herbs in a juice, e.g. water or wine. During cooking the flavours of the meat, vegetables and herbs are released into the liquid. After cooking, the solid ingredients and any grease are removed and the liquid is strained until it is clear.

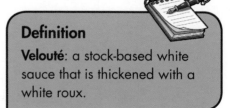

Definition

Aromatic: having a pleasant smell. Aromatic ingredients such as leaves, flowers, seeds, fruits, stems and roots are used essentially for their fragrance to enhance flavour of stocks.

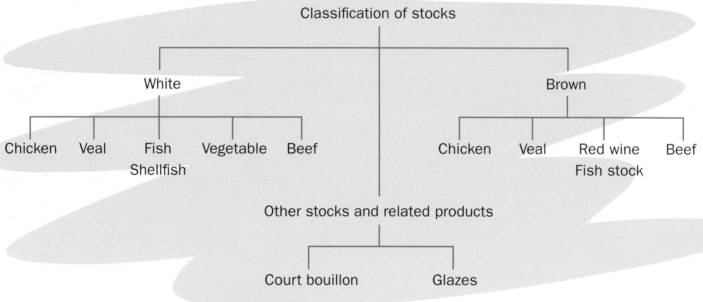

Figure 8.1 Classification of stocks

Types of stock

Stocks can be made from many different ingredients. The stocks covered in the Diploma are: vegetable, chicken, fish and beef.

Stocks can be either white or brown. For a white stock, the ingredients are simply added to the stock pot. White stock is used as a liquid to make soups, white stews and **velouté** sauce for poached poultry and fish dishes. For a brown stock, any bones are roasted and the vegetables are sautéed before being added to the stock pot. Brown stock is used as a liquid in soups, brown sauces, brown stews and for braising large cuts of meat. Both types of stock can be used in gravy.

Definition

Velouté: a stock-based white sauce that is thickened with a white roux.

Vegetable stock or nage

This is a light neutral base, which can be used in many soups and sauces. It can be used with other stocks and is suitable for use in vegetarian cookery. For maximum flavour do not strain the vegetables out immediately after cooking, but allow them to steep in the stock for up to 24 hours. Vegetable stock is used as a liquid for soups, sauces and for all preparations in vegetable cooking such as braised rice.

Chicken stock

This is a very versatile stock. It should have a good amber colour, without being too strong in taste. If a stronger-tasting stock is required, boil the stock until the quantity of stock is reduced to half to produce double chicken stock. Use fresh carcasses and winglets and if possible add boiling fowl, which may be removed later. Some recipes may need a darker or brown chicken stock. To make this, roast chicken carcasses in a hot oven for 15–20 minutes until golden brown (remembering to turn them frequently) and drain off the fat before using. Sauté any vegetables used to a golden brown and drain this also before using.

Fish stock

The best bones to use for fish stock are turbot and sole. Other fish bones can be oily, strong and even taste of ammonia, although hake, haddock and cod can be used. Always remove the eyes and gills, as these can have an effect on the flavour and colour of your stock. Also remember to rinse the fish bones and trimmings under cold water to remove traces of blood. Fish stock is used in the preparation of soups, fish sauces, velouté or white wine sauce. Fish stock is also used for shallow poaching and braising fish.

Fish stock can also be prepared with red wine for poached fish dishes.

Veal stock

This forms the base of many sauces. It is possibly the king of stocks, offering excellent body, richness and colour with a subtle flavour. As the bones are large they should be chopped smaller to enable them to release their flavour. It is possible to produce a white or a brown stock from these bones, but careful roasting of the bones will give a stock greater colour and flavour.

Did you know?

The ideal temperature for the following is:

cooking of stock	100°C
(except fish stock)	98°C
holding of stock	75°C
storage of stock	4°C.

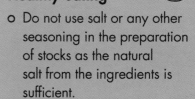

Healthy eating

o Do not use salt or any other seasoning in the preparation of stocks as the natural salt from the ingredients is sufficient.

o Make sure that all fat is removed from the meat and poultry bones before preparing stock.

o Always blanch the bones and refresh them in cold water to remove any excess fat (except fish bones).

Beef stock

Beef stock can be produced in the same way as veal stock. Beef stock is not very versatile and is best suited for use in beef dishes.

Other stocks and related products

Court bouillon

This is a light aromatic stock of vegetables, herbs, spices and white wine vinegar. It is used for poaching fish, crabs and other shellfish. This stock can be used two or three times before being discarded. Like other stocks it may be cooled and frozen for use at a later date.

Glazes

A glaze ('glace' in French) is a concentrated stock which is made through a process of reduction. It is used to enrich the flavour of sauces and dishes such as Parisienne potatoes. Before the stock is reduced, it should be passed through a very fine sieve or better still a piece of wet muslin cloth. Care should be taken through the reduction period to remove any scum that rises to the surface. This will help the glaze achieve its characteristic shine. The consistency of the glaze should be just flowing when warm and solid when refrigerated.

> **Healthy eating**
> o Avoid rapid boiling of stocks as fats are emulsified and dissolved in the liquid making it milky and unhealthy.
> o Avoid adding butter or oil while frying vegetables and bones for brown stocks. Always use the natural fat on the bones to give colour by roasting them in the oven.

> **Try this!**   Worksheet 32
> Close your book. List as many types of stock as you can remember.

Ingredients and equipment

White stock

White stock is a broth which has no colour. It has white meat bones and aromatic vegetables as a basis. The ingredients used are:

o chicken, beef, veal or game
o carrots, onions, leeks or celery
o thyme, bay leaf or parsley stalks
o liquid: water or white wine.

> **Remember!**
> If a small quantity of stock is required from a large pot in the refrigerator, never dip a utensil into it that is warmer than the stock itself.

Brown stock

This is a broth which has a light brown colour. The other term used to describe this stock is 'estouffade', which is a reduced brown stock. It has browned meat bones and sautéed aromatic vegetables as a basis. The ingredients used are:

o chicken, beef, veal or game
o carrots, onions, leeks, celery or garlic
o thyme, bay leaf or parsley stalks
o liquid: water.

Equipment

The equipment needed to make a stock:

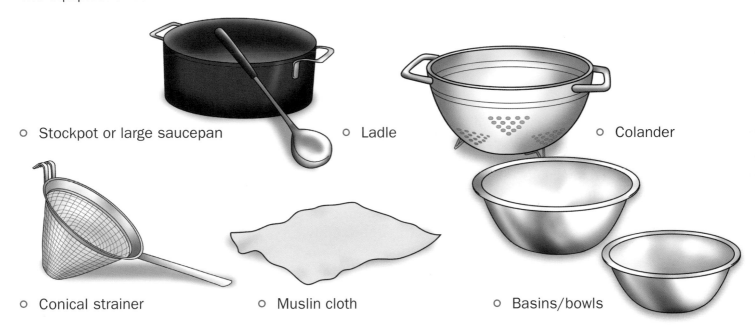

o Stockpot or large saucepan   o Ladle   o Colander

o Conical strainer   o Muslin cloth   o Basins/bowls

In addition, for a brown stock, a roasting tray or frying pan is needed.

Recipes for basic stocks

The minimum cooking times for different types of stock are:
o Vegetable stock – 30 minutes.
o Chicken stock – 2 hours.
o Fish stock – 20 minutes.
o Game stock – 2 hours.
o Beef stock – 4 hours.

Top marks!

Use all tools and equipment safely. Health and safety and food safety are very important. You will gain marks for good procedures and understanding.

White beef stock

For the stock:

beef shin bones	2kg
water, cold	6 litres
carrots	240g
onions, stuck with two cloves	120g

For the bouquet garni:

leeks	120g
celery	120g
parsley stalk and root	30g
bay leaf	1
sprig of thyme	1
Cooking time	6 hours
Makes	5 litres

Method

1 Cut or break the bones into 10cm pieces. Remove any marrow.
2 Wash and place into stock pot and add 6 litres of cold water. Bring to the boil and **skim** off the scum.
3 Add 100ml of cold water and wipe the sides of the stock pot clean with a damp cloth.
4 Add the vegetables whole, and the bouquet garni.
5 Allow the stock to simmer gently for six hours, during which time the fat which rises to the surface must be constantly skimmed off. The vegetables should be removed from stock after three hours.
6 Pass the stock through a muslin.
7 Reboil and place aside to cool.

Definition

Skim: to remove impurities from the surface of a simmering liquid with a ladle.

Points to consider when making white beef stock

All fat should be removed from the bones at the outset. The marrow should be put aside for use as a separate dish or as garnish. Stock should only simmer; if it is allowed to boil, it will become milky or cloudy.

The vegetables and bouquet garni should be easily accessible – tie bouquet garni to the handle of the pot with a long string and if there is a large quantity of stock, tie vegetables in a muslin or net. If allowed to remain in the pot too long the vegetables will begin

Chef's tip

Six to eight hours is the maximum time required to extract the full flavour – if cooked too long the flavour will suffer. Bones from which the flavour has been extracted may be re-boiled for a further six hours to produce jelly.

to disintegrate and/or lose their colour into the liquid, causing the stock to discolour. Discard scum. Save the fat which can be later clarified and used as dripping, for braising.

Do not allow any fat to remain on the surface as this will stop the heat escaping and may cause the stock to 'turn', that is, become sour.

Chef's tip

Whilst the bones should be a rich brown, burning will make the stock taste bitter.

Brown beef stock

good meaty bones, beef or veal, and trimmings of meat	2kg
beef fat	60g
carrots, diced (mirepoix) and fried	240g
onions, diced (mirepoix) and fried	240g
bouquet garni	1
ham bone	240g
water	6 litres
Oven temperature	250°C
Cooking time	6–8 hours
Makes	5 litres

Method

1. Cut or break the bones into 10cm pieces and place in a roasting tray. Add the trimmings and fat.
2. Roast the bones and trimmings in a hot oven until a rich brown colour.
3. Remove bones from fat and place in a stock pot. Cover with 6 litres of water, bring to the boil and skim.
4. Add the fried carrot and onion, the bouquet garni and the ham bone.
5. Allow the stock to simmer for six hours, skimming from time to time to remove the fat.
6. Strain through a muslin, reboil and use as required.

White fish stock

onions to slice	250g
butter	50g
fishbones: bones and trimmings of sole, whiting, turbot, brill and halibut, thoroughly washed before using	5kg
parsley stalks and root	30g
thyme sprig	1
bay leaves, small	2
white mushroom trimmings, well-washed	200g
lemons for juice	1–2
white peppercorns	approx. 20
white wine (optional)	300–400ml
water	5 litres
salt	20g
Cooking time	20–30 minutes
Makes	approx. 5 litres

Method

1 Peel and slice the onions, blanch, refresh and strain.
2 Melt the butter in a thick-bottomed saucepan. Add the onions and gently cook without colour five to ten minutes.
3 Add parsley, mushroom trimmings, lemon juice, thyme, bay leaf and chopped fish bones. Cover with buttered greaseproof paper and a lid.
4 Cook gently on the side of the stove for 15–20 minutes. This will reduce the volume of the bones so less water will be required and the stock will be stronger and better quality.
5 Add the white wine, water and salt. Bring to the boil, cover with a lid and simmer for 15–20 minutes.
6 Add peppercorns in the last five minutes; skim.
7 Pass stock through a muslin and reserve until required.

Chef's tip

Excess cooking will make the stock bitter and cause it to deteriorate.

Chef's tip

Only use white mushroom trimmings, as any black pieces will discolour the finished product.

Video presentation

Watch *Prepare fish stock (1) sweat* and *Prepare fish stock (2) boil, skim, simmer and strain* to see this being made.

Points to consider when making fish stock

Fish stock should be clear rather that milky and have a delicate fish flavour. Do not season it. The stock should be fat-free and gelatinous.

After gently cooking the fish bones for 20 minutes (end of step 3 above) you will notice that there is an extraction of juices at the bottom of the pan. These juices are reduced fish stock. They can be strained off and used for enhancing the flavour of fish sauces. Wine or water is then added to the bones to make a stock as in steps 5–7 above.

Holding, serving, chilling and storing stocks

Stocks for immediate use are held in a bain-marie at 75°C. Stocks not required for immediate use should be chilled as quickly as possible. When cooling stock, the pan should be raised on a trivet so that cold air can circulate round it. Other methods of chilling are blast chilling or placing the hot stock in an ice water bath. When cold, the pan should be covered with greaseproof paper and labelled with the type of stock and date. Stocks should be stored at 4°C in the refrigerator. The most efficient method of storing stock is to reduce it to a glaze. This prolongs the storage life.

Test yourself!

1 Name four different types of stock.

2 Give four important points to remember about preparation and cooking of white and brown stock.

3 What are the reasons for:
  a white fish stock being cloudy
  b brown chicken stock tasting bitter
  c white beef stock lacking flavour
  d brown vegetable stock being greasy?

4 What are the cooking times for:
  a Fish stock
  b White chicken stock
  c Brown beef stock
  d Vegetable stock?

5 State four quality points to look for in the finished stocks.

Basic soups

Types of soup

There are many different types of soup:

○ **Unpassed soups** such as Scotch broth, Chicken broth, Mutton broth and chowder.

○ **Clear soup (Consommé)** is a **clarified** stock that uses egg whites, finely minced shin of beef and vegetables. In fact, clarification is not essential if the stock is prepared perfectly by simmering the liquid over a period of time and continuously skimming any impurities that rise to the top.

Did you know?
The word 'soup' derives from 'sop' – originally the bread over which a broth or other liquid was poured.

Definition
Clarification: the process used to purify stocks, making the cloudy liquid clear using egg whites and albumen from the minced lean shin of beef.

241

- **Purées**, where the main ingredient of the soup gives a name and body to the end product e.g. purée of lentil.
- **Cream soups**, where vegetables are puréed and added to the béchamel sauce which gives body to the soup. Velouté is another name for a soup when velouté sauce replaces béchamel sauce.
- **Bisque** is a unique term given to the preparation of soup made from shellfish such as lobster or crab.
- **Cold soups** can be from clear soup such as jellied consommé or from vegetables and fruits such as potage vichyssoise, gazpacho soup and chilled cherry soup.

> **Investigate!** Worksheet 33
> Find three recipes for each soup category: unpassed, purée, clear, bisque, cream, velouté and cold soup.

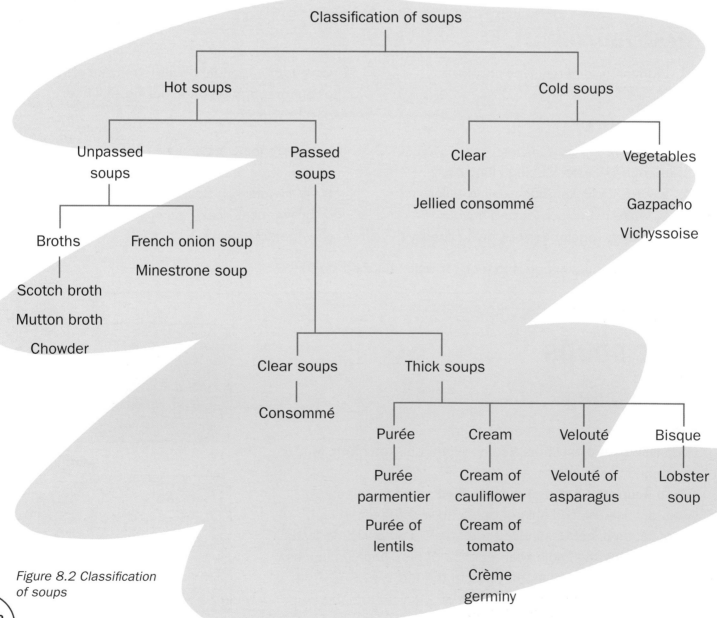

Figure 8.2 Classification of soups

242

Thickening agents for soups

The table below shows the thickening agents used in different types of soup.

Thickening agent	Types of soup
Barley Beans, pasta Rice Lentils Potatoes, cream crackers	Scotch broth Minestrone Bisque Game soup Chowder
Main ingredient of the soup, e.g.: Potatoes Lentils Beans	 Purée parmentier Purée of lentils Bean soup
White roux	Cream soup
Blond roux	Cream of tomato soup
Brown roux	Brown windsor soup
Béchamel sauce	Cream of cauliflower or celery
Velouté sauce: Chicken Fish	 Velouté of asparagus Velouté of lobster
Espagnole (basic brown) sauce	Kidney soup
Fresh cream and egg yolk liaison	Crème germiny
Breadcrumbs	Gazpacho

Figure 8.3 Thickening agents used in different soups

Healthy eating

o Use an alternative to a roux in the preparation of cream and velouté soup. The soup could be thickened with cornflour.
o Replace butter in the preparation of the roux with vegetable fat or margarine.

Liquids used in the preparation of soups

Type of liquid	Types of soup
Water	Lentils Beans
White stock	Chicken Beef or veal Fish Vegetable
Brown stock	Game Beef or veal
Vegetable and fruit juices	Tomato Beetroot Orange
Beer and wines	Swedish bean soup Consommé (Clear soup) Oxtail soup

Figure 8.4 Liquids used in different soups

Garnishes and accompaniments

Garnishes are defined as food items which are served in the soup.

Garnishes	Soups
Julienne	Velouté of celery
Brunoise	Scotch broth
Paysanne	Minestrone
Small florets of cauliflower	Cream of cauliflower soup
Savoury pancake julienne	Consommé
Rice	Cream of tomato soup
Tapioca	Cream of green pea soup

Figure 8.5 Garnishes

Accompaniments are food items which are served separately alongside soups.

Accompaniments	Soups
Croûtons	Purée soups, e.g. Purée of lentil soup
Croûtes	Clear soups, e.g. minestrone soup
Cheese straws	Turtle soup, Lobster bisque
Grated parmesan cheese	Minestrone soup, French onion soup
Duck patties	Borsch soup

Figure 8.6 Accompaniments

Definitions

Croûtons: 1cm cubes of white bread, shallow-fried to a golden brown colour in clarified butter.

Croûtes: sliced bread flutes toasted or evenly baked in the oven to a golden brown colour.

Finishing of soups

Finish	Soups
Knobs of butter	Purée soups
Fresh cream	Cream soups
Fresh cream and egg yolk liaison and knobs of butter	Velouté soups
Wines White wine Red wine	Fish soup Red haricot bean soup
Fortified wines Sherry Madeira Port Marsala	Consommé Turtle soup Oxtail soup Consommé **Bisques**

Figure 8.7 Finishing of soups

Definition

Bisque: a shellfish soup where the shellfish is puréed to add flavour.

Equipment used in the preparation of soups

The equipment you will need when preparing soups includes:

- large saucepan
- sauteuse
- wooden spatula
- wooden spoon
- ladles
- conical strainer
- colander
- sieves and **wooden mushroom**
- pestle and mortar
- whisks
- balloon whisk
- chopping board
- set of knives
- muslin cloth
- tammy cloth
- bain-marie.

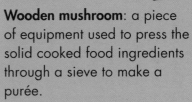

Definition

Wooden mushroom: a piece of equipment used to press the solid cooked food ingredients through a sieve to make a purée.

Figure 8.8 Equipment used in the preparation of soups. Can you name each item?

Soup recipes

Unpassed soup

Minestrone soup

haricot beans	80g
butter	60g
small lardons, blanched	100g
onions, chopped	250g
white of leek, **paysanne**	200g
celery, paysanne	100g
carrots, paysanne	250g
cabbage, paysanne	250g
turnips, paysanne	250g
salt and pepper	to season
white chicken stock	3 litres
bouquet garni	1
peeled potatoes, **paysanne**	400g
french beans, in lozenges	100g
peas	100g
patna rice	50g
spaghetti	50g
tomato purée	10ml
tomatoes for **concassées**	400g
garlic cloves, crushed	2
fresh pork fat, finely chopped, lard gras	60–80g
parsley, finely chopped	20ml
fines herbes	
grated parmesan served separately	
bread rolls or toasted sliced flûte bread served separately	
Cooking time	1 hour
Serves	6–8

Method

1. Wash and soak haricot beans overnight in a cool place. Cook separately for about one hour.
2. Put the butter and small lardons into a thick-bottomed saucepan. Gently cook and very lightly colour. Add the onions, leek, celery, carrots, cabbage and turnips.
3. Season lightly. Cover with greaseproof paper and cook slowly without colouring for 30–40 minutes, stirring occasionally.
4. Add the stock, bouquet garni, potatoes, French beans, peas, patna rice and spaghetti.

Definition

Concassées: finely diced skinned tomato flesh (seeds and juice removed).
Fines herbes: a mixture of aromatic herbs such as chervil, tarragon, chives and parsley.
Paysanne: a small cut of vegetables in a variety of shapes, such as triangles, squares, circles and oblongs.

Chef's tip

Other herbs which may be added with the parsley and fines herbes are sage leaves, basil, marjoram and chives.

Did you know?

Minestrone soup is from Italy. It is sometimes called 'minestra'. There are several variations of recipes according to the regions.

5 Cook until all the ingredients are tender. Add tomato purée. Mix in well, remove the bouquet garni.

6 Add the cooked haricot beans and the tomates concassées. Reboil, taste for seasoning. Rectify the thickness. The consistency of this soup should be fairly thick.

7 Crush the skinned garlic with finely chopped pork fat, adding chopped parsley and fines herbes. Toss in a little hot butter then added to the soup, mixing in well with a ladle.

9 Serve with toasted shredded bread or rolls, or toasted sliced flûte bread and grated parmesan cheese as an accompaniment.

Did you know?

'Chowder' comes from the French word 'chaudière', an iron cauldron used by fishermen to make soup on their boats. It has since been used to describe a soup from New England.

New England clam chowder

live clams	1.5 litres
water	1 litre
green bacon	150g
onions	200g
potatoes	250g
salt	to season
ground pepper	to season
butter	30g
milk	½ litre
double cream	½ litre
cream crackers	4
Cooking time	1 hour
Serves	10 portions

Method

1 Wash and scrub the clams. Put them in a saucepan with the water.

2 Cover the saucepan and cook over a high heat until all the clams are opened, approximately 10 minutes.

3 Remove the clams from their shells and strain the liquid through a muslin cloth.

4 Finely mince the clams and put in the refrigerator.

5 Finely dice the green bacon. Blanch it and then sauté in a saucepan. Finely chop the onions. Add them to the saucepan.

6 Add the cooking liquid from step 3 and simmer gently.

7 Cut the potatoes into paysanne and add them to the soup.

8 Add clams and check the seasoning.

9 Finish the soup with butter, milk and fresh double cream.

10 Place some crushed cream crackers in the soup tureen and pour over the soup.

11 Serve hot.

Clear soup

Clear soup (*Consommé*)

minced shin of beef	1kg
egg white	1
mirepoix of onions	125g
mirepoix of carrots	125g
mirepoix of celery	125g
mirepoix of leeks	125g
cold, white beef stock	5 litres
bouquet garni	1
peppercorns	15–18
salt	to season
Cooking time	3 to 4 hours
Serves	6–8

Method

1 Soak the minced shin of beef in cold water for about 20–30 minutes, adding salt to withdraw blood. Add egg white and mix well.

2 Prepare the mirepoix of onions, carrots, celery and leeks. Add these vegetables to the beef and cover with good beef stock.

3 Add bouquet garni and peppercorns.

4 Bring it just to the boil slowly over a gentle heat, stirring occasionally.

5 Give a last stir and let the consommé simmer gently over a low heat. Cook it for approximately two hours without stirring.

6 Strain the consommé through a muslin cloth.

7 Use kitchen paper squares to remove all fat from the top.

8 Check the seasoning and colour, which should be a delicate amber.

9 Bring the consommé just to the boil again and serve in a warm soup tureen.

Chef's tip

Consommé can be prepared by using a variety of stocks such as chicken, game and veal. There are numerous classic garnishes which can be added to finish the soup.

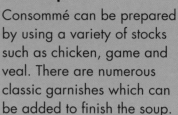

Did you know?

Clear soup should never be boiled as this makes it cloudy. If it gets cloudy, the process of clarification must be repeated.

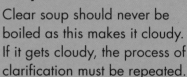

Healthy eating

Make sure clear soups are free from traces of fat.

Purée soup

Purée of lentil soup

lentils, red	250g
butter for vegetables	25g
pork or bacon rind	30–40g
onion, diced	30–40g
carrot, diced	30–40g
water	1.25 litres
bouquet garni	1
salt	to season
butter, clarified	15g
milk, boiling	150–200ml
bread for croûtons	100g
Cooking time	1 hour
Serves	6

Method

1 Wash the lentils well and soak for half an hour.
2 Lightly sauté the diced bacon or pork rind in 25g butter, using a thick-bottomed pan.
3 Add the diced carrot and onion, lightly colour.
4 Add the strained lentils and stir. Cook gently for 10–15 minutes.
5 Add water and bouquet garni. Cover with a lid, simmer until the lentils are tender and fully cooked, add salt in the last ten minutes.
6 Remove bouquet garni. Pass the soup through a sieve.
7 Reboil, pass through a fine chinois.
8 Reboil, taste for seasoning. Check the thickness, adding a little boiling milk if necessary. The consistency of the soup should be like thick double cream.
9 Add the clarified butter (15g) to complete the soup. Check the seasoning and add salt, if necessary.
10 Serve croûtons separately.

Healthy eating

o Purée soups are healthier than cream of velouté soups.
o Avoid the use of fresh cream, butter or cream and egg yolk liaison to finish the soups.
o Avoid over-seasoning the soups.
o Serve toasted croûtons instead of croûtons shallow-fried in butter.

Chef's tip

Omit the pork or bacon rind for a vegetarian option.

Cream soup

Cream of cauliflower soup

white of leek	500g
butter	300g
cauliflower, without leaves	2kg
water or cauliflower stock or white stock	2 litres
bouquet garni	1
béchamel, boiling	3 litres
cream, boiling	600ml
salt and pepper	to season
sprigs or leaves of chervil	
Cooking time	1 hour
Serves	6–8 portions

Method

1 Wash and shred the white of leek. Cook in half the butter without colouring.
2 Wash the cauliflower. Reserve 300g of cauliflower in small florets to be boiled and used for garnish.
3 Shred the bulk of cauliflower. Add to the leeks, mix well and season. Cover and continue to cook without colouring, until tender.
4 Add the liquid and the bouquet garni. Simmer for 15–20 minutes.
5 Remove the bouquet garni. Pass the soup through a sieve. Reboil and add boiling béchamel. Mix well, taste for seasoning. Pass through a fine chinois. Reboil then add the boiling cream and work in the rest of the butter.
6 Finally, add small cooked florets of cauliflower. The vegetable stock can be used to adjust the consistency of the soup. Taste again for seasoning. Cover and keep hot in a bain-marie.
7 Add the chervil on serving.

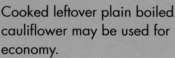

Chef's tip

Cooked leftover plain boiled cauliflower may be used for economy.
Blanched shredded onions can be used instead of leeks.

Chef's tip

It is very important to control the portion size in the service of soup. This depends on the occasion, e.g.
o table d'hôte menu   175ml
o á la carte menu   275 ml
The size of the portion is also reflected in the selling price.

Quality points to look for in finished soups

1 The colour and appearance is correct for the type of soup.
2 Correct consistency, in other words a proportionate amount of liquid added to the main ingredient.
3 Garnishes and accompaniments are consistent size and shape and are cooked correctly.
4 Well seasoned and appropriately finished.
5 Served at the correct temperature, hot or cold, depending on the type of soup.

Did you know?

The ideal temperature for the following is:

cooking of soup	100°C
holding of soup	75°C
service of soup	65°C
storage of soup	4°C.

Test yourself!

1 Name four different types of soup as they will appear on the menu.

2 Identify the main differences between the following:
   a Purée and cream soups
   b Broth and consommé
   c Velouté and cream soups.

3 Indicate the correct temperatures for the following:
   a Cooking of soup
   b Holding of soup
   c Service of soup
   d Storage of soup.

4 State four quality points to look for in the finished soup.

5 Suggest four ways of preparing, cooking and finishing basic soups to make them healthier.

6 Indicate the main difference between a garnish and an accompaniment. Give an example of each.

7 Indicate the finishing of the following soups:
   a Cream
   b Purée
   c Chowder.

8 Name four different thickening agents used in the preparation of basic soups.

Basic sauces

Types of sauces

Marinades were originally used to preserve and tenderise meat. Later they were also used to improve the flavour of dishes. Creative chefs transformed these marinades into sauces, to moisten a stew or accompany roast meats. Some sauces were originally devised to disguise the strong flavours of meat and game. Others, for example a creamy purée of beans or peas, helped to balance the saltiness of preserved meats.

The seventeenth century in France was the 'golden age' of sauce creation. During that period famous chefs developed a small group of basic sauces, also known as 'mother sauces', from which hundreds of variations came. The original mother sauces were stock-based brown sauce, velouté, milk-based béchamel and hollandaise made from egg yolks. Another basic sauce was added a century later when tomatoes arrived from the New World. At first chefs believed that the scarlet flesh of the tomato was deadly poison. Soon they realised that the flesh can easily be broken down and made into a **piquant** purée sauce.

> **Did you know?**
> The word 'sauce' comes from the Latin 'salsus', meaning 'flavoured with salt'.

> **Definition**
> **Piquant**: a pleasant, sharp taste.

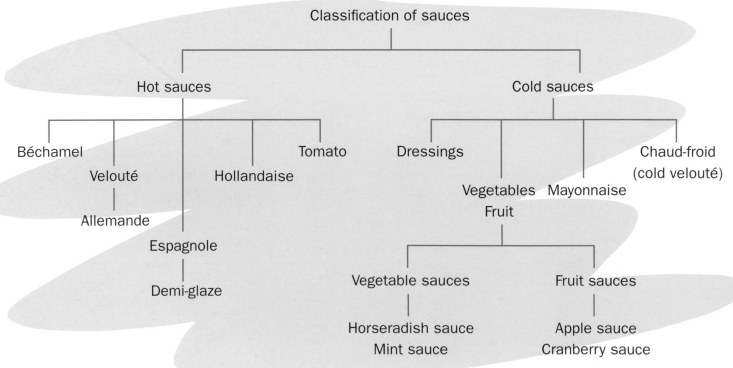

Figure 8.9 Classification of sauces

Thickening sauces

Thickening agents

Thickening agents used in the preparation of sauces include the following types:

1 **Roux**. This is an equal mixture of fat and flour, cooked slowly to break down the starch cells in the flour and allow thickening to take place. There are three types of roux:
   ○ white (used for e.g. béchamel sauce)
   ○ blond (used for e.g. velouté sauce)
   ○ brown (used for e.g. espagnole sauce).
2 **Egg yolks**. These are used for hot and cold sauces, e.g. hollandaise sauce (hot), mayonnaise sauce (cold).
3 **Sabayan**. A light, foamy sauce. Whisk egg yolks over a saucepan of simmering water until the sauce is thick. Remove from the heat and continue whisking until the mixture cools slightly.
4 **Beurre manie**. This is a mixture of butter and flour kneaded together to form a paste. Small pieces of this mixture are dropped in boiling liquid and whisked together to form a sauce.
5 **Bread**, e.g. bread sauce.
6 **Vegetables and potatoes**.
7 **Fresh fruit**, e.g. apple sauce, cranberry sauce.
8 **Cornflour and fécule** (starch from potatoes). These are used to thicken roast gravy (jus-lié).
9 **Butter**. This is used in an emulsified form, e.g. butter sauce, white wine sauce for fish.
10 **Sugar**, e.g. caramel sauce.
11 **Various nuts**, including peanuts, cashew nuts, pistachio nuts, e.g. satay sauce.

Vegetable-thickened sauces and coulis

Some sauces are produced without a thickening agent. Instead they are thickened by using the title ingredient which is puréed into the sauce, as in the case of vegetable-thickened sauces and coulis.

Type of sauce	Description
Carrot sauce	Carrots cooked in stock with thyme and garlic, sauternes and cream; liquidised and passed; finished with brunoise of blanched carrot.

Celery sauce	Celery cooked in bouillon, puréed in, mixed with cream sauce.
Fennel sauce	Fennel cooked in white stock with pernod, enriched with cream and butter.
Red capsicum coulis	Red capsicums cooked with garlic and shallots; moistened with white wine and cooked in vegetable stock before **liquidising** and passing through a fine sieve.
Tomato coulis	Tomatoes cooked with vinegar, tomato purée and olive oil. Processed and passed through a fine sieve.

Figure 8.10 Vegetable-thickened sauces

Fruit-thickened sauces

Type of sauce	Description
Apple sauce	Peeled apples cooked with sugar, water, lemon juice and a little cinnamon. Can be enriched with butter.
Cranberry sauce	Cranberries cooked in water, orange juice and port with sugar.
Gooseberry sauce	Gooseberries cooked with sugar and puréed.
Cherry sauce	Reduction of port wine, mixed spice and orange juice; with redcurrant jelly and stoned cherries.

Figure 8.11 Fruit-thickened sauces

Pulse-thickened sauces

These purée-type sauces can be made with any pulse vegetable. They require some hard physical work as they need to be passed firmly through a fine sieve to remove the fibrous outer shells.

Puy lentil sauce: puy lentils cooked in stock with shallots, garlic and thyme, liquidised and passed through a fine sieve.

Miscellaneous sauces

Some sauces fail to fit into any of the groups mentioned and are put into the miscellaneous group. Sauces that may appear here include:

○ Bread sauce: thickened by the starch from bread.
○ Curry sauces: the word 'curry' comes from the Tamil word for sauce.
○ Sweet and sour sauce: thickened using arrowroot.

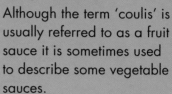

Did you know?
Although the term 'coulis' is usually referred to as a fruit sauce it is sometimes used to describe some vegetable sauces.

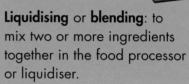

Definition
Liquidising or **blending**: to mix two or more ingredients together in the food processor or liquidiser.

Preparing sauces

Liquids used

1 White stock (see page 238)
2 Brown stock (see page 239)
3 Milk, cream and yoghurt
4 Vegetable and fruit juices
5 Water, beer, wines (white and red), vinegar, various oils, lemon juice
6 Meat juices
7 Court-bouillon.

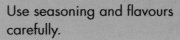

Top marks!
Use seasoning and flavours carefully.

Flavourings used

o Herbs: parsley, thyme, chives, chervil, tarragon, marjoram, basil, bay leaves, oregano, mint and rosemary.
o Spices: black peppercorns, white peppercorns, nutmeg, cloves, saffron, mace, allspice, cayenne pepper, juniper berries.
o Bouquet garni: the following, tied in a bundle: thyme, bay leaf, parsley stalk, celery stick, piece of leek, green.
o Mirepoix of vegetables: roughly diced onions, carrots, celery.
o Proprietary sauces: soy sauce, Worcester sauce, tomato ketchup.

Equipment required

The equipment you will need when preparing sauces:
o saucepans
o sauteuse
o wooden spatula
o wooden spoon
o ladles
o conical strainer
o colander
o sieves and wooden mushroom
o pestle and mortar
o whisks
o balloon whisk
o chopping board
o set of knives
o muslin cloth
o tammy cloth
o bain-marie.

Healthy eating
o Use an alternative to roux as a thickening agent in the preparation of hot sauces.
o Replace butter in roux with vegetable fats or margarine.
o Ensure that the stocks used for sauces are free from traces of fat.
o Do not use butter, fresh cream or egg yolks to finish the sauces.
o Reduce the level of salt and seasoning in the sauces.
o Avoid the use of alcohol in finishing the sauces.

Common faults when making sauces

Type of sauce	Common faults
Fruit/pulse/vegetable thickened sauce	Not using enough fruit/pulse/vegetable or using too much. Cooking time too short. Cooking temperature too high. Insufficient liquid.
Cream-thickened sauce	Heat too high, causing it to burn. Over-**reducing**. Under-reducing. Using the wrong type of cream: double cream is usually the correct cream to use. Using aluminium pans, which discolour the sauce.
Jus	Over-reducing. Under-reducing. Too much thickening agent in the case of jus-lié. Fat not drained from tray, resulting in a greasy jus. Not skimmed. Not strained.
Reduction	Under-reduced. Over-reduced. Not skimming. Seasoning too soon, causing the salts to concentrate. Placing over too low a heat. Reducing at the wrong stage, e.g. while bones are in the liquid.
Brown stock	Bones not browned enough. Bones browned too much. Boiling too rapidly, causing it to go cloudy. Not skimming enough. Using unfit bones. Not cooling quickly.
White stock	Boiling too rapidly. Not skimming enough. Seasoning with salt. Using unfit bones. Too much liquid in relation to bones.
Meat glaze	Over-reducing, producing a bitter glaze. Not straining. Seasoning and becoming too salty, if there are enough natural salts. Under-reducing. Not skimming.

Figure 8.12 Faults in preparing sauces

Definition

Reduce: to concentrate or thicken a sauce. This is done by boiling it to make the water evaporate and reduce the volume of the sauce.

Derivatives of sauces

Basic sauce	Derivative
Béchamel	Parsley sauce Mustard sauce
Velouté	Suprême sauce Mushroom sauce
Espagnole	Chasseur sauce Madeira sauce
Hollandaise	Mousseline sauce Béarnaise sauce
Mayonnaise	Tartare sauce Marie rose sauce

Figure 8.13 Derivatives

Classic combinations of sauces and dishes

The table below shows a selection of classic sauces and the dishes they are most commonly served with.

Sauce	Dish
Hollandaise sauce	Poached egg
Tartare sauce	Fried fillet of sole in breadcrumbs
Apple sauce	Roast loin of pork
Mint sauce	Roast leg of lamb
Bread sauce	Roast chicken
Horseradish sauce	Roast sirloin of beef
Parsley sauce	Boiled ham
Cranberry sauce	Boiled cauliflower
Piquante sauce	Grilled pork chop

Figure 8.14 Combinations of classic sauces with typical dishes

The main function of sauces

○ To thicken soups and stews, e.g. béchamel sauce for cream of leek soup and velouté sauce for white veal stew.

○ To enhance the flavour of the dishes, e.g. tomato sauce served with fried fillet of cod in batter.

○ To provide the main body for savoury and sweet dishes, e.g. béchamel sauce for Welsh rarebit and custard sauce for savoury trifle.

○ To moisten savoury and sweet dishes, e.g. curry sauce with corn croquettes and apricot sauce with pineapple fritters.

○ To increase the nutritional content of dishes, e.g. hollandaise sauce with fresh asparagus served hot and mornay sauce with boiled cauliflower.

Top marks!
Always be on time, make sure your uniform is clean, make sure your hair and nails are clean and tidy and that you are not wearing any jewellery.

Hot sauces

Béchamel

When preparing béchamel sauce, the 'boiling out' process gives body and stability to the sauce. This is especially important if the sauce is used as a base for soufflés. If the sauce has thickness, but no body or stability, a soufflé will tend to 'spew', or sink.

Béchamel sauce

butter	480g
flour	480g
boiling milk	4 litres
salt	30g
white pepper	pinch
grated nutmeg	pinch
onion, studded with cloves	1
sprig of thyme	1
Cooking time	30 minutes
Makes	4 litres

Method

1 Use the butter and flour to make a white roux and cool it.
2 Gradually add the boiling milk, stirring vigorously. Make sure the sauce is quite smooth before adding each small quantity of milk. If this instruction is not followed – or the milk is added too quickly – the sauce will become lumpy.
3 When all the milk has been added, bring to the boil – still stirring – then remove to the side of the stove. Add the seasoning, onion and thyme. Allow to cook gently for one hour.
4 Remove from the heat. Pass through a tammy cloth.
5 Cover with a circle of buttered paper from which the centre has been cut out.
6 Place to one side to cool. If required hot, place in a bain-marie with a few small knobs of butter on top to prevent a skin forming.

Video presentation

For guidance on how to make a roux watch *Prepare velouté sauce (1) make roux.*

Espagnole sauce

Espagnole is the basic sauce for many others. As good sauces cannot be produced from faulty bases, the espagnole must be right from the word 'go'. Therefore, the brown stock used must be of a good flavour, good colour and clear. Do not burn the roux or it will give a bitter flavour to the sauce.

The finished sauce should be 'bright', smooth and clean. Vegetables must be removed before they break up and cloud the sauce. The scum must not boil back into the sauce.

Make sure your strainer and pots are quite clean – many good sauces have been ruined by **passing** them into a dirty saucepan or through an unclean strainer.

Definition

Passing or **straining**: to separate food from marinade, water or cooking liquor using a strainer, colander or sieve.

Espagnole sauce

dripping or white fat	480g
flour	480g
brown beef stock	10 litres
carrots	480g
onions	480g
sticks celery	60g
tomato purée *or*	120g
fresh tomatoes, crushed	1kg
bouquet garni	1
Cooking time	16 hours
Makes	5 litres

Method

1 Use the dripping or white fat and flour to make a brown roux and cool it.
2 Add boiling brown stock gradually, making sure that the stock and roux are smoothly combined before adding more. Stir vigorously with a wooden spatula. This prevents the cooking flour from becoming lumpy.
3 When all the stock has been added, stir until the sauce boils and then put the pan on the side of the stove to simmer gently. Allow to simmer for eight hours, skimming any thick scum and fat.
4 Make a mirepoix of the carrots, onions and celery by dicing. Fry them to a golden colour in a little clean fat. Add this, the bouquet garni and the tomato purée or the fresh tomatoes and continue simmering for a further two hours.
5 Remove from the heat. Pass through a fine strainer (chinois).
6 Simmer the sauce for a further six hours, skimming constantly.
7 Strain and put aside for further use.

Velouté

Velouté sauce

butter	480g
flour	480g
white veal stock	6 litres
salt	to season
white mushroom liquor	400ml
Cooking time	45–60 minutes
Makes	5 litres

Method

1. Use the butter and flour to make a blond roux and cool it.
2. Gradually add the boiling stock to the roux as described in espagnole.
3. Reboil, stirring well.
4. Add the mushroom liquor and allow to simmer for one hour, removing any scum during the process.
5. Remove from the heat. Pass through a tammy cloth or fine strainer. Coat with a little butter to prevent skin formation and put aside for future use.

Allemande sauce

white veal stock	400ml
velouté of veal	1 litre
egg yolks	5
mushroom liquor	400ml
lemon juice	from ½ lemon
cream	400ml
butter	60g
Cooking time	30–45 minutes
Makes	1 litre

Method

1. Place the veal stock, velouté, mushroom liquor and egg yolks together in a thick-bottomed sauté pan. Mix well.
2. Reduce to one litre over an open flame while stirring and keeping the bottom clear from burning with a spatula.
3. Add the cream and reboil.
4. Remove from stove and work in the butter. Add the lemon juice.
5. Pass through a fine strainer or muslin.
6. Cover with a buttered circle of greaseproof paper with a small hole in the centre through which the steam escapes.

Video presentation

Watch *Prepare velouté sauce (1) make roux* and *Prepare velouté sauce (2) mix, boil and simmer* to see this being made.

Chef's tip

Velouté should not be milky in appearance but should be bright and have body.

Chef's tip

To make mushroom liquor, first wash mushroom stalks and trimmings. Put them in a buttered pan with a few drops of lemon juice. Cover them with buttered paper and sweat them out. Finally, strain off the moisture.

Tomato

Tomato sauce

diced bacon trimmings, blanched	80g
butter	125g
diced carrots for mirepoix	80g
diced onions for mirepoix	80g
plain flour	125g
tomato purée	300g
garlic, crushed cloves	2
white stock	3 litres
bouquet garni	1
salt	to season
pepper	to season
sugar	15g
Cooking time	2 hours
Makes	2 litres

Method

1 Place the butter and bacon into a thick-bottomed straight-sided pan. Allow to colour slightly.
2 Add the diced onion and carrot. Cook gently and lightly colour.
3 Add the flour and mix well.
4 Cook to a blond roux, then cool a little.
5 Add tomato purée and garlic.
6 Gradually add the boiling stock, mixing well.
7 Add the bouquet garni and salt.
8 When boiling remove the spoon, clean inside the saucepan with a palette knife.
9 Cover with a lid. Simmer for one hour.
10 Pass sauce through a sieve with pressure. Reboil, check the thickness and seasoning.
11 Add sugar to counteract the acidity of the tomato purée.
12 Pass the sauce through a fine chinois into a sauce bain-marie.
13 Butter the surface, cover with a lid, keep hot in the bain-marie.

Chef's tip
For large amounts this sauce can be cooked in a moderately hot oven.

Investigate!
Worksheet 34

Find as many derivative sauces as you can for each of the following basic sauces: béchamel, velouté, espagnole, hollandaise and tomato.

Gravy

This is made from the meat juices after roasting, e.g. chicken, beef, lamb or pork. Gravy should not really be thickened. A good-quality gravy should be free from fat and have a strong meaty taste.

The flavour of gravy can be improved by the addition of alcohol such as white wine or red wine. It is normally served as an accompaniment with roast meat and poultry and the dish is described as 'au jus'.

Jus–lié

This is a rich, smooth and lightly thickened sauce made from meat juices. The thickening agent used in the preparation of jus-lié is cornflour or arrowroot.

1 Mix the cornflour or arrowroot with a little cold water and then add slowly to the rich brown stock or reduced meat juices from the pot-roasting tray.
2 Bring to the boil and simmer for 20–25 minutes.
3 Strain through a conical strainer and use.

Temperatures for the cooking, holding and serving of sauces are:
o Cooking of sauces   100°C
o Holding of sauces   75°C
o Service of sauces   65°C
o Storage of sauces   4°C.

Finishing sauces

Methods of finishing sauces include:
o Monter: this method involves finishing the sauce with a few pieces of butter at the last minute prior to serving, e.g. white wine sauce for fish dishes or madeira sauce for tournedos.
o Adding whipped double cream: this is folded into warm sauce as a glazing for a fish dish.
o Adding fresh cream and egg yolk liaison: to finish sauces for dishes such as chicken fricassee.
o Adjusting consistency: e.g. adding potato flour diluted in cold water to meat juices from the roasting tray, e.g. jus-lié.
o Garnishing: e.g. adding short julienne of gherkins to sauce charcutière.
o Seasoning: e.g. adding mustard to mustard sauce.

Definition
Jus: juice.

Did you know?
Jus-lié can also be prepared by just reducing rich brown stock to a shiny glaze. The gelatinous nature of brown stock will help to thicken the sauce.

Try this!   Worksheet 35
How many of the words can you find in the wordsearch?

Storage

All sauces should be strained through a conical strainer or fine chinois. In some cases, the sauce might have to be passed through a muslin or tammy cloth.

Sauces which are to be used immediately should be stored in a bain-marie with a few knobs of butter placed on top to stop a skin forming. Cover the bain-marie with a lid and label it. Sauces which are prepared for later use should be stored in a bowl and covered with a circle of buttered greaseproof paper from which the centre has been removed. This is to allow heat to escape. The bowl should be raised on a trivet to allow air to pass round and under it to speed cooling. When cold – and only when cold – the sauces may be placed in a refrigerator. The sauce bowl should be labelled and dated. Sauces should be used in rotation – first in, first out.

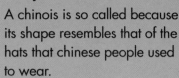

Did you know?
A chinois is so called because its shape resembles that of the hats that chinese people used to wear.

Test yourself!

1 Name four basic sauces.

2 What is the difference between:
  a Béchamel sauce and velouté sauce?
  b Gravy and jus-lié?
  c Espagnole sauce and tomato sauce?

3 What is the correct temperature for:
  a cooking of sauces?
  b holding of sauces?
  c service of sauces?
  d storage of sauces?

4 State four quality points to look for in the finished sauces.

5 Name four different thickening agents used in the preparation of sauces.

6 State four different methods of finishing sauces.

7 Write down four different ways of making healthier sauces.

8 Give two uses of each of the following basic sauces:
  a Béchamel sauce
  b Espagnole sauce
  c Velouté sauce
  d Tomato sauce.

Practice assignment tasks

Prepare and cook stocks, soups and sauces

Task 1

Write a report on the basic principles of making stock. You will need to:

○ Produce a table listing the main types of stock.

○ Explain how to make chicken stock. Include quality points, key stages, cooking times, cooling time and storage.

○ Work out a time plan for making chicken stock including the tools and equipment required to make it.

Task 2

Write a report to identify different soups and say how they are produced and served. To do this:

○ Identify the different types of soup.

○ Choose a soup to make.

○ List all the equipment required to make that soup.

○ List the key preparation and cookery skills used in making that soup.

○ Identify five different soups and list the appropriate accompaniments.

Task 3

Write a report about sauces. You need to:

○ List the types of sauces.

○ Explain why sauces are used to accompany different types of food.

○ State the two different finishing methods.

○ State the storage procedures for sauces.

Fruit and vegetables

9

This chapter covers the following outcomes from Diploma unit 208: Prepare and cook fruit and vegetables

- Outcome 208.1 Prepare fruit and vegetables
- Outcome 208.2 Cook fruit and vegetables

Working through this chapter could also provide evidence for the following Key Skills:

C2.1, C2.2a, C2.2b, C2.3, N1.2, N2.2, ICT2.1, ICT2.2, ICT2.3, LP2.1 LP2.2, LP2.2, PS2.1, PS2.2, PS2.3

In this chapter you will learn how to:

Identify commonly used fruit and vegetables and their seasons

Group them into their classifications

Identify their quality points

Identify and practise correct storage procedures

Identify and use preparation, cooking and preservation methods

Identify and use additions and coatings used in preparation

Identify tools and equipment and their use

Hold and serve cooked fruit and vegetables

Demonstrate safe and hygienic practices.

Identifying fruit

A vast array of fruit is available to the modern chef. This versatile produce is popular eaten both raw and cooked in desserts. Fruit is a source of fibre and is high in vitamin C. It is low in calories and so can usually be eaten in large quantities. Children in particular should include a large amount of fruit in their diet.

Fruit can be spilt into five categories:

- soft, e.g. strawberries, raspberries, blackberries, redcurrants blackcurrants and gooseberries
- hard, e.g. apples and pears
- stoned, e.g. plums, damsons, peaches and apricots
- citrus, e.g. oranges, lemons and grapefruit
- tropical and other, e.g. bananas, pineapples, mangoes, melons and pawpaw.

Soft fruit

Strawberries

Strawberries are one of the most popular summer fruits. They grow throughout the UK and Europe from July to November. Although they can now be obtained year round, the flavour is not as good when they are out of season. The fruit is soft and sweet. They are a popular dessert either on their own or in pies, flans and other cold desserts. (See Chapters 15 and 17 for recipes.) Choose strawber ries which are bright red and plump with the green stalk still attached. This will help them keep longer. Remove the stalk and wash them just before they are required for use. Strawberries are very popular preserved as jam or **conserve**.

Figure 9.1 Soft fruit: a strawberries, b raspberries, c blackberries

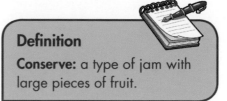

Definition

Conserve: a type of jam with large pieces of fruit.

Raspberries

These are a delicious soft fruit, usually sweet with a slightly acidic taste. They have a central **hull** and are normally purchased already hulled. They are therefore very delicate and easily crushed. They are a great dessert on their own with a little sugar and cream or in pies, flans, mousses and all other desserts. See the recipes for Pavlova and Coulis on pages 476 and 494.

See the recipes for Pavlova and Coulis on pages 476 and 494.

> **Definition**
> **Hull:** The part of a soft fruit that you do not eat.

Blackberries

Blackberries can be found growing wild over the countryside. Blackberries lose flavour rapidly once picked and should therefore be eaten quickly. They have a central hull similar to raspberries and are therefore easily crushed. Blackberries are popular in desserts such as pies, flans and other cold desserts. They are also preserved in jams. See page 491 for a recipe for Compote.

Currants

Currants are small and delicate. Red- and blackcurrants have a slightly sour taste but redcurrants are slightly sweeter and can be eaten raw. White currants are less popular. They are white/green and have a delicate flavour. Currants are commonly used to make jams and preserves and are also used in hot and cold desserts. All three types can be used together. Blackcurrants are used to make cassis (a liqueur). Buy currants still on the stem and choose very glossy ones.

Figure 9.2 different types of currant

Gooseberries

Gooseberries are usually green and look a bit like grapes. They are fleshy with large seeds in the centre and can be hairy. They are very sour and usually used in pies, puddings and desserts. Wash them thoroughly before use. Dessert gooseberries are sweeter and can be eaten raw but this variety is not very common. Their colour can vary from green to light red.

Hard fruit

Apples

There are many different varieties of apple with different sizes, appearances and flavours. Apples can be divided into dessert or cooking apples. Cooking apples are very sour and need sugar to sweeten them but are delicious in pies and puddings. Dessert apples, e.g. Cox's orange pippin and granny smith, can also be cooked in puddings and pies because they have a good texture and flavour. However, they are best eaten raw in fruit salads or as an accompaniment to cheeseboards. All apples should be kept in a cool dry place for no longer than two weeks before being eaten or used. They should be unblemished and free from damage. Once peeled or cut, apples will discolour so put cut apples in **acidulated water** or brush them with lemon juice. See recipes for Apple fritters and Fruit crumble on pages 482 and 492.

Figure 9.3 hard fruit: a apple, b pear

Definition

Acidulated water: water with lemon juice added to it.

Pears

Pears come in many different varieties, shapes and sizes. They have a bell shape – narrower at the top and fatter at the bottom – and a short stalk at the top. Pears are soft, juicy and very sweet when ripe. Ripe pears deteriorate very quickly so they should be eaten within a couple of days. Pears can be eaten with cheese or poached as a dessert. If pears are to be poached they should not be firm. See page 491 for instructions on how to poach pears.

Stoned fruit

Plums

Plums are a soft fruit with a stone in the centre. They come from a tree. The colours vary from purple to yellow dependent on the type, which also affects their size and shape. All plums can be cooked or stewed as well as eaten raw on their own or in fruit salads. They are a popular fruit to preserve in jams and conserves. Plums damage easily because of their soft flesh and should not be used if very damaged. They should be eaten soon after they have ripened. See the recipe for Fruit compote on page 491.

Figure 9.4 stoned fruit: a damson, b peach, c plum, d apricot

Damsons

Damsons are similar to plums but smaller in size and tarter in flavour. They are generally cooked for pies or puddings and also used in preserves. They are blue/purple in colour and have yellow flesh. They have a stone in the centre.

Peaches

Peaches are very popular. They are not generally grown in the UK as it is not warm enough. They are plump, sweet and a yellow/orange colour. Peaches have a large stone in the centre. Peaches can be eaten raw or can be poached quickly and used in other desserts. They bruise easily and should be checked for damage before use. If the skin is bruised the flesh will be damaged too.

Nectarines

Nectarines are similar in appearance to peaches although the skin is smooth to touch whereas a peach is fuzzy. The ripe fruit is sweet smelling, slightly soft to the touch and juicy. Once ripe they will turn quickly. Nectarines can be chopped up and added to fruit salads or eaten as they are. Nectarines grown in the UK are available from May through to September, while imported nectarines are available from January through to April.

Apricots

Apricots are small stoned fruits, similar in size to plums. They have velvety soft flesh and are an orange/yellow colour. Unripe apricots are hard and sour. Once ripe the flavour improves but if they are left to overripen they taste bland and floury. Apricots make good jam, can be eaten raw or can be used in puddings. Apricot jam is often used in the pastry kitchen, see Chapter 16.

Citrus fruits

Oranges

Oranges are usually eaten fresh and raw. They are high in vitamin C. Their flesh is segmented which is a trait of citrus fruit. Surrounding the **segments** is a tough outer skin. Remove the peel and white pith before using oranges in fruit salads and desserts. Some types of orange are easier to peel than others. Citrus fruit is acidic. The flavour of oranges varies from sour/tart to sweet. Seville oranges are bitter and used in **marmalade** while the Valencia oranges are much sweeter.

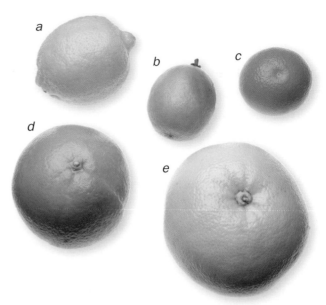

Figure 9.5 citrus fruit: a lemon, b lime, c satsuma, d orange, e grapefruit

Satsumas

Satsumas are a seedless, orange citrus fruit with a thin leathery skin that can be peeled very easily. Satsumas are delicate and will bruise easily if handled roughly.

Mandarins

Mandarins (also known as tangerines) are similar to satsumas but they are squatter and have seeds. They are grown in tropical and subtropical regions. Mandarins can be used in desserts such as Fruit salad (see pages 488–9) and damage easily if not handled carefully.

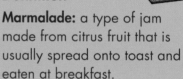

Definition

Marmalade: a type of jam made from citrus fruit that is usually spread onto toast and eaten at breakfast.

Segment: a section of a citrus fruit.

Lemons

Lemon juice or zest is frequently used in cooking to flavour sauces, meat, fish and desserts. Lemons are extremely sour and are not eaten on their own. Lemons have bright yellow, moist-looking skins and generally feel heavy for their size. See the recipe for Lemon meringue flan in Chapter 15 (page 493).

Grapefruit

Grapefruit are large, round and juicy. Pink grapefruit are sweeter than yellow ones. Peel the skin before eating the flesh. The flesh is segmented and the tougher membranes are usually cut away before eating. Grapefruit is a bitter-tasting fruit, which can be served at breakfast. Grapefruit juice is very healthy as it can help to reduce cholesterol.

Limes

Limes are green, firm and have a sharp, distinctive flavour. Limes can be used with lemons or as an alternative to them.

Peel

The peel of citrus fruit is used to make candied fruit and mixed peel, which can be used in desserts and cakes. Candied fruit can be served as petits fours. The peel is soaked in increasingly stronger stock syrup (see page 489) until the water in the peel is replaced with concentrated stock syrup. The crystallisation process of the sugar in the stock syrup acts as a preservative.

Top marks!

In fruit-based dishes, your understanding what is ripe and what is not will affect the product. Learn how to determine what is ripe and of good quality and what is not.

Tropical and other fruits

Bananas

Bananas are easily recognisable by their elongated shape. They have a soft fleshy inside which is high in fibre and makes a healthy meal. Unripe bananas are green. They will ripen quickly if you store them in a dark place. Ripe bananas are yellow. Once the skin darkens this is an indication of overripeness but the banana will also be sweeter which is more appealing to some. They are popular in dishes such as fruit salad (see pages 488–9), ice cream, cakes and hot desserts but they discolour quickly when peeled, so brush them with lemon juice if left raw, e.g. in a fruit salad.

Figure 9.6 tropical fruit: a melon, b mango, c pineapple, d bananas

Pineapples

Pineapples are large and oval with prickly outer skins and sweet, juicy yellow flesh. If you can pull one of the leaves away from the top, the pineapple is ripe. Pineapples have a tough woody core, which should not be used. The flesh is used in sweet and savoury dishes.

Did you know?

A bunch of bananas is known as a hand.

Mangoes

Mangoes have a very large flat stone running through them and a tough outer skin. They have a sweet orange flesh. To cut a mango into bite-sized pieces first cut it in half, leaving the skin on. Then score the flesh into cubes without cutting through the skin. Push

271

the skin inside out and slice off the cubes. Mangoes are used in many sweet dishes and once ripe must be used within three days. Avoid using bruised or wrinkled mangoes, as the flavour and taste will be affected.

Melons

Melons come in many colours, shapes and sizes. Melons feel heavy for their size and are a firm fruit with a tough outer skin. Melons have pips or seeds in the centre surrounded by a fragrant flesh. Because of their high water content melons are extremely healthy as part of a balanced diet. Melons can be eaten on their own, in fruit salads or served with cold meat and fish starters. They are a good source of vitamins A and C.

Watermelons are large with a green skin and red, juicy, black-seeded flesh. They have a high water content and when ripe have a subtly sweet flavour. They can be cut into manageable bite-sized pieces for fruit salads or into segments.

Cantaloupe melons are much smaller than watermelons. They have a pale green ribbed skin and orange flesh with seeds in the centre cavity. Ripe cantaloupe melons have more flavour and are sweeter than watermelons. They are excellent in fruit salad, in segments or as an accompaniment to prawns in a cocktail. Their season is October to February but they are available all year round from some suppliers.

Honeydew melons are yellow, the size of a coconut and oval. They have greenish-yellow flesh. When ripe they are sweet and very juicy and can be eaten in salads and appetisers or in segments.

Galia melons look similar to cantaloupe melons but they are larger and have greenish-yellow flesh. They are sweet and aromatic.

Pawpaw

Pawpaw is also known as papaya. It is a similar shape to a pear and has orange/yellow flesh, surrounding a mass of black round seeds at the centre cavity. This fruit is ripe when soft and can be cut into wedges and eaten whole or added to other cold dishes or fruit salads.

Top marks!

Fruits are readily available from suppliers all year round, but to score top marks it is beneficial to know when these fruits are traditionally in season. When deciding what to choose from the menu, your customers want what is seasonal and in its prime.

Fruit seasons and quality points

All fruit is seasonal as it needs time to grow and ripen. Figure 9.7 below identifies when UK fruit is in season and at its best. It is cheaper to buy fruit in season because it is available locally. Food that is out of season is always more expensive because of the cost of transporting it. The table also shows quality points to look out for.

Fruit	Quality points	Months in season
Strawberries	Good colour, clean appearance, fragrant smell, no damage	Jun, Jul, Aug, Sep, Oct
Raspberries	Good colour, clean appearance, fragrant smell, no damage	Jul, Aug, Sep, Oct
Blackberries	Good colour, clean appearance, fragrant smell, no damage	Sep, Oct, Nov
Redcurrants/ blackcurrants	Free from impurities such as dirt, good sheen, no bruising	Jul, Aug, Sep, Oct
Gooseberries	Free from impurities such as dirt, good sheen, no bruising	Jul, Aug
Apples	Good colour, no bruises or blemishes, firm to touch	Jan, Feb, Mar, Apr, Sep, Oct, Nov, Dec
Pears	No bruises or blemishes, firm/soft to touch	Jan, Feb, Mar, Apr, Oct, Nov, Dec
Plums	Clean, good sheen, firm to touch, fragrant aroma, no damage	Oct, Nov
Damsons	Clean, good sheen, firm to touch, fresh aroma	Oct, Nov
Peaches	Pleasant smell, firm, no blemishes or bruising	All year round as imported
Apricots	Firm/soft to touch, good colour, no bruising	Jan, Jun, Jul, Dec
Oranges	Moist appearance to skin, bright colour, good smell	All year round as imported
Lemons	Moist appearance to skin, bright colour, good smell	All year round as imported
Grapefruit	Moist appearance to skin, bright colour, good smell	All year round as imported
Limes	Moist appearance to skin, bright colour, good smell	All year round as imported
Bananas	Firm, even colour, no bruising.	All year round as imported
Pineapples	No damage or bruising to outer skin, good size and weight.	All year round as imported
Mangoes	Firm fruit, no wrinkling or damage to exterior, pleasant smell.	All year round as imported
Melons	Fragrant smell, no external damage, slightly soft to touch.	All year round as imported
Pawpaw	Firm, no wrinkling or damage to exterior, pleasant smell	All year round as imported

Figure 9.7 Fruit season and quality points

Identifying vegetables

Vegetables accompany most meals. In vegetarian dishes they are sometimes the main ingredients. You can probably already identify many different types of vegetables and pulses. What you may not know is where they come from and how to cook them.

Pulses are seeds and pods which are harvested for drying. Commonly used pulses include some types of peas, lentils and beans.

Many items, e.g. chives and potatoes, are available all year round as suppliers obtain them from abroad when they are out of season in this country.

Vegetables within this chapter are split into these categories:

○ root vegetables
○ bulbs
○ flower heads
○ fungi
○ tubers
○ leaves
○ stems
○ vegetable fruits
○ pods and seeds
○ pulses
○ nuts
○ squash
○ vegetable protein
○ seaweed.

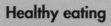

Healthy eating

Root vegetables are usually peeled to remove the outer skin before being cooked. They will have been in contact with the soil and may be dirty. However, you can scrub root vegetables with water and cook them with their skins on, as the skin contains valuable nutrients.

Root vegetables

Carrots, parsnips, beetroot, turnips, radishes and swede are all examples of root vegetables. They grow in soil. The root is the edible part of the plant. The stalks grow above the soil and are usually thrown away and not eaten. Root vegetables are a good source of fibre and vitamins A and B. They normally have a firm or hard texture, as this helps them to survive in the soil.

Figure 9.8 Root vegetables: a carrot, b parsnip, c beetroot, d turnip, e radish, f swede

Carrots

Carrots are tapered orange vegetables which vary in size. The younger they are, the smaller and sweeter they are. Carrots are a common addition to many British dishes and are generally boiled or steamed. They are a good source of vitamins A and C.

Swede

Swede is a round vegetable with a thick outer skin. The flesh is yellow and has a distinctive sweet flavour. This vegetable is usually boiled or steamed and can be served diced or mashed.

Celeriac

Celeriac looks similar to swede but its flesh is white rather than yellow. It has a slightly bitter flavour, a bit like celery. It can be steamed or boiled and served on its own diced or mashed. It can also be combined with mashed potato.

Investigate!

The Scots have a special name for swede or turnip. What is it? These are eaten along with 'tatties' (potatoes) on a special night of the year. Find out what this is.

Turnips

Turnips have a similar shape to swede but are smaller. They may be purple and white or greenish-white depending on the variety. The tough outer skin is peeled away leaving a white flesh, which is usually boiled.

Beetroot

Beetroot is a smaller round vegetable, which is easily recognised by its deep red colour. It is generally used in salads and in soups such **borsch**.

Definition
Borsch: a traditional Russian soup made with beetroot.

Parsnips

Parsnips look similar to carrots but are a creamy beige colour. They can be roasted in batons to accompany a roast dinner, puréed in a soup, boiled and served as mash or even steamed whole.

Radishes

Radishes are small round vegetables with a red outer skin. They have a bitter flavour and are used in salads or as a garnish rather than for cooking.

Bulbs

Bulbs grow in soil but their stalks are above the ground surface. They are recognisable by the layers which form at their base. Examples of bulb vegetables include onions, leeks, chives and garlic.

Onions

Onions are probably the most common and popular type of bulb vegetable. They are used in cookery worldwide for a large range of dishes, e.g. casseroles, stir-fries and sauces. Most onions have a dry inedible skin which is peeled and thrown away during preparation. Onions vary in size, shape and colour.

Shallots are small and either red or white. Traditionally they are available between September and October, although now you can get shallots all year round.

Red onions are dark red. They are sweeter in flavour than other onions and are good in salads.

Spring onions are used raw in salads. Some outer layers are removed from the stalk and bulb to remove dirt or damage. They are now available all year round.

Button onions, as the name suggests, are small. They are white. They are used as garnishes in dishes such as coq au vin because they are bite-sized and can be served whole.

Spanish onions are the largest. They are sliced or diced in various dishes, e.g. stews and casseroles, or accompany convenience products, e.g. hot dogs and burgers.

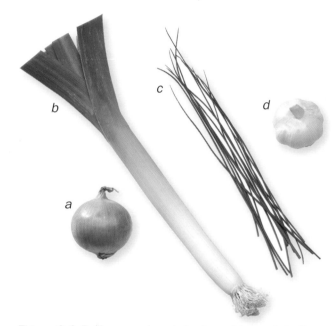

Figure 9.9 Bulbs: a onion, b leek, c chives, d garlic

Figure 9.10 Types of onion: a shallot, b red onion, c spring onion, d button onion, e Spanish onion

Leeks

Leeks have a white base and stem which changes to green at the top. Leeks have a lot of dirt in their layers so it is important to wash and trim leeks properly. Leeks vary in size and can be used in a variety of ways.

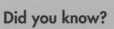

Did you know?
The leek is the national symbol of Wales.

Try this!
Leek and potato soup can be served either hot or cold. Make the soup, taste it hot and then cold to see which temperature you prefer.

Chives

Chives are usually used as a herb or garnish and are not served as a dish. Chives are available all year round.

Most items are now available all year round from suppliers. However, if a supplier gets a product from abroad it will generally cost more.

Garlic

Garlic is a versatile vegetable. It is not usually served on its own but is crushed or sliced and added to dishes such as soups, sauces, meat dishes or marinades to enhance flavour. Garlic is usually grown in France and can vary in size from a standard bulb to jumbo or elephant garlic.

Chef's tip
Garlic has a very overpowering flavour, which can linger on your hands, breath and clothes. Always ensure you use the correct amount according to the recipe. If you use too much, the dish will be overpowered by the garlic flavour.

Flower heads

Broccoli, asparagus and cauliflower are common examples of flower head vegetables. As the name suggests, the flower head is the part of these plants which is eaten. Flower heads deteriorate quite quickly so it is important to ensure they are fresh.

a

b

Figure 9.11 Flower heads: a cauliflower, b broccoli

Cauliflower

A cauliflower has tightly packed florets or flowers making a compact, round, white head. The flower head is usually surrounded by thick green leaves, which are discarded during preparation. Cauliflowers are available all year round, but the price will vary.

Did you know?
Cauliflower leaves can be used to make soup.

Broccoli

Broccoli is a deep greenish-purple colour. Poor quality is indicated by discoloration – the head starts to seed and goes yellow. The stem from which the florets are cut is edible so by leaving the stem intact with the floret you have a greater yield from the vegetable.

Fungi

Not all fungi are edible. In fact some fungi could kill you or your customer if eaten so it is really important to obtain your fungi from a reputable supplier. Most people do not possess the skills to pick their own mushrooms or fungi in a wood; the consequences of picking the wrong fungi, e.g. a death cap, mean it is not worth taking the risk.

Reputable suppliers will have many different types of edible fungi and mushroom available, e.g. grey and yellow oyster, hon-shimeji, field and paris brown. They will vary in price due to their availability and the season.

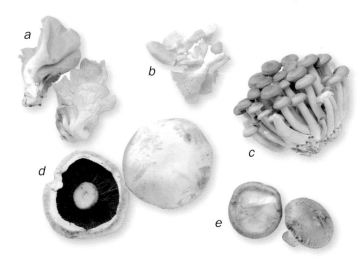

Figure 9.12 There are many types of mushrooms available to caterers, including: a grey oyster, b yellow oyster, c hon-shimeji, d field, e paris brown

Mushrooms

The most commonly used mushrooms are button mushrooms and open flat mushrooms. These are generally white but can be dark brown. Freshness is essential and should be checked before use. Mushrooms must be washed thoroughly as they are found in or around decaying trees and plants or are artificially cultivated in soil heavily treated with manure or animal waste. Mushrooms are usually cooked by frying.

Figure 9.13 A death cap mushroom

Tubers

Tubers are swellings or nodes on the roots of plants. The rest of the plant is discarded for cooking. They grow under the soil. The main vegetable in this group is the potato. Potatoes are round or oval, yellowy-white on the inside with an outer skin, which is peeled or scrubbed before cooking. Sweet potatoes have an elongated shape and red/pink skin. They have orange flesh and a sweeter flavour than normal potatoes. They are excellent roasted or boiled then mashed. They come from the West Indies and Caribbean where they are called yams.

Figure 9.14 Potatoes: a baby new potatoes, b maris piper, c desiree

There are at least 40 different types of potato ranging from small Charlotte potatoes to red Desiree potatoes. Maris Pipers make the best chipped potatoes. Potatoes differ in size from bite-sized baby new potatoes to large King Edwards, which can be bigger than your hand.

Potatoes are split into 'new' and 'old'. New potatoes are available between May and August and old potatoes are available between September and April.

Did you know?

A potato is made up of layers, which can be seen if the potato is cut.

Leaves

Leaf vegetables are the prepared leaves of the plant. They include cabbage, sprouts, spinach and lettuce.

Cabbage

Several varieties of cabbage are commonly used in cooking:

Traditional or **white cabbages** are greenish-white balls of flat leaves tightly packed together. The thick-stemmed leaves are trimmed to aid the cooking process.

Savoy cabbages have a distinct flavour and ruffled appearance. The leaves are green or yellow. They are not as tightly packed as white cabbages.

Figure 9.15 Leaf vegetables: a savoy cabbage, b red cabbage, c spinach, d iceberg lettuce, e green cabbage, f white cabbage

Red cabbages are similar in shape and texture to white cabbages, but the leaves are a deep purplish-red. Red cabbages generally take a little longer than normal cabbages to cook because of their density and the thickness of their leaves.

Sprouts

Sprouts, which we all traditionally turn our noses up at during Christmas, are a type of miniature cabbage with a very distinctive flavour. The small, tightly packed balls of leaves are attached to the long sturdy stem of the plant. Extremely nutritious, Brussels sprouts are a valuable source of folic acid which is important for pregnant women.

Spinach

When cooked, spinach reduces to a dark-green, soft texture. Because it reduces in volume so much on cooking, a great amount is needed if a large yield is required.

Lettuce

Lettuce is traditionally used in salads. Lettuce must be washed thoroughly, as soil can easily get into the heart. Lettuce leaves should be firm, clean and fresh.

Stems

This group of vegetables includes celery and asparagus.

Celery

Celery is the most commonly used stem vegetable. It has a distinctive taste and is often used in salads, although it can be braised or made into soup. The long green stem has a fibrous string-like outer skin, which should be removed to enhance its quality.

Asparagus

The base of asparagus is quite woody, so cut it away. The remaining stem has a small flowering head, which has usually not flowered before cooking.

> **Chef's tip**
> Fruit, e.g. apple, is a good accompaniment for red cabbage.

> **Chef's tip**
> Nutmeg is a great addition to spinach.

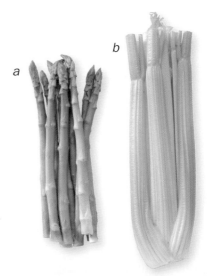

Figure 9.16 Stem vegetables: a asparagus, b celery

> **Did you know?**
> Asparagus is classed as a flower head if just the tips are cooked. However, asparagus is usually cooked whole with its stem.

Seaweed

With the increased interest in Asian cooking, especially Japanese cooking, seaweed is used in many kitchens. Many types of seaweed are used in cooking and it is used in a variety of dishes including salads, ice cream, puddings, bread, soups and stocks. These are some different types of seaweed:

- **Kombu**: also known as kelp, this can be used in rice or bean dishes, or used to make soups or stock.
- **Wakame**: this can be added to soup.
- **Nori**: can be eaten on its own, in soups or sprinkled over food.
- **Arame** and **hijiki**: traditional Japanese seaweeds.
- **Agar agar**: occasionally used in desserts. Processed agar agar can be used as a gelatine substitute for vegetarians.
- **Dulse** and **sea palm**.
- **Samphire**: is a common and popular seaweed which is used to flavour soups and salads.

Seaweeds are very rich in minerals. For example, they contain between seven and 14 times as much calcium as milk, depending on the type of seaweed. Seaweed is eaten cooked, dried or fresh depending on the dish, and can be obtained from Asian restaurant suppliers.

Chef's tip
Finely shredded deep-fried seaweed is a great accompaniment to an Asian dinner.

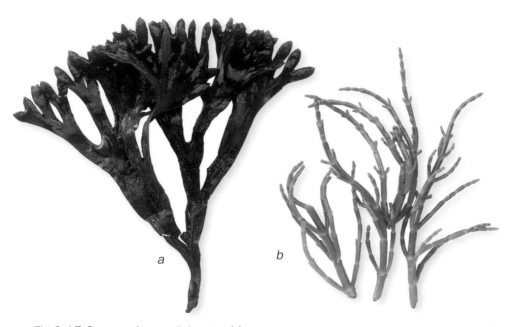

Fig 9.17 Seaweed: a nori, b samphire

Vegetable fruits

These vegetables are the ripened fruit of the plants they grow on. They include aubergines, capsicums (peppers), cucumber, avocados, tomatoes, courgettes, marrow and sweetcorn.

Figure 9.18 Vegetable fruits: a aubergine, b capsicums, c cucumber, d avocado, e beef tomato, f tomato, g cherry tomatoes

Aubergines

Aubergines have a firm to spongy texture. They are bell-shaped and black or purple in colour. They are generally used with other vegetables, e.g. tomatoes, courgettes, garlic and onions for ratatouille. Aubergines can be grilled with olive oil for an hors d'oeuvre (starter) or used as the vegetable layer in moussaka. Aubergines are a Mediterranean vegetable and are a popular element in that style of cookery.

Capsicums

Capsicums are commonly known as sweet peppers. They can be red, orange, green or yellow. The colour depends on the age of the capsicum, i.e. a green capsicum will eventually turn red. These versatile vegetables are used in salads and many Mediterranean dishes. They can also be blanched and stuffed with other food, e.g. rice, to create vegetarian dishes.

Cucumbers

Cucumbers are long green baton-shaped vegetables, which are not usually cooked but are used for cold food and salads.

Avocados

Avocados originally came from South America but are now grown in many different countries. They are oval in shape and are a green or brown colour. The skins are tough and inedible. Once peeled, avocados may discolour rapidly. Avocados contain a large seed or stone in the centre. When ripe the flesh feels soft to touch. It can easily be puréed. They have a high fat content for a vegetable.

Try this!

Take a piece of raw red capsicum and taste it. Now brush it with oil and grill it till the skin is black. Remove the skin and taste the capsicum. The difference is astonishing — the sweet flavour of the capsicum really comes through when grilled.

Tomatoes

Tomatoes are very versatile and are used in many dishes and salads. They are instantly recognisable from their round red appearance, although they do come in other shapes as well, e.g. the long plum tomato from Italy. Their colour varies and a good indicator of flavour is a deep red colour. Tomatoes supplied on the vine are considered to be better quality and the flavour should be sweeter. Cherry tomatoes are baby tomatoes and have a sweeter taste than normal tomatoes. Beef tomatoes are the largest variety. They are very fleshy and juicy with a sweet flavour. They are ideal in Greek salad and can be cooked by grilling or shallow frying as an accompaniment to a meal.

> **Top marks!**
> Do you recognise all the different types of fruit and vegetables? Many people connot identify half the vegetables in a supermarket if the label is removed. Top marks if you learn to identify all the fruit and vegetables and the groups they belong to.

Squashes

Courgettes

Courgettes are similar in appearance to marrows, but they are smaller. They taste quite bland so they are usually sautéed or stir-fried with other vegetables, e.g. onion and garlic, to add flavour. Overcooking courgettes makes them soggy and unattractive.

Marrows

Marrows are much larger versions of courgettes with similar preparation and cooking methods. Marrows are not popular as their high water content makes their flavour quite bland. Overcooked marrows are extremely unappealing and mushy.

Figure 9.19 Squashes: a marrow, b pumpkin, c courgette

Pumpkin

Pumpkins are large and round with a tough outer skin. The hard orange flesh can be steamed, boiled or roasted. It also makes excellent soup. Pumpkins have a large central cavity which contains many seeds. Once roasted, these make a very healthy, tasty snack. Pumpkins are usually harvested in late summer and autumn. They range dramatically in size depending on how long they have been left to grow.

> **Try this!**   Worksheet 16
> Close your book and list as many vegetables as you can for each category.

Fresh peas, beans and seeds

Peas and beans are the seeds (e.g. garden peas) and the seed pods (e.g. mangetout, French beans, runner beans and broad beans) of plants. Vegetables such as garden peas are usually blanched and then frozen.

Some seed pods grow to yield large seeds, e.g. broad beans, from which the pod is discarded and only the seed is used for cooking. Other types, e.g. runner beans and French beans, are picked with the pod and seed still intact and are prepared together. These vegetables contain high levels of vitamin C.

Mangetout is a pea pod inside which the peas have not yet grown. They are very delicate and do not take long to cook. Quick cooking methods such as stir-frying are suitable for mangetout as they can become wilted and mushy very quickly.

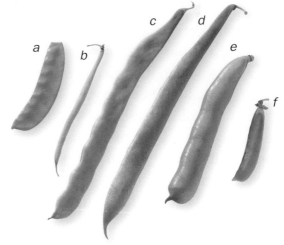

Figure 9.20 a mangetout, b French bean, c flat bean, d runner bean, e broad bean, f garden peas

Sweetcorn was originally grown in America but is now grown all over the world. The yellow corn **kernels** – cob – are surrounded by green leaves. Fresh sweetcorn should be boiled whole in salted water. It can be served whole or the kernels can be stripped off. This popular vegetable can be bought canned, frozen or fresh.

Figure 9.21 A sweetcorn cob and kernels

Definition
Kernel: the seed contained within a husk.

Nuts

Nut is the term given to a single seed or dry fruit encased in a shell. There are many different types of nuts. They are high in protein, vitamins, minerals, fats and fibre. Nuts are used in vegetarian cooking as a meat substitute, in baking and in sauces. Nuts can also be eaten as a snack. They can be shelled, flaked or ground.

Figure 9.22 Nuts: a brazil nuts, b almonds, c walnuts, d hazelnuts, e coconut

Almonds

Almonds are seeds from a tree similar to a peach tree. There are two varieties. One is bitter and used to make oils and essences. It should not be eaten in great quantities. The other is sweet and is used split, whole or flaked in cakes. Sweet almonds can be ground to a paste and added to a variety of dishes, e.g. macaroons. Almond paste can be used to thicken and flavour sauces, e.g. **korma sauce**. To remove the skins before use, blanch almonds in boiling water for 10 seconds, and then rub the skins off.

> **Definition**
>
> **Korma sauce:** a mild, creamy Indian sauce.

Walnuts

Walnuts are popular worldwide. They have round crinkly shells and wrinkled kernels. They are available in the shell or shelled, whole, chopped or ground. Walnuts have a moist oily flavour and can be used in cakes, stuffing and salads.

Hazelnuts

Hazelnuts are small round kernels, which accompany chocolate very well. They can be bought whole, chopped, ground or as oil. Blanch them to remove the skin.

Brazil nuts

Brazil nuts are large, dark, three-sided, oval nuts. They have a very hard shell. They can be eaten whole or used in salads, vegetarian meals, desserts or sweets.

Coconuts

Coconuts are the fruit of the palm tree and grow in all tropical areas. They have a hard, hairy, brown shell and firm white flesh. Once the coconut is cracked, the rich milk can be used in Asian cooking. The flesh can be eaten raw, blended, desiccated or shredded and can be used as an ingredient in cakes and pastries and in ethnic cooking. It is also processed into coconut milk. When selecting a coconut make sure it is heavy and shake it to ensure it contains milk (liquid). There should not be any sign of mould.

Pulses

Pulses are the edible seeds of plants, harvested for drying.

Pulses, e.g. chickpeas, lentils, split yellow peas, split green peas and beans, can be obtained dried or cooked and canned. The pulses you are likely to use in the Diploma will be dried, and most of these will need soaking before use. Pulses are a high source of fibre, protein, iron and B vitamins.

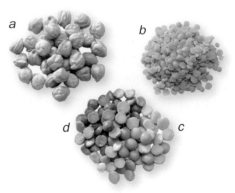

Figure 9.23 Dried pulses: a chickpeas, b lentils, c split yellow peas, d split green peas

Peas

- Split green peas disintegrate easily and are very starchy. They are often used as an ingredient in soups and broths.
- Chickpeas hold their shape well and are used, as with other pulses, in vegetarian dishes. In some parts of the world they are ground into flour to make breads, batters, etc. They have a slightly nutty flavour.
- Marrowfat peas, like split green peas, disintegrate easily and are very starchy. They are often used as an ingredient in soups and broths.

Healthy eating
Pulses contain no saturated fats and are a healthy alternative to meat.

Beans

Many types of beans are available to caterers, e.g. red kidney beans, white haricot beans, mung beans, butter beans, borlotti beans, broad beans and soya beans.

- Red kidney beans contain an enzyme which if not destroyed will cause food poisoning. Rapid boiling for ten minutes destroys the enzyme. This cooking time enables the heat to penetrate the bean and kill the enzyme.
- Haricot beans are used in baked beans.
- Butter beans are also known as lima beans. They are large, flat and yellowy-brown. They have a buttery taste when cooked.
- Borlotti beans are similar to kidney beans and are a good substitute for kidney or haricot beans in dishes. They are very moist and tender and have a nice texture in dishes.
- Soya beans are high in fat and protein. Soya bean products are increasingly popular. They are processed into flour, milk, meat substitutes (e.g. tofu or tempeh), margarine and even soy sauce.

Remember!
Red kidney beans must always be boiled for at least ten minutes before use.

Lentils

Lentils are the seeds of a small branching plant. They resemble small peas. They can be used whole or split and do not necessarily need to be soaked before cooking. Lentils are rich in protein. They are named and identified according to their colour: red, yellow, green and brown. Red and yellow lentils disintegrate when cooked, while green and brown remain whole.

Investigate! Worksheet 17

Find more information about pulses. For each type of pulse write a description, a note of its uses, nutritional information and any other key facts you discover.

Vegetable protein

Quorn

This is a high-protein vegetable used by vegetarians as a meat substitute. This myco-protein is processed from a tiny plant of the mushroom family. Egg white (albumen) is used to bind it and then other flavourings and colours are added. In its natural form it resembles grey mincemeat. An increasing number of ready-made products can be purchased, e.g. sausages and fillets. It is not suitable for vegans because of the egg white.

Try this!

Substitute Quorn for minced beef and make a cottage pie in the same way. You will be surprised how similar the taste is.

Soya

Soya is an excellent source of high-quality protein and is a popular Asian vegetable. Soya foods include: tofu, tempeh, soy sauces and oils, miso and margarine.

- **Tofu** is the bean curd made from thickened soya milk. The beans are soaked, crushed and heated to produce soya milk. Calcium is added and this thickens the soya milk and makes it more solid so it forms a soft cheese-like product.
- **Tempeh** is fermented soya bean paste mixed with a healthy mould. Under controlled conditions these components merge to produce a good meat substitute suitable for deep-frying, shallow frying, baking and steaming. Tempeh is easily recognisable by its chewy texture, black speckling and distinct flavour.
- **Miso** is the fermented condiment of soya beans, rice or barley salt and water. Miso is used to give flavour, colour, texture and aroma to soups, stews, casseroles and sauces. Many non-meat eaters use soya as a meat substitute because of its high protein yield and textured quality.

How to judge quality of fruit and vegetables

It is essential that you can recognise good-quality fruit and vegetables and select those suitable for use. Common sense should always be used when selecting fruit and vegetables of appropriate quality. Always consider size, shape, colour, smell, damage and texture. The table below lists vegetables, the quality points to look for and when they are in season. See Figure 9.7 for more information about fruit.

Vegetable or pulse	Quality points	Months in season
Potato	No excessive soil, no eyes or roots growing from the tuber, no weeping, bruising or damage to the skin. Good even size for type required.	(New) Jun, Jul, Aug, Sep (Old) Jan, Feb, Mar, Apr, May, Oct, Nov, Dec
Carrot	Good tapered straight shape, vibrant orange colour, no woody appearance, no insect or spade damage or wrinkling of skin.	Jan, Feb, Mar, Apr, Jul, Aug, Sep, Oct, Nov, Dec
Turnip	Firm with no damage to the exterior. Outer skin is not wrinkled, no insect or spade damage. Pliable to touch.	Jan, Feb, Mar, Oct, Nov, Dec
Swede	Firm with no insect or spade damage to the exterior. Outer skin is not wrinkled and pliable to touch.	Jan, Feb, Mar, Apr, Sep, Oct, Nov, Dec
Parsnip	Firm with no insect or spade damage to the exterior. Outer skin is not wrinkled. Pliable to touch.	Jan, Feb, Mar, Apr, Sep, Oct, Nov, Dec
Radish	Even size, good red colour. No insect or spade damage to outer surface. Healthy fresh-looking green leaves.	Apr, May, Jun, Jul, Aug, Sep, Oct, Nov, Dec
Onion	Firm and dry exterior, no moisture at top. No sign of stem growth.	Jan, Feb, Mar, Jul, Aug, Sep, Oct, Nov, Dec
Garlic	Firm and dry exterior, no moisture at top. No sign of stem growth.	Available all year round
Chives	Good green colour, no discoloration, no signs of wilting.	Available all year round
Spring onion	Bulb and stem clean in appearance, no damage to stem, leaves or bulb. No slime, no moist leaves.	Jul, Aug, Sep, Oct, Nov, Dec
Leek	No excessive soil, no damage or slimy feel to exterior layers or leaves.	Jan, Feb, Aug, Sep, Oct, Nov, Dec
Cabbage	No discoloration or evident damage, clean and fresh appearance. No wilting.	Jun, Jul, Aug, Sep, Oct, Nov
Courgette	No bruising or damage to the exterior surface. Firm flesh.	Jul, Aug, Sep, Oct
Marrow	No bruising or damage to the exterior surface. Firm flesh.	Aug, Sep, Oct
Sprouts	Compact leaves, no yellow discoloration, clean fresh appearance.	Jan, Feb, Dec

Lettuce	No wilting leaves, no excessive soil, no contamination from insects such as snails and slugs. Colour should be bright and vibrant.	May, Jun, Jul, Aug, Sep, Oct, Nov
Spinach	Crisp leaves, fresh appearance, no slimy leaves, deep green colour.	Apr, May, Jun, Jul, Aug, Sep, Oct
Cauliflower	Tightly packed heads, no discoloration or damage to the head. Leaves surrounding the flower head intact and not wilting. Not too many leaves.	Jan, Feb, Mar, Apr, Aug, Sep, Oct, Nov, Dec
Broccoli	Fresh green colour, no discoloration (yellow). Stems firm and crisp, not spongy or flexible.	Jan, Feb, Mar, Apr, Sep, Oct, Nov, Dec
Asparagus	Firm flower heads, good size, base not too woody, no discoloration or damage.	Jun, Jul
Celery	Firm stems with no damage or discoloration to the vegetable. Stems tightly packed together. Breaks crisply when separated.	May, Jun, Jul, Aug
Mushrooms	No slime or bad odour, appears clean and dry, no discoloration to the cap.	Available all year round
Tomato	No damage to skin, firm to touch, good colour.	Apr, May, Jun, Jul, Aug, Sep, Oct
Avocado	Good green or brown colour, skin firm but with some give to show ripeness. No damage to exterior.	Available all year round
Aubergine	Firm, no damage or soft spots.	May, Jun, Jul, Aug, Sep
Cucumber	Long firm and straight. Skin clean and a good green colour. No sign of wilting or wrinkling. No soft spots.	Jun, Jul, Aug, Sep
Capsicum	No wrinkling, good vibrant colour, no soft spots or damage.	Available all year round
Broad bean	Pods undamaged and not too large. Evenly sized.	May, Jun, Jul, Aug, Sep
Mangetout	Crisp, flat, evenly sized pods, good green colour, no discoloration.	May, Jun, Jul, Aug, Sep
Peas	Plump and crisp, no discoloration.	Jun, Jul
Runner beans	Even size, not too big, good green colour, no discoloration, snaps crisply when broken.	Jul, Aug, Sep, Oct, Nov
French beans	Even size, not too big, good green colour, no discoloration, snaps crisply when broken.	Jun, Jul
Dried pulses	Free from contaminants such as insects; feels clean, dry and smooth.	Available all year round

Figure 9.24 Quality points to look for in vegetables and pulses

Try this!

Worksheet 18

Close your book. List the quality points you should look for in a delivery of fresh vegetables.

Food value and healthy eating

Fruit, pulses and vegetables are an essential part of a healthy, well-balanced diet. The wrong cooking method or cooking time will affect the nutritional value of the food so it is important to understand and apply the correct preparation and cooking methods.

Most fruit and vegetables contain large amounts of vitamins B and C. These vitamins dissolve in water; therefore over-boiling vegetables to a mush means they will not be as nutritious. Fruit is not cooked as often as vegetables but its nutritional value will be reduced if it is.

The table below identifies the nutritional value of vegetables.

Type	Fats (grams per 100g)	Protein (grams per 100g)	Carbohydrates (grams per 100g)	Vitamin content
Potato	0.2	3.9	31	B, C
Carrot	0.3	0.6	7.9	A, B, C, K
Turnip	0.3	0.9	4.7	B, C
Swede	0.3	5.0	1.9	B, C
Parsnip	1.1	1.8	12.5	B, C, K
Beetroot	0.3	0	9.0	A, B, C
Radish	0.1	0.8	2.9	C
Onion	0.2	1.2	7.9	B, C
Garlic	1.0	7.0	15.0	C
Spring onion	1.0	2.0	3.0	B, C
Leek	0.5	1.6	2.9	B, C
Cabbage	0.5	2.1	3.9	B, C
Courgette	0.4	1.8	1.8	C, K
Sprouts	1.0	2.8	2.0	A, C, K
Lettuce	0.3	0.7	1.9	C
Spinach	0.8	2.8	1.6	A, B, C, K
Cauliflower	0.9	3.6	3.0	B, C, K
Broccoli	0.9	4.4	1.8	A, B, C, K
Asparagus	0.6	2.7	1.1	C
Celery	0.3	0.3	0.9	C
Mushroom	0.5	1.8	0.4	B, C, K

Tomato	0.4	0.7	2.8	A, B, C
Avocado	28	2.0	2.0	B, C, E
Aubergine	0.4	0.9	2.2	B
Cucumber	0.1	0.7	1.5	C
Capsicum	0.4	1.0	6.4	A, B, C
Broad beans	0.8	5.1	5.6	B, C
Peas	0.7	4.8	7.8	B, C
Runner beans	0.4	1.6	2.0	A, C
Haricot beans	1.6	21.4	49.7	B
Lentils	1.5	24.0	48.8	B
Soya beans	7.3	14	5.1	B
Chickpeas	5.4	21.3	49.6	C

Figure 9.25 Nutritional value of vegetables

Preparation tools and techniques

Washing

Vegetables grow in, on or above the ground. They can become contaminated by the soil, which contains many types of harmful bacteria, e.g. clostridium perfringens and bacillus cereus, so it is important to wash them carefully. Also, insects and other animals, e.g. slugs, can be trapped within the leaves. Another reason for washing vegetables is to remove any residue from chemicals and pesticides, which may have been sprayed onto the vegetables to deter birds and insects. This also applies to fruit.

It is important to inspect the product first to make sure it is the right quality. Then strip away any unnecessary leaves or remains from when the vegetable or fruit was joined to the plant, e.g. removing the tomatoes from the vine.

Next wash the fruit or vegetables in cold running water. The type of fruit or vegetable will determine how robustly you clean it. You may use a brush to scrub the mud from potatoes but you would be more careful washing a tomato. Once the items have been washed thoroughly, they should be drained of any excess water.

Figure 9.26 A brush can be used to clean potatoes

Video presentation
Watch *Washing and peeling vegetables.*

Mastering these cuts takes time because they are very precise and a lot of skill is involved. Good knife skills are essential for a chef, and practising these cuts is good preparation for developing other knife skills.

Clumsy knife skills and poorly cut vegetables will detract from the presentation of a dish. They could even affect the cooking, as larger pieces will cook more slowly than smaller ones.

Slicing

Slicing is a general term for cutting food with a knife. Vegetables such as onions are usually sliced. If the bulb is whole, slicing across the diameter of the onion will create onion rings. Halving the bulb will produce slices of onion, which are suitable as general garnish, e.g. with steaks.

Slice to the specific size or shape stated in the recipe. Slicing can be done by hand or by a mechanical food processor, depending on the size of the catering outlet.

Trimming

Trimming is the removal of food parts not required for a particular dish. For vegetables this includes peeling, removing the thick stems in the centre of cabbage leaves and removing the outer leaves of a cauliflower.

Grating

Root vegetables and other vegetables of a firm texture may be grated to yield fine strands of the vegetable. Carrots are grated for salads and coleslaw.

A grater is a metal utensil which has a sharp rough surface and is perforated. As a vegetable is passed over this surface, strands of it are shaved through the perforations. Graters come in all shapes and sizes, from hand graters to industrial machinery which will grate large quantities in a short space of time. Food processors normally have grating utensils.

Video presentation

Choosing the right knife and *Sharpening a knife* will give you important background information. *Classic cuts* shows you how these essential cuts are made.
Watch *Preparing and chopping an onion* to see a skilled chef doing this.
Watch *Preparing leeks* for a demonstration of trimming.

Remember!

At all times ensure your own and others' safety. Never use any equipment you have not been trained on how to use.

Figure 9.32 An industrial food processor

Soaking

Pulses are generally dried. They need soaking or reconstituting before cooking. This means soaking them in water to put the water content back into the vegetable to make it soft.

The type of pulse will determine how long it should be soaked for. Usually pulses should be soaked in twice the volume of water to pulses and between 4 and 8 hours.

It is advisable to soak pulses in the fridge as warm temperatures during the soaking process can have an adverse effect on them.

Once pulses have been soaked they should be re-washed, as there will be some sugars in them which are hard to digest.

Coatings and additions

Most fruit and vegetables can be coated. Cauliflower florets can be coated in egg and breadcrumbs and then deep-fried. When served with a tomato sauce this makes the dish Cauliflower portugaise. Apple slices can be battered and then deep fried to make Apple fritters (see page 482). Other ingredients such as nuts, fruit herbs, oils, spices and batters can be added to many vegetable dishes, salads, pulse dishes and some fruit dishes. A duxelle stuffing can be added to tomatoes before they are roasted.

Preserving fruit and vegetables

For more information about the methods see pages 228–230.

Chilling and freezing

Always cover fruit or vegetables to prevent cross-contamination and possible freezer burn. Chilled or frozen fruit and vegetables should be stored near the top of a fridge or in a separate area to prevent cross-contamination.

When soft fruit, e.g. berries, is frozen the berries are frozen individually and very quickly. If you freeze berries at home they take longer to freeze. This means the structure of the fruit is broken so when the fruit is defrosted the fruit collapses and some of the flavour is lost.

Vacuum-packing

Fruit and vegetables can be vacuum-packed.

Bottling and pickling

Bottling fruit lengthens the shelf life of the fruit and in some cases enhances the flavour of the fruit (e.g. sour fruit can be sweetened by being bottled in sweet sugary syrup). The process of bottling is quite simple and means the fruit can be stored in manageable quantities for future use. Fruit is commonly bottled after being cooked in a sweet stock or syrup (see page 489). The high sugar content means that fruit can be preserved for a long period but there are limitations to the use of the fruit afterwards. Boil fruit, add pectin and allow it to cool. Put it into a sterilised jar or bottle with a sealed lid. Fruit suitable for bottling includes apples, apricots, backberries, peaches, plums and cherries. Bottling ensures fruit is available out of season. Fruit can be kept whole or large fruit can be halved or quartered. Vegetables can also be bottled.

Pickling vegetables ensures a longer shelf life, although it does not entirely stop the spoilage process. It enables vegetables to be stored in manageable quantities and also allows additional flavours to be added which infuse into the vegetables from the pickling solution.

Drying

Fruit is dried to make it last longer. The drying process removes most of the moisture which increases the natural sugar content and fruit becomes sweeter. This increase in the sugar content prevents the development of bacteria which would otherwise cause the fruit to deteriorate. Large quantities of fruit can be stored in a relatively small space as the fruit shrinks when dried.

Prunes are dried plums while currants and sultanas are dried grapes. Dried orange peel and cherries can be used in cakes (see Chapter 17). Stoned fruits lose their freshness quickly and so drying is a good preservation method. Vegetables can also be dried. Tomatoes can be tied to strings and dried in the sun.

Figure 9.33 A fruit dehydrator

Dried fruit and vegetables can look drab and the outer skin will be wrinkled but there will still be adequate nutrients.

Dried fruit needs to be soaked in water before use unless the dish does not require it to be soaked or it is supplied ready to eat. Some dried fruit is supplied pre-washed but it is better to wash, pick over and dry it yourself to remove any dirt, stones or stalks.

Canning

Canning fruit or vegetables is a common process. You can buy fruit pie fillings, cooked vegetables, e.g. pulses and beans, and cooked root vegetables, e.g. carrots. Canning keeps the flavour and shape of the fruit and increases its shelf life.

Cooking methods, tools and equipment

Blanching

Blanching is used to kill the enzymes in fruit and vegetables that cause their quality to deteriorate. Blanching can also be used to remove skins from vegetables and nuts.

To blanch fruit and vegetables immerse them in boiling water for between ten seconds and two minutes depending on the type. Remove them from the boiling water and refresh them (make them cool again) by immersing them in iced water or running cold water over them.

Once drained, fruit and vegetables which have been blanched may be stored fresh or frozen for later use or the next stage of preparation.

Over-blanching a fruit or vegetable will cook it for too long and the quality will be affected. If a tomato is blanched for too long the flesh after peeling will be very mushy and unsuitable for use.

Have to hand:
○ a cloth to stop you burning yourself
○ a pan with boiling water
○ a spider or perforated spoon
○ a perforated basket if the quantity is large enough
○ an industrial boiler if the quantity is large enough
○ a container with iced water or cold running water.

Top marks!
Skills such as cutting and piping are important when preparing fruit and vegetables. Good skills reduce wastage. Good skills mean confidence.

How to blanch tomatoes to remove their skins

① Use a paring knife to remove the eye of the tomatoes. Make a cross-incision on the underside of the tomatoes.

② Use a slotted spoon to plunge the tomatoes into boiling water for ten seconds.

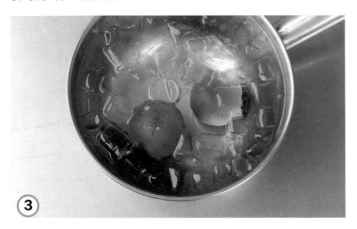

③ Remove the tomatoes and immediately refresh them in a bowl of iced water.

④ When cool, the skin should easily peel away with the help of a paring knife.

Capsicums can also be blanched to remove their skins. Oil rather than water is used because the skins are very tough and difficult to remove. There are three ways to remove the skins:

1 Brush the capsicum with oil and grill it until the skin is black, then peel it off.
2 Deep-fry the capsicum until the skin comes off.
3 Roast the capsicum, then deep-fry it and put it in a plastic bag. The skin will come off.

The equipment needed for blanching capsicums is either a grill or a deep fryer, a spider or perforated spoons, cloths and suitable trays to lay out the vegetables.

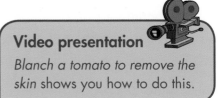

Video presentation

Blanch a tomato to remove the skin shows you how to do this.

Ratatouille

tomatoes	200g
onion, diced	100g
garlic, chopped	hint
green capsicums	100g
red capsicums	100g
olive oil	50ml
herbes de Provence	good pinch
courgettes	200g
aubergines	200g
salt and pepper	to taste
chopped parsley	good pinch
Cooking time	1 hour
Serves	10–12

Method

1 Blanch the tomatoes (see method above). The skin should split for easy removal. Peel off the skin and chop including the seeds.
2 Chop the onion and garlic.
3 Clean the capsicums, cut into small strips.
4 In a large cooking pot with thick bottom, put in olive oil, onions and chopped garlic. Add the capsicum. Cover to keep in the moisture. Cook for 20 minutes, stirring frequently, and add olive oil as necessary to prevent burning.
5 Add the peeled tomatoes and herbes de Provence. Stir well and cook for another 15 minutes.
6 Cut the aubergines and courgettes into chunky bite-size pieces.
7 Add the aubergine and courgettes to the pot. Cook for another 25 minutes.
8 Season to taste and garnish with parsley.

Boiling

Not all vegetables are suitable for boiling, e.g. courgettes have a high water content and will disintegrate if boiled. Vegetables which are suitable for boiling include:

- potatoes
- carrots
- runner beans
- broad beans
- dried pulses, e.g. lentils, beans and peas
- fresh peas

- broccoli
- cauliflower
- beetroot
- Brussels sprouts
- cabbage
- parsnips
- turnip
- swede.

Boiling lowers the nutritional value of the vegetable. Vitamins B and C are commonly found in vegetables. These vitamins dissolve in water and are absorbed into the hot liquid during boiling.

Over-boiling can leave a vegetable limp and lifeless, so correct cooking times are important to ensure a good-quality product. Different types of vegetables have different cooking requirements. For more information see page 220.

Boiling root vegetables and tubers

The flesh of root vegetables and tubers, e.g. potatoes, is firm and dense. The boiling process breaks down the structure of the vegetable, making it pleasant and easy to eat. These types of vegetables should be put into cold water and brought to the boil. They will need boiling for 15–20 minutes. Test them by inserting a sharp implement, e.g. a skewer, into the flesh. It should enter easily. Some root vegetables, e.g. carrots, should not be too soft. They should still be quite firm with a slight crunch.

Remember!
Root vegetables must be cooked in cold water brought to the boil. Green vegetables must be cooked in water that is already boiling.

Definitions
Baton: a cut of a vegetable, evenly sized 2.5cm long × 0.5cm × 0.5cm.
Skim: to remove any surface impurities from a liquid using a spoon or similar implement.

Glazed baton carrots

carrots	600g
butter or margarine	50g
sugar	15g
salt	to taste
chopped parsley	good pinch
Serves	6–8

Method

1 Wash and peel the carrots and cut them into **batons**.
2 Place them in a pan and add the butter, sugar and salt.
3 Add enough water to half cover the carrots.
4 Cover them with a lid until the liquid boils.
5 Remove the lid. **Skim**.
6 Serve in a hot dish, season to taste and sprinkle with chopped parsley.

Boiling stem vegetables

Asparagus is expensive and care must be taken to cook it correctly. The tips cook quicker than the stem so use a special asparagus kettle which boils the stem and steams the tips. If an asparagus kettle is not available, bundle the stems, tie them with string and cook them standing up in a wide pan.

Figure 9.34 An asparagus kettle

Asparagus and prosciutto

fresh asparagus	1kg
salt	5ml
prosciutto, cut into thin slices	250g
parmesan cheese, grated	60ml
butter	200g
Oven temperature	180°C
Cooking time	8–10 minutes
Serves	10

Method

1 Preheat the oven to 180°C.
2 Clean the asparagus, cutting off the tough ends. Add salt to the boiling water. Place the asparagus in the water, cover and cook for five minutes.
3 Lift out with tongs and drain the asparagus on paper towels.
4 Divide the asparagus into bundles, wrap each bundle with two strips of prosciutto, securing with a toothpick or similar implement.
5 Place the asparagus and ham bundles in a greased ovenproof dish and sprinkle with the parmesan cheese.
6 Heat in the oven for three minutes.
7 Melt the butter in a saucepan. Put the bundles on a warm serving plate and pour melted butter over them.

Boiling leaves

Leaf vegetables are less dense and require a much shorter boiling time. They should be added to water that is already boiling and cooked for only a few minutes. This also helps to reduce the amount of vitamins and minerals lost during the cooking process.

Boiling pulses

Pulses are usually cooked by boiling. Red kidney beans must always be boiled for ten minutes to kill off poisonous enzymes contained in them before they are used. Pulses are usually boiled before being made into other dishes, e.g. hummus, fritters and rissoles.

Cooking times for pulses vary:
○ Borlotti beans: 1 hour
○ Haricot beans: 1–1½ hours
○ Broad beans: 1½ hours
○ Lentils: 15–30 minutes
○ Chickpeas: 1–1½ hours
○ Dried peas: 45 minutes
○ Kidney beans: 1 hour
○ Soya beans: 30–45 minutes.

Boiling fruit

Fruit is usually boiled to make jam or other types of preserves. To make fruit compote the fruit is washed, then peeled if necessary. A small amount of liquid is then added. The fruit is boiled so that it softens and breaks down. Soft fruit, e.g. strawberries, take much less time to soften than hard fruit, e.g. apples.

Strawberry jam

strawberries, hulled	1.6 kg
lemon juice	45 ml
sugar	1.4kg
butter	knob
Makes	Approx 2kg

Method

1 Put the strawberries and lemon juice in a large saucepan.
2 Simmer gently for 20–30 minutes, stirring occasionally.
3 Take the pan off the heat. Add the sugar and stir until it dissolves. Add the butter.
4 Bring the mixture to the boil, stirring frequently, for about 20 minutes. Remove any scum with a slotted spoon.
3 Spoon the hot mixture into sterilised jars. Leave a 1cm gap at the top.
4 Put the lid on and store in a cool, dark place.

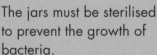

Remember!
The jars must be sterilised to prevent the growth of bacteria.

Steaming

Many vegetables are suitable for steaming. The vegetables that are most often cooked this way are:

○ potatoes
○ carrots
○ cauliflower
○ broccoli
○ asparagus
○ swede
○ turnip
○ Brussels sprouts
○ beans and peas.

Steaming will not colour the vegetables but will enhance their colour as long as they are not overcooked, e.g. broccoli will be greener, carrots will be more orange. For more information see page 221.

Stewing

Most vegetables are suitable for stewing, either on their own or as an accompaniment to meat in meat stews. Root vegetables need longer cooking times than softer vegetables such as aubergines. Care must be taken to ensure the dish is not overcooked. A vegetable curry is a good example of a stewed vegetable dish, as are ratatouille and petits pois français (which is made from peas, lettuce and small onions).

All pulses are suitable for stewing, and chickpea curry is a suitable meat substitute in an Indian restaurant. For more information see page 223.

Healthy eating
Steaming is healthier than any other method of cooking vegetables and pulses.

Remember!
Steam can be extremely dangerous. It can cause severe burns if you do not use equipment correctly.

Top marks!
Well-seasoned vegetables can make the difference between a good and a bad dish. Understand how to season and learn what vegetables require what seasoning to enhance their flavour and give a balanced dish.

Mixed bean curry

dried red kidney beans	50g
dried black-eyed beans	50g
dried haricot beans	50g
dried flageolet beans	50g
vegetable oil	30ml
cumin seeds	5ml
mustard seeds	5ml
cloves of garlic, crushed	2
onion, finely chopped	1
ginger	2.5cm piece
fresh green chillies, chopped	2
curry paste	30ml
chopped tomatoes, canned	400g
tomato purée	30ml
water	250ml
fresh coriander, chopped	30ml
Cooking time	2¼ hours
Serves	10

Method

1 Soak all the beans in water overnight.
2 Drain the beans and put them in a heavy-based saucepan with at least double the volume of cold water.
3 Bring to the boil and boil vigorously for ten minutes, then simmer for 60–90 minutes or until the beans are soft.
4 Heat the oil in a pan and fry the cumin, mustard seed, garlic, onion, ginger and chillies until the onion is soft.
5 Stir in the curry paste.
6 Add the tomatoes, tomato purée and water. Adjust the seasoning and simmer for five minutes.
7 Add the drained beans and coriander. Cover with a lid and simmer for 30 minutes until the sauce has thickened.
8 Serve and garnish with extra coriander.

Top marks!

Portion sizes affect the balance of a meal. The main item can be dominated by too many vegetables or too much potato.

Most fruit is suitable for stewing to eat on its own or as part of a dessert. See the recipe for Fruit compote on page 491 and below.

Rhubarb fool

rhubarb, chopped	455g
light brown sugar	100g
orange, zest and juice	1
whipping cream	360ml
Serves	6–8

Method

1 Put the rhubarb, sugar, orange juice and zest into a large saucepan. Stew until the rhubarb goes soft.
2 Allow the mixture to cool.
3 Whip the cream until soft peaks form.
4 Fold the cream into the fruit mixture.
5 Serve in glasses or coupes.

Gooseberries or strawberries can be used instead of rhubarb.

Frying

Nearly all vegetables are suitable for shallow- or stir-frying. Different vegetables have different textures and cooking times will vary. For more information see pages 223–224.

Top marks!
Use all tools and equipment safely. Health and safety and food hygiene are paramount when preparing and cooking any food. You will gain marks for good procedures and understanding.

Mixed vegetable stir-fry

vegetable oil	15ml
clove of garlic, chopped	1
ginger	2.5cm piece
baby carrots	225g
broccoli florets	350g
asparagus tips	175g
spring onions	125g
green cabbage	175g
light soy sauce	30ml
apple juice	15ml
sesame seeds, toasted	15ml
Cooking time	10 minutes
Serves	4–6

Method

1 Heat the oil in a wok and sauté the garlic over a low heat.
2 Raise the heat. Add the ginger, carrots, broccoli and asparagus tips and stir-fry for four minutes.
3 Add the spring onions and green cabbage and stir-fry for another two minutes.
4 Drizzle over the soy sauce and apple juice and toss over the heat for one to two minutes.
5 Sprinkle the sesame seeds on top and serve.

Courgettes provençale

courgettes	600g
garlic clove	1
olive oil	25ml
chopped tomatoes	300g
salt and pepper	to taste
chopped parsley	
Cooking time	6 minutes
Serves	6–8

Method

1 Wash the courgettes and slice them to 5mm thickness.
2 Crush and chop the garlic.
3 Use olive oil to mask bottom of a heated pan then fry the garlic off with the courgettes. Only a little colour should be achieved.
4 Add the tomatoes and season to taste.
5 Serve sprinkled with chopped parsley.

Top marks!
Even portion sizes willl aid presentation. Make sure your portion sizes are appropriate for the main dish.

Top marks!
Using evenly sized items will improve cooking times. For example, if you are roasting potatoes, any large pieces will take longer to cook than the small pieces.

Deep-frying

The most commonly used deep-fried vegetable is chipped potatoes. Pulses are also deep-fried, e.g. fritters. Tofu can be deep-fried. This improves the flavour if you want to eat it on its own. Tofu is a particularly good source of food (myco-protein) to deep-fry because of its texture. Its texture is very durable and can be cut into appropriate shapes and coated with cornflour easily without losing shape or breaking up. Tofu can be marinated before cooking. It is served with soy sauce. It is very popular in Japan, and can be used as a vegetarian alternative.

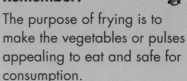

Remember!

The purpose of frying is to make the vegetables or pulses appealing to eat and safe for consumption.

Falafels

dried chickpeas	150g
onion, chopped	1 large
cloves of garlic, chopped	2
parsley, roughly chopped	60ml
cumin seeds	5ml
coriander seeds	5ml
baking powder	2.5ml
vegetable oil	500ml for deep-frying
salt and pepper	to taste
pitta bread	
salad	
natural yoghurt	
Oil temperature	180°C
Cooking time	3 minutes
Serves	approx. 6

1. Soak the chickpeas in a bowl of water overnight.
2. Put the chickpeas in a large pan and cover them with water. Make sure they are covered by 5cm of water.
3. Bring to the boil and boil for ten minutes. Then simmer for 60–90 minutes until soft.
4. Put the chickpeas in a food processor. Add the onion, garlic, parsley, cumin seeds, coriander seeds and baking powder. Process until a fine paste is formed.
5. Shape the paste into walnut-sized balls.
6. Deep-fry in batches.
7. Serve with pitta bread, yoghurt and salad.

Sautéing

This method of frying means cooking quickly in a small amount of hot fat. The food is tossed in the pan so that it browns all over.

Did you know?
The name comes from the French word 'sauter' which means 'to jump'.

Mushroom sauce

onion, chopped	20ml
butter	60g
flour	4 tbsp
salt	½ tsp
beef stock or consommé	500ml
fresh mushrooms, sliced	250g
pepper	$\frac{1}{8}$ tsp
Cooking time	15–20 minutes
Serves	4–6

Method

1 Over a medium to low heat, sauté the onion in three-quarters of the butter.
2 Add the flour and salt, cook the roux until the flour and butter are smooth and blonde.
3 Add the beef stock or consommé, reboiling each time liquid is added to the mixture.
4 Sauté the mushrooms in the remaining butter.
5 Add the mushrooms to the sauce.
6 Bring to a boil once again, adjust seasoning with salt and pepper.
7 Serve immediately.

Lyonnaise potatoes

potatoes	2kg
olive oil	20ml
onions, thinly sliced	4
garlic, chopped	2 tbsp
butter	50g
salt	to taste
ground white pepper	to taste
fresh parsley, finely chopped	1 tbsp
Oven temperature	200°C
Cooking time	10 minutes
Serves	8

Method

1. Peel potatoes and cut into ½-inch slices. Place in a pot and cover with water.
2. Bring to the boil. Allow to boil for 2 minutes, then drain and set aside.
3. Heat a large overproof frying pan over a medium heat. Pour in olive oil, then add onions.
4. Sauté until lightly caramelised, 8 to 10 minutes. Stir in garlic and sauté until onions are deep brown and garlic is soft.
5. Place pan back on stove over a low heat. Melt the butter and sauté the potatoes until they are cooked and have a good golden colour.
6. Add the onions for the last 5 minutes.
7. Bake in a pre-heated oven for 10 minutes.
8. Season with salt and pepper and sprinkle with chopped parsley just before serving.

Grilling

Grilling is a quick cooking process. For more information see page 224. Vegetables are usually brushed with butter or oil to aid the colouring process and to prevent the vegetable from drying out. Your skill and experience are required to identify when vegetables are cooked. Cooking times vary depending on the type and thickness of the vegetable. Suitable vegetables for grilling are:

o mushrooms
o tomatoes
o capsicums
o onions
o aubergines
o pre-prepared potato dishes such as **duchesse potatoes**.

Baking and roasting

Both processes make vegetables and pulses easy to eat and digest and more appealing to the consumer. For more information see page 225. Some vegetables and pulses suitable for roasting and baking are:

o potatoes
o carrots
o capsicums
o parsnips
o lentils (when making a loaf or vegetarian dish).

Remember!
Overcooking vegetable or pulse dishes by grilling will make the food dry out.

Definition
Duchesse potatoes: mashed potato piped onto trays, and then grilled before service.

Did you know?
Vegetables such as courgettes and cucumbers have a high moisture content and will soften rather than become crispy when roasted.

Top marks!
Some fruit and vegetables can be substituted if others are not readily available. Learn what vegetables and fruit complement each other and which can substitute for each other.

Potatoes dauphinoise

mixture of milk and whipping cream	250 ml
salt	¾ tsp
pepper	½ tsp
garlic, minced	1 clove
potatoes	1kg
gruyère cheese, grated	200g
Oven temperature	190°C
Cooking time	45 minutes
Serves	8

Method

1 In a heavy saucepan, combine the milk and cream, salt, pepper and garlic.
2 Bring the liquid to the boil over a medium heat.
3 Immediately remove from the heat. Set aside and keep warm.
4 Peel the potatoes and then using a sharp knife or mandolin, cut into very thin slices.
5 Pour 75ml of the milk mixture into a greased 10-inch (25cm) dish. Layer with half of the potato slices, overlapping slightly. Repeat this layering.
6 Pour remaining milk mixture over the top of the potatoes.
7 Cover the potatoes with gruyère cheese.
8 Bake in the oven for about 20 minutes or until milk mixture starts to bubble up the sides. Using a spatula, press down the potatoes to submerge.
9 Bake for about 25 minutes longer or until potatoes are tender and the top is golden brown.
10 Let the dish stand for 15 minutes before serving.

Investigate!
What country is the dish potatoes dauphinoise associated with?

Remember!
Always use a dry cloth when handling trays from the oven to reduce the risk of burning yourself.

Roast potatoes are a popular dish for Sunday roast lunch. To make roast potatoes, peeled potatoes are covered in oil and put into a hot oven. The oil fries the potatoes while in the oven, producing brown and crispy potatoes ready for the table.

Roast potatoes

potatoes	5kg
oil	75ml
salt	to taste
parsley	for garnish
Oven temperature	190–200°C
Cooking time	60–90 minutes
Serves	10–15

Method

1 Pre-heat the oven.
2 Wash, peel and re-wash the potatoes.
3 Cut the potatoes into even sizes.
4 Fry and colour the potatoes in shallow hot oil.
5 Season the potatoes with salt. Place them on a tray and put them in an oven.
6 Baste the potatoes at regular intervals.
7 When they are soft inside and crisp on the outside, place them in a dish. Sprinkle them with parsley and serve.

Braising

A vegetable dish such as braised celery is started on the top of a stove. The vegetable can be fried to give colour (brown braising) or left as it is (white braising), before being added to a liquid, e.g. white stock or jus-lié (see Chapter 8). The ingredients are brought to the boil, covered with a lid and then placed in an oven.

Vegetables suitable for braising are:

o celery
o onions
o artichokes
o pulses such as chickpeas
o stuffed cabbage
o leeks.

For more information see page 223.

Combination cooking

A cauliflower cheese gratin dish is a good example of combination cooking as it uses two methods of cooking. The cauliflower is boiled, then put in a dish and covered with cheese sauce. It is finished and coloured in the oven or under a grill. For more information see page 226.

Cauliflower cheese

cauliflower	1 whole
butter	25g
plain flour	25g
mustard powder	½ tsp
warm milk	300ml
Cheddar cheese	150g
salt and pepper	to taste
Oven temperature	180–200°C
Cooking time	20–30 minutes
Serves	4–6 depending on size

Method

1 Cut the cauliflower into florets. Cook the cauliflower by boiling or steaming and place it in a dish suitable for the oven.
2 Melt the butter in a pan.
3 Add the mustard powder and flour.
4 Cook into a white roux.
5 Add the warm milk and make sure there are no lumps.
6 Add the grated cheese and stir until smooth. Season to taste.
7 Pour the sauce over the cauliflower and bake it in the oven until a good glaze appears.
8 Sprinkle with chopped parsley and serve.

Holding and serving

Holding vegetables and pulses at the right temperature is very important. The Food Safety Act 1990 states that hot food must be served and held at a temperature of at least 63°C. Cold salads must be served at or below 5°C. These temperatures make sure that potentially harmful bacteria will not multiply and harm the consumer.

If vegetables must be kept warm (e.g. if they are bulk cooked), they can be stored in a thermostatically controlled hot cupboard for no longer than 90 minutes. Ideally, however, food should be served freshly cooked so it is at the optimum temperature of 63°C and above. If the dish is covered in tin foil it will hold heat for a short period.

Test yourself!

1 What are the six traditional French cuts of vegetables?

2 What are root vegetables? What are bulbs? Write descriptions.

3 Which vitamins are water-soluble?

4 What is blanching? What equipment do you need to blanch tomatoes?

5 At what temperature should vegetables be deep-fried?

6 Why must kidney beans be boiled rapidly for ten minutes before use?

7 What particular quality points should you check for in the following vegetables and pulses?
   a Potatoes
   b Radish
   c Mangetout
   d Dried pulses.

8 Identify appropriate cooking methods for the following types of fruit:
   a Banana
   b Pineapple
   c Rhubarb
   d Apple.

9 What is the difference between a cantaloupe melon and a galia melon?

10 Which vitamins are in melons?

11 List four different types of citrus fruit and the dishes that can be made from them.

12 Why is it important to sterilise jars before jam making?

Practice assignment tasks

Prepare fruit and vegetables

Task 1

Produce a table listing up to 20 different types of fruit and 20 different types of vegetable:

○ Write the name of the fruit or vegetable.

○ Add the classification, e.g. soft fruit, root vegetable.

○ Write down the main nutrients.

○ Give examples of how they can be prepared, e.g. peeling, trimming, portioning.

○ Note as many methods of cookery as possible.

○ List the preservation methods.

○ Identify the quality points to look for when purchasing.

○ Note any additional information that you think may be helpful, e.g. place in cold water and bring to the boil.

Task 2

Identify 20 recipes for potatoes and produce a chart outlining:

○ the name of the dish

○ the cookery method(s)

○ additional ingredients used

○ preparation method(s).

Task 3

Identify three vegetarian dishes that use vegetables as the main ingredient and analyse their nutritional content. Make recommendations for how one of these meals can form part of a balanced menu.

Meat and offal

10

This chapter covers the following outcomes from Diploma unit 209: Prepare and cook meat and offal

- o Outcome 209.1 Prepare meat and offal
- o Outcome 209.2 Cook meat and offal

Working through this chapter could also provide evidence for the following Key Skills:

C2.1, C2.2a, C2.2b, C2.3, N, N1.2, N2.2, ICT2.1, ICT2.2, ICT2.3, LP2.1, LP2.2, LP2.3, PS2.1, PS2.2, PS2.3

In this chapter you will learn how to:

Identify the types of meat and offal and their quality points

State the most commonly used joints and cuts of meat and offal and their portion sizes/weights

Describe the methods of preservation and their advantages and disadvantages

Use the correct tools and equipment for preparation and cooking

Use the correct methods and principles to prepare, cook and finish the poultry

Determine when the meat and offal is cooked

Safely store meat and offal

Types of meat

Figure 10.1 Domestically farmed animals

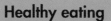
Meat is the flesh of domestic farmed animals. It is taken from the carcass in various cuts and joints. The following types of meat are relevant to your Diploma:

○ beef

○ veal

○ lamb and mutton

○ pork

○ ham

○ bacon.

Beef

Beef is a red meat from cattle. Cattle are usually slaughtered between the ages of 18 months and two years. Different breeds of cattle (Aberdeen Angus, Welsh Blacks, Hereford, Sussex and shorthorn) may be used and the quality of the beef can vary according to the age and type of cattle.

Once the animal is slaughtered, the carcass is hung for between 7 and 21 days. A carcass which has been hung for longer will produce a more tender meat as the natural enzymes within the carcass will start to break down the meat tissue. This hanging process is strictly controlled in both temperature and process and regular checks are carried out so there is no risk to consumers. The outcome is tender meat for cooking.

Figure 10.2 Aberdeen Angus cattle produce high-quality beef

Cuts and joints of beef

The quality of meat varies depending on which part of the **carcass** the meat is taken from. You must know where on an animal a cut of meat is from, as this will have a bearing on how the meat is cooked, as well as its preparation method.

After **slaughter** the head is removed and the carcass is split in half lengthways giving two sides. Figure 10.3 is of a side of beef, showing where the different cuts and joints are to be found.

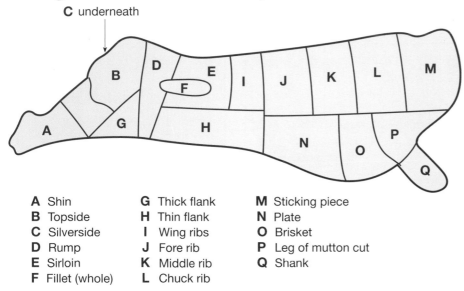

A	Shin	**G**	Thick flank	**M**	Sticking piece
B	Topside	**H**	Thin flank	**N**	Plate
C	Silverside	**I**	Wing ribs	**O**	Brisket
D	Rump	**J**	Fore rib	**P**	Leg of mutton cut
E	Sirloin	**K**	Middle rib	**Q**	Shank
F	Fillet (whole)	**L**	Chuck rib		

Figure 10.3 The different cuts and joints that can be found on a side of beef

The table below gives more information on the cuts and joints from Figure 10.3 that you will use most often. It provides information on cooking methods and suitable portion sizes. Each cut or joint has a distinctive shape. Remember these shapes to help you recognise the different cuts.

Position	Name of cut/ joint	Appearance	Suggested cooking methods	Weight per portion
A	Shin		Boiling, stewing	180g
B	Topside		Roasting, braising, stewing	180–200g
C	Silverside		Roasting, braising, stewing, boiling	180–200g

Definition

Carcass: the dead body of the animal.
Slaughter: the killing of an animal for food.

Healthy eating

Lean cuts of beef (less than 5 to 9 per cent fat), are almost as healthy as a chicken breast. In some cuts such as fillet, beef has only 1g more saturated fat than a skinless chicken breast.

Healthy eating

Beef is extremely high in nutrients, especially vitamins B12 and B6, riboflavin and iron.

D	Rump	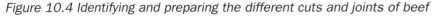	Roasting, braising, grilling, frying	180–360g
E	Sirloin		Roasting, grilling, frying	180–300g
F	Whole fillet, chateaubriand, tournedos, filet mignon		Roasting, grilling, frying	120–360g
G	Thick flank		Braising, stewing	180g
H	Thin flank		Boiling, stewing	180g
J	Fore rib		Roasting	120–210g
O	Brisket		Braising, boiling, stewing	120–210g
Q	Shank		Stewing	120–160g

Figure 10.4 Identifying and preparing the different cuts and joints of beef

Checking beef quality

When checking beef before preparation you must make sure it is of the right quality. A poor-quality piece of meat will inevitably end up as a poor-quality dish. If you are unsure about the quality, always check with your supervisor.

The following points should be considered when checking the quality of beef:

○ It should have a fresh aroma and not smell stale or unpleasant.

○ There should be a sufficient amount of fat in proportion to the meat present.

○ The fat should be smooth and creamy in colour.

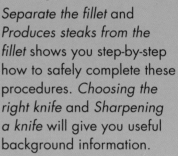

Did you know?

If stored correctly, a well-aged sirloin steak (7–21 days) will be brown rather than the normal red colour, but it will be perfectly safe and extremely tender.

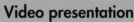

Video presentation

Separate the fillet and *Produces steaks from the fillet* shows you step-by-step how to safely complete these procedures. *Choosing the right knife* and *Sharpening a knife* will give you useful background information.

Top marks!

Are you able to identify which breed of cattle yield the best-quality meet and why? Understanding where your produce comes from – its origins and its suitability for certain dishes – will set you apart from the rest.

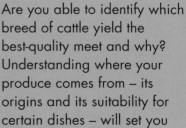

- The meat should be clean and bright in appearance. It should not look slimy.
- Flecks of fat run through some cuts of meat, this is called 'marbling'.
- It should be an appropriate temperature (1–5°C if fresh and –18 to –25°C if frozen) and stored correctly.
- It should be firm and a deep red colour with a sheen.
- It should be the correct cut or joint for the dish you are preparing.

Problems with beef are usually associated with the condition and quality of the meat. Cattle are now subject to rigorous checks by vets prior to slaughter.

Veal

Veal is the flesh of a calf (usually **culled** at three months of age). The meat is classed as white meat and is usually pale pink as the calf's diet is cow's milk. The texture of the meat is fine and lean because of the age of the animal.

Cuts and joints of veal

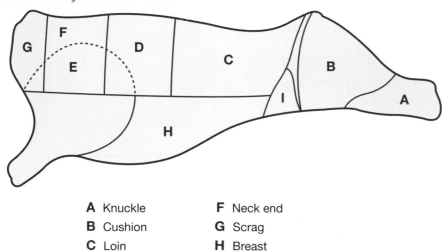

A Knuckle	**F** Neck end
B Cushion	**G** Scrag
C Loin	**H** Breast
D Best end	**I** Thick flank
E Shoulder	

Figure 10.5 The different cuts and joints on a side of veal

The table on page 320 lists the cuts and joints from Figure 10.5 that you will use most often. It provides information on cooking methods and average weights of each cut.

Remember!

Meat may well have a lot of fat or glands on it as well as bones still within the cut or joint, and as the chef you will need to know how to prepare it. Some cuts of meat are expensive, so mistakes can be costly.

Definition

Cull: to kill an animal.

Top marks!

Demonstrate a full understanding of the portion sizes of meat, average weights of joints and best cooking methods – this will enable you to score higher.

Position	Name of cut/joint	Suggested cooking methods	Average weight
A	Knuckle	Boiling, stewing	1–2kg
B	Cushion	Roasting, frying, braising	4–6kg
C	Loin	Roasting, frying, braising, grilling, griddling	4–6kg
D	Best end	Roasting, frying, braising, grilling, griddling	5–7kg
E	Shoulder	Roasting, braising, stewing	3–5kg
F	Neck end	Boiling, stewing	3–4kg
H	Breast	Stewing	2–3kg
I	Thick flank (cutlets)	Roasting, frying, braising	6–8kg

Figure 10.6 Preparing the different cuts and joints of veal

Checking veal quality

Issues regarding selection, quality and potential problems concerning the use of veal are similar to those of beef as the origins are the same (see pages 318–319).

Lamb and mutton

Lamb is meat from domestically farmed sheep which are less than 12 months old. Meat from sheep over the age of 12 months is classed as mutton.

The breed of sheep used for lamb and mutton is varied and can depend on the region. The meat from sheep usually has a delicate, sweet flavour and the flesh can vary in colour from pink to a deep red. The fat is usually quite hard and white in colour.

Lamb can be slaughtered at three different ages. This will have a bearing on the colour and flavour of the meat. The ages are:

○ 30–40 days, weighing 8–10kg
○ 70–150 days, weighing 20–25kg
○ 180–270 days, weighing 30–40 kg.

Mutton can be from rams (male sheep) or ewes (female sheep). Rams produce better quality mutton than the ewes, whose meat is of an inferior, fattier quality. The best quality mutton is taken from a **castrated** ram over 12 months old.

Did you know?
The loin and best end of veal are joints, which are used in the same manner as lamb.

Did you know?
Lamb or mutton generally has a higher fat content than beef. Its calorific value can be as much as 250 calories per 100g of meat.

Healthy eating
Lamb and mutton are a rich source of protein and vitamin B12.

Definition
Castrated: testes removed before sexual maturity.

Cuts and joints of lamb

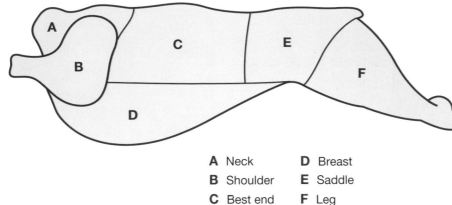

A Neck   D Breast
B Shoulder   E Saddle
C Best end   F Leg

Figure 10.7 The different cuts and joints on a side of lamb

The table below identifies the cuts and joints from Figure 10.7. It provides information on cooking methods (which are explained later) and average weights of each cut.

Position	Name of cut/joint	Appearance	Suggested cooking methods	Average weight
A	Neck		Boiling, stewing	0.5–1kg
B	Shoulder		Roasting, braising, stewing	3–5kg
C	Best end		Roasting, braising, stewing	2–3kg
D	Breast		Roasting, stewing	1–2kg
E	Saddle		Roasting, grilling, frying	3–5kg
F	Leg	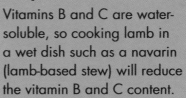	Roasting, grilling, frying	3–5kg

Figure 10.8 Identifying and preparing the different cuts and joints of lamb

321

Checking lamb quality

Prior to preparing lamb, its suitability and quality should be checked. Consider the following:

○ It should have a fresh aroma and not smell stale or unpleasant.

○ There should be a sufficient amount of fat in proportion to the meat present.

○ The fat should be smooth, creamy in colour and brittle (flaky).

○ The meat should be a dull red colour, with a clean appearance and no slimy exterior.

○ It should be at an appropriate temperature (1–5°C if fresh and –18 to –25°C if frozen) and stored correctly.

○ It should be the correct cut or joint for the dish you are preparing.

Chef's tip

Lamb and mutton do have a high fat content and consequently you may need to regularly skim the fat from the top of a dish such as an Irish stew.

Pork

Pork is a very popular meat taken from pigs. It is consumed in vast quantities throughout Europe. Other products such as ham and bacon are also produced from pork meat.

Male pigs are known as boars, females as sows and piglets as suckling pigs. A pig is usually slaughtered at the age of 10–12 months. Pigs are usually intensively fattened. The yield of meat from the carcass is generally quite high. Domesticated pigs for farming have shorter legs and a stockier appearance than wild pigs. There are many different breeds of pig farmed for their meat. The most common are the white Yorkshire, western white, Danish Landrace and Belgian Pietrain.

Healthy eating

Pork is high in protein. Nutrients such as the B vitamins and other minerals such as zinc are evident in pork.

Cuts and joints of pork

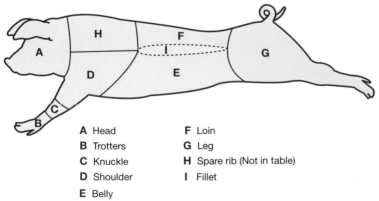

A Head   **F** Loin
B Trotters   **G** Leg
C Knuckle   **H** Spare rib (Not in table)
D Shoulder   **I** Fillet
E Belly

Figure 10.9 The different cuts and joints on a side of pork

Top marks!

Know about food fashions. Are today's restaurants serving traditional meat cuts such as shoulder of lamb or pork loin, or more diverse cuts such and cheek and offal? Knowing what is popular will set you apart and able to gain top marks.

The table below identifies the cuts and joints from Figure 10.9 that you will use most often. It provides information on cooking methods and weights of cuts and joints.

Position	Name of cut/joint	Appearance	Suggested cooking methods	Average weight
A	Head		Boiling	2–3kg
B	Trotters		Boiling	0.5kg
C	Knuckle		Boiling	1–2kg
D	Shoulder		Roasting, boiling	7–9kg
E	Belly		Roasting, boiling	2–3kg
F	Loin		Roasting, grilling, frying	4–6kg
G	Leg		Roasting, boiling	6–8kg
I	Fillet		Roasting, grilling, frying	0.5–1kg

Figure 10.10 Identifying and preparing the different cuts and joints of pork

Checking pork quality

The following quality points should be checked before using a piece of pork:

○ It should be lean and pale pink.
○ There should not be any slimy residue on the exterior of the meat.
○ The smell should be pleasant and not overpowering.

Remember!

Care must be taken when handling pork as it may contain harmful parasitic worms, and other harmful bacteria. The threat of **cross-contamination** is ever present if you do not use the correct skills when preparing and cooking pork. Washing your hands is essential after handling pork as the bacteria can infect any cuts or abrasions you may have on your hands.

Definition

Cross-contamination: the transfer of harmful bacteria from one food source to another by the food handler using the same equipment for different tasks, not cleaning their tools properly or not washing their hands before handling another food type.

- The fat should be evenly spread over the meat joints, but not in excess.
- The skin is very tough and this should be smooth and free from coarse hairs.
- It must have been stored correctly prior to use, either in a fridge (at the bottom to prevent any blood dripping onto other food) or in a freezer.
- It should be at an appropriate temperature (1–5°C if fresh and −18 to −25°C if frozen) and stored correctly.
- It should be the correct cut or joint for the dish you are preparing.

Ham

Ham is usually a cured and cooked prime leg of pork (e.g. York ham). Some hams can be eaten raw after they have been cured, e.g. Parma and Serrano ham. A curing or preserving process is applied to ham before cooking.

Gammon is a type of ham, but here the leg is not removed from the carcass until brining cures the carcass.

These are the different curing or preserving processes:
- Brining: injecting a salty liquid solution into the joint.
- Dry cure: rubbing a dry salt mixture onto the joint.
- Smoking: hanging in a room over a slow-burning regulated wood fire.

The time taken to cure the meat is usually three days, but this can vary depending on the type of ham required and whether the ham is to be eaten raw.

Figure 10.12 What sort of curing process is being used here?

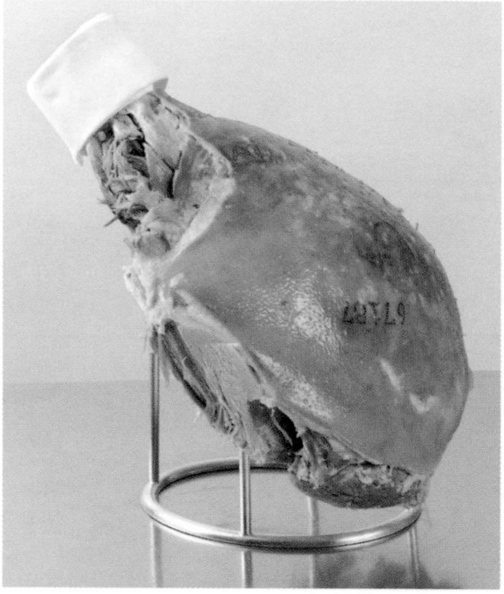

Figure 10.11 A York ham on a ham stand

> **Definition**
> **Curing**: the process of salting or smoking ham. The process varies depending on whether the ham is to be eaten cooked or raw.

> **Chef's tip**
> Make sure you soak ham in water to extract the excess salt from the meat before cooking.

Checking ham quality

The quality points to be considered for ham are the same as for pork (see pages 323–324) except that ham is ready to eat.

Bacon

Bacon usually comes from a large pig bred specially to produce bacon called a 'baconer'. The meat is cured (salted in brine) or smoked. There are two types of bacon: green, which is usually unsmoked bacon, and smoked. Bacon is usually cooked by frying and grilling but if kept in larger joints, as opposed to rashers, it can be boiled.

Cuts of bacon

There are usually four cuts from a baconer pig: back bacon, streaky bacon, middlecut bacon and gammon steaks. Back bacon is cut from the loin of the pig, while streaky is cut from the belly. Middlecut bacon is from the loin and the belly.

Checking bacon quality

Consider the following points:

- Streaky bacon has a higher fat content than back bacon because it is taken from the belly.
- Bacon should be firm to touch and dark pink.
- It should not be slimy to touch.
- It should not have an unpleasant smell.
- The fat should normally be creamy, but smoking can give the fat a brown tint.

Types of offal

Offal is the edible organs and parts taken from domestic farm animal carcasses. It is usually cooked in the same way as meat. The following types of offal are relevant to your Diploma:

- oxtail
- kidney
- heart
- tongue
- liver
- sweetbread
- pig's trotters.

Figure 10.13 a oxtail, b kidney, c heart, d tongue, e liver

You will need to know what parts of the animal offal comes from, as this will have a bearing on how the offal is prepared and cooked.

Investigate!   Worksheet 20

Find out about other types of offal, e.g. ox tongue and lamb hearts.
How big are they? How much do they weigh? How are they cooked?
Find a recipe for each type.

Liver

Liver is taken from many different types of animal and can be
cooked in a variety of ways, but it is usually fried, grilled or braised.
The size of the liver varies depending on the size of the animal
which it comes from. Calf's liver is the most popular type, followed
by lamb's liver. Ox liver is also used, but it is lower in quality and
has a much stronger flavour. Pig's liver is also used, but generally in
braised dishes and pâtés.

Checking liver quality

The following quality points should be checked before using a piece
of liver:

o It can deteriorate quite quickly if not stored correctly, so it is
   important that it is stored at the correct temperature (see Pork
   quality on page 324 for temperatures).

o It should be deep red, have a clean appearance and smell pleasant.

o Signs of discoloration, bad smells and a slimy appearance are
   indicators of poor quality.

Kidney

Kidneys are organs which vary in size depending on the animal from
which they are taken. Calf's kidneys are the best quality. Lamb's and
pig's kidneys are also good. Ox kidneys are used, but these take longer
to cook and need to be blanched before cooking. See page 222. The
usual cooking methods for kidneys are frying, grilling and braising.

Checking kidney quality

Consider the following points when selecting a kidney:

o It should be clean, reddish brown and have a pleasant aroma.

o The kidney should not feel slimy.

o The kidney should be below 5°C prior to preparation.

o If encased in fat the fat should be a creamy colour.

Remember!
Offal may have a lot of fat or
glands on it as well as bones
left inside it, and as the chef
you will need to know how to
prepare it.

Healthy eating
Liver has a high level of
vitamins and minerals
especially vitamins A, B and
C, and iron.

Did you know?
Liver is at its best if cooked
and served pink.

Healthy eating
Kidney is high in vitamins
A and K and has a strong
flavour.

Heart

Heart is another popular type of offal. Lamb's, calf's, pig's and cow's hearts are all acceptable for cooking. Lamb's heart is the smallest and most popular. Cow's heart can be five or six times larger.

To prepare hearts, first wash them thoroughly. Next, trim away any excessive fat, blood vessels, connective tissue and tubes as these have an unpleasant texture. Finally, soak them in salt water to ensure the finished dish will be of good quality. Lamb's and calf's hearts are moist and tender and can be grilled or sautéed. Be careful not to overcook them or you will make them tough. Cow's and pig's hearts are larger and should be braised or stewed. Hearts can be served whole and stuffed, sliced or diced.

Checking heart quality

When checking hearts for quality consider the following points:
- They should be dry.
- They should have a good aroma.
- There should not be any blemishes or signs of damage.
- Hearts should not be surrounded by excessive amounts of fat.

Oxtail

Oxtail can weigh 1–2 kg. It is usually skinned and cut into short lengths for cooking. Oxtail is a gelatinous meat and needs to be cooked slowly; it is usually stewed or braised. It is commonly used as an ingredient in soups. It can also be cooked and flaked then combined with other ingredients, e.g. prunes and a wine jus, then topped with potato. Oxtail can even be served in sections so customers have to separate the meat themselves. These latter two dishes are very rustic.

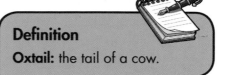

Definition
Oxtail: the tail of a cow.

Checking the quality of oxtail

These are the points to consider when checking the quality of oxtail:
- There should be a good proportion of lean meat, with a layer of firm white fat.
- The tail should be a good weight, approximately 1–1.5kg.
- It should have a fresh aroma and clean, dry appearance.

Tongue

The tongues of animals such as cows, sheep, and pigs are often cooked. The size of the tongue varies depending on the animal from which it came. Cow's and lamb's tongues are the most common and they are frequently boiled in a simple vegetable stock. A pig's tongue normally comes as part of the head but if you wanted it separately you could specify this to a butcher.

Pressed ox tongue is a popular and traditional dish, which is usually served cold with salads and pickles. It can also be braised and boiled and served with highly seasoned sauces such and piquant and charcutière.

Soak tongues in water for a couple of hours before boiling them. If the tongue has been bought already salted (see page 230) soak it for 4–5 hours before boiling. After cooking the tongue, you need to remove the skin and may also press it. Tongue is popular served cold and thinly sliced. (See the recipe on page 345.)

Checking tongue quality

Consider the following points when selecting a tongue:
- The tongue should be clean and have a fresh odour.
- It should be free from damage.
- Its weight should be appropriate to the type of animal it came from: lamb's tongue should weigh approximately 225g and cow's tongue should weigh 1.8–3kg.

Pig's trotters

The tenderness and delicious flavour of cooked pig's **trotters** makes them a delicacy, a tradition which began in France in the eighteenth century. Clean pig's trotters thoroughly before cooking; then boil or braise and simmer them for up to 6 hours.

Definition
Trotter: a pig's foot.

Sweetbreads

Sweetbreads are the throat and pancreas glands of calves and lambs. Lamb's sweetbreads are usually an average weight of 100g. Calf sweetbreads can weigh as much as 500g.

Healthy eating
Sweetbreads are a very good source of protein.

Checking the quality of sweetbreads

These are the points to consider when checking the quality of sweetbreads:

○ They are usually creamy white.
○ They should be soft to touch, dry and clean.
○ A good aroma is a sign of quality.

> **Investigate!** Worksheet 21
>
> Find out and record why vitamins B6, B12, C and the minerals iron, riboflavin, zinc and protein are important for health and which types of meat and offal contain them.

Preparing meat and offal dishes

Preparation methods

The table below lists the most popular cuts for each type of meat or offal.

Meat or offal	Cut or joint
Beef	Dice, steaks, strips
Veal	**Escalopes**, cutlets
Lamb	Leg, cutlets, chump chops, shoulder
Mutton	Dice
Pork	Chops, cutlets, dice, leg, loin
Bacon	Rashers, gammon
Ham	Slices
Kidney	Sliced, diced
Liver	Sliced
Sweetbreads	Sliced, pressed
Hearts	Whole, sliced, diced
Oxtail	In jointed pieces
Trotters	Whole
Tongue	Sliced

Figure 10.14 Popular cuts of meat and offal

> **Definition**
> **Escalopes**: large slices of veal cut from the leg and flattened before cooking.

> **Top marks!**
> Good clean butchery skills carried out safely will assist your progress in this qualification. Ensure you do not have too much wastage when trimming, boning and slicing meat and offal. Wastage in excess can cost a business money.

Cutting

It is essential that the correct knife and equipment is used and that you observe safe working procedures.

Ask yourself:
- Have I been trained to cut this food item?
- Do I know what to do next? (If not, ask!)
- Have I got the right knife?
- Is my knife sharp enough?
- Am I using the correct board?
- Am I dressed correctly?
- Have I selected the right equipment?
- Is my workstation tidy and suitable to prepare the food?

If your answer is 'Yes' to all of the above questions, it is safe to proceed.

In most cases a red chopping board is used for raw meat and the knife could be a red 7-inch boning knife, 10-inch chef's knife or 12-inch steak knife. Generally, you will need a knife with a sturdy blade so that it does not move when you are cutting the meat, as this could cause an accident. For slicing and dicing you will need a knife with a large heel.

Boning

Boning enables meat to be presented better and carved more easily. It creates a cavity which can be stuffed to add flavour. There are two type of boning: **external boning** and **tunnel boning**. Following external boning the cavity is filled and the joint tied to form a good shape. Tunnel boning is a more delicate and complex method.

How to tunnel bone the thigh bone from a leg of lamb

1 Find the H bone. This is part of the pelvic bone at the top of the leg of lamb.
2 Cut around the H joint at the top of the leg.
3 Separate the H joint from the ball joint and remove it.
4 Cut around the exposed ball joint.
5 Holding the knife almost flat against the bone, scrape and cut to ease the flesh away from the bone. As you do this, turn the leg inside out to make it easier.

Remember!
Make sure you use the correct knife and chopping board for the procedure, that your work space is clean and tidy and your hands are washed prior to cooking.

Remember!
Always cut away from yourself for safety reasons.

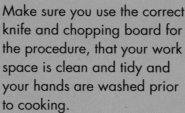

Definition
Boning: to remove the bones from a joint of meat.
External boning: to remove bones by cutting through the skin to expose the flesh and bone and then to cut away the bone from the meat.
Tunnel boning: to remove the bones from a bird or joint by cutting the flesh away from the bone without cutting through the skin.

Remember!
Take great care when boning meat. Boning is a skilled task that uses specialist knives. Lack of attention could result in cuts or a more serious injury.

6 Turn the meat back on itself so the skin is facing outwards again. There should not be any damage to the exterior of the joint as this will spoil the appearance.

7 Stuff and tie the joint. See pages 338 and 339.

Dicing

Meat which is off the bone can be diced. The meat or offal is cut into square cubes or evenly sized pieces to allow it to cook evenly.

Video presentation
Slice and dice chuck steak shows this being done.

How to dice beef

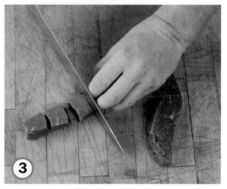

1 Use a 10-inch chef's knife. Cut across the beef (here a thick flank) to leave thick slices. You can trim off the end of each slice to neaten it.

2 Cut each slice into strips. Trim the end of each strip to make a neat square end.

3 Cut each strip into dice. Ensure they are evenly sized. Store on a tray and refrigerate until required.

Dicing is appropriate for dishes such as beef casseroles, navarins and blanquettes, where the meat is usually of a poorer quality and therefore requires longer cooking, e.g. braising, stewing and boiling.

Offal does not often need to be diced, but if it does, the process is the same.

Slicing

Slicing means to cut across a piece of meat or offal. Carving is a method of slicing cooked meat for presentation. If you cannot slice the meat correctly, then your final dish will not have the best presentation possible. Slicing is usually carried out by hand, but an electric slicer can be used for cooked, slightly frozen or raw meats.

Figure 10.15 Sliced kidney and sliced liver

Slicing meat requires patience and skill. The meat or offal may be raw or cooked. In either case you must hold your knife and the food firmly. You must use the correct knife and it must be sharp.

The carving knife should not be serrated as that could tear the meat. You should carve away from yourself for safety. Holding the joint firmly on a secure carving board will aid you when serving the customer and helps in maintaining a professional image.

How to slice ham off the bone

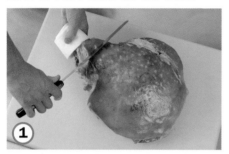

1 Cut straight across the neck of the joint near the bone.

2 Slice off the outer skin and excess fat.

3 Turn the board 180°. Cut the meat across the joint towards the bone.

4 Arrange the slices on a plate as you cut them.

5 Continue slicing until you reach the bone.

6 When you reach the bone turn the ham over and slice the other side.

Portioning

Portioning means cutting meat into the correct size, weight or shape during preparation or for it to be served. The correct size and amount depends on the dish. Slicing up a sirloin into individual steaks is portioning the meat.

The term is also used if carving cooked roasted meat, pies and other meat dishes before service. By cutting the cooked dish into servings (portions) a guaranteed **yield** of that dish is achieved.

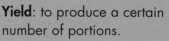

Definition

Yield: to produce a certain number of portions.

332

Portion sizes depend on the commodity. For example:

○ A portion of carved roast lamb leg should weigh approximately 120–150g.

○ A grilled rump steak would be one per portion as the steaks were pre-cut.

○ Sliced liver fried with bacon and onions may be portioned so that each customer has three slices per portion.

Trimming

Trimming means cutting away bone, excess fat, sinew, connective tissue or glands. Trimming improves the presentation of the meat or offal.

You must observe the following safe working procedures:

○ Ensure your workplace is clean and tidy.

○ Use a red chopping board for raw meat.

○ Use a 10-inch chef's knife.

○ Always cut away from yourself to avoid accidents if the knife slips.

○ Have a container ready to put the trimmings into and a dish to put the finished product into.

Beef has the skin removed, but sometimes there is a lot of fat lying around or in the meat which needs to be removed. Sirloin has a large area of sinew under the fat layer and above the meat layer. This fat and sinew must be removed. This process can be a little time-consuming as it is important to complete this task correctly, safely and without losing excess amounts of quality meat.

How to remove the fat and sinew from a sirloin

Chef's tip

The advantage of portioning your meat or offal before cooking is that you have a guaranteed number of servings for cooking and have enough food to feed everyone.

Remember!

Some trimmings may be suitable for stock, so do not just throw your trimmings in the bin.

Healthy eating

If fat is trimmed from meat it can make it a healthier option.

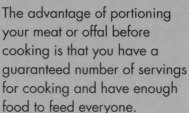

Video presentation

Trim a best end of lamb shows shows you more skills.

(1) This is the underside of the sirloin. The thick outer layer of fat is removed from the sirloin to reveal the sinew tight to the flesh.

(2) Using the point of a boning knife, lift and cut away the sinew. With the blade pointing upwards at a 45° angle, you will ensure only the sinew is removed. Push away the chain from the meat using your thumb. Cut the chain off.

Turn the meat over. Lift the end of the fat with your fingers. Slice the fat away with a sawing motion.

The trimmed sirloin.

How to trim liver

Liver varies in size. It is surrounded by a fine, transparent membrane which should be removed, because if it is left on during the cooking process it will shrink. The liver may also have some small glands (green or brown jelly-like spheres) and tubes or gristle. These should also be removed before cooking. After trimming liver should be cut into even thin slices – cut at a slant or angle. This is to ensure consistent cooking.

Video presentation

Prepare a whole lamb's liver shows you how to trim and slice a liver. Also watch *Prepare a chicken liver.*

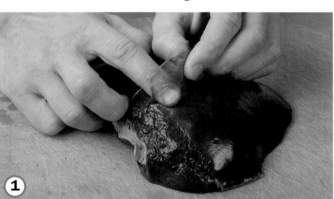

Use your fingers to remove the membrane without damaging the liver.

Remove excess fat, glands or valves. You will be left with a deep red liver with a soft gelatinous texture.

How to trim kidneys

Kidneys are usually cut through the centre to expose the white core, which must be removed. If large enough, they can be sliced thinly before cooking. Like liver, kidneys are surrounded by a membrane, which if left on during the cooking process will shrink, so this should be removed. They may also have some small glands (green or brown jelly-like spheres) and tubes or gristle, all of which should also be removed before cooking.

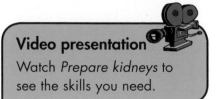

Video presentation

Watch *Prepare kidneys* to see the skills you need.

Pressing

Sweetbreads are usually blanched before cooking by bringing them to the boil. They are then washed, dried and pressed before being cooked. Calves' sweetbreads are sometimes passed through flour, egg and breadcrumbs then shallow-fried. Tongue is often pressed before being sliced thinly. You can press several at once. See the recipe on page 344.

Mincing

Mincing means passing meat or other ingredients through a piece of equipment which cuts and grinds the product into a fine texture. Mincing meat enables cheaper cuts of meat to be used and cooked using quick cookery methods, such as grilling or frying.

Minced meat can vary in quality depending on fat content of the meat and the cut of meat minced. Minced fillet steak for steak tartare is high-quality and low in fat compared to other cuts.

Mincing or grinding is used to make sausages. The meat is finely minced and then blended with other ingredients to make sausagemeat. Sausage skins are then filled with sausagemeat.

Another word for minced meat is forcemeat, as the meat is forced through a mincing machine, changing its appearance and texture.

Minced offal, e.g. liver, is used to make pâté and faggots. Pâté is smooth or coarse depending on how finely the offal is ground.

Skinning

Pork and bacon have a very tough skin, which is usually scored (for crackling) or removed to expose the fat layer beneath, which is in turn removed to an acceptable level. To remove the skin from a pork loin you need a sturdy firm-bladed knife. The process is the same as removing the fat from a sirloin of beef, but the pork fat is tougher.

Figure 10.16 Minced beef

Video presentation
Now watch *Prepare pâté from minced liver.*

Definition
Faggot: a type of meatball made from pork, pork liver, onion and breadcrumbs.

Try this!
Rather than throwing away the skin from the pork loin, replace it over the skinned loin when roasting as it keeps the pork moist and the skin crisps into a tasty accompaniment.

Video presentation
Watch *Prepare sweetbreads* to find out more.

How to remove the skin from a pork loin

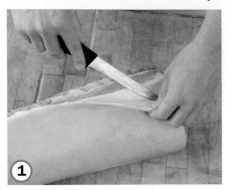

1 Keep the knife blade away from you and make a cut to separate the skin from the fat.

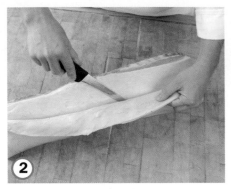

2 Remove the skin by cutting across the horizontal loin. Use gentle sweeping motions.

3 At the edge make sure you cut away only skin and not meat. The bone edges give you a clear cutting guide. Do not remove too much fat as this aids the cooking process and keeps the meat moist.

Coating

Coating can be as simple as covering a piece of liver in seasoned flour during preparation. It can also refer to covering meat, e.g. a veal escalope, in flour, egg and breadcrumbs to meet the requirements of a dish.

Coating with seasoned flour

This is commonly done when preparing pieces of offal for cooking, e.g. liver and kidneys. Each piece of meat or offal is dipped in a dish of seasoned flour, then the excess is shaken off. The flour helps to give colour to the meat or offal when it is fried.

Coating with flour, egg and breadcrumbs

Nearly all types of meat and offal can be coated in flour or breadcrumbs. The dish requirements will dictate whether or not this is necessary. Before you begin have ready three separate bowls: one bowl of well-seasoned flour, one bowl of beaten egg and one bowl of fine breadcrumbs. You should always follow the process below to make sure that the meat or offal is evenly coated.

Video presentation

Coat goujons of plaice demonstrates these skills but uses fish rather than meat.

How to coat a pork escalope with seasoned flour, beaten egg and breadcrumbs

1 Coat the pork with seasoned flour.

2 Gently pat the pork to remove the excess.

3 Put the pork in the beaten egg. Make sure it is completely covered.

4 Allow the excess to run off. Clean your hands.

5 Put the pork in the breadcrumbs. Ensure it is well coated. Gently pat off the excess.

6 Put the breadcrumbed portion on a suitable tray until it is required for cooking.

Once the meat or offal has been coated, it must be cooked fairly soon or the coating will become soggy. Do not stack portions of breadcrumbed products on top of each other as they may stick together and affect the appearance of the coating. Use greaseproof paper to layer many portions of coated meat or offal.

Coating meat in flour, egg and breadcrumbs helps it to remain moist during cooking, as it is sealed within a crispy coating, e.g. pork schnitzels.

Stuffing

Stuffing meat adds to its flavour, appearance and texture. Stuffing is added to the meat during the preparation stage. Ingredients such as meat, vegetables, rice and even fruit can be used for stuffing.

Video presentation
Watch *Stuff a belly of pork* to see this in action.

How to stuff a pork belly

Before you begin make light cuts in two-thirds of the skin to improve the flavour of the finished product. Trim the belly to form a square.

Trim to remove any excess fat.

Make the stuffing into a sausage shape. Put it in along the centre of the meat and spread it out.

Start to roll the meat around the stuffing.

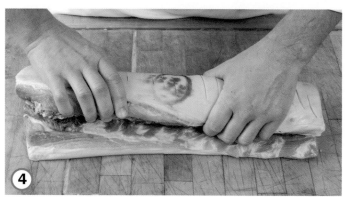

Continue to roll. The skin with the light cuts in it should be uppermost. Tuck the uncut skin inside the cut skin.

The equipment and tools used to stuff meat are:

○ Suitable knife

○ Chopping board

○ Piping bag to fill cavities in the meat (optional)

○ Spoons to prevent unnecessary handling of stuffing

○ String to tie the joint

○ Gloves

Before stuffing meat, it is important to check the quality of the product. If necessary, wash and dry the meat before stuffing. The stuffing or filling should always be at the correct temperature, which is 1–5°C. The meat should also be at this temperature. If possible, do not handle the filling – use a piping bag or spoon.

Offal, e.g. hearts and kidneys can also be stuffed. Pig's and cow's hearts are often stuffed and braised.

Tying

Tying holds meat joints or offal together before cooking, e.g. roast topside of beef, boned leg of lamb, stuffed pork loin, hearts or kidneys. Tying the meat joint with butcher's string means it retains its shape during cooking, especially if the meat joint is stuffed. Untied, the stuffed joint would fall apart and the quality of the dish would be affected. Strands should be tied about a thumb's width apart. Tying a joint also provides you with a guide to portion sizes and portions will not fall apart. Do not tie the meat too tight. If you do, the juices from the meat will be forced out during cooking and leave the meat dry.

How to tie a stuffed pork belly

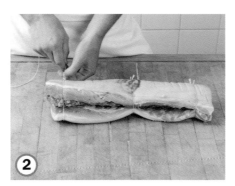

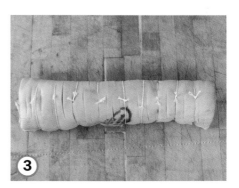

① Pass butcher's string under the meat in the middle and tie a simple slip knot. The string should be quite loose. Cut the string.

② Tie a string at each end. These should be a little tighter.

③ Fill in with more strings approximately a thumb's width apart. Keep the knots aligned as it is easier to remove the string afterwards.

Flavouring meat and offal

Various flavourings can be added to complement dishes. See pages 231–2 for more information.

Seasoning

Meat and offal are usually seasoned before cooking during the preparation stage.

If the meat you are preparing is for a wet cooking method, e.g. a casserole, navarin (a rich slow-cooked lamb or mutton stew) or blanquette (a French stew made from white meat, e.g. veal, lamb or poultry), the meat should be seasoned before cooking but the overall seasoning of the dish should be adjusted after cooking when all the flavours have combined.

Marinating

Meat or offal can be left in a marinade for varying lengths of time. It should be covered completely by the marinade.

Wrapping and topping

Meat and offal can be topped with or wrapped in puff pastry and baked in the oven. Short pastry can be used to make pies, e.g. chicken pie or mince and onion pie. Suet pastry can be used to line pudding basins and then to top raw beef steak and kidneys to make steak and kidney pudding. Mashed potato can be used to top minced beef to make cottage pie or minced lamb to make shepherd's pie.

Storage

Meat and offal, especially pork, can contain harmful bacteria and parasitic worms. This means that prepared meat or offal must be stored correctly before, during and after preparation:

○ Ensure that raw meat or offal is stored at the bottom of a refrigerator. This will prevent any blood or liquid dripping onto other food.

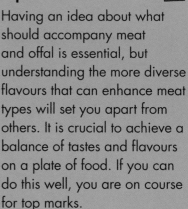

Top marks!

Having an idea about what should accompany meat and offal is essential, but understanding the more diverse flavours that can enhance meat types will set you apart from others. It is crucial to achieve a balance of tastes and flavours on a plate of food. If you can do this well, you are on course for top marks.

Did you know?

The term **marinade** comes from the Latin word *marinus*, which means marine (sea) and refers to the salt water used to preserve food for Roman sailors.

Figure 10.17 Always store your meat safely at the bottom of the fridge to avoid contaminating other food

- Clearly label the meat which has been prepared. The label should include the date so that it is possible to determine its shelf life.
- Store prepared meat and offal at 1–5°C.
- Do not stack prepared pieces of meat on top of each other as it can affect the appearance and quality of the end product. Food poisoning by cross-contamination can be caused if one meat is mixed with another type.

Preserving meat and offal

For more information about the processes see pages 228–230.

Preserving methods

Chilling and freezing

Meat and offal to be frozen should be labelled and covered to prevent cross-contamination and possible freezer burn. Chilled meat and offal should be stored near the bottom shelf of a refrigerator to prevent cross-contamination.

Vacuum-packing

Meat and offal can be vacuum-packed.

Smoking

This method is used to preserve meat such as pork. The pork is heated gently by a fire to dry and preserve it. Chicory wood chips, for example, are burned to give it a strong smoky flavour.

Canning

Meat and offal pie fillings are often canned.

Salting

This is one of the oldest methods of preserving meat for the winter. This is a cheap, easy and effective way to preserve meat but it makes it extremely salty.

Saltpetre is the common name for potassium nitrate. These small white crystals have been used to preserve raw and cooked meat for hundreds of years. Saltpetre can be mixed with salt to preserve meat. It taints meat pink through **oxidisation**. Saltpetre is harmful on its own and production is strictly regulated.

Pickling

Cooked and processed meat such as pork is often stored in brine.

Cooking and finishing meat and offal

Cooking methods

After meat or offal has been prepared it is important that the correct cooking method is used to ensure a quality dish. The cooking method chosen will depend on the dish required. A chef must work in a safe manner and use the correct tools, techniques and methods. The temperature of cooked meat and offal is also very important, as it will have a bearing on the quality of the served dish. Food safety may be at risk if meat or offal are not cooked to the correct temperature.

For more information see page 81.

Boiling

Tougher cuts of meat are normally boiled or cooked by other wet methods. Boiling is a simple process and does not require a lot of skill, although there is a need to **skim** the liquid to remove impurities and fat.

Boiling foods means that a lot of nutrients will be lost as they are water soluble. However, as the liquid may be used or consumed with the meat not all these nutrients will be wasted.

Definition
Oxidise: the chemical reaction that occurs when oxygen is mixed with another substance.

Remember!
Wet cooking methods are used for tough fibrous meats or offal.
Dry cooking methods are used for tender cuts of meat and offal.

Remember!
Before using any cooking equipment, ensure you are trained and competent to use it. If you have any problems with equipment or the ingredients to be cooked, always consult with your supervisor, head chef or line manager.

Figure 10.18 Boiling is a wet method of cooking meat using liquids like water or stock

The table lists cuts of meat and offal that are most often boiled.

Meat or offal	Cut or joint
Beef	Shin, thin flank
Pork	Trotters, cheeks, belly, gammon, ham
Lamb	Shin, shanks
Mutton	All cuts
Offal	Kidneys and sweetbreads

Figure 10.19 Cuts of meat and offal suitable for boiling

Cooking times are determined by the cut of meat and the dish to be cooked. Always refer closely to the menu or recipe; if you are unsure ask your line manager, head chef or supervisor.

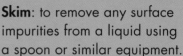

Definition

Skim: to remove any surface impurities from a liquid using a spoon or similar equipment.

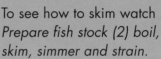

Video presentation

To see how to skim watch *Prepare fish stock (2) boil, skim, simmer and strain.*

Boiled bacon

piece of gammon or collar

carrots	2 medium
onions	2 medium
bay leaf	1
black peppercorns	4
parsley or onion sauce to garnish	
Cooking time	depends on size; 2kg would take 60–80 minutes
Serves	12–14

Method

1 Weigh the joint to calculate cooking time. Put in a pan of water and bring to boil. Drain off the liquid (this removes excess salt).
2 Place the joint in a large saucepan with the other ingredients, cover with cold water and bring to the boil. Keep removing any scum that forms at the surface of the liquid.
3 When cooked, cool slightly before removing the rind.
4 Serve hot and sliced with parsley or with onion sauce as an accompaniment.

Creamed sweetbreads

sweetbreads	450g
onion	1 small
carrot	1 medium
parsley stalks	bunch
bay leaf	1
salt and pepper	to taste
butter or margarine	40g
flour	60ml
milk	300ml
lemon juice	squeeze
chopped fresh parsley	to garnish
Cooking time	45 minutes
Serves	4

Method

1 Put the sweetbreads, onion, carrot, parsley stalks, bay leaf and seasoning in a saucepan with water to cover and simmer gently for 15 minutes until tender.
2 Drain the sweetbreads, keeping 300ml of the liquid for later use.
3 Melt the butter in a saucepan, stir in the flour and cook gently for a minute. Remove from the heat and gradually add the milk and cooking liquid.
4 Bring to the boil, stirring until thickened and add lemon juice.
5 Add sweetbreads to the sauce and simmer gently for five to ten minutes.
6 Garnish with parsley.

Top marks!

Understand cooking times and learn to recognise when food is at its optimum.
Should fillet be well done? Only if requested. Can you cook your meat and offal confidently to the correct specification – rare, medium or well done?

Cold pressed ox tongue

salted ox tongue	2–3kg
carrots, halved	2
onions, halved	2
celery stick, cut into chunks	1
bouquet garni	1
peppercorns	
Serves	30

Method

1 Soak the ox tongue in cold water for 24 hours. Change the water and wash the tongue occasionally.
2 Place the tongue in a large saucepan and cover with water. Bring to the boil and skim the surface as needed.
3 Add the remaining ingredients. Cover and simmer for 4 hours or until cooked. You should be able to pull out the small bones easily.
4 Remove from the heat and allow to cool.
5 When cool, remove from the liquid and drain on a board.
6 Remove the skin. Trim the root to remove any gristle or bone.
7 Roll the tongue so it fits into an 8-inch cake tin. It will be a tight fit.
8 Cover the tongue with a plate and stand a heavy weight on top.
9 Leave in a cool place or refrigerate for 12 hours.
10 Run a knife around the tin and turn out the pressed tongue.
11 Transfer to a serving plate. Serve sliced thinly.

Steaming

Steaming will not colour the meat and it will look quite natural. Meat is not usually steamed unless it is combined with other ingredients to make a dish such as steak and kidney pudding.

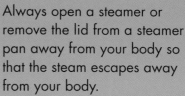

Remember!

Always open a steamer or remove the lid from a steamer pan away from your body so that the steam escapes away from your body.

Steak and kidney pudding

stewing steak	550g
ox's kidney	225g
onion	1 medium
chopped fresh parsley	30ml
plain flour	45ml
lemon rind, grated	1
salt and pepper	to taste
self-raising flour	275g
shredded suet	150g
butter or margarine for greasing	27g
Cooking time	5 hours
Serves	6

Method

1 Place the beef and kidney in a bowl with the onion and chopped parsley. Sprinkle in the flour and lemon rind and season with salt and pepper.

2 Mix the self-raising flour and suet and a pinch of salt. Stir in about 200ml of water and mix into a dough.

3 Roll out the dough and line a greased 1.7 litre pudding basin with the dough, leaving a piece big enough to top the basin.

4 Spoon the meat mixture into the lined pudding basin, add 120ml of water and seal the top of the basin using the remaining dough rolled out. Ensure the mix is well sealed by the dough by dampening the edges and rubbing them and turning in the edges to form a collar.

5 Cut a piece of greaseproof paper and foil and butter one side of the paper and lay it over the top of the basin and then tie the edge of the paper around the bowl. Then cover with the foil.

6 Place the pudding in a steamer and steam for about five hours. If using a saucepan steamer, ensure you check that the water does not boil away.

7 To serve, uncover, place on a serving dish and garnish with parsley.

Stewing

Stewing meat allows you to produce a good-flavoured dish from cheaper cuts of meat, e.g. mutton or beef shin.

Beef stew

vegetable oil	45ml
stewing steak	700–900g
onions	4 medium
carrots	350g
plain flour	30ml
beef stock	600ml
tomato purée	75g
salt and pepper	to season
bay leaves	2
Oven temperature	160–180°C
Cooking time	2¼ hours
Serves	4

Method

1 Heat the oil in a flameproof dish. When the oil is smoking, add the meat a quarter at a time.
2 Remove the meat when browned. Reduce heat and add onions and carrots and fry until lightly brown. Remove from casserole.
3 Sprinkle in the flour and stir well until blended with the remaining fat. Return to the heat until the roux turns a brown colour.
4 Add the stock, tomato purée and seasoning and stir the mixture until smooth. Add the meat and vegetable juices and bay leaf and slowly bring to the boil.
5 Cover the casserole and cook at 170°C for about 2¼ hours.
6 Uncover and stir once during cooking. Remove bay leaves before serving.

Blanquette de veau

veal	700g
onions	2 medium
carrots	2 medium
lemon juice	a squeeze
bouquet garni	1
salt and pepper	to taste
butter or margarine	25g
plain flour	45ml
egg yolk	1
single cream	30–45ml
bacon rolls, cooked	4–6
chopped fresh parsley	to garnish
Cooking time	90 minutes
Serves	6

Method

1 Put the meat, onions, carrots, lemon juice, bouquet garni and seasoning into a large saucepan with enough water to cover. Cover and simmer for one hour or until the meat is tender.

2 Strain off the liquid, reserving 600ml. Keep the meat and vegetables warm.

3 Melt the butter. Mix in the flour.

4 Gradually add the liquid, ensuring the liquid is boiled after every addition. Cook until the sauce thickens.

5 Adjust seasoning, remove from heat and add egg yolks and cream.

6 Add the meat, vegetables and bacon rolls and reheat without boiling.

7 Serve garnished with parsley.

Frying

It is essential to control the temperature and regularly turn and check meat during frying. Pork must always be cooked right through. Red meat and offal can be cooked to the customer's requirements.

Remember!

Thicker pieces of meat will take longer to cook. For example, a sirloin steak will take longer than thin strips of pork for a stir-fry.

Remember!

Hot oil can inflict serious injury if you are not careful during cooking.

Liver and onions

butter or margarine	25g
lamb's or calf's liver	450g
onions	450g
salt and pepper	to taste
mixed herbs (optional)	2.5ml
flour	for coating
Cooking time	5–10 minutes
Serves	4

Method

1 Melt the butter in a frying pan, add the onions and fry till brown. Add the herbs and seasoning. Cover and simmer for ten minutes.
2 Add the sliced liver to the onions and increase the heat slightly. Continue cooking for five to ten minutes.
3 Transfer to a warmed serving dish and serve.

Shallow-frying and stir-frying

Only good-quality meat should generally be fried.

To stir-fry meat, cut it into thin strips and place them into very hot oil in a wok. Cook the meat very quickly – normally for no longer than two to six minutes.

Video presentation

Watch the clip *Stir fry beef* to see this dish being made.

Try this! Worksheet 22

List as many meat dishes as you can that require stir-frying, deep-frying or shallow-frying.

Grilling

Beefsteaks, lamb cutlets, pork chops, veal, liver and kidneys can all be grilled, but you must ensure that the cut of meat is appropriate. See the table on page 351.

The meat can be placed on a tray or directly onto a clean grill. The meat may even be on skewers, e.g. kebabs. The meat is usually brushed with butter or oil (olive) to baste the meat during grilling. Meat such as pork, which has been marinated, is suitable for grilling. The heat colours the meat and helps to develop flavour.

The cooking time will vary depending on the type and thickness of the meat and it must be cooked to at least 63°C at the centre. Cooked grilled meat or offal should be firm to touch and resistant to pressure. Beef and lamb are an exception to this rule, as they can be served pink.

Healthy eating

Grilling is a healthy way of cooking meat as some of the fat drips from it.

Barbecued pork spare ribs

vegetable oil	30ml
onions	2 medium
garlic clove	1
tomato purée	30ml
malt vinegar	60ml
dried thyme	1.25ml
chilli seasoning	1.25ml
honey	45ml
beef stock	150ml
pork spare ribs	1kg
Oven temperature	190°C
Cooking time	1¾ hours
Serves	4

Method

1. Heat the oil in a saucepan, add the onions and cook for five minutes until softened.
2. Add all the remaining ingredients, except the spare ribs, and simmer gently for ten minutes.
3. Place the spare ribs in a roasting tray in a single layer and brush with a little of the sauce.
4. Roast in the oven at 190°C for 30 minutes.
5. Pour off the excess fat and spoon the remaining sauce over the ribs.
6. Cook for a further 1¼ hours, basting occasionally.

Griddling

Some griddles have bars running across them. This enables the meat to be **charred** or **seared**, providing a distinctive flavour and colour. Too much oil on the griddle can lead to excessive smoke and can hamper the cooking process.

Any type of meat or offal that can be grilled can also be griddled. The table below identifies what cuts from the meat types are suitable for grilling and griddling.

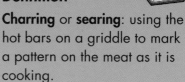

Definition

Charring or **searing**: using the hot bars on a griddle to mark a pattern on the meat as it is cooking.

Meat or offal	Prime or tender cuts or joints
Beef	Rump, sirloin, fillet
Veal	Loin, best end
Lamb	Best end, saddle
Pork	Loin
Bacon	Gammon, loin
Offal	Liver, kidneys

Figure 10.20 Cuts of meat and offal suitable for grilling and griddling

Roasting

Roasting meat gives a joint a good natural flavour and colours it nicely through the cooking process which adds to the appearance of the final dish. Meat such as lamb or beef can be rare, well-done or medium. This refers to how much the meat is cooked. Pork must always be well cooked. Undercooked pork runs the risk of giving someone food poisoning.

Place meat for roasting in a sturdy tray with handles. Roasting is normally started at a temperature of 200–210°C. The heat is then turned down to 160–180°C once the meat has coloured. Oven cloths and personal protective equipment must be used. A probe should be used to check that the centre of the joint of meat has reached an acceptable temperature and is safe to eat. The temperature is usually 63°C.

A probe is not always available. If this is the case, the juice from the meat can be used to test its condition. If the juice is pink and the meat is pork then continue to cook. A well-done joint of meat cooked throughout will have juices that run clear. Touch is another test. A resistant surface indicates that the meat is cooked.

Let the meat relax for 30 minutes before carving to allow the meat to cool slightly and make it tenderer to eat. This is particularly important with red meat, e.g. lamb and beef.

The roasting times for the main types of meat are as follows:
- Beef: 20 minutes per 450g plus 20 minutes.
- Lamb: 15–20 minutes per 450g plus 20 minutes.
- Pork: 25 minutes per 450g plus 25 minutes.
- Veal: 20 minutes per 450g plus 20 minutes.

The table below lists the types of meat and cuts suitable for roasting.

Meat	Cut or joint
Beef	Rump, topside, sirloin, fillet, ribs
Veal	Cushion, best end
Lamb	Best end, leg, shoulder, chops, saddle
Pork	Loin, leg, ribs, belly, shoulder
Bacon	Gammon

Figure 10.21 Cuts of meat suitable for roasting

Classic roast beef

piece of beef (sirloin, rib, rump or topside)	2kg
beef dripping (optional)	50g
salt and pepper	to taste
mustard powder (optional)	5ml
horseradish sauce	
Oven temperature	200–210°C until meat has coloured, then 160–180°C
Cooking time	See guidelines above
Serves	8–10

Method

1 Weigh the meat and calculate the cooking times.
2 Place the meat in a shallow roasting tin, preferably on a grid with the thickest layer of fat uppermost.
3 Add beef dripping if the meat is lean, season with salt, pepper, and mustard if preferred.
4 Roast the joint at 180°C for the calculated time, basting occasionally.
5 Remove from the oven and allow to rest for 20 minutes before carving. Serve with horseradish sauce.

Braising

The benefits of this cooking method are that the meat is very tender, flavours are able to merge and it allows cheaper, tougher cuts of meat to be used. The thickening agent for the liquid used when braising dishes is flour. A white or brown roux will be made and cooked into a sauce relevant to the dish.

Combination cooking

Lasagne is an example of a meat dish cooked using combination cooking. First the meat is sealed then it is stewed and finally it is finished by baking in the oven.

Combination ovens

A combination oven uses dry heat and an injection of steam to keep the food moist during cooking, e.g. lamb chops can easily become dry if overcooked in an ordinary oven. In a combination oven, the steam coupled with the convection heat will help to keep the meat moist and good to eat.

Did you know?
The thickening agent for the liquid used when braising dishes is flour. A white or brown roux will be made and cooked into a sauce relevant to the dish.

Hot holding, finishing and serving

Once you have worked hard to prepare and cook a dish it is important to serve it with the correct garnish and at the right temperature.

Hot holding

Holding the meat at the right temperature is also about being compliant with the law. The Food Safety Act 1990 states that hot food must be served and held at a temperature of at least 63°C. This temperature makes sure that potentially harmful bacteria will not multiply and harm the consumer.

Food is usually held at the correct temperature by either storing in a hot cupboard or hotplate which is above 63°C. Be aware that you may only hot hold food for a maximum of 90 minutes. Keep checking the condition of the food whilst hot holding as it can tend to become dry if it is not monitored correctly.

Finishing

Finishing a meat or offal dish correctly is very important. You should always check a dish before it is served and ask yourself the following questions:

○ Is the meat or offal at the correct temperature for service?
○ Does the dish have the correct flavour?
○ Does it need more seasoning?
○ Do I have the correct **garnish** or accompaniment for the dish?
○ Do I have the right equipment to finish and serve the dish?

The following are all appropriate garnishes for meat dishes:

○ Other cooked ingredients such as Yorkshire pudding for roast beef.
○ Accompaniments and sauces appropriate to the dish, e.g. apple sauce for pork or mint sauce for lamb.

Definition

Garnish: adding the final touches required to enhance a dish.

Yorkshire pudding

plain flour	125g
salt	pinch
egg	1
milk	200ml
vegetable oil	30ml
Oven temperature	220°C
Cooking time	40–45 minutes
Serves	4–6

Method

1 Add the flour, salt and egg in a bowl and mix.
2 Add half the milk and beat until smooth.
3 Add the remaining milk and beat until smooth.
4 Put a small amount of oil in a small roasting tray and pre-heat it in the oven.
5 Pour the batter into the hot tray and cook until risen and golden brown.

Serving

The equipment required to finish and serve meat can include:

○ serving platters (earthenware, plate or metal)

○ serving utensils, e.g. spoons, tongs, slices or forks.

The surface of a dish should be clean and presentable and maintained in an appropriate condition during service so that it is appealing to customers.

The final dish needs to be appealing to you and your customer. This is an aspect of catering where your flair will play an important part in shaping your career.

Figure 10.22 Serving is as essential as the preparation and cooking in creating an appealing dish

Test yourself!

1 Where should a pork joint be stored and at what temperature?

2 What is offal? Name two different types.

3 What is the most preferred type of liver used in offal dishes?

4 Which meats are classed as high risk?

5 What are the quality points to check for when selecting a pork loin for roasting?

6 What is the minimum temperature for pork to be cooked to?

7 Why is it important to cook pork thoroughly?

8 What type of pig does bacon come from?

9 What are sweetbreads?

10 What are the accompaniments for roast beef, lamb and pork?

Practice assignment tasks

Prepare and cook meat and offal

Task 1 — Beef

Produce a chart that identifies three cuts of meat from the hind-quarter of a cow and find a suitable recipe for each one.

List the equipment required to prepare and cook the dishes.

Identify suitable alternative meat cuts for each dish and describe the quality points of the cuts.

Task 2 — Pork

Produce a table to show the cuts of meat from a side of pork. For each cut:

○ state two quality points
○ list as many methods of cookery as you can
○ list up to three different methods of preparation, e.g. diced, jointed
○ identify two dishes and include notes on portion size and appropriate garnishes.

Produce a table to show the types of pig offal.

○ State two quality points for each type.
○ List as many cookery methods as you can.
○ List the methods of preparation.
○ Identify two dishes that can be prepared for each type.

Task 3 — Lamb

Find three different recipes for lamb dishes and adapt them to make them healthier.

Identify the offal available from a carcass of lamb. Select a recipe for each type and state the basic preparation method.

Draw a lamb carcass and identify all the cuts. For each cut indicate one method of cookery.

Poultry

11

This chapter covers the following outcomes from Diploma unit 210: Prepare and cook poultry

- Outcome 210.1 Prepare poultry
- Outcome 210.2 Cook poultry

Working through this chapter could also provide evidence for the following Key Skills:

C2.1, C2.2a, C2.2b, C2.3, N, N1.2, N2.2, ICT2.1, ICT2.2, ICT2.3, LP2.1, LP2.2, LP2.3, PS2.1, PS2.2, PS2.3

In this chapter you will learn how to:

Identify the types of poultry and their quality points

State the most commonly used cuts of poultry and their portion sizes/weights

Describe the methods of preservation and their advantages and disadvantages

Use the correct tools and equipment for preparation and cooking

Use the correct methods and principles to prepare, cook and finish the poultry

Determine when the poultry is cooked

Safely store poultry

You will learn to prepare and cook basic poultry dishes, including:

- sauté chicken bonne femme
- poached breasts of chicken with mushroom sauce
- chicken in red wine sauce
- marinade for chicken
- chicken kiev
- roast duck.

Types of poultry

What is poultry?

Poultry is the generic term used for domestic farmyard birds, e.g. chickens, ducks and turkeys. Geese and guinea fowl are also included in this group. Poultry is an increasingly popular source of protein, because it is versatile and adaptable in modern cooking.

> **Remember!**
> If you are unsure or have a problem with the poultry you are preparing or cooking then always seek advice from your supervisor, line manager or head chef.

Figure 11.1 Poultry includes many different species of bird (duck, turkey, chicken, guinea fowl, goose)

Chicken is the most popular type of poultry. It can be found in most domestic fridges as well in restaurants and industrial kitchens worldwide.

> **Did you know?**
> Corn-fed chickens are yellow. The cooked fat has a yellow tinge to it because of the food the bird is fed.

Quality points

The following quality points apply to all poultry:

○ There should not be any bruises or cuts on the skin of the bird.
○ The skin should be dry and not slimy.
○ Good-quality poultry should be odourless or at least have a fresh smell to it.
○ The poultry should not be discoloured.
○ The bird should be the right size for the dish you are to prepare. For example, a chicken for roasting should be about 1.3kg. Other birds, e.g. duck or turkey, can vary in weight but you should check the size against the requirements of the dish.
○ The **cavity** should not contain any excess blood or yellow fat, nor show any signs of damage to the inside of the carcass.

> **Definition**
> **Cavity**: the hollow space left inside the bird once all the innards have been removed.

- The poultry should be the correct temperature (below 8°C if fresh and −18 to −25°C if frozen).
- Packaging should not be damaged on initial receipt or before preparation.

To ensure the finished dish is of good quality, check:
- The poultry is correct type for the dish.
- There is minimal waste during preparation to ensure the correct quantity is available for cooking.

Potential problems

Poultry is a high-risk food, as it can contain harmful bacteria, e.g. salmonella. Bacteria can multiply if poultry is not stored or cooked correctly and this could lead to food poisoning. It is important to follow these food safety guidelines strictly:
- Poultry should be stored correctly at an appropriate temperature (1–5°C if fresh and −18 to −25°C if frozen).
- Always store raw meat on the bottom shelf of the refrigerator to stop the juices dripping onto the shelves below.
- Thoroughly defrost frozen poultry before cooking. Otherwise the meat in the thickest parts may not be cooked through and the harmful bacteria could remain.
- Always cook poultry to a temperature of above 63°C.
- Check there is no sign of uncooked flesh before serving.

Chicken

Chickens are farmed or reared in three different ways:

1 **Free-range**: the birds are usually left to roam freely.
2 **Battery**: an intense method of farming where the birds are kept packed in pens with little if any freedom of movement.
3 **Organic**: birds are fed on natural and traditional foods. Information is always readily available regarding organic poultry from either the label or organisations relevant to the product.

Did you know?
Chicken is high in protein and full of vitamins, especially vitamin B.

Healthy eating
The breast meat of chicken is low in fat and the leg meat has lower fat content than other more traditional red meats. The young age of the chicken (12 weeks) means that the meat is tender and very adaptable.

There are many types of chicken for cooking; the most common are shown in the table below.

Type	Description	Average portion yield	Appearance
Poussin	4–6-week-old bird	1	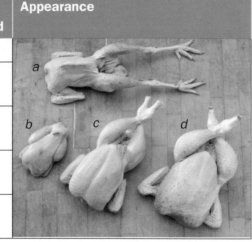
Double poussin	6-week-old bird	2	
Roasting chicken	12–14-week-old bird	4–8	
Boiling fowl	Older bird, over 14 weeks	6–8	
Large roasting chicken	Young fattened cockerel	8–12	

Figure 11.2 Types of chicken for cooking

a boiling fowl, b poussin, c roasting chicken, d capon

Cuts of chicken

The bird you will most commonly prepare is the traditional roasting chicken, which may come pre-packed. It can range in size from 1.3kg to 3kg. The chicken will have already been plucked and cleaned of its innards. It will therefore be ready for dish preparation and cooking.

A chicken can be cooked:

○ whole
○ **jointed** from the carcass into two breasts and two legs (see page 366)
○ cut into eight pieces for sautéing (see pages 367–8)
○ spatchcock (with the backbone cut out and flattened) for grilling or barbeque
○ removed from the bone and diced or cut into **emincé**.

Checking quality of chicken

When selecting chicken for use in the kitchen, it is important to check for the following quality points:

○ It should be plump and of appropriate size (1.3kg–3kg).
○ There should not be any damage, breaks, blemishes or bruising.
○ It should be clean, with a fresh smell and it should not be slimy to the touch. An unpleasant odour indicates that the chicken may be unsuitable for use.

Healthy eating

A skinless chicken breast is an appropriate low-fat meat option as part of a healthy well-balanced diet. A chicken breast has only 120 calories per 100g.

Definition

Jointed: cuts of poultry removed from the carcass during preparation, e.g. legs and breasts.
Emincé: a cut of meat or poultry – even, thin strips which are suitable for stir-fries.

Remember!

Chicken breasts can be expensive so there must not be too much wastage during preparation.

○ Make sure there is minimal fat and that the cavity does not contain a high proportion of yellow fat inside it, as this indicates poor quality or an old bird.

Using the wrong type of chicken will result in a poor-quality dish and affect your kitchen's reputation. For example, you should not use a boiling fowl if you are supposed to be producing roast chicken.

Duck

It is believed that duck was first domesticated in China hundreds, maybe thousands, of years ago. Today many types of duck are reared for cooking. Some commonly used types of duck are:

○ Pekin or Long Island
○ Barbary or Muscovy
○ Aylesbury.

Barbary and Aylesbury are the most commonly used ducks in cooking. The Aylesbury duck has a higher fat content than the Barbary duck. Ducks are generally quite large birds. They should have long plump breasts and smaller legs in proportion to the breasts. The flesh is usually a deep red.

Cuts of duck

Duck is versatile and can be prepared and cooked in many ways:
○ It can be cooked whole.
○ It has two breasts and two legs which can be jointed from the carcass.
○ The legs can be cut off and cooked slowly for **confit**.
○ It can be spatchcocked or flattened but duck is very fat to be cooked in this way.

Duck has a rich flavour, well-suited to sweet accompaniments.

Checking quality of duck

When selecting a duck for use check for the following points:
○ The skin is light in colour.
○ The duck is plump, especially in the breast region.
○ The skin must be clean and free from damage, blemishes or bruising.
○ It should smell fresh.

Figure 11.3 Duck breasts. Note the deep red flesh

Did you know?

Peking duck is roasted duck, which has been shredded. It is served in a light pancake with strips of spring onion and cucumber and plum sauce. Bombay duck is not duck at all. It is a dried fish!

Healthy eating

Duck contains a lot of fat, so should not feature too regularly in a healthy diet. It is a good meat choice for special occasions.

Definition

Confit: a method of preserving meat. The meat is salted and cooked slowly in its own fat. It is then put into a container and covered with the fat. The container is then sealed.

Healthy eating

Duck is high in protein, B vitamins and some minerals.

Portioning

The advantage of **portioning** the poultry before cooking is that you have a guaranteed number of servings. If you are preparing chicken for 200 people then portioning will assure you at an early stage that you have enough food to feed everyone.

Definition

Portioning: cutting meat into the correct size for it to be served. The correct size depends on the dish being made. Poultry is usually cut into four pieces (two breasts and two legs). If the poultry is a poussin (see table on page 00) it may also be prepared for grilling.

How to portion a chicken into four

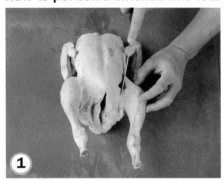

1 With your knife make small cuts at the top of the leg where it is attached to the main carcass.

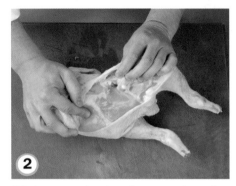

2 Dislocate the leg by popping the leg joint out of the socket and pulling back the leg.

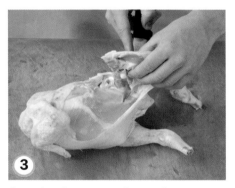

3 Cut the leg away from the carcass by following the natural line of flesh. Make sure you remove the oyster. Repeat on the other side.

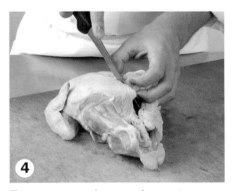

4 To separate the two breasts follow the natural line of the breast bone and cut down through the carcass and wing joint. The wings remain attached.

5 Trim each breast to remove any sinew, bone or excess fat.

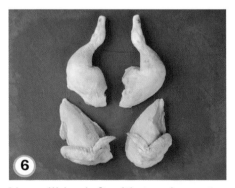

6 You will be left with two breasts and two legs.

Dicing and slicing

These methods of cutting are used for meat which is off the bone. Dicing makes you think of square cubes but with poultry, evenly sized pieces of any shape are needed. Cutting poultry into evenly sized pieces allows the meat to cook evenly. Dicing and slicing into strips is appropriate for stir-fries.

The principles listed on page 365 should be followed to ensure personal and food safety when dicing and slicing poultry meat.

Cutting poultry for sauté dishes

Sautéing is a relatively quick method of cooking and therefore the meat must be cut into small manageable pieces of approximately the same size. This preparation method is carried out on whole chickens.

How to cut a chicken into eight pieces for sauté

1 Make sure all the giblets have been removed. Clean the cavity – if necessary wash it out under cold running water and wipe it with a kitchen towel.

2 To remove the wishbone, pull the skin back around the neck area. Use an 8–10-inch chef's knife to rub the flesh on each side to expose the wishbone. You can see where the wishbone is joined to the shoulder blade.

3 Using the point of the knife cut through the bone on each side.

Remember!

Throughout this process ensure you work safely with the knife. Always work away from you, so if you slip you do not inadvertently stab yourself. If you are unsure of any process seek advice from your line manager.

Definition

Sauté: to cook meat, fish or vegetables in fat until brown using a sturdy frying pan.

4 Run your finger along each side of the bone to the top. At the top there is an oval-shaped piece of bone attaching the wishbone to the breast. Pinch this and pull to remove the wishbone.

5 Cut above the wing joint. Scrape flesh back to expose a clean bone.

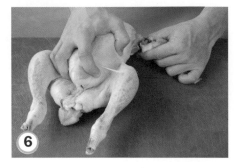

6 Snap off the wing at the joint. Repeat on the other side.

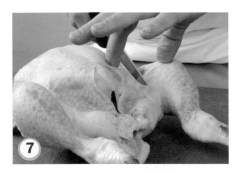

7 Pull out the leg and make a small cut through the skin to expose the flesh.

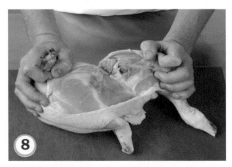

8 Push the thigh backwards to expose the bone. Hold the leg and pop the bone from the socket.

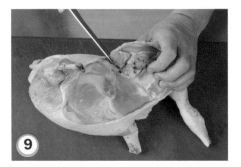

9 Work around the small piece of flesh on the back. This is the 'oyster'.

10 Remove the leg. Repeat to remove the second leg (2 pieces).

11 Cut the flesh at the bottom of the drumstick and scrape it back to the joint.

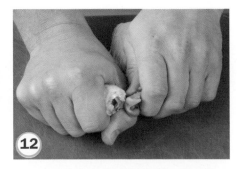

12 Snap the joint, leaving a small piece of clean bone exposed.

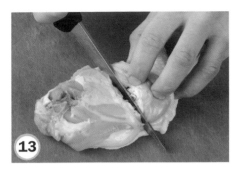

13 Smooth the skin. Put the meat skin side down. There should be a visible line of fat. Using this as your guide, cut through between the drumstick and thigh. Repeat on the other leg (4 pieces).

14 Remove the ball joint from each drumstick. Press down with the heel of the knife to cut off the bone. Repeat with the other leg.

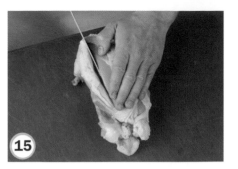

15 Have the cavity end towards you. Follow the feather lines along the breast, cutting through the shoulder.

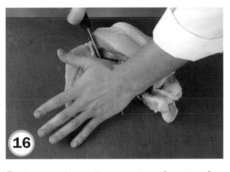

16 Put your hand over the front of the knife to steady it. Push the knife down to cut right through the bones. Remove the wing with part of the breast. Repeat on the other side (6 pieces).

17 Turn the chicken onto its side. Cut the remaining carcass from the breast.

Video presentation
Prepare a whole chicken for sauté shows a professional chef working through this process.

18 Cut across the breast bone. You will need to press on the heel of the knife to cut through the bone.

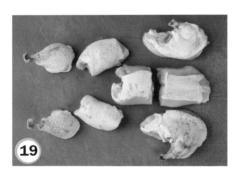

19 Reassemble the 8 portions on a tray, tidying the skin as you do this.

Boning

Boning is usually carried out so the legs of a bird can be stuffed, e.g. the thigh bone of a turkey, although a whole bird can also be boned out. It is much easier to carve a joint that has been boned and it also looks more attractive. There are two types of boning: tunnel boning and external boning.

External boning means cutting through the flesh to the bone and then removing the bone using a boning knife (a knife with a sturdy, tapered blade about 7-inches long). The cavity can then be filled and the joint tied to form a pleasing shape. Tunnel boning is a more delicate and complex method.

How to tunnel bone a thigh bone from a turkey leg

1 Cut around the ball joint at the top of the leg.
2 Holding the knife almost flat against the bone, scrape and cut along the thigh bone to manipulate the flesh away from the bone. Turn the leg inside out as you do this to make it easier.
3 Once the joint above the drumstick is exposed, cut through the joint to remove the thigh bone.
4 Turn the leg back in so the skin is facing outwards again. There should not be any damage to the exterior as this would spoil the appearance of the finished dish.
5 Stuff the leg.

Stuffing or filling

Stuffing or filling poultry adds to the flavour, appearance and texture of the dish. Stuffing, e.g. sage and onion, is often put into the neck cavity. Legs can also be filled or stuffed. Before stuffing a cavity it is important to check it to ensure the quality of the bird. If necessary, wash and dry the inside of the cavity. The stuffing or filling should always be at the correct temperature, which is 1–5°C. If possible do not handle the filling; use a piping bag or spoon.

Definition

Boning: to remove the bones from a joint of meat or poultry.

Remember!

Be very careful when boning poultry so that you do not cut yourself.

Figure 11.5 A boning knife

Remember!

Temperature is important when preparing poultry. The meat may contain harmful bacteria, which multiply rapidly at room temperature. Adding hot filling to a cool chicken cavity could lead to food poisoning. Always allow hot fillings or stuffing to cool below 8°C before adding them to the poultry.

How to stuff a turkey breast

1

Remove the breast from the turkey. Cut into the fattest part of the breast along its length. This cut almost slices all the way through the breast, creating a pouch or envelope effect.

2

Put the cooled stuffing in this 'envelope' or 'pouch', using a spoon or your hands, as long as they are clean.

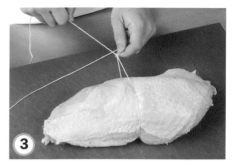

3

Tie the breast back to its original shape before cooking, using butcher's twine or another similar string. Do not use plastic-based string as this can melt and contaminate the meat.

How to stuff a leg

1 Remove the thighbone from the bird. This gives a natural cavity.
2 Put the stuffing in this cavity.
3 Sew, tie or wrap the leg in foil so that it keeps its shape during cooking.

Equipment and tools used to stuff a bird:

○ suitable knife
○ chopping board
○ piping bag to fill cavities in the meat
○ spoons to prevent unnecessary handling of stuffing
○ string to tie the bird or joint
○ gloves, which the food handler can use when stuffing poultry.

Video presentation

Watch *How to stuff a chicken leg for ballotine* to see how it's done.

Mincing

Turkey mince is probably the most common minced poultry meat although pâtés, raised pies, stuffings and **forcemeats** all use minced poultry. Most kitchens have a mincing machine and the poultry is passed through the machine to form a fine minced meat.

Generally leg meat or offcuts are minced. Poor-quality poultry, e.g. boiling fowl or older birds, can provide suitable meat for mincing as the texture of the mince is determined by the additional ingredients.

Definition

Forcemeat: finely chopped or minced meat used in stuffings. It is usually combined with other flavourings such as eggs, herbs and breadcrumbs.

371

Flavouring

Most dishes are enhanced with complementary flavours. See pages 231–2.

Seasoning

A chicken or turkey for roasting is usually seasoned before cooking, during the preparation stage. If the poultry you are preparing is for a **wet method** of cookery, e.g. stewing or braising, the poultry should be well-seasoned before cooking. The overall seasoning of the dish should be adjusted after cooking when all the flavours of the ingredients in the casserole have combined.

Marinating

Marinating poultry is done by combining a cooked or uncooked liquid with the bird or joints in a dish. The poultry can be left in the marinade for between 30 minutes and 48 hours, depending on the dish. The poultry should be covered completely by the liquid.

Some marinades are used after the poultry has been removed from them to create a sauce to accompany the dish. Tandoori is a well-known chicken dish in which the sauce is created from the marinade.

Did you know?

The main seasoning in chicken chasseur is the herb tarragon.

Definition

Wet method: a dish which is cooked and served in a liquid.
Dry method: a dish which is cooked using a dry method of cookery (e.g. roasting, grilling).

Top marks!

Knowing how different flavours incorporate with different types of poultry will indicate to tutors how astute you are.

Did you know?

Marinating can prolong the shelf life of poultry, as it may cure the meat.

Chef's tip

As a chef you can experiment with creating your own marinades by combining flavours and adding those to different base ingredients.

Basic marinade for chicken

chicken	1 portioned into 4 or 8
salt and pepper	to season
chopped shallots	2
thyme	1 sprig
bay leaf	1
chopped parsley	1 tablespoon
garlic clove, crushed	1 small
clove	1 small
black peppercorns	12
lemon juice	from 2 lemons
olive oil	375ml
Serves	4

Method

1 Season the chicken with salt and pepper.
2 Mix the other ingredients together in a bowl. Add the chicken and make sure it is covered in marinade.
3 Cover the dish and put it in a refrigerator for 2–12 hours.

Coating

Coating poultry can be as simple as covering it in seasoned flour during preparation. It can also refer to covering a piece of poultry in flour, egg and breadcrumbs to meet the requirements of a certain dish, e.g. Chicken Kiev.

Coating with sauce

Some poultry dishes are accompanied by a sauce. The sauce must have the correct consistency otherwise it will either run off or form a skin and look thick and stodgy.

Coating with seasoned flour

This is commonly done when preparing pieces of poultry for sauté. Dip each piece of poultry in a dish of seasoned flour and shake off the excess. The seasoned powder combines with the poultry to create a well-coloured and crisp texture when sealing the meat.

Coating with flour, egg and breadcrumbs

Coating poultry in flour, egg and breadcrumbs for Chicken Kiev allows the garlic butter to be held in the poultry leg or breast during cooking. A breadcrumb coating adds a different texture to the dish.

Always follow this process to make sure the poultry is evenly coated:

1 Take three bowls: one bowl of well-seasoned flour, one bowl of beaten egg and one bowl of fine breadcrumbs.
2 Coat the poultry with the flour and shake off any excess.
3 Place it in the beaten egg mix. Make sure the poultry is completely coated in egg mix. Shake off the excess.
4 Place it in the breadcrumb bowl. Make sure the meat is well coated.
5 Put the breadcrumbed poultry on a suitable tray until required for cooking.

Once the poultry has been coated it must not be left very long before cooking or the coating will become soggy. Do not stack portions of breadcrumbed products on top of each other or the quality of the coating and its appearance will be affected. Use greaseproof paper to layer many portions of coated poultry.

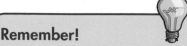

Remember!

It is important to use the correct tools, equipment and techniques when preparing poultry in order to ensure safety, to meet the dish requirements and to be economic, efficient and reduce wastage.

Try this!   Worksheet 23

List as many poultry dishes as you can that are coated in flour, egg and breadcrumbs.

Chicken Kiev

chicken breasts	2
butter	50g
lemon juice and zest	½ lemon
garlic clove	1
chopped parsley	20g
salt and pepper	to taste
flour	50g
white breadcrumbs	100g
eggs, beaten	2
watercress as garnish	
Cooking time	8–10 minutes
Serves	2

Method

1 Flatten the chicken breasts slightly.
2 Mix the butter, salt and pepper, lemon juice, crushed garlic and chopped parsley in a bowl.
3 Shape the butter mixture into fingers to fit inside the breasts.
4 Cut a pouch in each chicken breast big enough to put the butter in.
5 Put the butter into the chicken breasts and cover it with the surrounding flesh.
6 Coat each chicken breast in flour, egg and breadcrumbs. Make sure none of the chicken meat is left exposed. Refrigerate for one hour.
7 Deep-fry the chicken breasts for about six minutes until golden brown. Finish in a hot oven if required.
8 Serve with watercress.

Trussing

To **truss** a bird, use a trussing needle and butcher's string. A trussing needle is a long steel needle with a curved sharp end that is adapted for passing through poultry carcasses. Butcher's string is sturdy and will not alter when heat is applied. There are several ways to truss a bird and one method is shown below.

> **Definition**
>
> **Trussing**: a method of securing the bird in an appropriate shape during the cooking process.

How to truss a chicken

Use a string that is approximately four to five times the length of the bird.

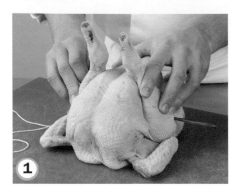

1 Insert the needle between the drumstick and the thigh on one side, through the cavity and out between the thigh and drumstick on the other side.

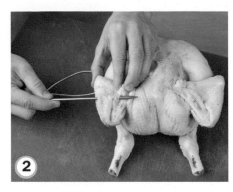

2 Turn the bird over and pass the needle between the two wing bones.

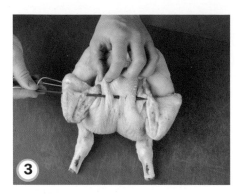

3 Sew down the neck flap.

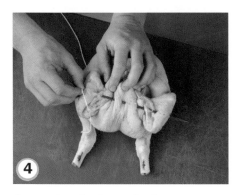

4 Come back through the opposite winglets.

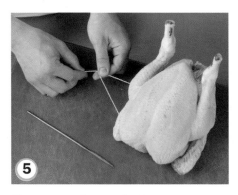

5 Tie securely producing a neat shape.

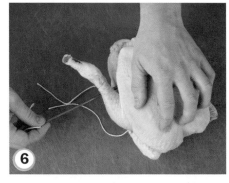

6 Insert the needle through the leg below the bone. Go through the cavity and exit through the other leg below the bone.

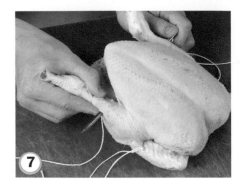

7 Go back through, just above the bone.

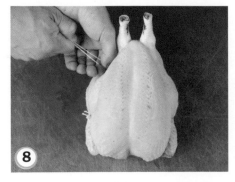

8 Pull the string tight to produce a nice neat shape and tie off.

9 A trussed bird.

Storing prepared poultry

Poultry can contain harmful bacteria, e.g. salmonella. This means it is necessary to store poultry correctly before, during and after preparation:

○ Ensure that raw poultry is stored at the bottom of a refrigerator. This will prevent any blood or liquid dripping onto other foods.
○ Clearly label poultry which has been prepared. The label should include the date so that it is possible to determine its shelf life.
○ Store prepared poultry at 1–5°C.
○ Do not stack prepared poultry on top of each other as it can affect the appearance and quality of the end product.

Preserving poultry

For more information on the processes see pages 228–230.

Preserving methods

Chilling and freezing

Poultry can be stored for 3–4 days in a fridge or for up to 12 months in a freezer. Poultry to be frozen should be labelled and covered to prevent cross-contamination and possible freezer burn. Chilled poultry should be stored near the bottom shelf of a refrigerator to prevent cross-contamination.

Vacuum–packing

This is a very effective method of storing poultry.

Smoking

This method is used to preserve some poultry such as duck, goose or chicken. The poultry is heated gently by a fire to dry and preserve it. Chicory wood chips, for example, are burned to give it a strong smoky flavour.

Canning

Few poultry dishes are canned except for those cooked in a wet sauce, e.g. chicken stew.

Cooking poultry dishes

Cooking methods

After poultry has been prepared correctly, it is important that the correct cooking method is used to ensure a quality dish. The cooking method adopted depends on the dish required. As the chef, you must make sure that you work in a safe manner and that the correct tools, techniques and methods are used.

It is useful to remember that a tough and fibrous bird is best cooked using wet methods of cookery, e.g. stewing, braising or boiling. For tender poultry, dry methods of cooking are appropriate, e.g. roasting, grilling, etc. Overcooking poultry makes it dry and unappealing to eat. For more information on cooking methods see pages 220–227.

Steaming

Poultry can be steamed.

Poaching

White stock (see page 235) is usually used to poach poultry. To test whether the poultry is cooked, prick the meat gently. The juices should run clear or white.

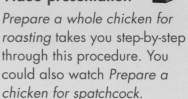

Video presentation

Prepare a whole chicken for roasting takes you step-by-step through this procedure. You could also watch *Prepare a chicken for spatchcock.*

Top marks!

Learn to understand cooking times and recognise when food is at its optimum. Should poultry be well done? Only if requested. Can you cook poultry to the correct specification?

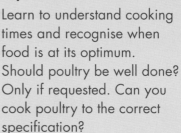

Chef's tip

Adding carrots and onions to the poaching liquor can give a delicate flavour to a poultry dish. Leeks and fennel are other good flavours for poultry.

Poached breasts of chicken with mushroom sauce

skinless chicken breasts	4
white stock	350ml
butter	25g
mushroom sauce	500ml
mushroom caps	8
salt and pepper	to taste
chopped parsley	to garnish
Cooking time	30 minutes
Serves	4

Method

1 Poach the chicken breasts in white stock for 20 minutes.
2 Slice the mushroom caps.
3 Shallow fry the mushroom caps in butter.
4 Heat the mushroom sauce.
5 Garnish the poached chicken breasts with the cooked mushroom caps, **napper** with the sauce and decorate by sprinkling the chopped parsley over it.

Definition

Napper: a French term meaning to coat or mask a tray of food.

Stewing

Stewing allows you to produce a good-flavoured dish from cheaper cuts of poultry, e.g. the legs or thighs. Vegetables and stock can be added and cooking slowly enables the flavours to infuse or merge.

Towards the end of the cooking time, you may need to thicken a stewed poultry dish. This can be done by **reducing** the liquid so it thickens itself or by using a roux or starch-based sauce method (see Chapter 8).

Definition

Reducing: to boil the liquid rapidly until it reduces in volume.

Coq au vin (chicken in red wine)

chicken	1	**For the garnish:**	
oil	50ml	button mushrooms	100g
bouquet garni	1	lardons of bacon	100g
red wine	100ml	button onions	100g
chicken stock	50ml	croutons, fried	4
meat glaze	12g	chopped parsley	
butter	25g		
flour	25g		
Oven temperature	140–160°C		
Cooking time	1–1½ hours		
Serves	4		

Method

1 Cut the chicken for sauté (see pages 367–9).
2 Put the oil in a pan and heat it until there is a blue haze. Put the chicken in the pan.
3 Season chicken and **seal** and colour it quickly.
4 Remove the chicken and place it in a stewing vessel with the bouquet garni.
5 Sauté the onions, mushrooms and lardons in the same pan the chicken was coloured in.
6 **Deglaze** the pan with the wine and stock. Bring it to the boil.
7 Pour the liquid over the chicken and put a tightly fitting lid over the dish. Cook it in the oven until the chicken is tender.
8 Remove the chicken and garnish it with the mushrooms, lardons and onions.
9 Reduce the sauce by a third and add the meat glaze.
10 Put the butter and flour into a clean bowl. Combine the butter and flour into a paste (beurre manie).
11 Add small amounts of the paste to the liquid.
12 As the liquid boils whisk to obtain the required consistency: thick enough to coat the back of a spoon.
13 Adjust the seasoning.
14 Pour an appropriate amount of the sauce over the chicken and garnishes. Serve with the fried croutons on top, sprinkled with chopped parsley.

Definition

Sealing: colouring meat in hot fat to prevent excessive juices leaking from the dish, e.g. the breadcrumbed breast of chicken for Chicken Kiev is sealed in hot fat to provide its colour and prevent the garlic butter from escaping during cooking.

Definition

Deglaze: to add wine or stock to a pan used for frying in order to lift the remaining sediment to make a sauce or gravy.

Frying

Regular turning and checking of the poultry during frying is essential to ensure that the food is cooked right through. Remember that thicker pieces of meat will take longer to cook. For example, chicken drumsticks will require longer cooking than thin strips of breast.

Deep-frying

Pieces of poultry which are deep-fried must be closely monitored to make sure they are thoroughly cooked. Temperature probing or piercing the flesh at the thickest part to see if blood runs from the joint is a good indicator.

Shallow-frying, sautéing and stir-frying

Only good-quality poultry should be used for sauté as the pan is deglazed and a sauce is made from **residues**.

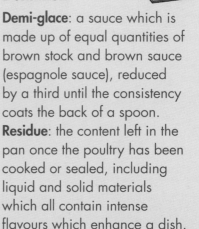

Definition

Demi-glace: a sauce which is made up of equal quantities of brown stock and brown sauce (espagnole sauce), reduced by a third until the consistency coats the back of a spoon.
Residue: the content left in the pan once the poultry has been cooked or sealed, including liquid and solid materials which all contain intense flavours which enhance a dish.

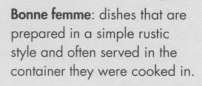

Definition

Bonne femme: dishes that are prepared in a simple rustic style and often served in the container they were cooked in.

Sauté chicken bonne femme

chicken cut for sauté (see page 367)	1
lardons of bacon, blanched and sautéed	100g
white wine	100ml
demi-glace	400ml
button onions for garnish	100g
cocotte potatoes	100g
salt and pepper	to season
Cooking time	45 minutes
Serves	4

Method

1 Sauté the chicken. Ensure that the poultry is cooked and coloured evenly. Keep an eye on the poultry as you do not want it to burn; regulate the heat if necessary. Fry off the lardons in the same pan, until they have a slight golden brown colour.
2 Deglaze the sauté pan with the wine.
3 Reduce the liquid by half.
4 Add the **demi-glace**, adjust the seasoning if required, add the garnishes (lardons, potatoes and onions), and serve.

For stir-frying, the poultry is cut into thin strips and cooked very quickly – normally for no longer than three to six minutes. This maintains its tenderness and succulence.

Grilling

Chicken or duck breasts are often grilled. When grilling poultry the meat can be placed on a tray or directly onto a clean grill plate. The poultry may be on skewers if you are preparing kebabs. Poultry is usually brushed with butter or (olive) oil to **baste** the meat during grilling. Poultry which has been marinated (see page 232) is suitable for grilling.

Chicken and other poultry must be cooked to at least 63°C. Cooked grilled poultry should be firm to touch and resistant to pressure. Duck breast is an exception to this rule, as it is usually served pink. An average duck breast takes 12 minutes to cook correctly. Overcooking poultry by grilling will make the meat dry and tough.

Griddling

A little oil may be used to assist in griddling, or the poultry itself may have been marinated with a little oil before cooking.

Roasting

Roasting usually changes the colour of the meat and adds to the meat's appeal. When roasting poultry, place the bird or jointed bird into a hot oven to colour and then turn the temperature down to allow the bird to roast slowly. This keeps the meat moist.

Roasting times for poultry are:
○ Chicken: 200–230°C for 20 minutes per 450g plus 20 minutes.
○ Turkey: 180°C for 15–20 minutes per 450g plus 20 minutes.
○ Duck: 180°C for 30 minutes per 450g.

Try this!   Worksheet 24

List as many poultry dishes as you can that require stir-frying, deep-frying, sautéing or shallow-frying.

Remember!

Grilling poultry is a healthy way of cooking food, as the meat does not absorb much fat. A grilled skinless chicken breast contains only 120 calories per 100g.

Definition

Baste: to moisten with liquid, fat, gravy, etc.

Top marks!

Do you know the appropriate cooking methods for different cuts and types of poultry? Would you roast or shallow fry a chicken breast? Would you braise or grill an old fowl? This is essential learning.

Roast chicken, turkey or duck

turkey, chicken or duck	one whole bird
oil	25–35ml
salt and pepper	to season
bed of root	1
Oven temperature	200–230°C for 20 minutes, reducing to 190°C for the remaining time
Cooking time	See page 217 for roasting times
Serves	4 if chicken or duck 6–12 if a turkey

Method

1 Wash the poultry and remove any excess fat.
2 Coat the bird in oil, season and put it on a **bed of root** on its side.
3 Roast for 20 minutes. Reduce the heat. Turn the bird onto its other side. Continue to turn at intervals of 20 minutes to obtain good even colour all over the bird.
4 Finish cooking breast side up.
5 Check internal temperature to ensure bird is cooked correctly.
6 Serve roast chicken with gravy, bread sauce, game chips and watercress. Serve roast turkey with cranberry sauce. For a duck, a fruit-based sauce such as orange or plum is a lovely accompaniment.

Video presentation

Watch *Prepare a whole chicken for roasting* before following this recipe.

Definition

Bed of root: chopped root vegetables which act as a base to put the bird on to prevent sticking and burning on the tray.

Combination cooking

Combination cooking means that more than one method of cooking is used in making a dish. For example, chicken croquettes are a dish where the poultry is boiled or poached, then diced and bound with other ingredients, e.g. mashed potatoes, flour, egg and breadcrumbs, and then deep-fried.

A combination oven uses two different methods of cooking within the same oven. An example of its use is for turkey, which if roasted whole can easily become dry when cooked in an ordinary oven. In a combination oven, the steam coupled with the convection heat will ensure the meat remains moist and of good eating quality.

Hot holding and finishing

Once you have worked hard to prepare and cook a dish, it is really important to be able to serve it with the correct garnish and at the right temperature.

Hot holding the poultry at the right temperature is also about complying with the law. The Food Safety Act 1990 states that hot food must be served and held at a temperature of at least 63°C. This makes sure that potentially harmful bacteria will not multiply and harm the consumer.

Finishing the poultry dish correctly is very important. You should always check a dish before it is served and ask yourself the following questions:

○ Is the poultry at the correct temperature for service?
○ Does the dish have the correct flavour?
○ Does it need more seasoning?
○ Do I have the correct garnish for the dish?
○ Do I have the right equipment to finish and serve the dish?

You can finish poultry by:

○ coating it with a sauce, e.g. duck is often coated with orange sauce
○ glazing it by brushing it with butter, oils or dish residue to add an attractive gloss, e.g. a barbecue marinade.

Garnishing means adding the final touches to enhance a dish. Appropriate garnishes for poultry dishes are other cooked ingredients, e.g. bacon rolls, stuffing and bread sauce for roast chicken, or a sprinkling of parsley over a casserole to add colour. Dough products, pasta, potatoes or vegetables may also be used.

Serving

The equipment required to finish and serve poultry includes:

○ serving platters (earthenware or metal)
○ serving utensils, e.g. spoons, tongs, slices or forks.

The service area for a dish should be clean and presentable and appealing to customers at all times.

Try this! Worksheet 25

List as many garnishes as you can that would be suitable for the following dishes:

○ Roast chicken
○ Chicken bonne femme
○ Chicken Maryland
○ Turkey fricassee
○ Roast turkey
○ Peking duck
○ Duck in orange sauce
○ Roast duck.

Test yourself!

1 State two actions to be taken when a problem is encountered with quality of poultry.

2 List two ingredients which can be used to garnish a roasted chicken.

3 What is the correct holding temperature for cooked poultry?
   a 62°C
   b 63°C
   c 64°C
   d 65°C

4 What internal temperature should poultry be cooked to?
   a 62°C
   b 63°C
   c 64°C
   d 65°C

5 State two ways to reduce fat in poultry dishes.

6 List five different types of poultry.

7 What is the correct temperature for stuffing or filling?
   a 1–5°C
   b 2–6°C
   c 3–5°C
   d 5–8°C.

8 For how long would you roast the following birds?
   a A chicken weighing 3kg.
   b A chicken weighing 1.5kg.
   c A turkey weighing 5.5kg.

Practice assignment tasks

Prepare poultry

Task 1

List the types of poultry. For each type describe:
- the quality points
- the preparation methods and cuts
- the weight and yield.

Task 2

Develop a two-course menu that includes one type of poultry in one of the courses. Produce a time-plan and food order to make the meal within two hours. The time-plan should include the following points:
- time
- activity
- duration
- temperatures
- special points, i.e. things to remember.

Indicate the method of service and garnishes.

Fish and shellfish

12

This chapter covers the following outcomes from Diploma unit 211: Prepare and cook fish and shellfish

- Outcome 211.1 Prepare fish and shellfish
- Outcome 211.2 Cook fish and shellfish

Working through this chapter could also provide evidence for the following Key Skills:

C2.1, C2.2a, C2.2b, C2.3, N, N1.2, N2.2, ICT2.1, ICT2.2, ICT2.3, LP2.1, LP2.2, LP2.3, PS2.1, PS2.2, PS2.3

In this chapter you will learn how to:

Identify the types of fish and shellfish and their quality points

State the most commonly used cuts of fish and their portion sizes/ weights

Describe the methods of preservation and their advantages and disadvantages

Use the correct tools and equipment for preparation and cooking

Use the correct methods and principles to prepare, cook and finish the fish and shellfish

Determine when fish and shellfish are cooked

Safely store fish and shellfish

You will learn how to prepare and cook basic fish and shellfish dishes, including:

- sea bass with capers
- deep-fried cod in batter
- moules marinière.

Types of fish and shellfish

Types of fish

White flat fish

This category includes the following types of fish:

o dover sole

o brill

o halibut

o turbot

o lemon sole

o plaice.

White flat fish have white flesh and are flat. Turbot, brill and halibut are very large flat fish, but are readily available from suppliers and popular in many fine restaurants. The cuts of flat fish are different to those of round fish.

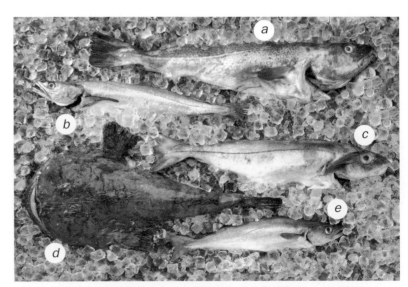

Figure 12.1 a Dover sole, b brill, c halibut, d turbot, e lemon sole, f plaice

White round fish

The following types of white round fish are included in the Diploma:

o cod

o hake

o haddock

o monkfish

o whiting

o huss.

These round fish are relatively common in UK coastal waters. Like flat fish, their flesh is white but the cuts are different.

Figure 12.2 a cod, b hake, c haddock, d monkfish, e whiting

Oily fish

This category includes the following fish:

o mackerel

o salmon

o trout

o tuna

o herring

o sardines

o anchovies.

All oily fish are round and the flesh is darker than that of white fish. White fish contain oil, but only in their livers, whereas oily fish have oil throughout their bodies.

Figure 12.3 a mackerel, b salmon, c trout

Types of shellfish

Crustaceans

Crustaceans often used in cooking:

o prawns

o shrimp

o crab

o lobster

o crayfish

o langoustine (Dublin bay prawn).

Definition

Crustaceans: soft-bodied creatures with legs and sometimes claws and whose exterior is a hard shell, e.g. crab.

Figure 12.4 crab

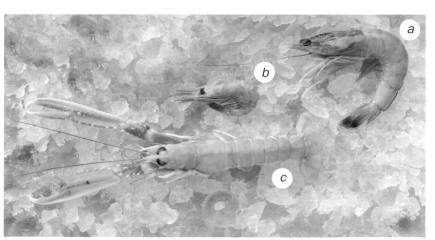

Figure 12.5 a tiger prawn, b shrimp, c langoustine

Molluscs

Molluscs included in the Diploma:

○ mussels

○ cockles

○ clams

○ squids (a cephalopod).

Other types of mollusc used in cooking:

○ oysters (a bivalve mollusc)

○ scallops (a bivalve mollusc)

○ whelks (a univalve mollusc)

○ cuttlefish (a cephalopod)

○ octopus (a cephalopod)

Figure 12.6 a palourdes clam, b amande clam, c mussel, d squid

Quality of fish and shellfish

Fish and shellfish can be obtained fresh, canned, salted, pickled, vacuum-packed or frozen. It is best to purchase only fresh fish and shellfish. Once killed, fish and shellfish will deteriorate very quickly if not stored correctly. If you are unsure of the quality of the fish or shellfish, do not use it. Ask your supervisor for advice.

The quality points below can indicate freshness in all types of fish (whole, fresh or frozen):

○ The eyes should be clear and raised, not sunken.

○ It should not smell of ammonia or have an unpleasant smell.

○ There should be slime on it and its skin should be moist.

○ Its gills should be bright and pink.

○ It should be firm in texture.

○ It should have no external damage, e.g. cuts, damaged fins.

○ The scales should be firmly attached and shiny.

○ It should have a good colour, e.g. orange spots on the skin of a plaice.

○ It should be of a good weight, appropriate to its size, indicating a good yield.

○ It should be kept at the correct temperature (−18 to −25°C for frozen, under 5°C for fresh).

○ If frozen, there should be no evidence of freezer burn.

○ Once thawed it should have firm flesh.

Definition

Molluscs: soft-bodied creatures contained in a hard shell, e.g. mussels.

Figure 12.7 whelks

Figure 12.8 winkles

Listed below are quality points for shellfish, alive and frozen:

○ It should be kept at the correct temperature (–18°C or below for frozen, under 5°C for fresh).
○ There must be no freezer burn on the flesh or skin.
○ Fresh shellfish should be alive and intact.
○ The open shells of mussels or clams will close if tapped. If they do not, discard them.
○ It should have a fresh salty smell.
○ All claws and legs should be intact and not damaged.
○ Live shellfish, e.g. lobster, should be lively not limp.
○ There should not be too many barnacles on the shells.
○ Shellfish should be a good weight in proportion to their size.

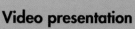

Video presentation
Watch *Quality points of fish* to see this.

Remember!
Any shellfish that has its shell open before preparation is probably dead.

Investigate!   Worksheet 26
Visit a fish market or supermarket and make a list of all the types of fish and shellfish. Categorise the fish into flat, round and oily. Categorise the shellfish into cephalopods, bivalves or univalves.

Preparing fish and shellfish

Preparation methods

Washing

Washing fish and shellfish is important during the preparation phase. Washing should be carried out regularly during preparation as fresh fish can be quite messy and the washing process should be thorough. Fish and shellfish should be run under cold water. The reasons fish and shellfish should be washed:

○ To wash any slime away from the skin before preparing.
○ To wash away any liquid which may have built up while being stored.
○ There may be blood or traces of scales or stomach contents after gutting and these must be removed.
○ There may be impurities such as sand and other physical contamination that must be removed.
○ The shells may have had barnacles removed, so washing will remove any loose debris.
○ To keep them clean.

Top marks!
Preparation of shellfish and crustaceans is quite testing. Presentation of the final dish is crucial and will determine better marks. Practise the skills shown to you in lessons and you will achieve optimum results.

Shelling

Shelling means removing the shell to leave the soft edible flesh of the mollusc or crustacean. While shellfish can be cooked with their shells intact, some dishes require the shell to be removed. Oysters must have their shells opened before being served raw. Scallops may have the shell removed.

How to shell a prawn

Prawns may be shelled before or after cooking. The process in both cases is the same.

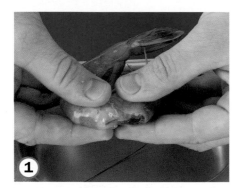

① Pull the head from the prawn. Put it in a separate bowl.

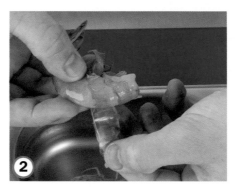

② Starting from the underside, peel away the shell in a rolling motion. The body will separate from the shell.

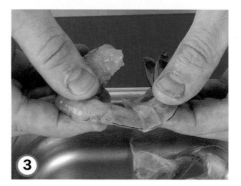

③ The tail section will require a gentle pull to extract it from the shell.

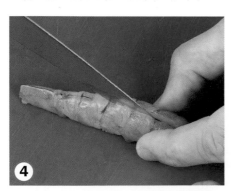

④ Make a shallow cut along the back of the prawn to expose the intestinal tract.

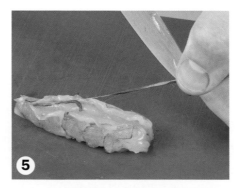

⑤ Grasp the intestinal tract between your thumb and the blade of a paring knife. Gently extract ensuring the entire tract is removed.

⑥ Rinse the prawns and put them in a clean bowl until required.

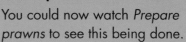

Video presentation
You could now watch *Prepare prawns* to see this being done.

How to prepare mussels

Purge mussels in a container of cold water for several hours.

Mussels must only be used if they are perfectly fresh. Check each one by tapping it against the side of the sink.

The shell of a fresh mussel should be closed or should close when tapped to indicate it is still alive. Discard any that do not close.

Wash under cold running water while scraping with a small paring knife to remove barnacles.

Remove the byssus threads by pulling with your fingers or use your thumb and the paring knife.

Video presentation
You may wish to watch *Prepare mussels* to see this being done.

How to remove a mollusc from its shell

Shellfish open their shells when cooked. Removing a mollusc is simple. Use either your hands or a small knife to pull the mollusc from its attachment.

Did you know?
All fish and shellfish contain high levels of vitamins A, B and D.

Cuts

Numerous cuts can be taken from flat and round fish. The table below identifies these.

Cut	Description of cut	Appearance
Fillet	This is flesh which is free from bone. It is usually the whole fillet and will therefore vary in size. A plaice fillet will be much smaller than that of a salmon.	
Supreme	A piece of fillet that has been cut across a large fillet at an angle. This cut is usually reserved for larger types of fish such as cod or salmon.	
Goujon	A strip cut from a large fillet. A goujon is usually coated in breadcrumbs before cooking.	
Paupiette	A flattened piece of filleted fish, which is then stuffed and rolled.	
Delice	A neatly folded and trimmed flat fish fillet.	
Medallion	Similar to a supreme but trimmed further to form a round or oval shape. (Monkfish is often cut into medallions.)	
Darne	A slice cut across the bone from a round fish.	
Tronçon	A finger-shaped cut from a flat fish across its body width. The thickness will vary depending on the type of flat fish.	

Figure 12.9 Different cuts of fish

Try this!   Worksheet 27

Look at the table above. Cover up the writing. Can you identify the photographs of the different cuts?

Video presentation

For guidance on how to make these cuts watch: *Prepare a whole halibut and cut tronçons; Prepare a whole cod and cut darnes; Cut supremes of salmon; Prepare paupiettes of plaice; Prepare delices of plaice; Cut goujons of plaice.*

Trimming

Trimming fish means to remove the fins, gills, eyes, head and scales. Gills, eyes and fins are usually removed by cutting them out or off using kitchen scissors. Kitchen scissors are used as they are robust and sturdy.

Shellfish (e.g. mussels) have byssus threads (threadlike attachments) hanging from their shells. They use these to attach themselves to rocks or other static structures. Use a knife to pull away these strings, and wash the shellfish again.

Video presentation

Watch *Trim a whole salmon* for more information.

How to remove the scales from a fish

Here we use a medium-sized serrated knife which is suitable for the removal of scales from a large fish such as salmon. A filleting knife would be more suitable for a smaller fish, e.g. herring or trout. Fishmongers sometimes use a special type of wire brush.

Lay the fish on a blue chopping board. Cut off the fins using fish scissors.

Scrape the knife blade against the scales of the fish in the opposite direction to that in which they lie. Ensure you hold the fish firmly by the tail to prevent accidents. This scraping motion will lift the scales and any surplus slime from the fish's body. Wash the fish.

Top marks!

Have a good understanding of what yield you will have from your fish. What type of fish is it? What type of cut? What will be the portion size of the finished dish? This is the difference between a well-presented or a clumsy dish. Don't forget that a lunch portion is usually smaller than a dinner portion.

Filleting

Filleting is a complex knife skill, which is an essential part of preparing fish. Filleting is the removal of the flesh from the bones and skin.

The equipment and tools used for filleting fish are:

○ a blue chopping board, secured to a flat work surface
○ suitable filleting knife with a sharp, flexible blade
○ container for waste products
○ tray for the fillets.

You may also need:

○ tweezers to remove pin bones (small bones) left in the fillet
○ kitchen scissors which can be used to trim away fins.

The process for filleting a flat fish is different from that of filleting a round one. Usually the preferred knife to use is a 7-inch blade which is flexible to aid the filleting process. If the flat fish is large (e.g. a turbot), a knife with a sturdy blade is needed for safety.

Figure 12.10 The tools required for filleting fish

How to fillet a flat fish

1 Lay the fish flat on the chopping board. Cut around the head with the point of the knife until you reach the lateral line.

2 Cut down the central lateral line until the knife reaches the rib bones. Then cut along the lateral line as far as the tail.

3 Bending the flexible blade, sweep the knife smoothly against the bones to remove the flesh. Cutting motions will leave flesh on the bone and affect the presentation of the fillet.

4 Cut the fillet away from the fins and place it on a tray. Turn the fish round and remove the other fillet in the same manner.

5 Trim up the fillet to remove the fins.

How to fillet a round fish

The fish must already be gutted and trimmed.

1

Lay the fish flat on the chopping board. Use a knife which has at least a 7-inch flexible blade and is sharp. Cut behind the fins and gills to give access to the backbone.

2

Cut along the backbone of the fish around the rib cage. Lift the fillet off the bones as you are cutting.

3

Continue to cut, lifting the fillet off the bones.

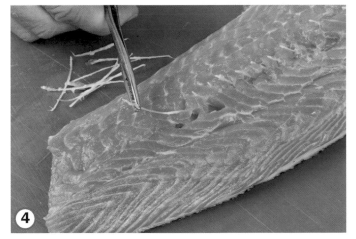

4

Place the fillet on the chopping board. Run your fingers along the flesh to locate any pin bones and remove them using tweezers.

Repeat the process on the other side of the fish.

Try this!   Worksheet 28

Close your book and write down the five steps you should follow to fillet a flat fish.

Video presentation

Watch *Fillet a salmon* to see this in action.

Skinning

While skin is usually edible on fish, some dish requirements mean that it needs to be removed. This is quite difficult. When skinning, you must not damage the flesh of the fish, so specific knife techniques are needed.

Skinning usually occurs once the fillets of the fish have been removed. The exception is a whole flat fish. In this case the whole skin is removed by making an incision at the tail and then pulling the skin from the flesh to the head.

The equipment needed for skinning is:

o a blue chopping board
o a flexible filleting knife
o salt or a clean cloth
o a container for waste products
o a tray to place the skinned fillets on.

How to skin a fillet

To provide grip when you grasp the tail end of the fillet either dip your fingers in some salt before you begin or use a cloth to hold the tail.

Did you know?
Fish contains high levels of monosaturated fat, which has no impact on cholesterol levels.

Video presentation
Watch a skilled chef at work in *Skin a salmon fillet.*

① Place the fillet on the chopping board. Cut into the end of the tail section until the knife is touching or lying on the skin at an angle of 45°.

② Take a firm hold of the tail skin and keep a firm grip on the knife. Use a sawing action, moving both the skin and knife at the same time. You will see the fillet come away from the skin and the angle of the knife will mean that no flesh will remain on the skin.

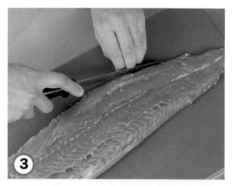

③ Trim any untidy pieces of fillet away to leave a neat, clean skinned fillet.

Preparing a whole fish

Fish such as trout, salmon, sole and plaice can be prepared whole ready for cooking.

How to prepare a whole round fish

1 Remove the eyes and gills.
2 Gut the fish (removing innards).
3 Remove the scales and trim the fins.
4 Wash thoroughly.

How to prepare a whole flat fish

1 Remove the eyes and gills.
2 Gut the fish.
3 Remove the skin (see skinning on page 398).
4 Wash thoroughly.

Stuffing

Some fish or shellfish dishes require stuffing, e.g. stuffing squid for a Mediterranean dish.

To stuff a whole fish simply fill the cavity which is left after gutting with a suitable stuffing – try filling a trout with herb stuffing. To make paupiettes spread mousse, or an appropriate stuffing mixture, along a flat fish fillet, then roll to make a paupiette. You could try this with plaice fillets.

How to stuff a squid

1 Remove the head and wash the body thoroughly.
2 Simply rub away the outer skin to reveal the white rubbery flesh.
3 Remove the skeletal cartilage, which resembles plastic. To do this you will need to turn the squid inside out. This becomes the presentation side.
4 Spoon or pipe the stuffing into the cavity which resembles a cannelloni pasta tube.

How to stuff a crab

1 Cook the crab and extract the meat.
2 Extract the meat and separate it into dark meat and white meat.
3 Dress and season the meat. Add other ingredients according to the recipe.
4 Stuff the crab, lining up white meat and dark meat to contrast.
5 Serve chilled.

> **Top marks!**
> Clean, safe working practices and workstations will ensure top marks when working. Organisational skills are as important as your practical skills in producing the dish.

> **Remember!**
> At all times take care to ensure food safety. For example, do not add hot stuffings to cold fish.

Preserving fish and shellfish

For more information see pages 228–230.

Preserving methods

Chilling and freezing

Fish or shellfish to be frozen should be labelled and covered to prevent cross-contamination and possible freezer burn. Chilled fish and shellfish should be stored near the bottom shelf of a refrigerator to prevent cross-contamination.

Vacuum-packing

Fish and shellfish can be vacuum-packed.

Smoking

This method is used to preserve fish such as herrings (kippers), salmon and trout. The fish is heated gently by a fire to dry and preserve it. Chicory wood chips, for example, are burned to give the fish a strong smoky flavour. Smoked fish is a special requirement for certain dishes.

Canning

Fish and shellfish suitable for canning includes tuna, salmon, crab, lobster, prawns and shrimps.

Salting

This preservation method is achieved by covering fish, e.g. cod, in salt. The problem is that it makes the fish extremely salty. Before it can be eaten water must be added to draw out the salt.

Pickling

This method which is used for both fish, e.g. herrings, and shellfish, e.g. whelks, winkles and mussels. They can be pickled when raw or cooked first. Raw herrings can be put into a pickling solution. Whelks and winkles can be boiled in a vinegar pickling solution and then preserved in a jar until required. Fresh shellfish have a short life span and can be stored for longer periods of time once pickled. However, pickled fish and shellfish have limited uses as the flavour is so strong.

> **Try this!**   Worksheet 29
>
> Using your book, the internet and any other resources complete the crossword.

Figure 12.13 Salted fish

Test yourself!

1 Name three different types of shellfish.

2 What are the categories of fish?

3 What equipment is used to trim the fins of fish?

4 What equipment is required to fillet a round fish?

5 List three quality points to look out for when selecting fresh fish for preparation.

6 What equipment is used to poach a whole salmon?

7 What cooking methods are applicable to shellfish?

8 List some traditional accompaniments and garnishes for fish and shellfish.

9 What should you do if any problems occur while cooking fish or shellfish?

10 What are the advantages and disadvantages of smoking and pickling?

Practice assignment tasks

Prepare and cook fish and shellfish

Task 1

You have been asked by your local tourist information centre to help them produce a short pamphlet on the commonly used fish and shellfish of the UK. You should include as much information as possible but the format needs to be simple and visual. At the minimum you must:

o Select one or two types of fish from each of the following groups: flat, round or oily.
o List the different cuts. For each cut give examples of two suitable fish.
o Identify the different flavourings that can be used to prepare fish.
o Write about a typical dish that is commonly served in the UK.

Task 2

Produce a chart/poster showing: the commonly used shellfish; their classification; and the preparation and cookery methods. Provide an example of a dish for each type of shellfish.

Rice, pasta, grain and egg dishes

13

This chapter covers the following outcomes from Diploma unit 212: Cook rice, pasta, grains and eggs:

- Outcome 212:1 Prepare and cook rice
- Outcome 212:2 Prepare and cook pasta
- Outcome 212:3 Prepare and cook grains
- Outcome 212:4 Prepare and cook eggs

Working through this chapter could also provide evidence for the following Key Skills:

C2.1, C2.2a, C2.2b, C2.3, N, N1.2, N2.2, ICT2.1, ICT2.2, ICT2.3, PS2.1, PS2.2, PS2.3, LP2.1, LP2.2, LP2.3

In this chapter you will learn how to:

Check that the rice, pasta, grain, egg and other ingredients meet dish requirements
Identify and use the tools and equipment correctly
Prepare and cook the rice, pasta, grain, egg and other ingredients to meet requirements
Strain and mould the rice or grain as required
Make sure the dish has the correct flavour, colour, texture and quantity
Present the dish to meet requirements
Make sure the dish is at the correct temperature for holding and serving
Safely store any cooked dishes not for immediate use

You will learn to cook basic rice, pasta, grain and egg dishes, including:

- risotto
- baked rice pudding
- ravioli
- Scotch oatcakes
- millet croquettes
- Spanish omelette.

Rice

Rice is a type of grain which grows on dry and wet land. It has been a food source for well over 3,000 years and is the second largest cultivated food source in the world.

Rice is grown in many countries, but mainly in China, India, Bangladesh, Africa and America. Rice can be eaten hot or cold, and used in savoury or sweet dishes.

Rice seeds are covered in a husk or tough outer skin. The seeds are milled to remove the husk and produce brown rice. With further milling the **germ** and the **bran** of the plant are removed, producing white rice.

Types of rice

The three main types of rice available are long grain, short grain and round grain.

Long grain rice is shaped like a narrow missile with a point. It is ideal for use with plain boiled rice dishes or savoury dishes. The grains remain separate during cooking because it has a tough hard texture and holds its shape. It is usually white and slightly see-through. Long grain is the rice most usually found in kitchens. When cooked, long grain rice has a light fluffy texture.

Short grain rice is round and looks a little like wheat. When cooked, it has a softer texture than the long grain type and the grains stick together easily. It has a light colour, sometimes golden but normally creamy white. Because this rice sticks so well, it is ideal for risotto and paella dishes.

Round grain rice is very much like short grain rice. When cooked, it has a soft texture, is almost see-through and goes sticky. It is used mainly for sweet rice dishes like puddings and is also known as pearl or pudding rice.

Although rice is broken down into long, short and round grain categories, these categories also contain different types of rice and have many differernt names and uses.

Figure 13.1 A rice plant growing in a paddy field

Definition
Germ: the heart of the seed.
Bran: the hard outer layer of the rice seed.

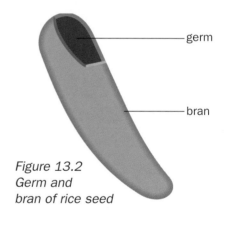
Figure 13.2 Germ and bran of rice seed

germ

bran

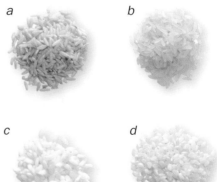
Figure 13.3 Types of rice: a brown long grain, b long grain, c round grain, d arborio

You will come across the main types when shopping for rice, and these include brown basmati, jasmine, japonica and arborio; all of these types of rice are available in most supermarkets.

Other rice types that are not so well know are carnaroli, vialone nano, baldo and carolina rice.

Brown rice: This is a very nutritious long grain rice. It has a sandy colour. When cooked, brown rice has a chewy texture with a mild nutty flavour.

Basmati: This is an Indian long grain rice. It is sometimes called the king of rices because of its great flavour; when cooked it has a nice aromatic quality and is best used as plain boiled rice to accompany spicy dishes.

Japonica: This is a Chinese long grain rice often used in sushi dishes; it is almost black and when cooked has a nutty mushroom-type flavour. It can be used in stir-fries and casseroles, but also as a stuffing.

Arborio or **risotto rice**: This is an Italian round pearl grain rice; it is most often used in risotto dishes but can also be used in puddings.

Vialone nano: This is an Italian short grain rice ideal in risotto, paella and puddings. This rice should ideally not be washed before use.

Jasmine: This is Thai long grain rice; when cooked it is less sticky that most other long grain rices and is best suited to plain boiled or fried rice dishes.

Carnaroli and baldo: These are Italian short grain rices mainly used in risotto and paella dishes; they are also good for puddings.

Carolina: This is an American white long grain rice; it is perfect for plain boiled rice, fried rice and used cold in salads.

Quality points for rice

Most rice, dried pasta and grains come packed and treated and are usually quite clean, but you must still check their quality.

When selecting rice it is very important to check for imperfections. Before using rice, dried pasta or grains always check the following:
- It has been correctly stored, off the ground in a waterproof container or a storage bin that has a lid.
- It has been stored in a cool well-ventilated store free from damp.

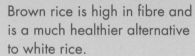

Healthy eating
Brown rice is high in fibre and is a much healthier alternative to white rice.

Remember!
If you find problems with any ingredient you should:
- inform your supervisor or line manager immediately
- ask your supervisor for a substitute or replacement ingredient
- never use the problem ingredient
- separate the problem ingredient from the others before use.

- o It does not have any other physical contaminants, e.g. stones or anything that may have fallen into the storage container.
- o If it is still in the original packaging, that it is free from tears, rips or general damage.

Preparation methods

It is important to check the dish requirements before you begin preparing your dish. You should check what type of rice you need (long, short, round, brown) and the quantity you require, as this reduces unnecessary wastage.

Before preparing and cooking rice, pick through it with your fingers. Look for imperfections in the rice grains or anything that may have fallen in. Throw away any imperfect grains. Wash it under cold running water to remove unwanted starch left over from milling and packaging. Also, as rice is tightly packed the grains rub against each other and leave a fine floury substance in the packet which needs to be removed. Washing the rice before cooking means it is less likely to stick.

It is important to weigh rice carefully to reduce wastage as rice gets larger and fluffs up as it cooks.

Cooking methods
Boiling

Boiling is the easiest and most usual way to cook rice. It is an ideal way to cook rice for serving with curries or meat dishes.

The rice (usually long grain) is plunged into boiling salted water for 15–20 minutes. When the rice is light and fluffy, but still with a little bite, it is cooked. Drain the rice in a colander and wash it off well to remove starch before service.

To safely store boiled rice for use in cold dishes, e.g. salads, drain the boiled rice under cold running water in a colander until cooled, allow to drain then put it in a covered container and refrigerate until required.

Plain boiled rice can be moulded and used as a decoration or a base for some meat dishes. The most common way of moulding rice is to tightly pack the cooked hot rice into a buttered ramekin mould and turn it out onto the serving plate. This is known as a timbale. Cold rice can be used as a decoration for salads.

Top marks!

Choosing the correct type of rice is vital to the success of a recipe. Get to know the best uses of each type of rice and the correct cooking times.

Did you know?

For a main dish the ideal portion of uncooked rice is 65g (2½ ounces) per person.

Steaming

Steamed rice is popular in Chinese-style cookery. It is simple and quick, and most types of rice can be steamed. Steamed rice is eaten plain or used as a garnish for meats and fish.

There are two ways to steam rice. The first way is to put washed rice over boiling water in a steamer; this takes 20–40 minutes.

The second, and more common, way is to combine boiling and steaming. Put the rice into a pan and cover it with 1½ times as much water. Cover with a tight-fitting lid, bring to the boil, then turn down the heat and cook until all the water has been absorbed by the rice or evaporated.

Stewing

Rice can be stewed in stock, water or milk. Set up as for boiling but keep the rice on the heat until most of the liquid has gone. It is important to keep stirring to prevent the rice sticking to the side or bottom of the pan.

Frying

Countries like China, Nepal and India use fried rice as part of many of their dishes. After you have boiled rice you can fry it, which is a good way to give the rice flavour. You can add other ingredients, e.g. vegetables or meat.

Investigate! Worksheet 36

Visit the website for 'The Cook's Thesaurus' and go to the rice section. A link has been made available at www.heinemann.co.uk/hotlinks. Just follow the links and enter the express code 4103P. Choose ten types of rice and find out:

- country of origin
- uses
- cooking method and time
- a recipe for each.

Fried rice

rice	5kg
oil	1 tsp
Cooking time	25 minutes
Serves	40

Method

1 Boil and cool the rice.
2 Put the cooked rice in a deep frying pan with some oil or butter or margarine.
3 Heat it over a low heat and stir often to stop it sticking.
4 Remove from heat. Transfer to a serving dish and serve hot.

Egg fried rice

rice	5kg
eggs	25
Cooking time	25 minutes
Serves	40

Method

1 Boil and cool the rice.
2 Lightly scramble the eggs in a frying pan.
3 Add the cooked rice, season and mix with the egg.
4 Fork through the rice. Transfer to a serving dish and serve hot.

Baking

This method is best suited to puddings. The best rice to use is round or short grain.

Milk is the most common liquid used with baked rice and forms the basis of rice pudding. Put the rice into the boiling liquid. Other ingredients may be added to help flavour the rice. Put this mixture into an oven and bake until the liquid has been soaked up by the rice.

Baked rice pudding

milk	500ml
round grain or pearl rice	160g
sugar	120g
nutmeg, grated	pinch
Oven temperature	190°C
Cooking time	30–35 minutes
Serves	4

Method

1 Put the milk into a medium-sized milk pan. Bring the milk to the boil and slowly add the rice. Remember to stir while you add the rice. Allow to boil for one minute.
2 Take off the boil. Slowly add the sugar and nutmeg.
3 Pour the mixture into an ovenproof baking dish, then put the dish into a medium/deep baking pan.
4 Pour boiling water into the baking pan so that it comes 1cm up the side of the baking dish, creating a bain-marie.
5 Cook in a preheated oven.
6 Remove the pudding from the oven, allow it to cool slightly.
7 Clean the outside of the dish and serve.

Braising

The common term for this method of preparing rice is pilaf or pilau. Long grain rice is the best type to use.

To prepare dishes such as pilaf, paella or risotto, **sweat** the rice in butter or oil to begin the cooking process. This coats the rice in fat. Add liquid, e.g. water or stock, and braise in an oven or over heat.

Pilaf or pilau of rice

onions, finely chopped	80g
butter	40g
white long grain rice, washed	260g
stock or water	750ml
Oven temperature	200°C
Cooking time	16–18 minutes
Serves	4

Method

1. Using a deep frying pan, sweat the onions in half the butter, being careful not to brown them.
2. Add the washed rice and stir until it becomes almost transparent.
3. Add the boiling stock or water and season.
4. Place a cartouche (buttered greaseproof paper) on to the liquid and rice, cover with a lid and put the pan into a preheated oven. Alternatively, transfer the rice and liquid to an ovenproof dish and proceed as before.
5. Remove the pan or ovenproof dish from the oven and allow the rice to stand for five minutes.
6. Stir in the remaining butter with a fork to separate the grains and transfer the rice to a serving dish.

Definition

Sweat: cook rice in a pan over a low heat.

Video presentation

If you would like to find out more about sweating food watch *Prepare fish stock (1) sweat*.

Did you know?

Au gras is cooked in the same way as pilaf rice but the rice is cooked with fat bouillon stock of chicken or beef.

Risotto

onion, finely chopped	30g
cooking oil	30g
short or round grain rice	350g
white stock	1.5 litres
salt	to season
bay leaf	1
butter	15g
finely grated Cheddar or Parmesan cheese	60g
Cooking time	15 minutes
Serves	5

Method

1 Using a medium-sized pan, sweat the finely chopped onions in the oil. Do not let them colour.
2 Add the rice and heat through.
3 Add the stock, season well and bring to the boil.
4 Add the bay leaf and simmer gently over a low heat. Stir frequently as the stock is absorbed by the rice.
5 When the rice is cooked, fork in the butter and grated cheese.
6 Serve sprinkled with grated cheese.

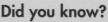

Did you know?
Medium or long grain rice absorbs up to three times its weight in liquid.

Microwaving

Rice can be reheated in a microwave but you must be very careful as it is a high-risk food. (See Safe use and storage of rice below.)

Adding flavour to rice

Rice can be quite bland if not added to or mixed with other ingredients. Dishes such as fried or braised rice can have flavour added by using herbs and spices. These are added to the dish when the rice is about to be fried, as the rice absorbs the flavours while frying. Some common herbs and spices used are: tarragon, mint, cumin, coriander, paprika, crushed black pepper and chilli powder. Care must be taken not to add too much spice and overpower the dish.

Safe use and storage of rice

Safe service and storage of rice dishes, whether hot or cold, is very important. The following points must be remembered:

Remember!
Rice is a high-risk food. Make sure the rice is properly cooked, cooled and stored.

- Hot rice dishes should be served at a minimum of 63°C. If you are hot-holding the dish for any length of time, e.g. on a hotplate, it should be kept at or above this temperature.
- Reheated rice should have a core temperature of 75°C before service. Only reheat rice once.
- Rice for service as a cold dish should be served at a temperature of 5°C and eaten as soon as possible afterwards.
- When using pre-cooked rice for dishes, e.g. salads, it is important that the rice has been properly stored in a refrigerator at a temperature of 3°C–5°C.
- Any rice stored after cooking should be covered and labelled showing the date.
- Do not use rice that has been refrigerated for more than three days (check label for the date).

Test yourself!

1 Write down three cooking methods for long grain rice.

2 Why is brown rice a healthier option than white rice?

3 What temperature must reheated rice reach before service?
   a 60°C
   b 65°C
   c 73°C
   d 75°C.

4 At what temperature should rice be served when used as an ingredient in a hot dish?
   a 60°C
   b 65°C
   c 73°C
   d 75°C.

5 What is the best rice to use for puddings?
   a Long grain rice
   b Round grain rice
   c Brown rice
   d Arborio.

6 What weight is an ideal portion of uncooked rice?
   a 55g
   b 60g
   c 65g
   d 70g.

7 Draw and label a diagram showing the parts of a rice seed.

8 Which four ingredients do you need to make a Baked rice pudding?

9 Rice is grown in many countries. Write down the names of three of them.

10 Before cooking rice what should you do?

Pasta

Traditionally, Italian pasta is made from wheat flour, eggs and oil. Sometimes water is used instead of eggs. The ingredients are mixed together and kneaded like dough. Pasta may be flavoured during the mixing stage by adding purées of vegetables, which can also colour it.

Types of pasta

Pasta has many varieties and comes in many shapes. Some well-known pasta varieties are spaghetti, cannelloni, macaroni, tortellini and ravioli. Pasta can be eaten plain, filled with vegetables, meat or cheese, fish and shellfish or simply eaten with a sauce.

Fresh pasta

Common colours for fresh pasta:
○ Light yellow: the colour for fresh pasta. It has a plain taste.
○ Green: this pasta may have had spinach added. It is called pasta verde.
○ Red: this comes from adding tomato purée and is called pasta rossa.

More colours can be created by adding unusual ingredients:
○ Black: add diluted cuttlefish ink.
○ Purple: add beetroot juice.
○ Brown: add bitter chocolate powder.

Once mixed, the fresh pasta is kneaded, shaped, filled, rolled or cut as needed. Fresh pasta can easily be formed into different shapes.

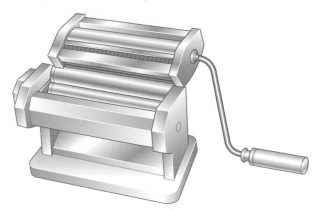

Figure 13.4 A pasta machine rolls the dough very thin

Did you know?
It is quite common for people, especially when young, to have an allergy to eggs.

Did you know?
'Pasta' is an Italian word meaning 'paste' or 'dough'.

Chef's tip
Fresh pasta dough should be smooth to touch with an elastic feel.

Did you know?
You can buy machines to roll out pasta very thin. It can then be cut into shapes, sheets or strips.

Basic pasta dough

flour (durum wheat flour, plain flour, brown flour or semolina)	500g
salt	pinch
eggs *or*	5
cold water	200ml
oil	15ml
Serves	10

Method

1 Sift the flour with the salt.
2 Make a bay, add the eggs *or* water. Add the oil and mix to a stiff paste.
3 Knead together well and allow to relax for 20 minutes.
4 Dust with a little flour or semolina to reduce sticking and use as required.

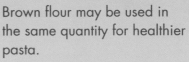

Healthy eating

Brown flour may be used in the same quantity for healthier pasta.

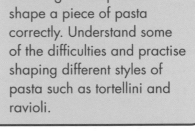

Top marks!

Pasta can be made in a number of different shapes. It takes practice and good handling techniques to shape a piece of pasta correctly. Understand some of the difficulties and practise shaping different styles of pasta such as tortellini and ravioli.

Dried pasta

Dried pasta is simply fresh pasta that has been dried. Dried pasta has a long shelf life. Generally, the plain unfilled dried pasta, e.g. conchiglie or spaghetti, can be kept for as long as two years provided it is kept dry and covered. Other dried and filled pasta such as tortellini lasts less time. Always check the 'use by' dates on the package before use (see page 135).

Shaped pasta

Fresh, kneaded pasta dough can be shaped by hand or using a machine. The dough comes out in the selected shape and is cut to size ready for drying or cooking.

Figure 13.5 Tortellini being shaped around a finger

421

In the table are examples of some popular pasta shapes:

Pasta shapes	Description of use
Rigatoni	Very good for heavier sauce dishes, e.g. bolognese or thick cheese sauce.
Cannelloni	Stuffed, covered with a sauce and baked.
Spaghetti	Good with almost any sauce, and can also be stir-fried after it has been boiled.
Linguine	A thin, long flat shape, good with sauce or in a salad.
Twists or rotini	The twist can hold meat, vegetables or cheese. This shape is ideal baked, as a pasta salad or stir-fried.
Farfalle	A 'butterfly' shape – ideal with a light sauce.
Vermicelli	Like thin spaghetti, this is ideal with light sauces.
Penne	This shape is a good choice to mix with a sauce, or use in a soup or salad.
Macaroni	A small, shaped pasta – ideal with heavy sauces, e.g. cheese or cream-based.

Figure 13.7 Popular pasta shapes

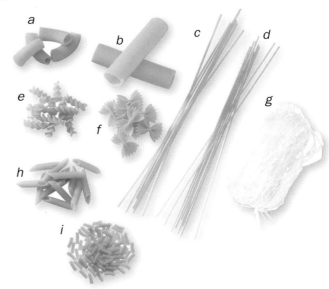

Figure 13.6 Pasta shapes: a rigatoni; b cannelloni; c spaghetti; d linguine; e twists; f farfalle; g vermicelli; h penne; i macaroni

Flat pasta

To make flat pasta, e.g. tagliatelle or lasagne, the dough is rolled very thin and then cut to a required shape: long strips, short strips or square sheets. The pasta dough can be passed through a machine which will flatten and cut it, or rolled out using a rolling pin and cut with a sharp 9-inch chef's knife.

Stuffed pasta

Stuffed pasta dishes are very popular as the pasta shapes are filled with meat, vegetables or cheese. This type of pasta makes an excellent meal on its own.

Stuffed pasta includes cannelloni, tortellini and ravioli (see page 426), all of which can be served with a sauce and can be baked.

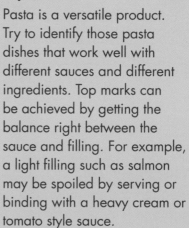

Top marks!

Pasta is a versatile product. Try to identify those pasta dishes that work well with different sauces and different ingredients. Top marks can be achieved by getting the balance right between the sauce and filling. For example, a light filling such as salmon may be spoiled by serving or binding with a heavy cream or tomato style sauce.

Cannelloni can be bought dried and filled with the stuffing of your choice. To make fresh cannelloni, follow the steps below.

1 Roll out some pasta dough to 10cm squares, 1.6mm thick.
2 Take a piping bag with a 12.5mm nozzle and pipe your filling in a line down the centre of the square.
3 Lightly egg wash one side of the square and roll it up like a sausage roll.
4 Put the cannelloni in a dish and cover it in a sauce ready for baking. Alternatively, you can cook flat sheets of cannelloni in boiling water for 15 minutes, drain them and serve with a separate sauce.

Figure 13.8 Rolled stuffed cannelloni ready for cooking

Noodle paste

Noodle paste is very similar to pasta but is made with more starchy flours, such as mung bean flour (for glass noodles), arrowroot flour, rice flour or buckwheat flour. Noodles are very thinly cut strips of dough. They cook very quickly.

Quality points for dried pasta

The quality points for dried pasta are the same as those for rice. See page 413.

Cooking methods

To cook fresh pasta, plunge it into boiling salted water for 3–8 minutes depending on the variety. Filled pasta takes around two minutes longer to cook. Stir pasta regularly during cooking.

Cook dried pasta in the same way but for 8–15 minutes.

Certain varieties of pasta may be combined with other ingredients and baked, e.g. lasagne.

It is important to test pasta while cooking. To test whether pasta is cooked, remove a piece of pasta from the pan and taste it. It should be firm with no floury taste but still stiff enough to need chewing. This is called 'al dente'. It is easy to overcook pasta. When overcooked, pasta becomes stodgy, swells up, and then breaks apart.

Chef's tip
Dried pasta cooking times can vary. Always follow the instructions on the packet carefully.

Pasta can be cooked, cooled and chilled for use in salads or pre-cooked and used at a later date for stir-fries. Boil the pasta, strain it in a colander and refresh it under cold running water until cold. Store it covered in a refrigerator until it is needed. It is important to note that filled/stuffed pasta is not ideally suited for use in salads.

Many pasta dishes are finished or accompanied by sauces, which can be light or heavy. These are some common sauces:

- **Carbonara**: a light binding sauce with a cream base, cooked bacon pieces or Parma ham. This sauce is traditionally seasoned with crushed black peppercorns. It has many varieties. Many chefs like to include mushrooms and onions to change the flavour of the sauce.
- **Napoletana** or **Neapolitan**: a tomato-based sauce, which is quite thick and often has other ingredients, e.g. ham, onions, mushroom, garlic, and herbs such as oregano or thyme. This sauce is often poured over the pasta allowing the customer to mix the sauce into the dish themselves.
- **Bolognese** or **Bolognaise**: traditionally this is a minced meat-based sauce; it contains a little tomato or tomato purée, onions, garlic and herbs, and is usually served with spaghetti.
- **Pesto**: a green sauce made with a mixture of olive oil, crushed pine nuts, basil and parmesan cheese. It can be served with pasta or Italian bread.
- **Cheese sauce**: a béchamel or velouté-based sauce made with parmesan or strong cheddar, used commonly with lasagne or macaroni. It is also used to coat some baked pasta dishes which are usually **gratinated**. Pasta velouté sauce is traditionally made with chicken stock and used as a coating or binding for dishes with chicken- or duxelle-based stuffings.

Definition

Gratinated: finished in the oven or browned under the grill.

Try this!

Write out how to cook perfect pasta.

Worksheet 37

Spaghetti bolognaise

For the Bolognaise sauce:

onions, chopped	60g
olive oil	30ml
lean minced beef	280g
garlic clove, crushed	1
tomatoes, peeled and diced	220g
mixed herbs	pinch
beef jus/brown sauce	280ml
salt and pepper	to season
Cooking time	45 minutes

Method

1 Sweat the onions in the oil until tender. Do not colour them.
2 Add the garlic and the minced beef.
3 Cook until the beef separates into individual small pieces, then add the tomato and mixed herbs.
4 Add the beef jus or brown sauce and bring to the boil. Season and simmer for 30 minutes.

For the spaghetti:

spaghetti	600g
butter	60g
Bolognaise sauce (see above)	800g
salt and pepper	to season
Parmesan cheese, grated	60g
parsley	14g
Cooking time	15–18 minutes
Serves	5

Method

1 Boil the spaghetti in salted water for 10–15 minutes for dried pasta, 5 minutes for fresh pasta. When cooked, drain in a colander and lightly refresh under cold water.
2 Heat the butter in a shallow saucepan. Add the spaghetti, season well and stir until thoroughly reheated.
3 Place the spaghetti in a serving dish with the hot bolognaise sauce in the centre.
4 Sprinkle the spaghetti with Parmesan cheese, sprinkle the bolognaise sauce with chopped parsley. Serve.

Ravioli

pasta dough	250g
egg	1
filling of your choice (savoury mince, ricotta cheese, **duxelle**, shrimp and lemon, tofu)	100g
tomato sauce	200ml
Cheddar or Parmesan cheese, grated	30g
Cooking time	15–20 minutes
Serves	5

Method

1 Divide the dough into two equal pieces and roll out each piece to 1.5mm thick. Keep the pieces an even size.
2 Cover one piece in egg wash.
3 Put the filling into a piping bag.
4 Pipe portions of filling the size of a hazelnut 2.5cm apart onto the egg-washed piece of dough.
5 Cover with the second piece of dough and press down between each row of filling in both directions.
6 With the blunt end of a 2.5cm round cutter, press down around each portion of filling.
7 Cut the dough into equal-sized squares with the filling in the centre of each square.
8 Cook in boiling salted water for 10–15 minutes. Remove and drain in a colander.
9 Arrange the ravioli neatly in a baking dish and cover with the tomato sauce.
10 Sprinkle with cheese and lightly grill until the cheese melts.
11 Serve immediately.

Definition

Duxelle: this is made up of very finely diced shallots, mushrooms or other vegetables, sautéd together in a little butter, cooked and dried out by slow cooking. It is a quick and cheap filling for pasta. Cuttings and stalks from mushrooms can be used.

Safe use and storage of pasta

The safe use and storage of pasta is the same as that of rice.
See page 418 for detailed information.

Pasta has a short shelf-life after cooking because of its high water content. Use refrigerated pasta within two days. (Check information on the label for the date.)

Test yourself!

1 List the three main ingredients used to make pasta dough.

2 Give two cooking methods for pasta.

3 What happens to pasta when it is overcooked?

4 What is Neapolitan sauce?

5 How many days can you keep pasta in a refrigerator?
   a One day
   b Two days
   c Three days
   d Four days.

6 For how long should you cook fresh pasta?
   a 1–5 minutes
   b 2–8 minutes
   c 3–8 minutes
   d 5–10 minutes.

7 For how long should you cook dried pasta?
   a 5–10 minutes
   b 8–15 minutes
   c 10–15 minutes
   d 15–20 minutes.

8 Which of these pasta types can be stir-fried after it has been boiled?
   a Penne
   b Farfalle
   c Linguine
   d Spaghetti.

9 Which of these pasta types has a 'butterfly' shape?
   a Penne
   b Farfalle
   c Linguine
   d Spaghetti.

Grains

Grains are also known as cereals. They are grown in greater quantities worldwide than any other crop. They are cheap to produce.

Grains are the main source of carbohydrates for many developing countries but also contain some protein, fats and vitamins.

Types of grain

Barley

Barley is a cheap, very nutritious food. Barley is a good ingredient for soups and stews, where it is used to thicken the dish.

Two types of barley are available:
- **Pearl barley**: the most common form of barley. Pearl barley is stripped of a nutritious bran layer during processing, leaving just the 'pearl' inside. Even with this bran layer taken off, pearl barley is still a nutritious food.
- **Pot barley or whole grain barley**: processed exactly like pearl barley, but the bran layer is left on. This type of barley is the most nutritious.

Pearl and pot barley are very common in health food stores as they are normally sold in their natural form.

Figure 13.9 Processed pearl barley grains

Buckwheat

Buckwheat has a nutty, earthy flavour and gives dishes a rough texture. Buckwheat seeds are triangular after processing and are a light golden colour. It is commonly ground down into flour and used to make everything from pancakes and tortillas to bread and noodles. The seed when ground into flour is gritty and dark and makes an excellent healthy substitute to normal flours. Buckwheat is also popular in some countries, e.g. America and Scotland, as a breakfast cereal.

Corn or maize

This is the only grain that is normally eaten as a fresh vegetable. Corn is high in vitamin A, fibre and other nutrients. Corn is also known as maize in some countries.

Healthy eating
Buckwheat is high in fibre and protein but very low in fat.

Did you know?
Buckwheat is free from gluten, so it is perfect for people with a gluten allergy. For more information on gluten see pages 169 and 446–8.

Corn bought fresh and raw in its husk (leafy outer covering) is called 'corn on the cob'. When buying corn on the cob fresh, break off one kernel (piece of corn) and bite it; the kernel should have a slightly sweet taste and be crisp. If the corn has no taste and is very dry, it is overripe.

Polenta

Polenta is made from ground corn called cornmeal. It looks like flour and can be rough or finely ground. It can be yellow or white. Polenta is very popular in Italy and is used in all sorts of recipes.

Polenta is most often served with simple meat dishes like pork chops, sausages or steaks. See page 432 for cooking instructions.

Figure 13.10 Polenta

Oats

Oats are highly nutritious. They contain protein, fat, iron, potassium, B vitamins and carbohydrates. They are high in fibre. Oats have a pleasant, nutty flavor and are fawn in colour.

Oats can be ground down into a meal and used to coat meat or fish. They can be rolled or crushed during processing and used to make breakfast cereals, e.g. porridge or muesli. They can also be used as an ingredient in biscuits or in crumble topping for pudding.

Figure 13.11 Rolled oats

Millet

Millet is very similar to wheat. It can be bought with its outer husk (hull) on or off. Millet seeds can be used to make flour, or used as part of breakfast cereals like muesli. The seeds are very tasty when toasted. Millet can be found in health food shops and is quite cheap.

Wheat

Wheat is used mainly in making flour; most flour available in the supermarkets is made from wheat. It can be used as grain in salads and also as an ingredient in pilaf dishes, muesli and cereal bars.

Wheat grain that has not been ground into flour has a nutty flavour. It is high in nutrients and gluten.

Healthy eating
Millet is very high in protein but is gluten-free.

Did you know?
Millet flour is very popular in India where it is used to make a flattened bread called bhakri.

429

Wheat is also processed into other ingredients like bulgar, semolina and couscous:

○ **Bulgar** or **burghul**: made from whole wheat that has been soaked and baked to speed up cooking time. It can be used as an ingredient in soup, bread and stuffing. It is a popular dish in the Middle East where it is used to make pilaf dishes. Bulgar comes whole, or cracked into fine, medium, or coarse grains. It is very high in nutrients and can be used as an alternative to couscous or rice.

○ **Cracked wheat**: whole wheat processed in the same way as bulgar, but which has not been parboiled. It is ideal boiled or steamed and has a distinctive nutty flavour.

○ **Semolina**: wheat that has been roughly ground or milled. It is often boiled and made into a pudding with sugar or another sweetener, e.g. jam. It can be flavoured with vanilla and eaten hot or cold.

○ **Couscous**: similar to semolina, but the wheat is ground a little finer. It is used as a side dish to meat or served under a stew or casserole. It is a very popular dish in Africa, Morocco and the Middle East where it is served with vegetables or as a separate side dish. To prepare couscous, soak it in cold water, then drain and wash it before steaming in a steamer or **couscousier**. Couscous can be served with meat or vegetable dishes.

○ **Rye**: very similar to a wheat grain, it is used in cereals once it has been rolled or bread and flour when ground. Rye is most famous as the staple ingredient in some types of beer, whiskey and vodka drinks.

Figure 13.12 Bulgar wheat

Figure 13.13 A couscousier

Quinoa

Quinoa is pronounced 'keen wah'. It is mostly used as an ingredient for breakfast cereals, but can also be cooked in the same way as rice. Quinoa contains more protein that any other grain. It is described as a perfect food because of the balance of nutrients.

Definition

Couscousier: a tall pot where stews or vegetables are cooked in the bottom and a smaller pot sits above with the couscous in it. The couscous cooks by steaming and absorbs the flavour from the meat or vegetables below it.

Investigate!   Worksheet 73

Look at the list of grains: barley, buckwheat, corn/maize, polenta, oats, milet, bulgar, cracked wheat, wheat, couscous, semolina, rye, quinoa.

Can they be used for:

○ classic main course dishes

○ garnishes

○ desserts?

Common uses for grain flours

Blini: a small, thick, round yeast-batter pancake, which varies in size from 5–15cm and looks like a crumpet. The yeast batter is made from wheat or buckwheat flour, with beaten eggs and whipped cream added just before cooking to make it light and fluffy. There should be small holes in the batter. Blinis are cooked in a frying pan with a little butter until golden brown and should be turned every few minutes. They are often served hot with whipped or soured cream and can be eaten at breakfast, mid-morning or during the afternoon.

Gnocchi: an Italian word that means 'lumps'. Gnocchi are best described as small dumplings made from flour, eggs and seasoning. Additional ingredients can be added if desired, such as chicken livers, spinach, beetroot or ricotta cheese. Traditional Italian gnocchi paste is made using semolina flour, but it can also be made using white flour, potato or choux paste. Gnocchi can be shaped or moulded into balls; turned using spoons into **quenelles**; or flattened and cut into 5cm roundels. Gnocchi is very similar to pasta, but it cooks much quicker. It is cooked in salted boiling water for a few minutes only and is often finished gratinated in an oven with parmesan cheese.

Figure 13.14 Gnocchi

Tortilla: a very thin pancake from Latin America made with cornmeal flour. The tortilla was traditionally approximately 20cm in diameter, cooked on an earthenware plate and served hot and flat with other ingredients spread on top (e.g. potatoes, minced or ground cooked beef or vegetables). Now it is more commonly served like a sandwich, both hot and cold, with a variety of fillings, e.g. spicy chicken breast or spicy vegetables. It also forms the main part of many other recipes, e.g. tacos, enchiladas and tostados, all of which use tortillas but are finished in a different way. They are often served with a spicy sauce to accompany the filling.

Definition
Quenelle: shaped like a rugby ball.

Figure 13.15 A tortilla

Quality points for grains

The quality points for grains are the same as those for rice. See page 413 for more information. In addition, look for signs of pest infestation. Grains are a favourite food for vermin and other pests. Check the grains for signs of mould, especially if the grains is stored somewhere near moisture.

Problems

See page 413 for more information about what to do if you have problems with ingredients. Report any signs of pest infestation immediately.

Safe use and storage of grains

The safe use and storage of grains is the same as that of rice. See page 418 for more information. Grain dishes that are cooked and finished may be frozen for later use. Put them in a suitable dish and cover them. Label with the date of cooking and freezing, and place in a freezer. Thaw the dish properly before re-use.

Cooking methods
Boiling and simmering

Most grains can be boiled. Both types of barley take around one to two hours to cook, usually by boiling or simmering, although pot barley can take up to three hours to become soft.

Polenta is normally boiled and quick-cook polenta can take as little as five minutes. Traditional polenta can take as long as an hour to cook. Polenta may be served hot and creamy with a little butter added. Extra ingredients, e.g. cheese, can be added just before service.

Oats can be made into porridge, a hot breakfast cereal, if you boil them in milk or water.

Quinoa can be boiled, stewed or baked. It is an ideal replacement for rice and can be treated in much the same way. It takes about 15 minutes to cook.

Top marks!

There are a wide variety of grains available, many of which can act as a healthy alternative to other ingredients. Find out some ingredients in dishes that can be replaced by grains and understand why they may be better.

Pilaf of pot barley

chicken or beef stock	440ml
pot barley (or pearl barley)	240g
spring onions, roughly chopped	3
celery stick, roughly chopped	1
mushrooms, sliced	220g
salt and pepper	to season
Cooking time	15 minutes
Serves	4

Method

1 Cook the barley in the simmering stock for approx. 45–50 minutes.
2 Drain the barley well and keep it warm. Keep around 100ml stock back.
3 Put the stock in a pan.
4 Add the spring onion and celery. Cook until the celery is soft.
5 Add the mushrooms. Cook until most of the liquid has gone.
6 Add the cooked barley. Mix gently.
7 Season with salt and pepper and serve.

This recipe can also be served cold as a salad.

Frying

Boiled polenta can be allowed to harden and then sliced and sautéed or fried before serving.

Grilling

Hardened polenta can also be sliced and grilled or fried before serving.

Baking

Millet croquettes

cooked millet	480g
celery, finely diced	120g
carrot, finely grated	60g
onion, finely diced	120g
chopped parsley	60g
dill	10g
oregano	5g
flour	120g
water	220ml
Makes	8–10 × 90g croquettes
Oven temperature	170°C
Cooking time	25 minutes

Method

1 Put the millet, celery, carrots, onion, parsley, dill and oregano into a bowl. Mix.
2 Add the flour. Gradually add the water and mix.
3 Form the mixture into even cigar-shapes, each 4cm long and approx. 90g.
4 Place on a lightly greased tray and bake.

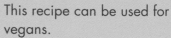

Chef's tip

This recipe can be used for vegans.

Basic simple cornbread

cornmeal	240g
wheat flour	240g
baking powder	20g
corn oil	50ml
water	330ml
sugar	30g
salt	pinch
Serves	8
Oven temperature	170°C/350°F
Cooking time	20 minutes

Method

1 Put all the ingredients into a bowl and mix well.
2 Put in a greased casserole dish.
3 Bake in the oven.

Scotch oatcakes

flour	60g
salt	pinch
baking powder	20g
oatmeal or rolled oats	300g
margarine	90g
milk	150ml
egg wash	1 beaten egg
Oven temperature	190°C
Cooking time	25 minutes
Makes	up to 10 cakes

Method

1 Sift the flour into a bowl.
2 Add the salt, baking powder and oatmeal or rolled oats. Mix together.
3 Rub in the margarine until the mixture has sandy texture.
4 Make a well. Add the milk and mix to a stiff paste.
5 Allow to rest for one hour.
6 Roll out to 5mm thick and cut into 75mm circles with a crimped cutter.
7 Place on greased trays and egg wash lightly.
8 Bake.

Test yourself!

1 Explain the importance of using the correct tools, equipment and techniques when preparing dishes containing grains.

2 Briefly explain how grain dishes should be stored.

3 Describe the action to take if you find any ingredient for your dish not suitable.

Eggs

Birds' eggs are a common food source. Many varieties of eggs can be cooked and eaten, e.g. eggs from ostriches, quails, ducks and chickens. The eggs most commonly used in cookery are chicken's or hen's eggs. They can be either white or brown, but they look exactly the same inside and taste the same when cooked. Hen's eggs for human consumption come from two different sources. These are free range or barnyard and battery:

○ Free range eggs are laid by hens that are allowed to run free in the farm area. The hens are not stressed in any way and these are considered to be the best eggs.

○ Barnyard eggs are laid by hens that are kept indoors, in large barns covered with straw and are separated into pens.

○ Battery or factory farmed eggs are laid by caged hens. The hens are not allowed to roam free and rarely see outside their battery.

Eggs are very nice on their own poached, fried or scrambled, and they are also found in all sorts of recipes, e.g. bread dough, batter, pasta and cakes.

The egg has a yellow centre called a yolk, which is surrounded by albumen, which usually called 'the white of the egg'. The yolk and albumen are covered by a shell which can be easily broken.

The contents of the egg can be used together in dishes, such as sponge cakes, that need both yolk and white, or separated, e.g. meringue only uses the white while béarnaise sauce needs just the yolk.

Egg whites make a good raising agent. Egg white proteins break and expand when whipped, forming elastic-walled cells that trap air. The air expands when subjected to heat.

The main protein in egg white is called albumen. This protein can be strengthened with the addition of an acid, e.g. lemon juice. Strengthened albumen is used when making meringues and royal icing as it provides more body.

Egg yolk proteins bind and thicken. The proteins are less stable than those of the egg white. When exposed to excessive heat, they harden and separate from the yolk's fat and water molecules, causing the yolk to separate and **curdle**.

Figure 13.16 Quail, chicken and ostrich eggs

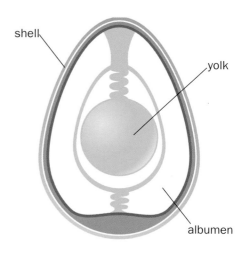

Figure 13.17 The parts of an egg

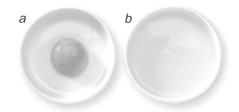

Figure 13.18 Separated eggs: a egg yolk, b egg white

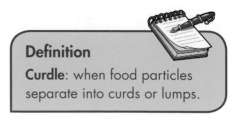

Definition
Curdle: when food particles separate into curds or lumps.

436

The setting temperatures of eggs are as follows:

○ Egg white starts setting at a temperature of 62°C and sets completely at a temperature of 70°C.
○ Egg yolk starts setting at a temperature of 65°C and sets completely at a temperature of 70°C.
○ The whole egg, white and yolk mixed, starts setting at a temperature of 63–65°C and sets completely at 70°C.

Eggs are available in their shells, as pasteurised whole eggs, pasteurised egg yolks, pasteurised egg whites, and even dried.

Raw eggs are the most common and have the most uses. However, they are a high-risk food, being associated with salmonella food poisoning. The following rules should be followed when using them:

○ Wash your hands after handling eggs.
○ Store fresh eggs in cool dry conditions.
○ Purchase fresh eggs from reputable suppliers.
○ Do not store fresh eggs with strong-smelling foods, because the shell is porous and can absorb smells from other foods.

An average hen's egg weighs about 50g and can be white or brown. Weight is used to measure the size of eggs. See the table below.

Size	Very large	Large	Medium	Small
Weight	Larger than 73g	63g–73g	53g–63g	Under 53g

Figure 13.19 Egg sizes

Quality points for eggs

Make these checks when selecting eggs for your dish:

○ The eggs are clean and free from dirt. If the shell has dirt on it, gently wash it with cold water.
○ There are no cracks in the shell.
○ Eggs in their shells have been stored in a dry cool room.
○ Eggs that have been shelled or separated have been covered and kept in a refrigerator.

Make these checks when cracking eggs:

○ The yolk of the egg is a nice bright yellow. Occasionally it may have a blood spot. This is not dangerous and the yolk can be used.
○ The white of the egg is a see-through off-white colour.
○ They have very little smell. If the egg does have a strong smell, throw it away.

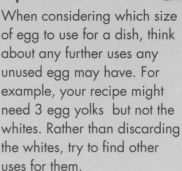

Top marks!

When considering which size of egg to use for a dish, think about any further uses any unused egg may have. For example, your recipe might need 3 egg yolks but not the whites. Rather than discarding the whites, try to find other uses for them.

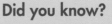

Did you know?

Eggs are often used as a symbol of life and fertility. Many ancient philosophers saw eggs as a symbol of the world and its four elements: the shell represented the earth, the white represented water, the yolk represented fire; and the air sac represented air.

- No shell gets into the egg yolk or white as this can be unpleasant for the customer later. If you notice shell in the raw egg after cracking or separating, gently remove it with a fork or spoon.
- Before and after handling and preparing eggs for dishes, you must wash your hands.

Problems

See page 413 for more information.

Cooking methods
Boiling

It takes eight to ten minutes to hard-boil an egg; this means that the yolk and white of the egg are cooked solid. Hard-boiled eggs can be served hot in their shell or cooled and used as garnish, in a salad or as a sandwich filling mixed with a light sauce, such as mayonnaise. They can be combined with other ingredients to form dishes such as Scotch eggs (cooked boiled egg, wrapped in sausagemeat and breadcrumbs, then deep-fried and finished in an oven and served with tomato sauce) or curried eggs (hot hard-boiled eggs, shelled, sliced in half lengthways, laid on rice and glazed with curry sauce). For more information on boiling see page 220.

How to boil an egg

1 Bring the water to boil and gently put the eggs into the water, using a perforated spoon or a basket.
2 Set a timer, or use a watch or clock, and simmer for 8–10 minutes, depending on how well cooked the eggs need to be for the finished dish.
3 Remove the eggs from the water.
4 If serving hot, place into an egg cup.
5 If using the eggs as part of a cold dish or garnish, cool them immediately under cold running water for a few minutes then store refrigerated in their shells until required.

Soft-boiling

Soft-boiled eggs have a runny yolk and a fully cooked or set white. Follow the same cooking method as boiled eggs, but reduce the time to three to four minutes.

Soft-boiled eggs cannot be used cold. They are usually eaten hot for breakfast.

Frying

See pages 223–4 for more information on frying. Shallow-frying can be difficult as eggs cook very quickly when fried.

How to shallow-fry an egg

1 Put a little oil or butter in a shallow frying pan and gently heat it.
2 Crack an egg into the pan. The egg will begin to cook straight away. The white will go very white, and the yolk will harden.
3 Gently remove the egg from the pan and serve.

Fried eggs can be served as part of a meal, e.g. breakfast, or served as an accompaniment with meat, e.g. gammon steak. They can also be eaten on their own as a snack with some bread.

Poaching

See page 000 for more information on poaching. Poached eggs are cooked in water with a little vinegar added. The acid in the vinegar helps to set the protein in the egg.

How to poach an egg

1 Put some water, a splash of vinegar and a pinch of salt into a pan.
2 Bring the water to the boil then allow it to simmer (just below boiling point).
3 Gently crack an egg into the water. Leave it to poach in the water for three to five minutes.
4 Use a perforated spoon to gently remove the cooked egg.
5 Trim, drain and serve immediately.

Poached eggs can be used as an accompaniment, or eaten on their own as a breakfast meal or as a starter dish to a main meal.

Poached eggs can be drained, cooled in iced water and stored in a refrigerator for later use. To reheat the poached egg, put it into very hot – but not boiling – salted water. When the egg starts to float, turn it once and leave it for one minute. Then remove it from the water using a perforated spoon. Drain then serve.

When used as a hot starter, some classic poached egg dishes combine the poached egg with another ingredient, e.g. a slice or a vegetable base. These are sometimes served in a cocotte dish and are usually coated in a sauce. Some variations include poached egg washington (mornay sauce) and poached egg benedict (hollandaise sauce).

Healthy eating

Low-fat or unsaturated margarines and oils can be used instead of plain cooking oil for a healthier option.

Chef's tip

Use a lower heat if using margarine, as it will heat and burn more quickly than oil.

Figure 13.20 A cocotte dish

Eggs benedict

slice toast, evenly buttered	1
fine slice of ham or cooked tongue	1
poached egg	1
hollandaise sauce	20ml
Oven temperature	100°C
Cooking time	5 minutes

Method

1 Cut a 7.5cm circle from the toast.
2 Cover the circle of toast with the slice of ham or cooked tongue and heat through in a warm oven.
3 Place a hot poached egg on to the toast and cover with hollandaise sauce.

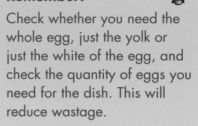

Remember!
Check whether you need the whole egg, just the yolk or just the white of the egg, and check the quantity of eggs you need for the dish. This will reduce wastage.

Griddling

To cook eggs using a griddle, follow the method for shallow-frying, but use less oil. The egg will cook very evenly on a griddle and can be turned to cook the yolk. The cooking times are very similar to the frying method. Make sure you have any equipment you need to hand before you begin cooking. See page 225 for more information.

Baking

When eggs are baked in a dish with other ingredients, they are usually used as the agent which binds the other ingredients together as it bakes in the oven.

Quiche lorraine (cheese and bacon flan) is a good example of using eggs in a baked dish. Another good example is baked egg custard. This dish can be cooked in a baking dish on its own or baked inside a sweet paste case to make a custard tart. The eggs are whisked together with sugar and milk and flavoured with vanilla.

Some sweet egg dishes, e.g. crème brûlée or crème caramel are baked in a bain-marie. Savoury baked egg dishes, e.g. eggs en cocotte (poached egg, placed in a cocotte dish and baked in a sauce) are also popular, especially as a starter dish. For more information on baking see page 225.

Quiche lorraine

For one flan case of 15cm:

shortcrust pastry	120g
oil	splash
onions, finely chopped	15g
cheese, grated	45g
ham, finely diced	30g
egg	1
milk	190ml
salt	pinch
cayenne pepper	pinch
Oven temperature	190°C
Cooking time	20 minutes
Serves	6

Method

1 Roll out the pastry to 5mm thick and evenly line a 15cm flan ring.
2 Heat the oil in a pan. Add the onions. Sweat the onions.
3 Put the cheese, ham and onions into the pastry base.
4 Put the egg, milk, salt and cayenne pepper into a bowl. Beat together.
5 Pour the egg mix into the pastry base.
6 Bake in the oven until cooked.
7 Remove from the oven. Carefully remove the quiche from the flan ring. Cut into evenly sized wedges.

Scrambling

Scrambling is a style of cooking eggs rather than a cooking method. The finished dish should be light and fluffy with a creamy texture. Scrambled eggs are most commonly used as a breakfast dish but are also used in recipes such as Scotch woodcock (anchovy fillets on toast covered by scrambled eggs topped with cheese).

Chef's tip

Use a small sharp 3-inch vegetable knife to help remove the pastry from the ring. Run the tip of the blade towards you slowly along the inside edge of the flan ring.

How to scramble eggs

1 Beat or whisk the eggs using a fork or whisk.
2 Lightly season with salt and pepper.
3 Melt some butter or margarine in a pan. Add the eggs.
4 Put over a gentle heat and stir with a spatula until just cooked.

Scrambled eggs can be cooked using a microwave. Put the beaten or whisked eggs into a heatproof dish and put into the microwave. Cook for 30–40 seconds at a time and whisk until a light and fluffy texture is achieved.

Omelettes

Omelettes can best be described as lightly scrambled eggs allowed to set and wrapped over a filling. However, Spanish omelettes are thick and served flat. Omelettes are a very quick dish to prepare and can be made more substantial by adding one more egg or a little more filling.

Chef's tip

A little cream or milk can be added to the egg at the whisking stage to make the dish even lighter and creamier.

Remember!

Scrambled eggs continue to cook for a short while after they have been served, so it is important to serve them as soon as they have set.

Cheese omelette

For one omelette:

eggs	2–3
salt	pinch
pepper	pinch
butter	15g
Cheddar or Parmesan cheese	30g
Cooking time	3–4 minutes
Serves	1

Method

1 Break the eggs into a small bowl. Add salt and pepper. Whisk with a fork.
2 Heat the butter in a small steel omelette pan until the butter stops bubbling.
3 Add the eggs. Stir with a fork until the eggs becomes creamy in consistency.
4 Allow the eggs to set for a few moments.
5 Add the grated cheese.
6 Fold the omelette in half with a fork and shape to a tidy 'D' shape.
7 Colour the omelette slightly.
8 Turn out onto a serving dish or plate and serve immediately.

Spanish omelette

butter	15g
onions, finely diced	30g
pimento, diced	15g
tomato **concassée**	60g
eggs	2
salt and pepper	to season

Method

1 Heat the butter in an omelette pan. Add the diced onions and cook until lightly coloured.
2 Add the diced pimento and tomato concassée and heat gently.
3 Put the eggs into a bowl and beat them with a fork.
4 Add the eggs to the pan and mix lightly. Allow to cook.
5 Serve flat, unfolded.

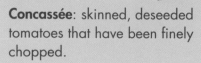

Definition

Concassée: skinned, deseeded tomatoes that have been finely chopped.

Safe use and storage of egg dishes

Safe service and storage of egg dishes is very important to keep the risk of food poisoning to a minimum. As eggs have a short shelf life after cooking, it is recommended that refrigerated cooked eggs are not used if they are more than two days old (check the date on the label). See page 437 for more information.

Try this! Worksheet 39

What are the five rules you must follow to reduce the risk of food poisoning caused by eggs?

List as many egg dishes as you can. Then describe the dish, including whether it's served hot or cold and whether it's sweet or savoury.

Test yourself!

1 Name three methods of cooking eggs.

2 What should you do if you notice that eggs are cracked before you use them?

3 Why would you add vinegar to the water for poaching eggs?

4 Which egg dishes might be baked in a bain-marie?

5 Why should you serve scrambled eggs as soon as they are set?

Practice assignment tasks

Prepare and cook rice, pasta, grains and egg dishes

Task 1

You have been asked by your Head Chef to develop a new vegetarian menu that includes at least three examples of dishes containing rice, pasta, grains or eggs.

Consider the colour, flavour, texture and overall balance of the menu so the dishes complement each other and the main ingredients do not overlap too much. Prepare a report outlining your choice of ingredients and make recommendations for the most interesting combinations.

Task 2

You have been asked to develop a 'concept menu' around the use of grains. The grains can be part of any of the courses on offer. Consider each type of grain and a produce list outlining:

- the different types of grains
- preparation and cookery methods
- nutritional content
- characteristics
- an example dish for each type of grain.

Task 3

A rice company is trying to increase people's awareness of the different sorts of rice available and their different characteristics, flavour and texture. It will provide some free rice to your restaurant and would like you to submit a brief description of the different types of rice. Include name and characteristics; typical uses in recipes; and sample recipes for each type of rice.

Task 4

First, investigate the different methods used to produce eggs. Then identify as many different starters and main course dishes that include eggs as you can. State the method of cookery used for each.

Task 5

Give a PowerPoint presentation about the importance/history of pasta in the Italian diet. You can include information you have researched or produce handouts.

Choose two pasta dishes to be used for a:

- starter
- main course.

The pastry kitchen

14

This chapter covers part of the following outcomes from Diploma unit 214: Prepare and cook bakery products

- Outcome 214.1 Prepare paste, biscuit, cake and sponge products
- Outcome 214.2 Cook and finish paste, biscuits, cakes and sponge products
- Outcome 214.3 Prepare fermented dough products
- Outcome 214.4 Cook and finish fermented dough products

Working through this chapter could also provide evidence for the following Key Skills:

C2.1, C2.2a, C2.2b, C2.3, N, N1.2, N2.2, ICT2.1, ICT2.2, ICT2.3, LP2.1, LP2.2, LP2.3, PS2.1, PS2.2, PS2.3

In this chapter you will learn how to:

Identify different types of, and uses for, paste, biscuit, cake, sponge and dough products

Identify the main ingredients and their quality points and quantities

Prepare and cook bakery products

Check, finish and decorate cooked bakery products

Identify the temperature for the cooking, holding, service and storage of finished bakery products

Adjust quantities of ingredients

Ingredients

Working in the pastry kitchen can be a very rewarding experience. It is very different to working in the hot kitchen. The pastry kitchen is more artistic and more scientific. Pastry items will not work correctly unless the balance of ingredients is right and they are handled well.

The key ingredients which are used in all pastry departments are:
o flour
o raising agents such as yeast
o sugar
o dairy products.

To get the best out of these ingredients you need to understand their characteristics and what to look for when things go wrong.

Flour

Flour is usually made from wheat. The wheat grains are crushed to remove the husks. The wheat germ, bran and endosperm are then used to make different types of flour.
o **Wholemeal** flour contains 100 per cent of the wheat grain – all the wheat germ, bran and endosperm.
o **Brown** flour contains 85 per cent of the original grain; some of the wheat germ and bran are removed.
o **White** flour contains 75 per cent of the wheat germ – the endosperm only.

Gluten

There are many important types of protein in flour. Two insoluble proteins called gliadin and glutamine are important in baking. When these are mixed with liquid a substance called **gluten** is formed. Gluten determines the strength of the flour and its best use. Gluten also develops if pastry is handled excessively.

Gluten is vital in baking because it is elastic enough to hold pockets of air in the mixture and strong enough to support the structure and stop the air escaping.

Top marks!
To help you get higher marks make sure you always check the quality and quantity of your ingredients.

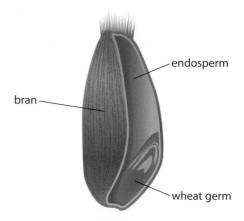

Figure 14.1 A wheat grain

Did you know?
Flour can cause fires and explosions in flour mills because of its fine particles and its heat-retaining properties.

Definition
Gluten: a protein found in flour which gives it its strength. The strength of the gluten is determined by the type of wheat and when and where it is grown.

Figure 14.2 shows the gluten contents of different types of flour.

Soft flour, also known as plain flour, can be white or brown. It can be used for a variety of tasks, e.g. sponges, cakes, biscuits, sauces and batters. It should be used within six to nine months.

Medium flour is for general use.

Strong flour is used to make bread and bun dough.

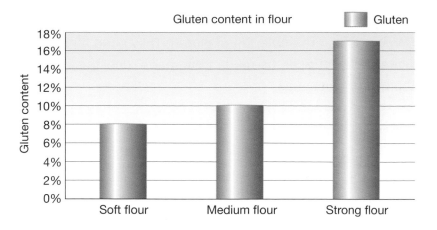

Figure 14.2 Gluten content in flour

Try this!
Squeeze some flour in the palm of your hand. If the flour holds together it is soft flour, but if it falls apart it is strong flour. This is very useful if the flour bins are not marked.

Try this!
To see gluten: put 200g of white flour into a bowl. Add 150ml cold water and mix into a paste. Allow to stand for ten minutes. Run cold water into the paste and wash it between your fingers until the water runs clear. The remaining sticky mass is gluten.

Brown and wholemeal flour

Brown and wholemeal flour have a higher fat content than white flour and this can make the finished product heavy. White flour can be added to the brown or wholemeal flour to help make the final product lighter in texture. Brown and wholemeal flour turns rancid more quickly than white flour because of its high fat content. Brown flour is best used within two to three months.

Self-raising flour

Self-raising flour is a mixture of plain flour and baking powder in a ratio of 480g flour:10g baking powder. It does not produce a consistent product, as some recipes need more baking powder. Self-raising flour is best used within six to nine months.

Gluten-free flour

Some people are intolerant of gluten. They need a gluten-free diet. Gluten-free flour can be made from maize, rice, buckwheat, potato, tapioca or chickpeas.

Storage of flour

Flour is normally supplied in 16kg bags and should be transferred into mobile storage bins, with lids. Flour must be kept dry and cool. Always wash and dry the containers before storing new flour and never put new flour on top of old flour.

Try this!
For more information on flour and bread, you can visit www. heinemann.co.uk/hotlinks and enter the express code 4103P.

Raising agents

Yeast

Yeast is a type of fungus and is a living micro-organism similar to a bacterium. Yeast is mainly used in breadmaking but may also be used in a variety of yeast batters, e.g. for fritters or blinis.

Like bacteria, yeast requires food, warmth, moisture and time in order to grow. Under the right conditions it produces carbon dioxide. This is what makes the dough rise.

Adding sugar to yeast will feed the yeast, but too much sugar will kill the yeast and prevent it producing carbon dioxide.

Adding tepid liquids like milk and water provides moisture and some warmth. A warm temperature during mixing and proving provides the warmth needed for yeast to generate carbon dioxide.

Salt improves the flavour and colour and stops the cooked products being sticky. Take care with the amount, as too much salt can kill yeast.

Warmth encourages the growth of carbon dioxide. Yeast starts to produce carbon dioxide at temperatures of 24–29°C. However, temperatures in excess of 49°C will kill yeast.

Yeast dough is usually left to **prove** in a warm, moist place, such as a prover. See page 459 for more information on **provers**.

Definition

Prove: to allow the yeast to develop carbon dioxide in the dough to make it rise before baking.

Prover: a cabinet that creates heat and moisture, helping dough products to rise evenly and assists in preventing products from drying out and skinning.

Using cold ingredients to slow down the growth of carbon dioxide can be an advantage, as it can produce different textures for different dough products, e.g. enriched dough products like croissants and Danish pastries.

Fresh yeast is normally supplied in 1kg blocks. When open it should have a pleasant smell and the surface should have a grey plastic look. It should be soft and crumbly, with a moist texture. As yeast gets older the surface colour changes to brown and looks dry and cracked. Yeast in this condition should not be used. Yeast should be kept covered in cool, moist conditions, ideally in a fridge at a temperature of 4–5°C.

There are two types of dried yeast, commonly known as baker's yeast and dried active yeast. Baker's yeast has large particles of dried yeast and has to be reconstituted in liquid and then treated as fresh yeast.

Dried active yeast is powdered and can be added directly to the flour according to the manufacturer's instructions. Dried yeast is used in smaller amounts to fresh yeast. Check the manufacturer's instructions prior to use for the exact amount to use. Dried yeast also needs food, warmth, moisture and time.

Baking powder

Baking power is a chemical raising agent that is made from one part bicarbonate of soda to two parts cream of tartar. When liquid is added, carbon dioxide is given off which makes products rise. Too much baking powder can have an adverse effect and cakes and sponges will collapse.

Bicarbonate of soda is an alkaline raising agent and needs acidic ingredients to work as a raising agent. Apart from bicarbonate of soda and egg white, all ingredients are acidic to various degrees, making bicarbonate of soda a good raising agent.

Cream of tartar is found in the juice of grapes, after they have been fermented in winemaking. It is classified as an acid and available in powder form. It cannot be used on its own as a raising agent.

> **Try this!** Worksheet 40
> Write down seven points you need to remember about fresh yeast.

Sugar

Sugar occurs naturally in all plants, in the fruit, the leaves and the stems. However, sugar for commercial use is obtained from two major sources, sugar cane and sugar beet. The sugar extracted from these sources is refined and cleaned to produce white sugar. It is then crystallised and sieved. The largest-holed sieve produces granulated sugar, the next size down produces caster sugar, and fine linen sieves are used to produce icing sugar. Loaf or cubed sugar is obtained by pressing the crystals together when slightly damp, drying them in blocks and then cutting them into squares. Sugar that has not been refined is coated in **molasses** and produces different types of brown sugar such as light brown sugar, soft brown and demerara sugar.

Sugar is used to add sweetness and texture to pastry products. Care needs to be taken to select the correct type of sugar for the dish you are making. Using the wrong type of sugar can affect the finished product.

Granulated sugar is a white medium crystalline sugar that is best used in products that require the sugar to be dissolved prior to use, e.g. when making caramel. If granulated sugar is used in pastry products it will not dissolve during cooking and will leave tiny crystals on the surface of the finished item.

Caster sugar is a white fine crystalline sugar that is best used in cakes, pastry and meringues. This type of sugar dissolves during the cooking process and gives these products the sweetness and texture they require.

Icing sugar is a white powdered sugar that is mixed with an anti-caking ingredient. This type of sugar is best used for decoration and icing, but there are a few other occasions when this very fine product is required as granulated or caster sugar will not dissolve sufficiently, e.g. when making tuille biscuits.

Nibbed sugar is not widely available and is normally only used in specialist confectionery shops. Nibbed sugar is sometimes used as a topping, e.g. on bath buns and rock cakes.

Cubed sugar can either be white or brown, and is the purest form of sugar you can buy. White sugar cubes do not allow any impurities to penetrate them and this make them very suitable for boiled sugar work. Brown sugar cubes are generally used to sweeten coffee.

Definition

Molasses: a dark, thick brown liquid obtained from raw sugar during the refining process. It is used to make syrup, e.g. golden syrup and black treacle.

Try this!

For more information about sugar you can visit www.heinemann.co.uk/ hotlinks and enter the express code 4103P.

Dark soft brown sugar is a very dark sugar with an intense flavour, and soft in texture. It is used in sticky toffee pudding and various cakes and sponges. If it is not stored tightly wrapped up, it will go hard and lumpy.

Muscovado sugar is similar to dark soft brown sugar, but lighter in colour. If a recipe suggests using this type of sugar but it is not available, use dark soft brown sugar instead.

Light brown sugar is similar in texture to dark soft brown sugar, but much lighter in colour, and milder in flavour.

Demerara sugar is a light-brown coarse sugar used for caramelising crème brûlée or in coffee.

Golden syrup is made from molasses that has been clarified. You should weigh it into a greased bowl to make it easier to use.

Black treacle is a thick, sticky dark syrup made from unrefined molasses.

Fats

Fats give pastry products taste and improve the texture. The fat coats the flour and prevents moisture activating the protein found in flour. Fats and oils contain essential fatty acids that provide the body with energy.

Unsaturated fats are derived from plants and are considered to be good fat. Saturated fats are made from animal fats and are considered to be bad fat because of their association with heart disease.

Butter is a fat made from cow's milk and is available unsalted or salted. Butter gives the final product a nicer taste than margarine, but it costs more. Butter has a fat content of 80 per cent.

Margarine is made from water and vegetable oils. Water and oil do not mix, so a stabilising agent is used to bond them together and this is known as an emulsion. It is often used as a cheaper alternative to butter. The fat content of margarine is 80–85 per cent, and it is a good source of vitamin D. Margarine has better creaming qualities than butter, but has less flavour.

Lard was originally made from pig fat. In order to promote healthier eating, lard is now usually made with vegetable oil.

Cream

Cream is the fat that rises to the surface of fresh milk when milk is left to stand.

It has different uses depending on its fat content:

- **Single cream** is made with 18–27 per cent of milk fat. It is used mainly for cooking or as pouring cream. It cannot be used for whipping because the fat content is under 30 per cent.
- **Whipping cream** is made with 33–36 per cent of milk fat. It is thicker than single cream and used mainly for whipping and in ice cream.
- **Double cream** is made with 40–48 per cent of milk fat. It is thick cream which is rich in flavour and easily whipped. It is used in mousses, cream cakes or as pouring cream.
- **Clotted cream** has a fat content of about 55 per cent and is very thick and rich in flavour. It is made by separating the cream from fresh milk, gently warming it over a low heat, then cooling it. It is traditionally served with scones.

Sour cream is a single cream that is soured with lactic acid fermenting bacteria. The bacteria also set the cream.

Crème fraîche is similar to sour cream, but double cream is used so it has a higher fat content.

Investigate!
Why do milk products taste better in summer than in winter?

Try this!
For more information on milk, visit www.heinemann.co.uk/hotlinks and enter the express code 4103P.

Fruit

Fresh and preserved fruit is often used in the pastry department to flavour desserts and pastry products and in its own right. See Chapter 9 for more information.

Adjust quantities of ingredients

A recipe gives quantities of each ingredient, usually stated as a weight in grammes. If you make up the dish using these quantities it will yield a certain number of portions. A good recipe will state how many portions it yields.

As a chef, you will often need to make more portions than those stated in the original recipe. In this case you need to know how to scale up the ingredients to yield the larger number of portions.

Remember!
When working out an amount in grammes you need to round your answers to the nearest whole number.

This example is for the Vanilla mousse recipe, on page 467. The original recipe yields 8 portions. These steps will show you how to find out the exact increase needed for each ingredient to meet a required yield of 27 portions.

on page 467

Chef's tip

A medium sized egg weighs approximately 50g.

You need to work out the weight of each ingredient required in order to make the increased number of portions. To do this:

○ divide the original weight of the ingredient by the number of portions in the original recipe in order to get the weight for one portion

○ then multiply the answer by the number of portions now required

Let's look at the first ingredient: leaf gelatine.

 original weight of ingredient ÷ original number of portions × required number of portions = new weight of ingredient required

$40 \div 8 \times 27 = 135$

The weight of leaf gelatine needed is 135g

Now you need to do the same calculation for each ingredient in the recipe.

Ingredient	Weight grammes ORIGINAL RECIPE	Weight grammes REQUIRED
Leaf gelatine	40	135
Caster sugar	150	506
Eggs	300	1,013
Milk	400	1,350
Vanilla pod	5	17
Double cream	700	2,363
Granulated sugar	150	506
Total weight of recipe	1,745	5,889
Number of portions	8	27
Weight per portion	218	218

Chef's tip

Notice that the weight per portion remains the same however many portions you make.

Try this!

A spreadsheet can take the hard work out of this calculation. Open the spreadsheet **recipe adjuster.xls** and follow the instructions.

Preparation methods

There are many different ways to produce patisserie items. Having an understanding of the basic methods, how they affect the product and what can go wrong will help you make the products well.

Rubbing in is the method used in making dough and pastry. It is done by placing the fat (usually butter or margarine) in the flour and rubbing the flour and fat together with the tips of your fingers. The tips of the fingers are the coolest part of the hand and mixture should not pass above the knuckle, otherwise the fat could start melting. Continue rubbing the fat into the flour until the fat is evenly distributed through the flour and the mixture looks like breadcrumbs or has a sandy texture. Do not overwork the flour and fat once it gets to this stage, otherwise they will bind together into an unusable lump which will have to be thrown away.

Rubbing the fat into the flour causes the fat to coat the flour particles. This prevents moisture developing the gluten in the flour, which ensures the product is not dry and tough. The ratio of fat to flour will affect the final product.

A low fat to flour ratio is used only for taste, e.g. bread rolls. The amount of fat to flour for bread rolls does not affect the gluten development so fat is used to improve the taste and lengthen the amount of time the product will keep. Bread can be made without using fat.

A high fat to flour ratio will make the product shorter and more difficult to use, e.g. sweet paste. Sweet paste should melt in the mouth and the high fat to flour ratio softens the gluten strands making the pastry more crumbly.

Creaming: In this method the fat (usually butter or margarine) and sugar (normally caster sugar) are placed into a bowl and beaten together until a light and fluffy mixture is achieved. The finished mixture should be almost white. It turns white because of the amount of air that has been added to the butter during beating.

Over-beating this mixture can affect the final product.

The air bubbles produced during creaming are used to trap liquid and bind the product during cooking. Without the bubbles, the mixture would curdle when liquid is added (normally eggs). The egg should be added slowly and beaten in well between each addition.

Figure 14.4 A chef rubbing in fat to flour

> **Try this!** Worksheet 41
>
> What does butter do to the flour in the rubbing in method?
>
> When using the rubbing in method why should you use the tips of your fingers? Why must you not overwork the fat and flour?
>
> What effect does the fat to flour ratio have on your dough?

Adding the liquid to the sugar/butter mixture too quickly will make the mixture curdle, as the bubbles need time to absorb the liquid.

Folding is a method of gently mixing ingredients into a mixture which has already been beaten or whisked to incorporate air. The idea is to mix in the new ingredients without losing air. Folding is normally done with a spoon which you use to cut through the mixture and turn over the remaining ingredients gently working around the bowl until all the mixture is bound together. It is sometimes called the 'cut and fold' method.

The term 'folding' is also used during the lamination process when making puff pastry (see Chapter 16 for more information).

How to cut and fold flour into cake mixture

| ① Make 3 cuts with your spoon in a downwards direction. | ② Make 3 cuts across to form a grid. | ③ Gently draw the spoon down and turn to fold in the flour. |

Beating is mixing ingredients vigorously in a bowl with a spatula until the required consistency is achieved, e.g. when making batter for pancakes.

Whisking is mixing the ingredients using a whisk to incorporate air into the mix. A balloon whisk is the best item to use, as its shape will assist in producing air, e.g. when making a fatless sponge or meringues. To use a balloon whisk correctly, use a round clean bowl, turn it slightly on its edge and use the whisk in either a figure of eight motion or in a circular motion from the wrist.

Equipment

Sieves

The best type of sieve for flour is a drum sieve Flour should always be sifted before use in order to:

o remove any lumps in the flour and to ensure an even distribution of flour particles throughout the final product

o remove any impurities in the flour

o start introducing air into the flour. This is the first stage in producing a light texture in the final product.

Weighing and measuring equipment

Weighing and measuring ingredients correctly is an important part of preparation for any recipe, but it is essential in patisserie, because the balance of ingredients has to be correct or the recipe will not work well.

Digital scales must be reset to zero before use. It is a good idea to test the scales before each use. Reset the scales to zero, then place a 1kg bag of sugar onto them and check the reading.

Measuring jugs are normally used for measuring liquids. If you do not have a measuring jug, then the liquid can be weighed: 1ml of liquid weighs 1g.

Some measuring jugs are designed to measure dry ingredients as well, so check to make sure you are using the right measurement.

> **Try this!**
> Measure 500ml of water then weigh it. Record your findings.

> **Top marks!**
> Check and gather all your equipment prior to the start of the assessment and try to determine what you will use each item for by running through the assessment in your mind. Allow for errors. This will prevent time loss, searching for equipment during the assessment.

> **Top marks!**
> Sort out and clean all service equipment to help you get higher marks.

Mixers

Planetary mixer: this is commonly called a Hobart machine, however Hobart is a manufacturer's name and not a type of machine. A planetary mixer has many different uses.

When using a planetary mixer, always follow the rules below:
- Make sure the guard is fitted before use.
- Do not insert anything into the bowl while the machine is turned on.
- Check the speed setting is low before turning the machine on.
- Do not leave the machine unattended during use.
- Switch off and unplug the machine before cleaning.

The guard is fitted to prevent fingers, arms etc. being inserted into the bowl during operation. The guard is fitted with a safety device which will turn off the machine if the guard is moved during use. The safety device is normally controlled by a series of magnets placed around the guard; these magnets have to line up otherwise the machine cannot be turned on.

Figure 14.5 A planetary food mixer with attachments

Planetary mixers come with many different attachments, e.g. a stainless steel bowl, dough hook, whisk and paddle. Some also have mincing machine parts.

Each attachment has a specific role:
- The **whisk** can be used to whisk egg whites for meringues or eggs for sponges. It can also be used to make batters to break down any lumps.
- The **dough hook** can be used to mix dough products, scones and even pastry.

Provers

Provers are used to control yeast dough during the proving stage; they can be used to slowly develop the carbon dioxide or to speed the process up. They use warm moisture or air to produce the warmth needed to prove yeast products.

The humidity can be controlled, which also prevents the dough forming a skin and ensures even proving.

Proving can be extended to develop flavour and produce a different texture in the yeast goods, e.g. Scottish morning rolls or ciabatta. Scottish morning rolls are proved slowly overnight, whereas dinner rolls can be proved for as little as 40 minutes.

Ovens

Deck ovens are normally found in bakeries because they are made specifically for bread and pastry products. Deck ovens are heated from the top and bottom, which bakes bread evenly and provides an extra lift to pastry and bread products.

Some deck ovens can introduce steam into the baking chamber; this stops the bread from drying out during baking or produces a crusty top if injected at the end of baking, e.g. French sticks.

Combination ovens can be used as a steamer, a dry oven or a mixture of both. With some you can control the humidity in the oven, which can be useful when cooking puff pastry products, as the extra moisture in the oven helps lift the pastry.

Combination ovens are fan-assisted and with some ovens you can control the speed of the fan, which is useful when baking soufflés as fans can cause the soufflé to rise in an uneven way.

Figure 14.6 A deck oven

Reduce the temperature by 10°C to 20°C for all fan-assisted ovens, as the heat is distributed more evenly than in normal ovens.

Convector ovens are similar to combination ovens, but they are not as versatile. Convector ovens are fan-assisted but do not have a steam facility. The heat is distributed evenly so the positioning of cooking trays is not as important.

Gas ovens are not fan-assisted and it is important to position the food correctly to achieve even cooking. If the heat source is at the back of the oven the tray should be placed in the middle of the shelf and parallel to the flames. The top of the oven is the hottest. During cooking the products may need to be turned.

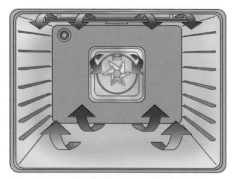

Figure 14.7 Direction of the heat flow in a fan-assisted oven

Electric ovens may or may not be fan-assisted. If they are not fan-assisted, it is important to position the food correctly to ensure even cooking. The top of the oven is the hottest. During cooking the products may need to be turned.

The position of the heat source inside the oven determines which way round a tray goes into the oven. If the heat source is at each side (normally electric ovens) then the tray should be placed in the middle of the shelf and parallel to the heat source.

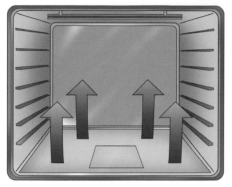

Figure 14.8 Direction of the heat flow in a conventional gas or electric oven

Test yourself!

1   What are the four key ingredients which are used in all pastry departments?

2   What is the minimum amount of fat in cream so it can be whipped?

3   What percentage of the wheat germ does white flour contain?
   a   60%
   b   75%
   c   80%
   d   55%

4   Name the two insoluble proteins that form gluten when mixed with a liquid.

5   At what temperature should you keep yeast?
   a   3–4°C
   b   4–5°C
   c   5–6°C
   d   6–7°C

6   What is baking powder made from?

7   Complete the sentence:
The rubbing in method is done by placing the _____ in the _____ and rubbing the _____ and _____ together with the _____ of your _____ .

8   There are three reasons why flour should always be sifted before use. What are they?

Desserts and puddings

15

This chapter covers the following outcomes from Diploma unit 213: Prepare and cook desserts and puddings

- Outcome 213.1 Prepare hot and cold desserts and puddings
- Outcome 213.2 Demonstrate how to cook and finish hot and cold desserts and puddings

Working through this chapter could also provide evidence for the following Key Skills:

C2.1, C2.2a, C2.2b, C2.3, N, N1.2, N2.2, ICT2.1, ICT2.2, ICT2.3, LP2.1, LP2.2, LP2.3, PS2.1, PS2.2, PS2.3

In this chapter you will learn how to:

Identify different types of hot and cold desserts

Identify the main ingredients and their quality points and quantities

Prepare hot and cold desserts and puddings

Cook hot desserts and puddings

Check, finish and decorate cooked desserts and puddings

Identify the temperature for the cooking, holding, service and storage of finished desserts and puddings

You will learn to make basic desserts and puddings including:

- ice cream
- vanilla mousse
- panna cotta
- crème caramel
- pavlova
- American-style pancakes
- fruit crumble

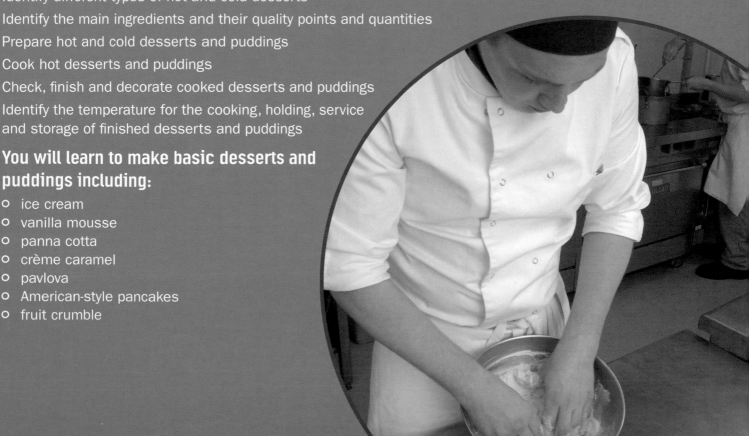

Types of desserts and puddings

Desserts and puddings all have one thing in common – most people love them. The art of making desserts and puddings can be learnt by everyone, but some chefs have a particular passion for creating them.

Basic hot and cold desserts and puddings include:

- **Ice creams**: made from milk, cream, sugar, eggs and flavouring, then churned in an ice-cream maker to achieve a smooth texture and consistency. Ice cream is available in many different flavours.
- **Mousses**: cold desserts such as chocolate or fruit mousse, generally light and airy in texture, often held together with a setting agent such as gelatine.
- **Egg-based desserts**: can be either served hot or cold. Cold desserts include crème brûlée, crème caramel and baked egg custard. Hot desserts include bread and butter pudding and cabinet pudding. Egg-based desserts also include meringues.
- **Batter-based desserts**: these are usually fried, e.g. pancakes and fritters.
- **Milk puddings**: can be served hot or cold. They may have fruit added. Examples include semolina and rice pudding.
- **Sponge-based desserts**: these include steamed sponges and bakewell tart.
- **Fruit-based desserts**: these include fruit flans, Eve's pudding, fruit crumble and summer puddings.

Ice cream

Ice cream is normally made using a sorbetière (ice-cream maker). It can be made using a normal household freezer, but the ice cream will not be such good quality.

A sorbetière slowly churns and freezes the ice-cream mixture. As the mixture freezes ice crystals are produced. These are kept small by the churning action. Small ice crystals mean high-quality ice cream with a smooth texture.

Freezing the ice-cream mixture in a normal freezer produces larger ice crystals so the texture is not so smooth.

Ice cream is generally made using high-risk products so it must be stored below –22°C. This temperature makes the ice cream hard to serve. Remove ice cream from the freezer and place it into the fridge before service to make it easier to serve.

Top marks!
If making individual items make sure each mould/dish is the same size.

Try this!
Draw a size chart to guide you on the correct sizes for all items.

Top marks!
Ensure there are sufficient garnishes for each portion but do not over/under garnish – sometime less is more!

Remember!
Melted ice cream must not be re-frozen.

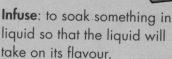

Vanilla ice cream

milk	1 litre
vanilla pod	½
egg yolks	5
caster sugar	375g
double cream	500ml

Method

1 Put the milk into a pan and warm it.
2 Split the vanilla pod and scrape out the seeds. Put the pod into the warm milk to **infuse**.
3 Put the egg yolks and sugar into a bowl and whisk together until light and fluffy.
4 Bring the milk to the boil and add to egg mixture. Mix with a spatula.
5 Put the mixture back into the saucepan.
6 Cook the mixture over a gentle heat until the mixture coats the back of the spatula. To test, stir the mixture well, take out the spatula and draw a spoon through the mixture. The mixture should not rejoin quickly.
7 Strain through a conical strainer and allow to cool.
8 When the mixture is completely cool, add the cream and freeze.

To freeze in a sorbetière: transfer the mixture into the sorbetière, churn and freeze. Once the mixture has doubled in volume and is firm transfer it to a clean container, cover and store in the freezer until required for service.

To freeze in a freezer: cover and put into the freezer. Stir every 30 minutes until firm. Freeze until ready for service.

This basic recipe can be used for many different flavours, by removing the vanilla pod and substituting other ingredients:
- **Chocolate**: added to the milk before boiling.
- **Fruit**: puréed and added after the double cream.
- **Dried fruits or nuts**: added just before the final freezing stage.
- **Alcohol**: added after the double cream.

There are many different-flavoured ice creams available commercially. Some establishments buy these in because they lack suitable equipment or qualified staff to make home-made ice cream. It may also make compiling and costing menus more effective.

Definition

Infuse: to soak something in liquid so that the liquid will take on its flavour.

Chef's tip

If the pan has any burnt milk left on it, use a clean pan.

Chef's tip

To stop the milk burning, sprinkle some of the sugar from the recipe onto the bottom of the saucepan, then add the milk but do not stir. The sugar on the base of the pan will protect the lactose and stop the milk from burning before it boils.

Chef's tip

Do not overcook the mixture for ice cream, bavarois or mousse or it will curdle and will have to be thrown away. Too much heat will cause the egg to cook and separate from the milk. Small pieces of egg will be evident in the milk and it will not thicken.

How to remove the Crème caramel from the moulds

1 Tilt the mould onto its side at 90° and loosen the edge of the custard from the mould. Continue all the way round.
2 Turn the mould upside down onto a serving plate, hold the plate and the mould and shake to loosen.
3 Remove the mould.
4 Any remaining caramel should be poured over the custard.

Crème brûlée

Crème brûlée translates as burnt cream, which indicates how the dessert is finished prior to service. Crème brûlée can be served hot or cold.

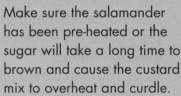

> **Remember!**
> The caramel should be rich and amber in colour, the surface of the cream should be smooth and not full of bubbles. The cream should stand proud and not dipped in the middle.

Crème brûlée

egg yolks	10
eggs	2
caster sugar	150g
double cream	1000ml
vanilla pod	1
demerara sugar	for topping
Oven temperature	180°C
Cooking time	30–40 minutes
Serves	8–10

Method

1 Make the custard as for egg custard. Then poach the custard in a bain-marie as for crème caramels.
2 Once set, sprinkle an even coating of demerara sugar onto the surface.
3 Glaze the sugar to a light brown colour under a salamander.
4 Once glazed, serve.

> **Chef's tip**
> Make sure the salamander has been pre-heated or the sugar will take a long time to brown and cause the custard mix to overheat and curdle.

Meringues

A meringue is a mixture of whipped egg whites and sugar. Usually, caster sugar is used as the grains are much smaller and more easily suspended in the bubbles of the whipped egg white.

When making hot or cold meringue, there are a few basic rules that must be followed:

○ All whipping equipment must be free from grease. Plastic bowls are not recommended; use either stainless steel or glass, as these can be scalded with very hot water to remove the grease. If you dry the bowl, use clean disposable tissue, not a cloth. A cloth could transfer grease to the surface of the equipment.

○ The easiest way to make meringue is by machine. However, if making by hand use a stainless steel balloon whisk. This type of whisk allows more air to be incorporated quickly.

○ Egg yolks consist mainly of fat and if any traces of yolk are present in the egg white, it will prevent the egg white whipping to a **stiff peak**.

○ Once made, the meringue mixture must be used straight away or the egg and sugar will start to separate and the egg white will start to turn back into liquid as the air escapes.

There are three different types of meringue:

1 **Cold meringue** (French meringue), used for cakes, sponges and pavlovas.
2 **Hot meringue** (Swiss meringue), used for piping shells and nests.
3 **Boiled meringue** (Italian meringue), used for mousses, ice parfaits and lemon meringue.

Definition

Stiff peak: when the peaks of the whipped egg white stand up without falling to one side. The final test is to turn the bowl upside down to see if the white drops out.

Chef's tip

A pinch of salt in the egg white helps the whipping process.

Cold meringue

1 part of egg white to 2 parts of caster sugar

For example:

egg white	100g
caster sugar	200g

Method

1 Whisk the egg white in a clean bowl on the highest setting of a mixing machine.
2 Whisk until tripled in size.
3 Slowly add the sugar in small amounts while the machine is still running on full speed.
4 Turn the machine off once all the sugar has been incorporated and use as required.

Hot meringue

1 part of egg white to 2 parts of caster sugar

Method

1   Put the sugar and egg white into a clean mixing bowl that will fit onto a machine. Combine using a hand whisk.
2   Put the bowl onto a bain-marie and whisk until the sugar has dissolved. To check this, remove the bowl from the heat and dip in a wooden spoon. Remove the wooden spoon and rub a finger over the spoon. If the mixture feels gritty return it to the heat and whisk until the sugar has dissolved.
3   Fit the bowl onto the machine, attach the whisk and whisk on the highest setting until the mixture is cold and in a stiff peak.
4   Use as required.

Video presentation

Watch *Finishing a flan* for an alternative method of making hot meringue. Try out both methods and see which you prefer.

Boiled meringue

granulated sugar	300g
water	90ml
cream of tartar	pinch
egg white	150g

Method

1   Put the sugar, water and cream of tartar in a clean saucepan. Combine with metal spoon.
2   Put the pan on a low heat. Wash the sides of the pan down with water and a clean brush (as for caramel for crème caramel).
3   Bring to the boil.
4   Boil the sugar mixture to 118°C. Test using a sugar thermometer. Do not stir the sugar, just let it boil.
5   In the meantime whisk the egg white to a stiff snow using a machine on the highest setting.
6   Once 118°C is reached remove from the heat and pour slowly into the whipped egg white while the machine is still running on full speed. Take care not to burn yourself.
7   Continue whipping until the mixture is cold and stiff peak.
8   Use as required.

Chef's tip

Meringues are normally one part egg white to two parts sugar. Weigh the egg whites and double the sugar to get the correct amount.

Granulated sugar is used in this type of meringue because it is a cleaner type of sugar with fewer impurities than caster sugar. In this method the sugar has to be boiled with the water and therefore the granulated sugar is more suitable.

Cream of tartar is found in the juice of grapes, after they have been fermented in winemaking. It is classified as an acid, available in the form of a powder and used in baking powder. It helps to stabilise meringue once it has been whisked.

Pavlova

Pavlova is a meringue dish that is soft and chewy inside with a crunchy outside. Cornflour and vinegar are added to the meringue.

> **Did you know?**
> Pavlova was named after Anna Pavlova, a Russian ballerina.

Pavlova

egg whites	100g
caster sugar	200g
vinegar	5ml
cornflour	5g
Serves	6–8

Method

1 Make meringue as previously described (cold meringue, steps 1–4).
2 Fold in the cornflour and vinegar.
3 Transfer onto silicone paper and bake at a temperature of 140°C for approximately two hours.
4 Cool and decorate with fruit and **Chantilly cream**.

Meringue shells, cases, nests and vacherins

These are all made with Swiss meringue and piped with star or plain piping tubes.

They can be dried on top of the oven overnight or dried in an oven on a low heat of about 90°C. This could take four to eight hours. Make sure that meringue products are not dried at too hot a temperature as they may discolour and lose their characteristic white colour.

Vacherins can either be large or individual round gateau-type meringues filled with fruit and cream and then decorated.

> **Definition**
> **Chantilly cream**: cream that has been sweetened, flavoured and lightly whipped (see Chapter 16 for recipe).

Fritters

Fritters can be either sweet or savoury. Examples of sweet fritters:

○ **Apple fritters**: peel and core apples, slice into four rings and keep covered in acidulated water (water with a squeeze of lemon juice). Drain well and dip the apple rings into flour and then into batter (see recipes below). Place into the deep fat fryer and cook on both sides until golden brown. Remove from fryer, drain well and coat in either plain or cinnamon sugar.

○ **Banana fritters**: do not prepare the bananas until required as they will turn black. Peel and cut the bananas into approximately 5cm pieces, place into the batter and cook as for apple fritters. Can be served with apricot sauce.

○ **Pineapple fritters**: remove the skin from the pineapple, slice into rings approximately 1cm thick, remove the core, and proceed as for apple fritters.

The frying batter is used to protect the items being fried, and gives them a crunchy texture.

A raising agent is needed for a frying batter to be light and fluffy. It could be whipped egg white, baking powder or yeast. The type of fritter and the establishment will determine the type of frying batter used.

After frying, transfer the cooked product to a colander and allow to drain. Serve as per menu requirements. Fritters are best served straight after cooking. Leaving them to cool will cause the batter to turn soggy.

> **Healthy eating**
> To encourage healthy eating, do not coat the fritters in sugar. They could be sweetened with honey as an alternative.

Frying batters

Egg white batter

soft flour	240g
salt	a pinch
cold water	300ml
egg whites	2

Method

1 Sift the flour and salt together into a bowl.
2 Gradually add the cold water, whisking well to a smooth batter.
3 Allow to rest for a minimum of 20 minutes before using.
4 Whisk the egg whites until they are stiff.
5 Fold the egg whites into the batter.
6 Use straight away.

Baking powder batter

soft flour	240g
salt	a pinch
vinegar	30ml
yellow colouring	4 drops
water	280ml
baking powder	20g

Method

1 Sift the flour and salt together in a bowl. Add the vinegar and colouring.
2 Gradually add the cold water, whisking well to form a smooth batter.
3 Add the baking powder just before cooking and whisk well.

Yeast batter

strong flour	240g
salt	a pinch
fresh yeast	30g
yellow colouring	4 drops
water	300ml

Method

1 Sift the flour and salt into a bowl. Add the yeast and colouring.
2 Gradually add the cold water, whisking well to form a smooth batter.
3 Prove for 30–40 minutes before using.

Did you know?

The vinegar in the batter helps to make the batter crispy and reacts with the baking powder to create carbon dioxide. The yellow colouring helps to make the batter turn golden brown during cooking.

Remember!

Test the temperature of the fat in the deep fat fryer by dropping a small amount of batter into the hot oil; it should rise to the surface and start to cook. Once brown it should be crisp but not greasy.
If the test piece is greasy but light in colour, the fat is too cold. If it is golden brown but raw inside, the fat is too hot. Adjust the temperature to suit the product.

Sponge-based desserts

Sponge-based desserts can be a combination of different products or a simple steamed sponge pudding. For more information about making sponges, see Chapter 17.

Bakewell tart

To make Bakewell tart, coat the base of a sweet paste case with raspberry jam. Fill the case with frangipane (see page 535). Decorate it with lattice pastry strips then bake it and finish it with apricot glaze and water icing.

Steamed sponge pudding

Steamed sponge pudding is a sponge that is cooked in a steamer; it can be served with a variety of toppings and sauces:

- **Blackcap pudding** has currants on the top.
- **Golden sponge pudding** has golden syrup on the top.
- **Chocolate sponge pudding** has chocolate-flavoured sponge and is normally served with chocolate sauce. To make it, replace 50g flour with 50g cocoa powder.
- **Jam/marmalade sponge pudding** has jam or marmalade on the top.

Basic sponge pudding

soft flour	250g
baking powder	5g
butter	250g
caster sugar	250g
eggs	4 medium
Serves	10

Method

1. Sift the flour and baking powder together into a bowl.
2. Flour and butter ten individual moulds.
3. Cream together the butter and sugar until light and fluffy.
4. Beat in the egg a little at a time.
5. Add the sifted flour and baking powder. Lightly mix until incorporated. Do not over mix.
6. Use as required.

All the sponges can be prepared individually or for portioning.

Use **dariole moulds** or pudding bowls. The insides of these must be buttered and floured. Once they are prepared, do not touch the inside as this could cause the cooked pudding to stick to the mould.

Put the topping at the bottom of the dish and the sponge mixture on top.

Did you know?

Apricot glaze is made with apricot jam, sugar and water. It is used to make the surface of sweet products shine. Apricot jam is used because apricots are very low in **pectin**. The glaze does not stain or change the colour of the final product and does not affect the taste. However, if the apricot glaze burns it will darken and taste bitter.

Definition

Pectin: a natural setting agent found in fruit.

Definition

Dariole moulds: cylindrical moulds which are available in different sizes.

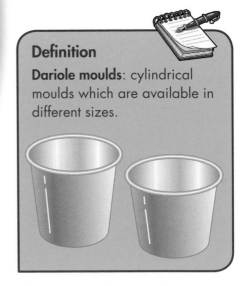

Do not over-fill the mould as the sponge will expand during cooking. Cover the top of the mould with a piece of greased greaseproof paper to prevent the steam penetrating the sponge.

Cooking times will depend on the size of the mould, but individual sponges can take up to 40 minutes, whereas large ones can take up to two hours.

Another popular sponge pudding is **Sticky toffee pudding**, which has soaked dates and is a soft sponge. Some recipes also have nuts and customers need to be informed in case one of them has a nut allergy.

Eve's pudding is a sponge and apple dessert. The apple is placed into a baking dish and covered with a basic sponge. It is then baked and normally served with fresh egg custard.

See pages 489–490 for how to prepare the apples.

Investigate! Worksheet 48

Find examples of 10 steamed puddings using different types of mix and an appropriate sauce for each.

Did you know?

Eve's pudding is so called because of the story from the Bible about Eve eating an apple in the garden of Eden.

Soufflés

Some people will not even attempt to make a soufflé because they are so worried about it rising and then collapsing. A soufflé is an easy dessert to make, as long as you follow these simple rules:
- Do not over-mix the egg white when folding into the base mix (panade).
- Butter and sugar the moulds well.
- Make sure the oven is set at the right temperature.
- Serve immediately.

There are three ways to make a soufflé:

Roux method: the roux and beurre manie methods produce a heavier, more pudding-like texture but this means the soufflé will not collapse so readily.

Beurre manie method: here the panade is made differently to the roux method, but otherwise the ingredients and method are the same.

Crème patissière method: this is the most popular method used in industry as it allows each order to be freshly cooked, therefore offering greater flexibility during service.

Cooking times and temperatures
- Large soufflés should be baked for 20–25 minutes at a temperature of 175°C.
- Individual soufflés should be baked for 7–10 minutes at a temperature of 205°C.

485

Vanilla soufflé

butter	60g, plus extra for lining dishes
caster sugar	60g, plus extra for lining dishes
eggs	5 medium
vanilla pod	1
milk	300ml
plain flour	60g
Oven temperature	205°C
Cooking time	7–10 minutes
Serves	8 using size 1 ramekin dishes.

Roux method

1 Butter and sugar the ramekin dishes. Clean off any sugar from the rim of the dish as this can cause the mixture to stick to the edge which will stop the soufflé rising correctly.
2 Separate the eggs.
3 Put the milk in a pan and heat gently.
4 Split the vanilla pod and remove the seeds. Add both to the milk to infuse.
5 Add half the sugar to the milk.
6 Melt the butter in another pan. Add the flour and make a roux.
7 Remove the vanilla pod from the milk. Slowly add the hot milk to the roux (as if making a white sauce). This makes the panade.
8 Allow the panade to cool slightly. Add the egg yolks one at a time and beat into the panade until smooth.
9 Whisk the egg whites to a peak. Be careful not to make them too dry or they will not fold into the panade easily.
10 Add a quarter of the egg white to the panade, and mix. This will loosen the panade and make it easier to fold the remaining egg white into the mix.
11 Add the remaining sugar to the remaining egg white and whisk. Gently fold this mixture into the panade.
12 Three-quarters fill the ramekins.
13 Put the dishes into a bain marie on the stove.
14 Simmer until the mixture reaches the top of the dish then carefully transfer the bain marie into the oven.
15 Bake in the oven until risen and golden brown on the top.
16 Turn out of the dishes before service.
17 Dust with icing sugar.
18 Serve immediately with Sauce anglaise (see page 495).

Beurre manie method

1 Follow steps 1 to 5 from roux method.
2 Cream the butter in a mixing bowl.
3 Add the flour. Mix to make the beurre manie.
4 When the milk is simmering remove the vanilla pod.
5 Add small amounts of the beurre manie to the hot milk and stir. Allow each piece of beurre manie to dissolve before adding more. The panade should be smooth and thick.
6 Continue with steps 8–17 from the roux method.

Crème patissière method

For the crème patissière base:

milk	300ml
vanilla pod	1
egg yolks	2 medium
caster sugar	50g
plain flour (sifted)	40g

Method

1 Put the milk in a pan. Split the vanilla pod and remove seeds. Add both to the milk. Warm gently to infuse the flavour.
2 Put the egg yolks and caster sugar in a mixing bowl. Whisk together until light and fluffy.
3 Sift the flour. Add to the egg/sugar mixture and beat until smooth.
4 Bring the milk to the boil. Remove vanilla pod.
5 Pour the hot milk onto the egg/sugar/flour mixture and mix well.
6 Return the mixture to the pan and cook out until thick and smooth.
7 Transfer to a dish and allow to cool.
8 Cover with a cartouche, to prevent skinning.

To complete the soufflé

butter	50g
caster sugar	75g
crème patissière base	8 tbsp
lemon juice	1
egg yolks	2 medium
egg whites	8 medium
Serves	6 using size 1 ramekin dishes.

Method

1 Butter and sugar 6 ramekin dishes.
2 Put 8 tbsp of crème patissière base in a mixing bowl. Add the lemon juice and egg yolks.
3 Follow steps 9–17 from roux method.

Chef's tip

Check the bottom of the pan before cooking out the crème patissière base. If the milk has caught use a clean pan. The lactose in the milk can cause the crème patissière to burn.

Different flavours can be incorporated into crème patissière base. Try adding 75g of grated chocolate to the milk and allowing it to dissolve. For a fruity flavour add the finely grated zest of 2 lemons, oranges or limes to the milk and warm gently to infuse the flavour (as with vanilla). The milk will separate but this will not affect the base when made into the panade.

When completing the soufflé, flavours can be added before the final the egg white, i.e. after step 10. For a hazelnut flavour add 120g ground hazelnuts. For a coffee flavour add 60g liquid coffee. For an almond flavour add 120g ground almonds. For a fruit flavour add 20g fruit purée.

Fruit-based desserts

Fruit-based desserts can be as simple as a Fresh fruit salad or a Rhubarb crumble. All fruit-based desserts have flexibility which can be adjusted to suit every establishment.

Syrup

When making Fresh fruit salad, keep the pieces of fruit roughly the same size.

Fresh fruit salads normally have a base syrup to stop the fruit discolouring after being prepared. Fruit has a natural sugar called fructose, so the base syrup does not need to be too sweet, however this does depend on the type of fruit being used.

Place all the fruit together and add sufficient stock syrup to cover the fruit. Just before service, peel and slice the bananas and add them. Gently stir to mix the fruit and syrup and serve.

The syrup could be a simple stock syrup or even an unsweetened fruit juice. Stock syrup is a mixture of sugar and water, dissolved and boiled together. See page 496 for flavours.

Stock syrup

sugar	720g
water	565ml

Method

1 Put the sugar and water into a saucepan.
2 Boil them and skim off any impurities.
3 Cool and use as required.

Preparation of fruit

All fruit should be washed and dried before preparing or eating.

Apples need to be peeled, cored and quartered. Apples tend to turn brown very quickly once peeled. To prevent this, peeled apples should be kept in acidulated water. There are hundreds of varieties of apples, from the common Granny Smith to pink lady. Each apple has its own level of sweetness and crispness.

Bramley apples are normally used for cooking but eating apples can also be cooked. They require less cooking time and less sugar.

For Fruit salad the quarters should be sliced into small pieces.

Cooking apples should be peeled, cored, quartered and kept in **acidulated water** until ready for cooking. The time of year and the variety of apple used will determine whether the apple needs additional water and sugar added during cooking. As a rough guide only, 1kg of cooking apples needs 125g sugar. After cooking, taste the apples and add extra sugar if required, or if too sweet add some lemon juice.

How to cook apples

1 Put sugar into a saucepan, add the drained apple slices and squeeze half a lemon over the top.

Healthy eating

The vitamins and nutrients found in apples are just under the skin, so use a vegetable peeler to remove the peel. To increase roughage in people's diets leave the peel on.

Definition

Acidulated water: water with lemon juice added to it.

2 Put a tight-fitting lid on and place on the heat to cook. The steam created should provide enough liquid to cook the apples. Water can be added if necessary.

3 Test to see if the apple is cooked by tasting a small piece. If using the fruit in pieces it should be soft but still firm. For purée, cook slightly longer until there is no bite left.

4 Remove the fruit from the pan and allow to cool.

5 To purée the fruit, use a food processor. Purée can also be made using a potato masher, but it will not be so smooth.

Oranges should be peeled and segmented, but the most important part is to make sure there is no pith left on the segments.

How to peel an orange

1 To peel the orange, top and tail it first, so that you can see how thick the skin is.

2 Run a vegetable knife from the top of the fruit to the bottom, judging the correct thickness to remove all the pith and skin.

3 Once the first slice has been removed it will allow the next piece to be removed more easily, as you can then see how much skin to remove each time to remove all the pith and skin. Continue removing slices round the orange until all the skin and pith has been removed. Try to keep the round shape of the orange.

How to segment an orange

The orange is then ready to cut into segments which should be free from pith, pips or the membrane which divides up the inside of the orange. There are two different methods to achieve this:

Method 1

1

Place a container underneath the orange. Hold the peeled fruit in one hand and run a paring knife down towards the centre of the fruit just inside the segment membrane.

2

Once the centre is reached push the segment away from the centre.

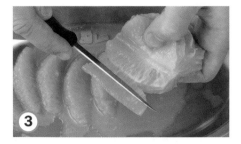

3

The segment should come away from the membrane on the other side. Continue until all the segments have been removed. Squeeze the remaining pulp to remove any juice that remains.

Method 2 This is similar to method 1, but instead of pushing the segment away from the centre, cut the other side of the segment away from the membrane too. Method 2 is slightly easier but can cause more waste.

Bananas should not be prepared until required for service. Bananas turn brown very quickly and in fruit salad they will go black and spoil the presentation of the fruit. Bananas can be coated in lemon juice to slow down but not stop the browning process.

Peel the banana and cut slices about 3mm thick. If using bananas for fritters, cut them into three or four depending on the size of the fruit.

Grapes should be halved and the seed removed.

Kiwi fruit should be topped and tailed and peeled in the same way as oranges. Once peeled, slice and use as required.

Pears are either red or green and are also available in many varieties. Some are suitable for cooking. The normal method of cooking pears is poaching.

Pears can be peeled with a vegetable peeler and cored, then cut into quarters and then into smaller pieces to go into fruit salad.

To poach pears, do not core them until after poaching as this will help stop them falling apart. Pears can be poached in stock syrup, red wine or even sweet dessert wine. It depends on the dessert being produced, but the method of poaching is the same.

Investigate! Worksheet 49

Find the names of four types of pears suitable for cooking and a suitable recipe for each.

How to poach pears

1 Peel the pears and keep them covered in acidulated water.
2 Bring the poaching liquid to the boil and remove from the heat.
3 Put the pears into the liquid and cover with a cartouche.
4 Put back onto the heat and simmer gently for 10–25 minutes depending on the type of pear and the liquid being used.
5 The pears will change colour slightly to a translucent pale colour.

Fruit compote

Fruit compote is a mixture of stewed fruit which can be made with soft fruit, hard fruit and dried fruit.

Soft fruit should be chosen, washed and covered in hot stock syrup. Cool and serve as required.

Dried fruit should be washed and soaked overnight in cold water. Then sugar is added and the fruit is gently cooked in its juice. It is cooled and served as required.

Hard fruit should be washed, prepared, put in a shallow dish and covered in stock syrup. Put a cartouche on top and place in the oven to stew until the fruit is tender. Allow to cool in the syrup and serve as required.

Fruit compotes can be served at breakfast or with sweet sauces and ice cream. They can also be flavoured with alcohol. The fruit should retain its original colour, so the correct preparation method is important.

Fruit crumbles

Crumbles are a very popular but simple baked dessert. A crumble has fruit on the bottom and a topping of butter, flour and sugar.

Sometimes the fruit is cooked before the crumble topping is placed on top. This depends on the type of fruit used. For example, apples, rhubarb and gooseberries should be cooked, whereas raspberries, blackberries and peaches can be used raw.

> ### Try this!
> For more general information on fruits, visit www.heinemann.co.uk/hotlinks and enter the express code 4103P.

Crumble

flour	450g
butter	200g
sugar	200g
fruit	1.5kg
Serves	8–10

Method

1 Rub all the ingredients together to achieve a sandy texture.
2 Put approx 1.5kg of prepared fruit in an ovenproof dish.
3 Sprinkle the crumble mixture on top of the fruit. Do not press the topping mixture down as this compacts the topping and makes it soggy.
4 Bake in a moderate oven until the fruit is cooked and the crumble topping is golden brown.

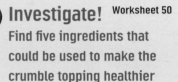

Investigate! Worksheet 50

Find five ingredients that could be used to make the crumble topping healthier to eat.

Fruit flans

Apple meringue flan is a simple dessert, but care is still needed to produce it well. An apple meringue is a blind-baked sweet paste flan (see Chapter 16), three-quarters filled with apple purée and with meringue piped on top.

To finish the flan, sprinkle caster sugar on top and bake in a moderate oven until the top is golden brown and the apple is hot.

When piping the meringue, keep it even and level as any peaks will burn during cooking.

Lemon meringue flan is prepared exactly the same as apple meringue; just replace the apple with lemon filling. Lemon filling is available pre-made or in powdered form, or it can be made from fresh ingredients.

Apple flan is a blind-baked sweet paste flan, three-quarters filled with apple purée, topped off with sliced raw apple. Sprinkle with sugar and cook in a moderate oven until the apple slices are cooked and browned. Coat with apricot glaze.

Fruit flans are completed differently from apple flans. First the case is filled with pastry cream and then fruit is overlapped on top to completely cover the pastry cream. It is then coated in apricot glaze to protect the fruit from discoloration.

Lemon filling for lemon meringue flan

sugar	120g
water	150ml
lemon juice	60g
cornflour	25g
butter	30g
egg yolks	2

Method

1 Put the sugar and half the water into a pan over a low heat.
2 Dissolve the sugar. Add the lemon juice. Bring to the boil.
3 Dissolve the cornflour in the remaining water to make a **slake**. Add to the water and lemon juice and cook until the mixture thickens.
4 Add the melted butter.
5 Whisk in the egg yolks.
6 Remove from the heat. Pour into a cooked flan case and allow to cool.

Video presentation

Watch *Finish a flan* to see this being produced. You may also find *Prepare sweet paste (rubbing in method)*; *Line a flan ring*; and *Bake blind* useful.

Definition

Slake: a mixture of cornflour or custard powder mixed with cold liquid.

Pastry cream

milk	850ml
vanilla pod	1 (can be replaced with essence or extract)
egg yolks	8
sugar	240g
plain flour	120g

Method

1 Put the milk into a saucepan. Split the vanilla pod and put seeds into the milk, add the pod and infuse over a low heat.
2 Put the egg yolks and sugar into a bowl and whisk together until light.
3 Sift the flour and add to the egg mixture. Mix to a smooth paste.
4 Bring the milk to the boil and remove the pod.
5 Gradually add the milk to the sugar mix and stir well.
6 Put the mixture into a clean pan and bring it back to the boil, stirring continuously.
7 Pour into a clean bowl and cover with a cartouche to prevent skinning. Allow to cool.

Sweet sauces

Coulis

A fruit coulis is made with soft fruit, e.g. strawberries or raspberries, and sugar. Icing sugar is normally used as it sweetens the fruit and provides a smooth sauce.

Did you know?
The word coulis means sifted.

Fruit coulis

soft fruit	25g
icing sugar	50g
lemon juice	3–4 drops
Serves	approx 4–6

Method

1 Wash and dry the fruit.
2 Liquidise the fruit, icing sugar and lemon juice.
3 Pass the mixture through a sieve into a clean bowl.
4 Check the taste. If the coulis is too tart (sour) add icing sugar to taste.
5 Check the consistency. If the coulis is too thick, add a little stock syrup (see page 489).

Cooked fruit sauce

This sauce could be made using apples, pears or apricots.

Cooked fruit sauce

fruit	450g
caster sugar	100g
water	150ml
lemons	1

Method

1 Prepare the fruit as required.
2 Put all the ingredients in a saucepan and simmer until the fruit is tender.
3 Liquidise and push through a sieve.
4 Check the taste. If the sauce is tart, add more sugar.
5 Allow to cool. Store in a refrigerator and use as required.

Custard sauce

This is sometimes called Crème anglaise.

Custard sauce

caster sugar	75g
milk	300ml
double cream	300ml
vanilla pod	1
egg yolks	8 medium
Makes	750ml

Method

1 Put the sugar into a saucepan.
2 Add the milk and cream.
3 Split the vanilla pod and remove the seeds. Add the pod and seeds to the milk/cream mixture.
4 Warm the mixture gently to infuse the flavour.
5 Whisk the egg yolks together until they are light.
6 Bring the milk/cream mixture to the boil.
7 Take off the heat. Remove the vanilla pod.
8 Pour the hot milk/cream mixture onto the eggs yolks. Mix.
9 Return the mixture to the pan and reheat until it thickens. Do not boil the mixture or it will curdle.
10 Test the sauce. It should coat the back of a spoon.
11 Serve immediately. Do not reheat.

> **Chef's tip**
>
> Any unused sauce can be used as a base for ice cream. See page 465 for more information.

Flavoured syrup

Flavoured syrup can be made by adding flavouring to simple stock syrup, see page 489. The thickness of the syrup is determined by the sugar content and how much it is reduced.

Flavour	Method	When added
Orange and cinnamon	Add orange zest and a cinnamon stick	At the cooking stage
Cinnamon	Add a cinnamon stick	At the cooking stage
Vanilla	Infuse a vanilla pod	Add once the syrup is the correct consistency and while it is still hot
Lemon	Add lemon zest	At the cooking stage
Chocolate	Add cocoa powder	Add at the cooking stage. After cooking, pass the syrup through muslin to remove the powder

Coffee	Add strong coffee	Once the stock syrup is the right consistency
Lime	Add lime zest	At the cooking stage
Rose	Add rose water to taste	Once the stock syrup Is the right consistency
Ginger	Use the syrup from crystallised ginger	Once the stock syrup Is the right consistency
Lavender	Add eight spikes of lavender	Add at the cooking stage. Allow the syrup to cool to infuse the flavour, then strain
Lime, lemon grass and ginger	Add lemon grass, kaffir lime leaves and chopped ginger root	Add at the cooking stage. Allow the syrup to cool to infuse the flavour, then strain
Mint	Add mint leaves	Add once the stock syrup is the right consistency. Allow to cool to infuse the flavour, then strain

Figure 15.5 Flavourings for stock syrup

These desserts and puddings are only a small sample of the vast selection available, but mastering them is the first step to understanding how to produce fantastic hot and cold desserts and puddings.

Figure 15.6 Dessert service

Test yourself!

1 What setting agent is used in mousse?

2 What is a sorbetière?

3 True or false? It is safe to re-freeze melted ice cream.

4 Why does milk boil over?

5 How would you prepare the following for a fruit salad:
   a bananas
   b kiwi
   c grapes
   d apples.

6 How can you reduce the risk of overheating the custard mix when making an egg custard-based dessert?

7 What ingredients do you need to make rhubarb crumble?

8 At what temperature should you store ice cream?

Practice assignment tasks

Prepare and cook desserts and puddings

Task 1

You have been selected to represent your restaurant at a local competition. You need to produce a trio of desserts (including hot desserts and cold desserts).

Design two desserts, one hot and one cold, which could be served in a trio of desserts, e.g. hot dark chocolate mousse, white chocolate ice cream and milk chocolate mousse.

Task 2

Complete a report on how eggs are used in the production of cooked desserts and puddings.

Task 3

Research how desserts and puddings can be adapted to be healthier options and complete a summary of your findings. Include four examples of adapted recipes.

Pastry

16

This chapter covers part of the following outcomes from Diploma unit 214: Prepare and cook bakery products

- Outcome 214.1 Prepare paste, biscuit, cake and sponge products
- Outcome 214.2 Cook and finish paste, biscuits, cakes and sponge products

Working through this chapter could also provide evidence for the following Key Skills:

C2.1, C2.2a, C2.2b, C2.3, N, N1.2, N2.2, ICT2.1, ICT2.2, ICT2.3, LP2.1, LP2.2, LP2.3, PS2.1, PS2.2, PS2.3

In this chapter you will learn how to:

Identify different types of, and uses for, paste, biscuit, cake and sponge products

Identify the main ingredients and their quality points and quantities

Prepare and cook bakery products

Check, finish and decorate cooked bakery products

Identify the temperature for the cooking, holding, service and storage of finished bakery products

You will learn to cook basic pastry products, including:

- short pastry
- sweet pastry
- suet pastry
- choux pastry
- puff pastry
- filo pastry
- convenience pastry.

Types of pastry

Pastry has many different uses from savoury starters to delicious desserts. The ingredients and proportion of fat to flour affects the pastry and what it can be used for. Generally, a soft flour with a low gluten content should be used. The exceptions are choux pastry and puff pastry. For these, flour with a high gluten content produces a better-quality final product.

There are three different ways to give pastry a lighter texture:
- Mechanical: whisking, creaming, beating, sifting.
- Chemical: baking powder, bicarbonate of soda.
- Lamination: layers of fat and pastry.

With the exception of suet paste, which is normally steamed, and some choux pastry goods which are deep-fried, pastry items are normally baked. The cooked product should be an even golden brown with a crumbly melt-in-the-mouth texture.

Pastry products include:
- **Short pastry**, commonly called short paste. This is an unsweetened paste that is normally used to make savoury dishes. When baked, short paste should be tender, easily broken and melt-in-the-mouth. Products that can be made with short paste include savoury flans (quiches), pasties and meat pies.
- **Sweet pastry**, commonly called sweet paste. It is a sweetened paste used to make sweet dishes, e.g. lemon tart and fruit tartlets.
- **Suet pastry**, commonly called suet paste. This is an unsweetened paste that is used for sweet and savoury dishes. These dishes are normally steamed. Products include: jam roly-poly, dumplings, meat puddings, steamed fruit puddings and steamed syrup pudding.
- **Choux pastry**, commonly called choux paste. This is a cooked mixture of fat, flour and water with a little sugar and salt in which eggs are beaten. It is used to make éclairs and profiteroles.
- **Puff pastry**, commonly called puff paste. This is a **laminated** paste where fat has been sandwiched between layers of dough through folding. Puff paste is versatile and used for sweet and savoury dishes. It is one of the most complicated pastries and it requires a lot of patience to make puff paste well. Savoury products using puff paste include sausage rolls, vol-au-vents,

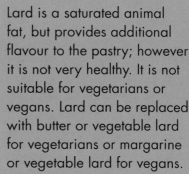

Healthy eating

Lard is a saturated animal fat, but provides additional flavour to the pastry; however it is not very healthy. It is not suitable for vegetarians or vegans. Lard can be replaced with butter or vegetable lard for vegetarians or margarine or vegetable lard for vegans.

Chef's tip

Paste that has not been used before will produce a better-eating product. Paste that has been rolled and used more than once will be tougher.

Definition

Lamination: forming layers of fat in pastry to create texture and lift as the pastry cooks.

bouches, cheese straws, beef Wellington and tops for pies. Sweet products made with puff paste include cream horns, Eccles cakes and apple turnovers.

o **Convenience pastry**: this is any bought pre-prepared pastry. It could be a powder that water is added to or pre-made pastry. Types of convenience pastry include:

- filo pastry, which is used to make baklava and strudels
- spring roll pastry, which is used to make spring rolls
- won ton pastry, which is used to make won ton and dim sum
- puff pastry
- short crust pastry.

Preparation and cooking methods

Short pastry

Short paste

soft flour	500g
cornflour	25g
salt	5g
butter	125g
lard	125g
cold water	200ml

Rubbing-in method

1 Sift the flour, cornflour and salt into a bowl.
2 Rub the butter and lard into the flour and salt.
3 Make a well. Add 160ml (80 per cent) water and mix to form a soft dough. Add more water if required.
4 Do not over-mix the paste once it has been made.
5 Wrap the pastry in cling film and allow it to rest in the fridge for at least 30 minutes.

Chef's tip

When making short paste make sure all the ingredients are cold, especially the water. The cold butter stops the water developing the gluten in the flour and makes the pastry crispier once cooked.

Did you know?

In short paste the proportion of fat to flour is 50 per cent. Recipes for other pastries will have higher proportions of fat. These pastries have different qualities and require different methods of preparation.

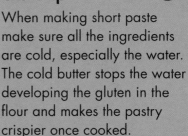

Chef's tip

Adding cornflour to the recipe softens the flour to help to produce a better-quality pastry.

Sweet pastry

There are three methods that can be used to make sweet paste. Each produces a slightly different sweet paste with its own properties and benefits. The choice of method depends on the product being made. The rubbing-in method will give a sweet paste with a close, firm texture that is easy to handle. It is generally used for apple pies, etc. Creaming method 1 will give a sweet paste with a light and loose texture. It can be difficult to handle. It is generally used for fruit flans, e.g. lemon tart and fruit tartlets. Creaming method 2 will give a sweet paste with a medium to soft texture, similar to creaming method 1, but easier to handle. It is used for similar products to creaming method 1.

Sweet paste

soft flour	500g
salt	pinch
butter	125g
caster sugar	300g
medium eggs	2

Rubbing-in method

1 Sift the flour and salt.
2 Rub the butter into the flour and salt.
3 Make a well. Break the egg into the well.
4 Add the sugar. Mix the sugar until it has dissolved.
5 Draw the flour into the egg and sugar mixture until a soft dough is achieved.

Creaming method 1

1 Make sure the butter is soft and not chilled.
2 Sift the flour and salt into a bowl.
3 Put the sugar and butter into another bowl and beat to a light and fluffy texture.
4 Crack the eggs into a smaller bowl and whisk to break the eggs down.
5 Add the egg to the butter and sugar mixture a little at a time and beat well. Too much egg will make the mixture curdle. If the mixture looks like little specks of butter it is starting to curdle. To stop this add a spoonful of the flour to the mixture and gently mix in. It is better not to add any flour if possible, though, as this starts the gluten development early.

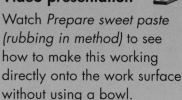

Video presentation

Watch *Prepare sweet paste (rubbing in method)* to see how to make this working directly onto the work surface without using a bowl.

Did you know?

One reason why pastry is chilled is that the gluten in the flour has been stretched and needs time to relax and spring back to its original size. If the paste is used straight away it will shrink during cooking. Chilling also makes the pastry easier to handle.

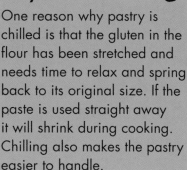

Chef's tip

The creaming method is a very good one for making sweet paste, but the paste is harder to use so it takes practice.

Chef's tip

When using a creaming method make sure the eggs are used at room temperature, as this reduces the risk of curdling.

6   When all the egg has been added, add the flour and gently mix it in until a soft dough is achieved. Do not over-mix.

7   Cover the pastry with cling film and allow it to rest in the fridge for at least 30 minutes.

Creaming method 2

1   Make sure the butter is soft and not chilled.

2   Sift the flour and salt into a bowl.

3   Crack the eggs into a smaller bowl and whisk to break the eggs down.

4   Dissolve the sugar into the eggs.

5   Cream the soft butter with half the flour until combined well.

6   Add the sugar and egg mixture.

7   Fold in the remaining half of the flour. If the pastry seems too soft, do not add any additional flour. Once the pastry has been chilled the fat will set and the pastry will be easier to handle.

8   Wrap the pastry in cling film and allow it to rest in the fridge for 30 minutes.

Chef's tip

Do not use too much extra flour when pinning the paste as this will change the balance of the ingredients and make the paste tough and harder to use.

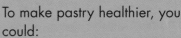

Healthy eating

To make pastry healthier, you could:

o   replace butter with margarine

o   replace some of the plain flour with wholemeal flour, or

o   use wholemeal flour instead of white flour.

Try this!

Worksheet 43

Using the three recipes above make three sweet pastries and compare them.

Chef's tip

To give a nutty flavour seeds can be added to the flour before making the pastry.

Lining a flan ring with pastry

Sweet paste is often used to make flans which are filled to make desserts. You should only roll out the required amount of pastry for one flan at a time and keep the remaining pastry chilled. Before you start lightly grease the inside of a flan ring and the tray that it is being cooked on.

How to line and finish a flan ring

① Pin out the paste until it is approximately 3mm thick. Dust the surface of the paste with flour to prevent it from sticking to itself and roll up the paste with the rolling pin inside. This helps to prevent stretching the paste.

② Transfer the paste over the flan ring. Remove the rolling pin.

Video presentation

Line a flan ring takes you through this procedure.

Chef's tip

Slide a palette knife under the pastry during pinning out to prevent the paste sticking to the table.

③ Lift the edge of the paste and gently ease the pastry into the flan ring. Do not tear the paste. Use your fingers to press the paste into the flan ring. Make sure the paste touches all of the ring and tray.

④ Roll the rolling pin over the flan ring to trim off the excess.

⑤ Pinch the paste around the flan ring.

⑥ **Crimp** the paste.

Definitions

Crimping: to give a decorative edge to pastry using forefinger and thumb or specialist tools.

Blind baking process

1 Dock the base of the pastry by using a fork or **docker** to make little holes. These will prevent air bubbles building up under the pastry during baking.

2 Line the flan with a **cartouche** and fill it with baking beans.

3 Chill the flan for 15 minutes.

4 Bake it in the oven. The oven temperature and cooking time will depend on the type of pastry, but should be roughly 200°C for 10–15 minutes.

5 When the sides are golden brown, remove it from the oven and allow it to cool slightly. Then remove the baking beans and cartouche.

6 Brush the inside of the flan with egg white to close the holes at the bottom of the flan. Return it to the oven until the base is golden brown.

Suet pastry

Suet paste

flour	500g
salt	10g
baking powder	25g
vegetable suet	250g
water	330ml

Method

1 Sift the flour, salt and baking powder into a bowl.
2 Add the suet and mix it in.
3 Make a well and add the water. Mix until combined well.
4 You can use the pastry straight away without resting or chilling.

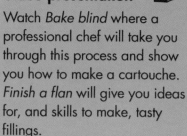

Video presentation

Watch *Bake blind* where a professional chef will take you through this process and show you how to make a cartouche. *Finish a flan* will give you ideas for, and skills to make, tasty fillings.

Definitions

Blind baking: cooking a flan case without the filling in it. The flan is lined with greaseproof paper (cartouche) and filled with baking beans. The beans help to keep the shape of the pastry during cooking.

Cartouche: a round piece of greaseproof paper used to line or cover.

Docker: a spiked tool used to put holes in flan cases to prevent them rising during baking.

Did you know?

The egg white will seal the holes so the flan case can be later filled with liquid fillings such as lemon tart or quiche mix.

Steaming

Suet paste products are normally steamed. This is a long, slow method of cookery. It does not have any negative effects on the other ingredients, e.g. steak and kidney in a pie. The suet paste needs to be covered well to prevent water getting into the paste and making it soggy.

Modern steamers are self-contained and form part of a combination oven with a steam mode. Combination ovens can be adjusted to increase the amount of humidity inside the oven and this can provide an effective lift to the pastry, as the steam assists the layer to rise. Make sure the oven is switched to steam mode before placing the suet paste item to be cooked.

Use caution. Before opening the door to any steamer, make sure no one else is close to the oven door. Turn off the oven, slowly open the door and allow the steam to escape. Then open the door fully and place the item inside. Close the door and restart the cooking process.

> **Remember!**
> Opening the door of a steamer too quickly can cause very hot water to burst out and scald you or someone else.

Choux pastry

Choux paste

butter	65g
water	185ml
salt	5g
caster sugar	7g
eggs	3
strong flour, sifted	130g
Oven temperature	200°C
Cooking time	30–40 minutes, depending on product

Method

1. Dice the butter and place it into a saucepan with the water, salt and sugar.
2. Cook until the butter melts, then bring to the boil.
3. Crack the eggs into a bowl and whisk them.
4. As soon as the mixture boils add all the flour. Mix with a spatula until all the flour has been absorbed.

> **Chef's tip**
> Do not use a metal spoon in a metal saucepan as the spoon may scratch the saucepan and this will turn the paste grey.

5 Cook out the flour or the mixture will not absorb the correct amount of egg to make the final product rise sufficiently. To do this, cook until the mixture comes away from the sides of the saucepan. Then cook for a further minute.

6 Place the mixture (**panade**) into a clean bowl to cool. Do not start adding the egg while the mixture is hot, otherwise the egg will cook before the mixture goes into the oven.

7 When the panade has cooled, place it back into the saucepan and slowly add the egg. Beat well between each addition until the paste is smooth. The eggs give the finished cases the light and open texture.

8 Continue adding the egg until a dropping consistency has been achieved. Lift up the paste on the spatula and slowly count to seven. The mixture should drop off. Add more egg if required.

9 Shape the paste as required (see below).

10 Cooking times are shown below.

Products you can make with choux paste

Éclairs

These are 3cm- to 12cm-long pastries filled with cream and decorated with chocolate or fondant. Pipe the mixture onto lightly greased trays with a medium tube and savoy bag, about 7cm long. Keep the tube at 90° to the tray.

To make sure the éclair is completely round do not let the tube touch the tray or the top of the mixture coming out of the tube. To pipe the éclair straight, only move the tube as fast as the mixture is coming out of the bag. Apply consistent pressure.

Apply an egg wash to give an even colour during cooking. Cook for approximately 15 minutes.

Paris Brests

These are choux rings filled with hazelnut cream. The rings represent the car rally route between the cities of Paris and Brest. Pipe with a medium tube. Use the same piping technique as for éclairs. Cook for approximately 15–20 minutes.

> **Did you know?**
> The main raising agent in choux paste is water. The water in the pastry gets hot during baking and turns into steam which reacts with the flour and eggs causing the choux product to rise. Keep the oven door closed for at least 10–15 minutes, otherwise the steam will escape and will not be able to react with the eggs and flour. This will result in a flat end product.

> **Definition**
> **Panade**: a paste of flour, butter and a little liquid.

Figure 16.1 Eclairs

Figure 16.2 Paris Brests

Profiteroles

These are small cases filled with chantilly or pastry cream (see page 494) and served with chocolate sauce. Pipe downwards onto lightly greased trays, to about the size of a ten pence piece. The tips will burn if they are allowed to remain proud; dampen a finger and press the mixture down to level it off. Cook for approximately 15–20 minutes.

Figure 16.3 Profiteroles

Choux pastry ring

Pipe in a large ring and decorate with flaked almonds. Bake for 20–30 minutes. Cut the ring in half. Fill with cream and dust with icing sugar.

Figure 16.4 Choux pastry ring

Swans

1 Pipe a teardrop shape. This will form the body and the wings.
2 Pipe the neck with a small nozzle in the shape of a number 2.
3 Bake for approximately 15–20 minutes.
4 Cut the teardrop shape in half. Use one half for the body.
5 Cut the other half in half again lengthways for the wings. Dip the top in chocolate.
6 Fill the body with whipped cream and insert the wings into the cream.
7 Push the neck in between the wings to complete the swan.
8 You can decorate the body with fruit and dust with icing sugar.

Choux paste fritters (*Beignets soufflés*)

These are small, walnut-sized pieces of choux paste, deep-fried in hot oil and served with apricot sauce.

Figure 16.5 Swans

1 Heat the oil to 190°C–200°C.
2 With two spoons, take uncooked choux paste about the size of a walnut and carefully drop into the hot oil.
3 Cook for approximately 10–15 minutes until brown.
4 Remove from the oil and drain well, sprinkle with caster sugar (it may be flavoured with cinnamon).
5 Serve fritters and apricot sauce separately.

How to check if choux pastry is cooked

1. Check the products are golden brown.
2. Open the oven door carefully and remove one piece from the tray, then close the door gently, leaving the rest in the oven.
3. Break open the product and touch the inside. It should feel slightly damp.
4. If it feels wet and sticky leave the products in the oven and check again in a few minutes.
5. Once cooked, cool on a cooling wire.

Storage of choux products

Filled choux cases must be stored in the fridge, unless they have been glazed with fondant icing; fondant icing will sweat in the fridge and fall off the case.

Unfilled cooked cases should be stored in airtight conditions to prevent them going soft and used within three days.

Chef's tip

If unfilled, cooked choux pastry cases go soft. Place them in an oven at 180°C (convection), 200°C or gas mark 6 (normal oven) for a few minutes to crisp up.

Puff pastry

This is one of the most complicated pastes used in patisserie. Few establishments make their own, because of the length of time needed to make it. Understanding how puff paste is made and works will help you when working with either commercial puff pastry or puff pastry made from scratch.

The proportion of fat to flour in puff pastry can be:
- 1kg strong flour to 1kg of fat – full puff.
- 1kg strong flour to 750g of fat – three-quarter puff.
- 1kg strong flour to 500g of fat – half puff.

Between 80 and 90 per cent of the fat used in puff pastry is pastry margarine. Pastry margarine has a higher melting temperature than normal margarine. This creates steam during cooking, which gives the pastry its light crispy texture.

Puff pastry is made using a lamination method which gives the pastry its distinctive layered effect when cooked.

Methods of making puff paste

There are three different methods of making puff paste:

1 **French method**: a ball of paste rolled out to a shape similar to an opened-out envelope; the pastry margarine is placed into the centre. The folds are then used to seal in the margarine. Then the paste is pinned and folded.

2 **Scotch method**: this is a quick way to make puff pastry but its quality is not as good as the French or English methods. It can also be messy. All the fat is cut into small pieces and added to the flour. Then the liquid is added and mixed to form a dough, with the fat pieces whole. The paste is then pinned out and folded.

3 **English method**: three-quarters of a rectangle of paste is covered with pastry margarine and folded in thirds to seal in the margarine. The paste is then pinned and folded as described below. This is the most popular method.

Puff paste

lemon juice	5ml
salt	5g
cold water	315ml
strong flour	500g
margarine (block)	60g
pastry margarine	440g

Method

1 Add the lemon juice and salt to the ice cold water. Stir to dissolve the salt.
2 Sift the flour into a bowl.
3 Cut the block of margarine into smaller pieces and rub it into the flour.
4 Make a well in the flour. Add the acidulated water and mix to make a soft, pliable dough – similar to short paste.
5 Gently knead the dough to a smooth paste.
6 Cut a cross in the top of the dough and cover it with an upturned bowl.
7 Allow the paste to rest in the fridge for 30 minutes. This allows the gluten to relax.
8 Follow the instructions on the next page to fold in the paste.

Remember!
A high cooking temperature is needed to create steam to make the pastry rise as the layers of margarine melt during cooking.

Video presentation
Did you know you can prepare puff paste by mixing it on the work surface rather than into a bowl? Watch *Prepare puff paste* to see how this is done. Then watch *Make puff paste (English method)*.

Did you know?
The lemon juice helps to strengthen the gluten.

How to fold puff pastry — English method

① Take a clean plastic bag about the size of an A4 sheet and open it out. Put it on the work surface. Cover two-thirds of one half of the plastic in sliced pastry margarine.

② Fold the other half of the plastic over the butter. Pin out to flatten the butter so that it fills the rest of the plastic and is of an even thickness. Put it to one side.

③ Lightly flour the work surface and place the prepared puff pastry dough onto it. Open out the corners of the cross in the top of the dough to make a square.

④ Pin out the dough into a rectangle a third longer and slightly wider that the pastry margarine.

⑤ Take the pinned out pastry margarine. Open up one side of the plastic. Put the margarine onto one end of the pastry and peel off the plastic. It should cover two-thirds of the pastry.

⑥ Fold the uncovered third of the pastry over to create 3 layers (2 pastry, 1 fat).

⑦ Use the pastry brush to remove any excess flour and fold over again creating 5 layers.

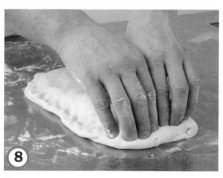

⑧ Seal the edges by pressing with your fingers.

⑨ Pin out the pastry again until it is just over 1cm thick.

10 Fold one third down. Brush away any excess flour as you go.

11 Fold the other third up and seal.

12 Turn the pastry and margarine envelope through 90° so the sealed edge is on the left. Wrap it in silicone paper and allow it to rest in the fridge for 20 minutes. This is one turn.

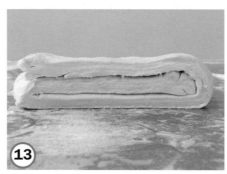

13 Repeat steps 9–12 until you have made 6 turns.

Cutting and cooking puff paste

When cutting puff paste use a guillotine method to prevent the layers of pastry causing distortion during cooking.

Do not twist pastry cutters when making vol-au-vents and bouches, as this will cause the pastry cases to rise unevenly.

Cooked puff pastry should be golden brown in colour, well but evenly risen, and have crisp texture. The bases should be cooked – turn them over and check.

Storage of puff paste

Uncooked puff paste should be covered in plastic to prevent skinning and stored in the fridge. All cooked puff pastry products not containing high-risk foods can be stored in airtight conditions to prevent them going soft. All products containing high-risk foods must be stored in the fridge.

Investigate! Worksheet 44

What does salt and lemon juice do for puff pastry? Use the internet to find five sweet and five savoury pastry recipes.

Filo paste

Filo paste is made by rolling and pulling the dough until extremely thin sheets of the paste are produced. Filo is made in a similar way to strudel dough. It is often bought because the commercial product is of a high and consistent quality.

Because it is extremely thin, filo paste needs to be kept moist or it dries and cannot be used. Melted butter is used to stick the sheets together and to keep the sheets moist until cooking. Any sheets not being used immediately should be covered with a damp cloth.

Filo paste can be used for sweet and savoury dishes. Baklava is traditionally eaten in the Middle East. It is made from layers of filo paste and walnuts which are baked and then soaked in rose flavoured stock syrup. Filo paste can also be used to make samosas.

Samosas

Samosas are popular and are the Asian equivalent to Cornish pasties. However, they are deep-fried rather than baked. Samosas are usually made with a paste similar to a short paste but filo paste can also be used. A variety of different fillings can be used. It is very easy to make a lamb filling but any dry vegetable or meat mixture can be used.

Lamb samosas

onions	1 large
green peppers	2
cooking oil	120ml
cinnamon powder	2g
chilli powder	5g
ground cumin	5g
garam masala	5g
ground black pepper	10g
minced lamb	500g
salt	to taste
frozen peas (optional)	120g
filo paste	1 packet
Makes	filling for 20+

Method

To make the filling

1 Finely dice the onions and green peppers.
2 Heat the oil in a pan. Add the onions and sweat them until softened.
3 Add the spices and black pepper to the pan and fry for 2 minutes.
4 Add the green peppers and minced lamb. Fry until cooked through.
5 Season with salt, to taste.
6 Add the frozen peas and mix gently.
7 Cool before use.

To wrap the samosas

1 Open the packet and unfold the filo paste.
2 Cut the paste lengthways into 2 or 3 strips.
3 Take 1 strip. Keep the other strip(s) covered or it will dry out.
4 Lightly water wash the top layer.
5 Put the filling near the top of the strip. Lift 2 or 3 layers of filo paste and fold them over to create a triangle.
6 Seal the edges.
7 Keep folding in the same way until you reach the bottom of the strip. Make sure the edges are sealed properly between each fold.
8 Seal the final edge to complete the samosa.
9 Heat the oil. Deep fry the samosas until crispy and golden brown.

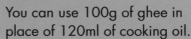

Chef's tip

You can use 100g of ghee in place of 120ml of cooking oil.

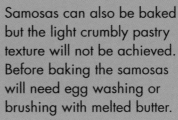

Did you know?

Samosas can also be baked but the light crumbly pastry texture will not be achieved. Before baking the samosas will need egg washing or brushing with melted butter.

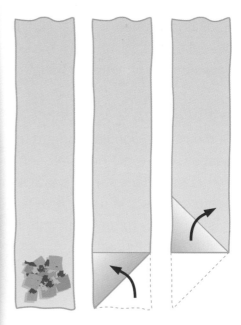

Figure 16.6 How to fold a samosa when using filo paste

Convenience pastry

Any pastry that is available commercially, including pre-made pastry and pre-mixed pastry mixes, is called convenience pastry.

Puff pastry and filo pastry are the most commonly used commercial pre-made pastes. Puff pastry can be purchased either frozen, chilled or in a pre-mixed mix. Filo pastry is available chilled or frozen and is made up of very thin sheets of pastry, which are very crispy when cooked.

Dry pre-mixed mixes normally only require liquid. The method of production should be in accordance with the manufacturer's instructions. They should be stored in airtight conditions.

Remember!
The manufacturer's storage instructions and 'use by' dates should be followed.

Test yourself!

1 When making short paste, what does the butter do to the flour?

2 Describe the creaming method for short paste.

3 When making short paste using creaming method 1, why should you not add all the egg in one go?

4 List five sweet and five savoury puff pastry products.

5 There are three ways to give pastry a lighter texture. What are they?

6 How is suet paste normally cooked?

Practice assignment task

Prepare and cook bakery products

Task

Collect a recipe example for each of the following types of pastry:

- short
- choux
- filo
- sweet
- puff
- suet.

Identify two products that can be produced from each type of pastry. Note down the main ingredient which gives the product its characteristic, e.g. nuts, fruit, eggs.

Cakes, sponges, biscuits and scones

17

This chapter covers part of the following outcomes from Diploma unit 214: Prepare and cook bakery products

- Outcome 214.1 Prepare paste, biscuit, cake and sponge products
- Outcome 214.2 Cook and finish paste, biscuits, cakes and sponge products

Working through this chapter could also provide evidence for the following Key Skills:

C2.1, C2.2a, C2.2b, C2.3, N, N1.2, N2.2, ICT2.1, ICT2.2, ICT2.3, LP2.1, LP2.2, LP2.3, PS2.1, PS2.2, PS2.3

In this chapter you will learn how to:

Identify different types of, and uses for, paste, biscuit, cake and sponge products

Identify the main ingredients and their quality points and quantities

Prepare and cook bakery products

Check, finish and decorate cooked bakery products

Identify the temperature for the cooking, holding, service and storage of finished bakery products

You will learn to cook basic cakes, sponges and scones including:

- Victoria sponge
- Genoise sponge
- Swiss roll
- Madeira cakes
- scones: plain, fruit, cheese, potato, drop
- steamed sponge.

Preparation, cooking and finishing methods

Cakes, sponges and scones are very popular either as a snack or for a formal afternoon tea. Unlike dough, the flour used for cakes, sponges and scones is soft flour and it should not be over-mixed. Over-mixing will cause a tighter crumb and make the product dry. It is important to weigh and measure the ingredients correctly and to sieve the flour before use.

Sponges, cakes and scones are available in a vast range of different textures, flavours, shapes, sizes and fillings. The texture of a cake or sponge will vary in accordance to the type and recipe used. However, they all should display the following qualities:

- a good even volume and uniform shape.
- a thin and even crust.
- not dry to the palate.
- a good flavour and aroma.

Texture and lightness are provided by different methods, which include:

- mechanical
- chemical
- physical.

Ready mixes

In some establishments ready mixes are used to save time and money or because the establishment does not have the skill base to produce cakes and sponges from scratch.

There is a huge variety of pre-mixes on the market. Most pre-mixes require the addition of liquid such as milk, water and sometimes eggs. The manufacturer's instructions must be followed.

Pre-mixes can be an excellent choice for producing cakes and sponges for those customers with special dietary needs, e.g. diabetic or gluten-free.

Weighing and measuring

o Check all ingredients are of the right quantity and quality.
o Dry ingredients should be sieved before use.
o Ensure scales are working correctly.

Methods of making cakes, sponges and scones

The different methods of making cakes and sponges:
o creaming/beating
o whisking
o rubbing-in.

Creaming/beating

The creaming/beating method is also known as the sugar batter method. It is suitable for Victoria sponges, Madeira cake, steamed sponges and slab cakes.

Cream the softened butter and sugar by mixing them together until light and fluffy. Next add the eggs a little at a time, beating well between each addition. Finally, fold in the dry ingredients.

Creaming the butter and sugar together brings air into the butter which traps the liquid. Curdling occurs when the egg is added too quickly, causing the fat and liquid to separate.

Whisking

The whisking method is used to make Swiss rolls, Genoise sponge and sponge fingers/drops.

Cold whisking: whisk together the eggs and sugar until the mixture increases three times in size. Use a mixing machine on the highest setting with the whisk attachment to speed up the process. Gently fold in the dry ingredients. The end product will have a closer texture than with the warm whisking method.

Chef's tip

When using the creaming method make sure the eggs are at room temperature to help prevent the mixture curdling.

Chef's tip

If the mixture starts to curdle before all the eggs have been added, mix in a little flour and then continue adding the rest of the egg.

Warm whisking, method 1: put the eggs into a mixing bowl. Warm the sugar on a tray in the oven until warm (do not melt the sugar). Pour the warmed sugar onto the eggs and quickly whisk together, and continue whisking until the mixture increases three times in size. Gently fold in the dry ingredients. This method can be used to save time. A mixer with the whisk attachment will also speed up the process.

Warm whisking, method 2: put the eggs and sugar into a mixing bowl and whisk over a bain-marie. Whisk until the mixture is three times the size. To test the consistency, lift the whisk and allow the mixture to fall. If the mixture sits on top of the main mixture without collapsing, then it is ready. This is known as 'ribboning'. Gently fold in the dry ingredients. This method produces a very light and airy texture.

Folding refers to ingredients being added gently and in stages, without knocking out air. The folding process usually occurs as the last stage in preparation. The following points should be remembered:

o Flour, raising agents and the other dry ingredients should be sifted before folding in.
o If adding butter it should be melted but not too hot.
o Butter should be folded into the egg at the same time as the flour.

Rubbing-in

This method involves rubbing the fat into the flour using your fingertips until the mixture has a sandy texture. Liquid and eggs are added at the end. This method is suitable for scones, rock cakes, and steamed sponges.

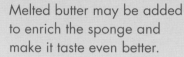

Chef's tip
Melted butter may be added to enrich the sponge and make it taste even better.

Other preparation and finishing techniques

Glazing: in cake making this means brushing the surface of the product with egg wash before baking in order to enhance its appearance and flavour, e.g. scones.

Greasing and dusting: this refers mainly to trays and cake tins that have been greased with melted butter and sometimes also dusted with a thin coating of flour to prevent the cake or sponge sticking to the tin. Grease tins or trays before starting to make the cake or sponge.

Lining: greasing a cake tin or baking tray and then lining with greaseproof or baking parchment, that has been cut to size.

Drumming when using a cake ring without a base this means adding a piece of greaseproof paper to the cake ring to prevent the cake mixture seeping out. The greaseproof paper looks like the skin of a drum.

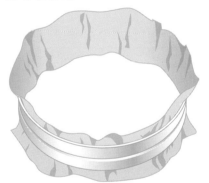  

Figure 17.1 How to drum and line a flan ring

Mixing: combining different ingredients together.

Portioning: can mean dividing a cake or sponge mixture before baking. Portioning after baking refers to dividing the finished product into equal portions.

Piping: this is mainly used when shaping sponge fingers or drops before baking to fill or decorate baked products.

Rolling: often referred to as pinning out, used, for example, in making scones.

Shaping: this means cutting or shaping out scones or sponge fingers or drops.

Baking: all cakes and sponge products must be baked as soon as they have been prepared. The longer they sit around the more air will escape and a denser end product will be produced.

Dusting: a finishing method used to decorate cooled cake and sponge products. Icing sugar or cocoa powder are used for dusting. A variety of stencils can be used to create different effects.

Filling: layering or rolling baked cakes and sponges with different creams, icing and/or jam.

Icing refers to covering the top and or sides of a cake or sponge with icing as a decoration.

Spreading and smoothing: methods used when filling or icing a cake or sponge product. A palette knife can be used to achieve a smooth, even coating or filling.

Trimming: cutting small amounts from the sides or top of a cake or sponge to create a cleaner, neater finish.

Biscuits

Biscuits help to provide texture and also help to clean the palate. They are often used to decorate desserts. They help to provide height when individual desserts are plated, thus making the dessert look more attractive. Of course, they can also be eaten alone or with a hot drink. There are many different types of biscuit – or cookie as they are known in America.

> **Try this!**　　　　　　　　　　　　　Worksheet 72
>
> List your five favourite biscuits, then say what their main flavour is and how they can be used. For example: Ginger, ginger, cheesecake base.

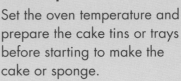

Chef's tip

Set the oven temperature and prepare the cake tins or trays before starting to make the cake or sponge.

Did you know?

A special sugar called 'neige décor' can be used to dust onto warm cakes or sponges. It does not melt when used on warm cakes or sponges.

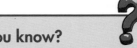

Chef's tip

To make biscuits it is best to use very soft plain flour, commonly known as biscuit or cake flour. If only strong flour is available, replace up to 50 per cent of the strong flour with cornflour. This will reduce the gluten content in the flour.

Shortbread

butter	200g
caster sugar	100g, plus extra for topping
soft plain flour	300g
Makes	12–15 biscuits
Oven temperature	200°C
Cooking time	20 minutes

Method

1 Put the butter and caster sugar in a mixing bowl. Cream together.
2 Sift the flour and add it to the mixing bowl.
3 Mix until a soft pliable paste is formed.
4 Wrap the paste in cling film and put it in the fridge for 20 minutes.
5 Take the paste out and pin it out to 5mm thick.
6 Cut the paste into your preferred shapes and transfer to a lightly greased baking tray.
7 Lightly dock the surface of each biscuit.
8 Sprinkle the surface of each biscuit with caster sugar.
9 Bake in the oven until a light golden brown.
10 Sprinkle again with caster sugar while still hot.
11 Cool slightly before transferring to a cooling wire.
12 Once cool store in an airtight container until ready for service.

Try this!

Rice flour can be used to lighten the texture of the biscuit. Replace 25g of flour with 25g of rice flour.

Different flavours and textures can also be added to the basic shortbread recipe.

For a nutty flavour add 25g of poppy seeds at the same time as the flour.

For a citrus flavour add 25g of lemon zest to the sugar and butter.

For a crumbly texture replace 50g of flour with either polenta or semolina.

Piped shortbread

caster sugar	120g
butter	360g
vanilla extract	to taste
eggs	1 medium
soft flour	240g
salt	pinch
Makes	18–20 biscuits
Cooking temperature	200°C
Cooking time	20 minutes

Method

1 Put the sugar, butter and vanilla extract in a mixing bowl. Cream together.
2 Crack the egg into a small bowl and beat. Add the beaten egg to the mixture a little at a time. Mix well between each addition.
3 Sift the flour. Add the flour and salt.
4 Mix to form a soft paste.
5 Using a Savoy bag and a medium star tube, pipe the paste into different shapes. Pipe onto a lightly greased baking tray.
6 Bake to a light golden colour.
7 Remove the shortbread from the tray and place onto a cooling wire.
8 Allow to cool.
9 Store in an airtight container until required for service.

Chef's tip

These biscuits can be decorated with glacé cherries before baking.

Did you know?

Shortbread is a well known Scottish biscuit which was traditionally pressed into decorative wooden moulds prior to baking.

Figure 17.2 A traditional shortbread mould

Viennese biscuits

Viennese biscuits

butter	240g
icing sugar	75g
egg	1 large
vanilla extract	to taste
soft flour	300g
salt	pinch
Oven temperature	200°C
Cooking time	15–20 minutes
Makes	16 biscuits

Method

1 Put the butter and icing sugar in a mixing bowl. Cream together until light and fluffy.
2 Crack the egg into a small bowl and beat. Slowly add the beaten egg to the mixture. Beat well in between each addition.
3 Add the vanilla extract.
4 Sift the flour. Add this to the mixture and gently mix to a soft paste.
5 With a Savoy bag and a medium star tube, pipe onto a lightly greased and floured tray into the required shape: rosettes, fingers, or shells.
6 Bake until a light golden brown.
7 Once cooked, allow to cool slightly and transfer to a cooling wire.
8 Dust with icing sugar prior to service.

Chef's tip

A delicious way to serve these biscuits is to dip the ends into melted chocolate and allow the chocolate to set. Next, sandwich two biscuits together with raspberry jam and butter cream. Finally, dribble chocolate over them. They can also be piped into petit four cases and served as **petit fours secs**. Use the same-sized nozzle.

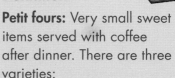

Definition

Petit fours: Very small sweet items served with coffee after dinner. There are three varieties:
o petit four secs which are dry biscuits
o petit four glaces which are finished with icing
o petit fours which are sweets like truffles and nougat.

Langue du chat biscuits

These biscuits are often used as accompaniments to mousses and ice cream. They can be wrapped around a round-handled spoon while they are still warm. They can also be used to decorate gateaux and as petits fours.

Langue du chat biscuits

butter	60g
caster sugar	60g
egg whites	2 medium
soft flour	70g
Oven temperature	215°C
Cooking time	7–10 mins
Makes	60 biscuits

Method

1 Put the butter and sugar into a mixing bowl. Cream together until light and fluffy.
2 Slowly add the egg white and beat well in between each addition.
3 Sift the flour. Add to the mixture and mix to a soft paste.
4 Using a Savoy bag and a 6mm plain tube pipe the paste into finger shapes approximately 4cm long. Pipe onto a lightly greased and floured baking tray. Allow plenty of space between the biscuits as they expand during baking.
5 Bake in the oven until the edges of the biscuits are tinged with a golden brown colour.
6 Put the biscuits on a cooling wire while they are still warm.

Biscotti

These popular Italian biscuits are traditionally served with a glass of wine. However, they are more commonly served with coffee. The biscuits are very hard because they are baked twice, so they are dipped into a cup of coffee or glass of wine to help soften them. This adaptable recipe can be used to make many different types of biscotti. (For more information visit the website 'Joy of Biscotti'. A link has been made available at www.heinemann.co.uk/hotlinks. Just follow the links and enter the express code 4103P.)

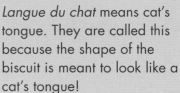

Did you know?

Langue du chat means cat's tongue. They are called this because the shape of the biscuit is meant to look like a cat's tongue!

Did you know?

Biscotti is an Italian word meaning twice-baked.

Hazelnut and chocolate chip biscotti

hazelnuts	100g
eggs	5 medium
granulated sugar	150g
vanilla extract	5g
plain flour	280g
baking powder	5g
salt	1g
powdered cinnamon	3g
chocolate chips	85g
Oven temperature	150°C
Cooking time	40–50 mins
Makes	24

Method

1. Put the hazelnuts on a baking tray and toast them in a hot oven at 200°C for a few minutes.
2. Take them out of the oven and wrap them in a cloth.
3. Wait a few minutes, then rub the hazelnuts through the cloth. This will help to remove the bitter outer skins.
4. Allow the hazelnuts to cool completely, and then chop roughly.
5. Put the eggs, sugar and vanilla extract in a mixing bowl. Whisk together.
6. Sift the plain flour, baking powder, salt and powdered cinnamon into a clean bowl.
7. Add all the flour mixture to the egg mixture. Beat well.
8. Add the chopped hazelnuts and chocolate chips. Mix to form a soft dough.
9. Put the dough on a lightly floured surface and divide it into two parts. Roll the dough into two logs.
10. Transfer onto a baking tray lined with a non-stick baking mat. Leave space between the logs as they spread during cooking.
11. Cook the logs for 35–40 minutes or until firm to the touch.
12. Remove from the oven and allow to cool for 10 minutes.
13. Using a serrated knife slice diagonally into finger-sized pieces. Arrange on the baking tray.
14. Cook for a further 10 minutes, or until firm to the touch.
15. Allow to cool and store in an airtight container until required.

Tuile biscuits

These are very thin and are often used to decorate desserts and ice creams. They also give a different texture to these dishes. Each establishment will have its favourite recipe. Different flavours can be added to the basic recipe below.

Tuile biscuits

icing sugar	450g
butter	360g
soft flour	360g
egg whites	9 medium
Oven temperature	180°C
Cooking time	5–6 mins
Makes	12 biscuits

Method

1. Sift the icing sugar. Put the icing sugar and butter into a mixing bowl. Cream together until light and fluffy.
2. Sift the flour. Add the egg white and flour to the sugar/butter mixture and mix to a soft smooth paste, like thick paint.
3. Chill the paste in the fridge for 30 minutes.
4. Spread the mixture into the pre-formed shape.
5. Place the former onto a lightly greased baking tray or a non-stick silicone mat.
6. Using either a palette knife or a pastry scraper smooth the tuile biscuit mixture into shape and smooth level with the former.
7. Remove the former.
8. Repeat steps 4 to 7 until the tray is complete.
9. Bake in the oven until light golden brown.
10. Re-shape as required while the biscuits are still warm.
11. Once cooled, store in an airtight container until service.

Pre-formed tuile biscuit shapes can be purchased commercially. However, the warm biscuits can be shaped over dishes, rolling pins, etc. They can be shaped into baskets in which to serve ice cream or sorbets.

To achieve a different flavour try one of the following options:
- add the zest of 3 lemons or oranges
- replace 50g flour with 50g ground almonds
- replace 50g flour with 50g cocoa powder.

Figure 17.3 A selection of formers

Cookies

Cookies are often mistaken for biscuits but they are much chewier. Many establishments offer home-made cookies as an alternative to biscuits.

Sultana and oat cookies

butter	120g
soft brown sugar	120g
caster sugar	120g
eggs	1 medium
soft flour	120g
baking powder	2g
rolled oats	150g
sultanas	150g
salt	pinch
vanilla extract	to taste
Oven temperature	200°C
Cooking time	15–20 mins
Makes	12 biscuits

Method

1 Put the soft brown sugar, caster sugar and butter in a mixing bowl. Cream together until light and fluffy.
2 Add all the egg and mix it in.
3 Add the remaining ingredients. Mix to form a soft paste. This is often known as cookie dough.
4 Shape into a thick sausage and wrap in cling film.
5 Chill in the fridge until the cookie dough is firm. This will make it easier to cut.
6 Cut into 12 pieces and place onto a lightly greased baking tray or non-stick mat. Allow plenty of space between the cookies as they spread during cooking.
7 Bake until light golden brown.
8 Allow to cool slightly and transfer onto a cooling wire.
9 Store in an airtight container until service.

Top marks!

When piping, e.g. biscuits, use the correct angle to the tray and tube to ensure sufficient mixture is piped. Use a constant even pressure and only move the tube as fast as the mixture is coming out. This will help you to pipe even shapes.

Sponge fingers or drops

The mixture is piped onto silicone paper in the shape of fingers or small discs, sprinkled liberally with caster sugar and baked.

Sponge fingers or drops

flour	150g
eggs	3 medium
egg yolks	35g (3–4)
caster sugar	150g
Oven temperature	200°C
Cooking time	5–10 minutes
Makes	48 fingers or drops

Method

1 Follow steps 1 to 5 of the recipe for Swiss rolls (see page 537).
2 Put the mixture into a savoy bag with a medium plain tube. Pipe into fingers approximately 8cm in length onto silicone paper or 4cm diameter circles.
3 Sprinkle liberally with caster sugar.
4 Bake until light brown. Once cooked transfer onto a cooling wire.
5 Sandwich together with whipped cream and jam or butter cream.
6 A **dredger** may be used to ensure the sugar coating is even. Place a finger onto the top when using to prevent the lid coming off.

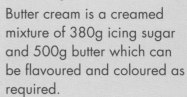

Chef's tip
Butter cream is a creamed mixture of 380g icing sugar and 500g butter which can be flavoured and coloured as required.

Did you know?
Another name for these biscuits is Biscuits à la cuillère.

Definition
Dredge: to sprinkle or coat food with flour and sugar to enhance presentation.

Sponges

Different methods can be used to make sponges but the balance of ingredients must always be correct.

Sponges can be either baked or steamed depending on the product. If baked, they should be light in texture and a golden brown colour. The amount of sugar in the recipe will determine the temperature of the oven.

Victoria sponge

Victoria sponge is made using the creaming method. When used for making sponges this method is also known as the sugar batter method.

Video presentation
Prepare a sponge cake mix shows you how to make a Victoria sponge mix for a sandwich cake. For the skills to make an excellent sponge you should also watch *Correct a sponge cake mix* and *Finish a Victoria sponge cake.*

Victoria sponge sandwich

butter	120g
caster sugar	120g
eggs	3 medium eggs
flour	120g
baking powder	5g
Oven temperature	180°C
Cooking time	25 minutes
Serves	6–8 portions

Method

1. Cream the butter and sugar in a bowl until the mixture is light and creamy.
2. Beat the eggs together in a smaller bowl and slowly add to the creamed butter mixture. Mix well between each addition.
3. Sift the baking powder and flour together in another bowl. Fold them into the sugar/butter mix. Do not over-mix.
4. Grease and flour two 15cm sponge sandwich pans.
5. Portion the mixture between the two sandwich pans and smooth with a palette knife.
6. Bake. To test if the sponge is cooked, gently press down the centre of the cake. If the cake is cooked it will pop back up again.
7. Once cooked, allow to cool slightly before turning out of the pans. Cooling will cause the sponge to shrink slightly, making it easier to remove from the pan. Turn out onto a cooling wire and allow to cool.
8. Using a palette knife, spread raspberry jam onto one of the Victoria sponge bases.
9. Pipe Chantilly cream over the jam or spread it using a palette knife.
10. Put the other Victoria sponge onto the cream and press gently.
11. Dust the surface of the cake with icing sugar.

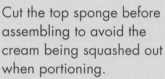

Chef's tip

Cut the top sponge before assembling to avoid the cream being squashed out when portioning.

Chef's tip

Use a doily or a cooling wire to decorate the top of the sponge. Put the doily or cooling wire on top of the sponge and then dust with icing sugar. When you remove the doily/cooling wire, it will leave a pattern.

Did you know?

The Victoria sponge was supposedly introduced by the Duchess of Bedford in the 1880s. She was one of Queen Victoria's ladies-in-waiting. Queen Victoria was so fond of this cake it was named after her and became a sensation at royal events.
Victoria sponge cake is as popular now as it was then.

Chantilly cream is lightly whipped double cream, sweetened with caster sugar and flavoured with vanilla.

Chantilly cream

fresh double cream	564ml
caster sugar	60g
vanilla extract or vanilla pod	to taste

Method

1. Put the cream in a bowl. Add the sugar and vanilla seeds to the cream.
2. Whisk together keeping the cream cold (whisk straight from the fridge, or over ice). Keep whisking until the desired consistency is achieved.
3. If using a vanilla pod, split the pod and remove the seeds, then add the seeds to the cream.

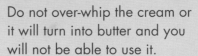

Remember!
Do not over-whip the cream or it will turn into butter and you will not be able to use it.

Basic slab cake

Basic slab cake uses a general sponge mix. Different flavours and fruit can be added to make different cakes.

Basic slab cake

flour	500g
baking powder	20g
caster sugar	500g
butter	500g
eggs	13 medium
Oven temperature	180°C
Cooking time	25–50 minutes, depending on size
Makes	35–40 pieces

Method

1. Make the sponge cake using the creaming method.
2. Grease and flour 20cm tins as required.
3. Bake in the oven.

Different types of slab cake can be made by following the ideas below.

For **Madeira cakes**, add the **zest** of four lemons. Adding the lemon at the creaming stage will enhance the lemon flavour but it can also be added with the flour.

For **cherry cakes**, add 250g of glacé cherries. To prepare the cherries, wash the sugar off them and dry them. Cut them in half and cover them with flour. Add the cherries to the cake mix at the same time as the flour. Do not over-mix as the cherries can sink to the bottom.

For **sultana cakes**, add 180g of washed and dried sultanas. Add the sultanas with the flour.

For **chocolate slab cakes**, exchange 30g of flour for 30g of cocoa powder. Sift the flour, baking powder and cocoa powder together.

Steamed sponge

Steamed sponge can be made using the creaming method or the rubbing-in method. The rubbing-in method will produce a heavier sponge and the keeping qualities will be affected.

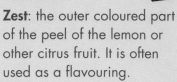

Definition

Zest: the outer coloured part of the peel of the lemon or other citrus fruit. It is often used as a flavouring.

Did you know?

Covering the cherries in flour helps to prevent them sinking.

Steamed sponge (rubbing-in method)

flour	340g
baking powder	20g
butter	170g
sugar	170g
eggs	1
milk	125ml
Cooking time	Steam for 40 minutes–2½ hours, depending on the size

Method

1 Sift the flour and baking powder together into a bowl, rub in the butter.
2 Make a well in the flour and add the sugar. Break the egg and add it to the well, then add the milk.
3 Dissolve the sugar and draw in the flour, gradually bringing in the flour from the sides into the main mixture.
4 Continue mixing until a smooth texture has been achieved.
5 Pipe into prepared moulds.
6 Steam.

Steamed sponge pudding (creaming method)

butter	250g
caster sugar	250g
eggs	4 medium
plain flour	250g
baking powder	5g
Cooking time	steam for 40 minutes–2½ hours, depending on the size
Serves	10

Method

1 Use the creaming method to achieve the desired mixture.
2 Pipe into pre-prepared moulds.
3 Steam.

Different types of steamed sponge can be made by following the ideas below:

Blackcap pudding has currants on the top.

Golden sponge pudding has golden syrup on top.

Chocolate sponge pudding is chocolate-flavoured sponge. Replace 50g of flour with 50g of cocoa powder. It is usually served with chocolate-flavoured sauce.

Jam or **Marmalade sponge pudding** has jam or marmalade on the top.

Frangipane

Frangipane is an almond sponge made using ground almonds instead of flour. The ground almonds provide texture and flavour to the sponge. Some of the almonds may be replaced with plain flour to achieve a lighter sponge. To make a lighter almond sponge, up to 50 per cent can be replaced with plain flour. Frangipane has lots of different uses, from desserts to cakes.

Frangipane

ground almonds	250g
almond essence	few drops, if needed
butter	250g
caster sugar	250g
eggs	6 medium

Method

1 Sieve the ground almonds. Almond essence can be used to enhance the flavour.
2 Follow the creaming method.

Cup cakes

The cup cake recipe can be used for small sponge cakes, fairy cakes, butterfly cake and castle cakes.

Cup cake mixture

butter	120g
caster sugar	120g
eggs	4 medium
flour	180g
Oven temperature	200°C
Cooking time	15–20 minutes
Makes	18

Method

1 Follow the creaming method.
2 Transfer the mixture into a Savoy bag with a medium tube and pipe the mixture into paper cases.
3 Bake in the oven.

Cup cake mixture can be used to make the following small cakes:

○ **Fairy cakes**: wash and dry some currants. Pipe the mixture into paper cases. Put the currants on top and bake.
○ **Butterfly cakes**: cook and cool the cakes. Cut the tops off, cut them in half. Pipe butter cream onto the cake and push the two halves of the top into the butter cream to make a butterfly.
○ **Castle cakes**: pipe the mixture into greased and floured **dariole moulds**. Bake and cool them. Dip them in boiling raspberry jam and then coat them with desiccated coconut.

Definition

Dariole mould: a small mould shaped like a flower pot.

Genoise

Genoise sponges can be used for many different types of desserts and cakes.

Genoise

flour	125g
caster sugar	125g
eggs	3 medium
melted butter	30g
Oven temperature	185°C
Cooking time	35–40 minutes
Makes	1 × 20cm ring

Method

1 Sift the flour.
2 Whisk together the sugar and eggs over a bain-marie until the mixture is thick and light. To test the consistency, lift the whisk and allow the mixture to fall. If the mixture sits on top of the main mixture without collapsing, then it is ready. This is known as 'ribboning'.
3 Once the mixture ribbons, remove it from the bain-marie and whisk gently until it cools.
4 Fold in the flour in three different stages.
5 Add the melted butter with the third flour stage. Be careful not to over-mix otherwise the air will be knocked out and the sponge will be heavy.
6 Put the mixture into the prepared cake ring. Do not press the mixture down or smooth it, as the air will be knocked out and the surface will be damaged.
7 Bake until the sponge is well risen and springy when touched. Do not slam the oven door as this can cause a vacuum and this will cause the cake to sink.
8 When it is cooked, leave the sponge in the cake ring to cool slightly.
9 Remove the cake ring and transfer the sponge onto a cooling wire.

For best results allow the sponges to rest for a few hours before use.

To make chocolate genoise, replace 25g flour with 25g cocoa powder and sift them together.

Fresh fruit gateau

Genoise sponge	1
Chantilly cream	600ml
fresh soft fruit (strawberries, raspberries, blueberries)	500g
lange du chat biscuits	25–35 biscuits
Serves	8

Method

1 Slice the Genoise sponge into three layers.
2 Spread Chantilly cream onto the first layer. Put some fruit on top.
3 Put the second layer of sponge on top. Spread cream onto the sponge. Put some fruit on top.
4 Put the final layer of sponge on top. Cover the sides and top with cream. Smooth off.
5 Decorate the sides with langue du chat biscuits.
6 Pipe scrolls of cream onto the top of the gateau to show portion sizes.
7 Decorate. The decoration should highlight the flavour of the gateau, e.g. use chocolate and raspberries.

Swiss roll

Swiss roll

soft flour	75g
cornflour	25g
eggs	4 medium
caster sugar	125g
extra caster sugar for dusting	
jam for filling	
Oven temperature	230°C
Cooking time	10–12 minutes
Makes	1 Swiss roll, suitable for 10–12 portions

Method

1 Grease, line and flour a Swiss roll tin.
2 Sift the flour.
3 Whisk the sugar and eggs together until they reach the ribboning stage.
4 Gently whisk until cold.
5 Fold in the dry ingredients in three stages, as for Genoise.
6 Bake in the oven.
7 Lightly dust a cloth or greaseproof paper with caster sugar.
8 Once cooked, turn the roll out onto the sugared cloth or greaseproof paper.
9 Remove the back paper.
10 Spread the Swiss roll thinly with beaten jam. Use a palette knife.
11 Start the rolling process with the hands and then pull the Swiss roll towards you with the aid of the cloth or paper.
12 Leave the Swiss roll wrapped in the cloth or paper as this prevents it unwrapping. Transfer to a cooling wire.
13 Once it is cool, remove the cloth or paper. Dust with caster sugar. Slice with a serrated knife to portion and serve.

To make chocolate Swiss roll, use 50g soft flour and 25g cocoa powder.

Fruit cakes

There are many varieties of fruit cake. They are made in a similar way but some are matured to improve their flavour. The most common is Rich fruit cake which has a lot of dried fruit and is coated with marzipan and either sugar paste or royal icing. It is often used for celebrations.

Rich fruit cake

This recipe is suitable for celebration cakes, e.g. wedding cakes. It needs to be matured for a minimum of six weeks to develop the flavour and make it easier to cut.

Rich fruit cake

currants	480g
sultanas	240g
raisins	240g
mixed peel (or other dried fruit)	130g
glacé cherries	130g
orange	1
lemon	1
brandy/rum	230ml
split almonds	75g
soft flour	240g
ground almonds	120g
mixed spice	5g
ground cinnamon	5g
butter	240g
soft dark brown sugar	240g
eggs	8 medium
Oven temperature	160°C
Cooking time	approx 4 hours
Makes	28cm round cake/ 25cm square cake

Method

1 Wash and dry all the dried fruit (currants, sultanas, raisins, mixed peel).

2 Wash the sugar syrup off the glacé cherries and cut them into quarters.

Chef's tip

Bake the cake in a bain-marie. This creates moisture in the oven and helps to prevent the cake drying out. Note that it also increases the cooking time.

Did you know?

Honey can replace up to 25 per cent of the sugar. Honey helps to attract moisture into the cake during the cooking and maturing processes.

3   Zest and juice the orange and lemon.

4   Put the dried fruit, the cherries, the zest and juice from the orange and lemon, the brandy/rum and the split almonds in an airtight container. Soak for 48 hours. Mix occasionally.

5   Sift the dry ingredients (flour, ground almonds, mixed spice and ground cinnamon) into a mixing bowl.

6   Grease and double line a deep cake tin with greaseproof paper.

7   Put the butter and brown sugar into a clean bowl. Cream together until light and fluffy.

8   Crack the eggs into a bowl and beat them.

9   Slowly add the beaten egg to the butter/sugar mixture. Mix well between each addition.

10   Sprinkle a quarter of the flour onto the fruit and mix. (The flour helps to stop the fruit sinking during cooking.)

11   Add the remaining flour to the butter/sugar mixture. Do not mix.

12   Add the fruit and any remaining liquid.

13   Slowly mix until all the flour has been absorbed. (It is best to mix by hand so the fruit does not break up. If you use a machine, choose the slowest speed and be careful not to over-mix.)

14   Transfer the cake mixture into the cake tin. Use the back of your hand to make a dip in the centre of the cake mixture. This helps to make the finished cake level.

15   Bake in the oven.

16   To test if the cake is cooked insert a skewer into the cake. It should come out clean and dry.

17   Once cooked, allow the cake to cool in the tin. This helps retain the shape.

16   Once cooled, remove from the tin. Leave the lining paper on the cake and wrap it in greaseproof paper and then in tin foil. Do not use cling film as it will restrict the maturing process.

Chef's tip

If the top of the cake starts to brown too much, put some paper on the top as this slows down the browning process.

Chef's tip

When you have transferred the fruit cake mixture to the tin, press it down with the back of your hand so that the mixture is concave.

Dundee cake

Dundee cake is a lighter fruit cake, flavoured with orange and decorated with split almonds. Despite its name it does not come from Dundee; recipes dating back to the 18th century can be found all over Scotland.

Dundee cake

currants	60g
sultanas	150g
mixed peel	45g
oranges, juice and zest	½
lemons, juice and zest	½
butter	150g
dark brown sugar	150g
eggs	4 medium
soft flour	150g
ground almonds	20g
milk	15g
split almonds	60g
Oven temperature	160°C
Cooking time	approx 90 minutes to 2 hours
Makes	16cm round cake

Method

1. Wash and dry the dried fruit.
2. Soak the dried fruit in the juice and zest of the orange and lemon. Leave it to soak while you prepare the cake mixture.
3. Grease and line a cake tin.
4. Put the butter and sugar into a mixing bowl. Cream together until fluffy.
5. Crack the eggs into another bowl and beat them. Slowly add the beaten egg, mixing well between each addition.
6. Sift the flour and ground almonds into a clean bowl.
7. Add the soaked fruit and flour to the butter/sugar mixture.
8. Mix gently until all the flour has been absorbed.
9. Transfer mixture to the pre-lined tin.
10. Make a dip in the middle of the mixture by dipping the back of your hand into the milk and pressing the mixture so it is higher at the edge than in the middle. Do not use too much milk or the surface will be crispy.
11. Decorate the top of the cake with split almonds.
12. Bake in the oven.
13. Once cooked, allow to cool in the cake tin on a cooling wire.
14. Once cooled, remove from the tin. Leave the lining paper on the cake and wrap it in greaseproof and then in tin foil.
15. Store in an airtight container. It will keep for up to two weeks.

Genoa cake

Genoa cake

currants	120g
sultanas	90g
mixed peel	30g
glacé cherries	120g
butter	120g
caster sugar	120g
eggs	4 medium
soft flour	180g
Oven temperature	180°c
Cooking time	1 hour, 15 minutes
Makes	16cm cake

Method

1. Wash and dry the dried fruit (currants, sultanas and mixed peel).
2. Wash the syrup off the cherries. Dry them and cut into quarters.
3. Grease and line a cake tin.
4. Put the butter and sugar into a mixing bowl. Cream together until light and fluffy.
5. Crack the eggs into another bowl and beat them. Slowly add the beaten egg to the butter/sugar mixture, mixing well after each addition.
6. Sift the flour. Add the flour, dried fruit and cherries. Mix gently until all the flour is absorbed.
7. Transfer to the pre-lined tin and bake.
8. Once cooked, allow to cool in the tin on a cooling wire.
9. Store in an airtight container. Use within 3–4 days.

Chef's tip

Always line a cake tin properly. If the paper is crinkled it will create a pattern on the cake. It will then be very difficult to achieve a smooth finish with marzipan and sugar paste.

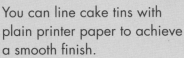

Did you know?

You can line cake tins with plain printer paper to achieve a smooth finish.

Try this!

To help prevent the edges of the cake going brown and crispy, line the outside of the cake tin with brown paper.

Scones

Scones are very popular. Some scones are baked, other cooked on a griddle, and some are even fried and eaten for breakfast.

The recipe for plain scones can be adapted to different types of scone with the addition or removal of different items.

Kneading is a technique used in the preparation of scones to combine ingredients after rubbing-in. Unlike the kneading of bread dough, it must be carried out in a gentle manner. Scones are made with soft flour so a full kneading process would ruin the final product. See Chapter 18 to compare techniques.

Plain scones

plain flour	500g
baking powder	30g
salt	good pinch
butter	100g
caster sugar	100g
egg	1 medium
milk	230ml
Oven temperature	225°C
Baking time	15–20 minutes
Makes	16 scones using a 5–6cm pastry cutter

Method

1 Sift the flour, salt and baking powder together into a bowl.
2 Rub in the butter.
3 Make a well. Add the sugar to the well.
4 Break egg into a jug. Add the milk.
5 Add the egg and milk mixture to the well and dissolve the sugar.
6 Draw in the flour and butter and continue mixing until a soft dough is achieved. Do not over-mix at this stage, but gently knead to smooth off the dough.
7 Pin out on a lightly dusted floured surface to a thickness of approximately 2cm.
8 Cut out using a scone cutter. Transfer onto lightly greased trays.
9 Knead the trimmings into a ball, pin it out and cut out as before.
10 Egg wash the tops and allow the items to relax for 15 minutes.
11 Put into the oven. To test if they are cooked, tap the bottom of the scone – it should sound hollow.
12 Allow to rest for ten minutes and transfer onto cooling wires.

Use these suggestions to make different types of scones:

o **Sultana scones**: add 125g washed and dried sultanas. Add them at the same time as the flour, before the liquid.

o **Cheese scones:** use 125g of grated cheddar cheese instead of sugar. Add a teaspoon of English mustard powder and a teaspoon of cayenne pepper. The spices bring out the flavour of the cheese.

o **Treacle scones**: replace 50g of the sugar with 50g of black treacle. Add the treacle with the milk.

o **Wholemeal scones**: replace 375g of flour with 375g of wholemeal flour. A little more milk may be required.

o **Potato scones**: replace up to 50 per cent of the flour with cold mashed potato and omit the sugar. Pin out to a thickness of 0.5cm and cook on a lightly oiled griddle.

Drop scones

Drop scones are more like a pancake and in some places they are known as Scotch pancakes. Traditionally they are cooked on a griddle.

Drop scones can be served with butter and jam.

> **Try this!** Worksheet 45
>
> **What methods are used to produce:**
> o *Victoria sponge*
> o *Swiss roll*
> o *steamed sponge*
> o *sponge fingers*
> o *genoise sponge*
> o *frangipane*
> o *plain scones*
> o *rock cakes?*

Drop scones

plain flour	250g
baking powder	5g
caster sugar	10g
eggs	2 medium
milk	200ml
Makes	12–18

> **Chef's tip**
> As an alternative, add 75g soaked sultanas to the drop scone batter.

Method

1 Sift the flour and baking powder together.
2 Make a well and add the sugar, milk and eggs.
3 Whisk to a thick batter.
4 Heat a lightly oiled griddle or a heavy-based frying pan.
5 Drop sufficient batter onto the griddle to make a circle approximately 5cm in diameter.
6 As the scone cooks, the surface will dry out. Once this has been achieved turn the scone over using a palette knife.
7 Once cooked remove from griddle and serve hot. The scones should be a golden brown colour.

Rock cakes

Rock cakes are similar to scones but are more rustic.

Rock cakes

plain flour	500g
baking powder	30g
salt	3g
butter	125g
currants, washed and dried	60g
mixed peel, washed and dried	25g
caster sugar	60g
egg	1
milk	225ml
eggs for egg wash	2
granulated sugar	25g
Oven temperature	225°C
Baking time	15 minutes
Makes	16 cakes

Method

1 Sift the flour, salt and baking powder together.
2 Rub in the butter until a sandy texture is achieved.
3 Add the dried fruit and mix.
4 Make a well in the centre and add the sugar. Add the egg and milk and dissolve the sugar.
5 Draw in the flour and make a soft dough. Do not over-mix.
6 Break off evenly sized pieces and place onto a lightly greased tray. Do not make them too uniform.
7 Brush the rock cakes with egg wash and sprinkle them with granulated sugar.
8 Bake until golden brown. Once cooked remove from the oven and allow to cool slightly. Then transfer them to a cooling wire.

Test yourself!

1 How many grammes are there in one kilogramme?

2 How many millilitres are there in one litre?

3 What protein is developed in flour during kneading?

4 What effect will it have in cakes?

5 Why is baking powder used?

Practice assignment task

Prepare and cook bakery products

Task

Produce an afternoon tea menu. Include as many of the following as possible: shortbread, scones, Genoise, sponge, Swiss roll, fruit cake. Suggest suitable accompaniments/fillings. Identify other suitable menu items to complete the menu.

Bread and dough products

18

This chapter covers part of the following outcomes from Diploma unit 214: Prepare and cook bakery products

- Outcome 214.3 Prepare fermented dough products
- Outcome 214.4 Cook and finish fermented dough products

Working through this chapter could also provide evidence for the following Key Skills:

C2.1, C2.2a, C2.2b, C2.3, N, N1.2, N2.2, ICT2.1, ICT2.2, ICT2.3, LP2.1, LP2.2, LP2.3, PS2.1, PS2.2, PS2.3

In this chapter you will learn how to:

Identify different types of and uses for dough

Identify the main ingredients and their quality points and quantities

Prepare and cook bakery products

Check, finish and decorate cooked bakery products

Identify the temperature for the cooking, holding, service and storage of finished bakery products

You will learn to make bakery products, including:

- buns
- bread
- soda bread
- focaccia bread
- pizza dough
- pitta bread.

Bread and dough products

People have been eating bread for thousands of years. In every culture in all parts of the world bread is a staple part of the diet. Whether it is Arabian flat bread or tiger bread the fundamental ingredients of flour, yeast, salt, and water do not change, even if different flavours and production methods are introduced.

These are some examples of bread and dough products:

- **Bread dough**: unsweetened yeast dough. Suitable for bread rolls, bread loaves and speciality breads such as focaccia bread.
- **Bun dough**: sweetened yeast dough that is enriched with butter, sugar and eggs. Suitable for Chelsea buns, hot cross buns, Bath buns, Swiss buns, jam doughnuts and ring doughnuts.
- **Soda bread**: bread made using bicarbonate of soda as the raising agent rather than yeast. Bicarbonate of soda is a chemical. Adding liquid causes a chemical reaction which means that the bread does not need time to prove before cooking. Bicarbonate of soda will start working as soon as it's mixed into the bread, so it does not need to be left to prove. The texture of the bread is firmer. Examples are white soda bread, wholemeal soda bread and soda farls (flat soda bread).
- **Naan bread**: can be made with yeast, bicarbonate of soda, baking powder or self-raising flour. It is classified as Indian flat bread and is traditionally cooked in a very hot clay oven called a tandoor oven. Traditionally, a tandoor oven is made from clay and heated by charcoal. Naan bread is only proved once. It is not proved again before cooking, unlike traditional bread.
- **Pizza dough**: unsweetened yeast dough made with olive oil which originates from Italy.
- **Pitta bread**: unsweetened yeast dough. It is classified as flat bread and is traditionally baked in a hot clay oven and the heat gives it a pocket. Best known in Turkey and Greece but served all over the Middle East. It is often stuffed with vegetables and meats.

Figure 18.1 Bread baking in a modern tandoor oven

Try this! Worksheet 42

Draw a picture of the following loaves: sandwich, farmhouse, plait, cob, cottage and bloomer. Then find examples of ethnic and speciality breads. Say what type of bread they are and give their country of origin, e.g. naan, lightly leavened, India.

Investigate!

Find out what types of bread your establishment uses.

Preparation methods

Mixing the dough

First, carefully weigh and measure the ingredients and sift the flour. Next, prepare the yeast. There are two main ways that yeast is used to produce carbon dioxide in bread and bun products:

○ sponging
○ bulk fermentation time.

Sponging

Sponging is a method where the yeast is allowed to produce carbon dioxide before it is added to the bulk of the flour. Sponging is the fastest method for making bun and bread products and will result in a light and open dough texture.

Put the tepid liquid into a bowl. Dissolve the yeast and add the sugar. Add enough flour from the recipe to mix to a batter (the consistency of paint). This mixture is then allowed to ferment for 10–15 minutes before being added to the rest of the ingredients.

Bulk fermentation time

In this method, the yeast liquid is mixed with all of the flour at once.

Bulk fermentation time (BFT) describes the length of time that the dough proves from the end of the mixing time until the **scaling** time. It can take 1–18 hours, depending on the recipe and the dough temperature. The end product will have a tighter texture with an improved flavour.

Put the tepid liquid into a bowl. Dissolve the yeast and add the sugar. Mix. Add this mixture to all of the flour and mix to form a dough. Then allow to prove.

For both methods, the water used to mix the dough should be at body temperature (37°C). If the temperature is too high (above 49°C) it will kill the yeast.

The amount of liquid suggested in the recipes is only approximate. The actual amount of liquid needed will vary, depending on the quality of the flour. For example, the gluten content can result in more or less liquid being needed.

Remember!
All types of flour must be sifted. The ideal type of sieve is a drum sieve. Sieving ensures that flour lumps are broken up, leading to a better leavened product. It also identifies physical contamination.

Figure 18.2 A drum sieve

Definition
Scaling: cutting and weighing the dough into the required size, e.g. for bread rolls scale dough into 60g pieces.

Chef's tip
To test the temperature of the water, place a finger into the water. If the water feels warm or cold, the water is not at the correct temperature.

Kneading

Once all the ingredients have been combined, dough is **kneaded** by working it with the ball of the hand or by machine. This helps to develop the gluten in the dough. Strong gluten results in a better structure to hold the carbon dioxide produced by the yeast.

How to knead dough

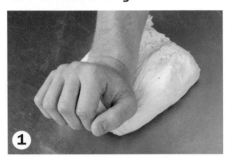

① Use the heel of your hand to push the dough down and out.

② Lift the dough back with your fingertips.

Proving

Proving allows the gluten in the flour to relax after it has been stretched by the kneading process. Insufficient proving will make the dough difficult to shape and it will contract during rolling, leading to a close, heavy texture.

There are several stages when proving dough:

- **First prove**: after sponging, cover and prove in a warm place until the yeast mixture starts to bubble and looks like honeycomb.
- **Second prove**: after the kneading process, cover and prove the dough in a warm place until double in size.
- **Final prove**: after scaling and moulding but before baking, dough products are proved, usually in a prover, until they double in size.

Dough products can be proved without a **prover** by lightly sprinkling the surface of the dough products with water and covering them with oiled plastic and then placing them somewhere warm. A new plant spray bottle with a fine spray will help to give a light and even coating of water.

It is important to cover dough products when they are proving to prevent **skinning**.

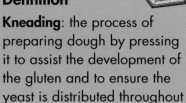

Definition

Kneading: the process of preparing dough by pressing it to assist the development of the gluten and to ensure the yeast is distributed throughout the dough.

Definition

Prove: to allow the yeast to develop carbon dioxide in the dough to make it rise before baking.

Prover: a cabinet that creates heat and moisture, helping dough products to rise evenly, and assists in preventing products from drying out and skinning.

Skinning: when dough is left uncovered and the surface of the dough starts to dry out and oxidise. If this is then mixed into the dough it will leave dry pieces of dough in the finished product.

Remember!

Sponging method uses first prove, second prove and a final prove. BFT method uses second prove and final prove.

Definition

Oxidise: a chemical reaction when oxygen causes the surface of the dough to dry out.

Knocking back and scaling the dough

Knocking back means removing the air produced during proving. It is done by kneading the dough again. This ensures the yeast is working before shaping and provides an even texture during baking. Removing all the air also assists in shaping the dough after scaling. The dough is now ready to be scaled, or cut and weighed, into pieces of the required size.

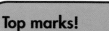

Top marks!
Weigh scaled dough pieces to assist in portion control.

Hand shaping

Shaping the dough is also known as 'moulding'. Hand shaping does take some practice but with time many different shapes can be achieved. The first two shapes to master are rounds and fingers.

How to shape rounds or balls

Mastering this shape will help you to make other shapes correctly.

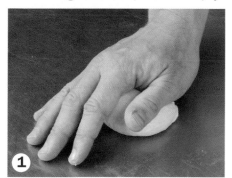

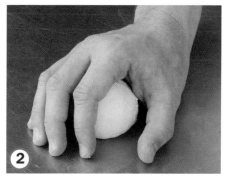

1 Take a scaled piece of dough and knead it briefly to remove any air. Then put the dough onto the work surface and cover it with the palm of your hand. Start to slowly rotate your hand while pressing down quite hard.

2 As the ball forms, slowly cup your hand until a nice smooth ball is achieved. The surface of the dough must be smooth with no cracks otherwise the roll will crack during proving and cooking.

3 Once the shape has been achieved, transfer the completed roll to a baking tray, lined with silicone paper, and repeat the process with the other pieces of dough. Allow them to prove until double their size. Unless you are using a steam prover, cover with oiled plastic to prevent skinning.

How to shape fingers

1 Shape as for rounds until the smooth ball has been achieved.
2 Roll the piece backwards and forwards until a finger shape has been made.
3 Transfer onto a baking tray and allow to prove.

Once the shaping of rounds and fingers has been mastered, there are many different shapes that can be achieved, including knots, double knots, three-strand plaits, five-strand plaits, twists, ropes, brioche shapes.

Cooking and finishing methods

Finishing methods applied before cooking

Before baking a product you may wish to apply a finish to the dough.

○ **Egg wash**: Use an egg wash to glaze dough products. Beat an egg well. Thin it down with a little milk or water if necessary. Brush onto the surface of products to give them a shine and a golden brown colour during baking. Dough products which can be egg-washed before baking include bread rolls, bread loaves, Bath buns. Dough products should be egg-washed before the final prove because they are fragile once proved and can collapse if touched.

○ **Toppings**: to give dough products an attractive finish, sprinkle them with different seeds, e.g. sesame, poppy, sunflower or pumpkin seeds, or oats.
For a more rustic look, dust bread dough products with flour.

○ **Cutting**: to achieve a different effect, make small cuts in the surface of the rolls or bread. Make the cuts before the final prove using a small sharp knife or a pair of scissors. Cutting the surface allows the cuts to expand prior to baking and gives the products an attractive finish.

Steaming

Before certain dough products are baked, steam is used to give them a high gloss and a crust, e.g. French sticks or crusty rolls.

Steam should be introduced into the baking chamber before you load the proved dough products. Some ovens have a timer which adds steam automatically, normally for 30 seconds, after which

Remember!
Do not allow the rolls to over-prove (no more than double their size) or they will collapse.

Figure 18.3 Bread rolls can be made in many attractive styles

Try this!
Cut an attractive pattern into bread roll dough using a pair of scissors or a small knife.

baking will start. To introduce steam to a normal oven, put a deep tray on the base of the oven 20 minutes before you want to cook something. When you are ready to cook, open the door and carefully pour 1 litre of cold water into the tray. Close the door for a few seconds then load the dough and bake as normal.

Modern combination ovens can be programmed to provide a mixture of steam and dry heat. Turn off the steam 2 minutes after loading the dough products and bake as normal.

Effects on the dough

The steam condenses on the surface of the dough causing the surface temperature to increase; this causes the flour starch to swell with water and fix the crumb structure. During baking this thin film of gelatinised starch forms a crust with a high gloss.

> **Remember!**
> Steamed dough products do not need glazing prior to baking.

Baking

Dough products are baked after the final prove. Times and oven temperatures are as follows:

o Bread rolls:
   – 230°C for 20–25 minutes
   – should be golden brown and when tapped on the bottom sound hollow.
o Bread loaves:
   – 230°C for 10 minutes or until a crust has developed, then reduce to 200°C for 25–45 minutes, depending on size
   – should be golden brown and when tapped at the bottom sound hollow.
o Bun dough:
   – 200°C for 20–25 minutes (a lower temperature is required due to the higher, sugar, fat and egg content in bun dough)
   – should be golden brown.

> **Healthy eating**
> o Fats could be replaced with low-fat products or vegetable oils.
> o Sugars could be replaced with natural sweeteners like honey.
> o Salt could be replaced with a low-sodium salt.

Cooling baked dough products

To cool bread rolls or bun dough:

o Remove from the oven, and allow to cool for a few minutes.
o Transfer them onto a cooling wire or rack. If products are left on the tray to cool down, the base of the rolls will go soggy as they cool down and create steam.

Flat breads

Naan and pitta bread are classed as flat breads. These types of bread do not require proving for a second time before cooking as they are generally thin and cooked at a high temperature.

Pitta bread

strong white flour	500g
sugar	30g
salt	10g
fresh yeast	25g
olive oil	10ml
tepid water	250ml
Oven temperature	240°C
Cooking time	20 minutes
Makes	8

Method

1 Sift flour, sugar and salt into a bowl, and mix.
2 Dissolve the yeast in a small amount of the water.
3 Add the oil and enough water to make a soft pliable dough.
4 Knead for ten minutes until smooth. Wrap in cling film and rest for 30 minutes.
5 Preheat the oven to 240°C.
6 Divide the dough into 100g balls and pin these out into flat oval shapes.
7 Place on baking sheets. Bake until the dough puffs up.
8 Remove from the oven and leave to cool a little. After ten minutes the bread will slowly collapse.

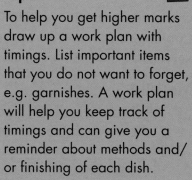

Top marks!

To help you get higher marks draw up a work plan with timings. List important items that you do not want to forget, e.g. garnishes. A work plan will help you keep track of timings and can give you a reminder about methods and/ or finishing of each dish.

Chemically raised bread

Bread made without yeast but with a chemical raising agent is a good alternative when time is short.

Soda bread

plain flour	340g
salt	5g
bicarbonate of soda	5g
buttermilk	290ml
Oven temperature	200°C
Cooking time	30 minutes

Method

1 Preheat the oven to 200°C.
2 Sift the flour, salt and bicarbonate of soda into a large bowl and stir.
3 Make a well. Pour in the buttermilk and mix quickly to form a soft dough.
4 Turn onto a lightly floured surface and knead briefly.
5 Form into a round and flatten the dough slightly before placing it on a lightly floured baking sheet.
6 Cut a cross on the top and bake for about 30 minutes or until the loaf sounds hollow when tapped. Cool on a wire rack.

Top marks!
Take care when weighing ingredients. Take the time to ensure each recipe is weighed correctly, as this will lessen the chance of things going wrong.

Bun dough

Bun dough can be made using either the sponging method or the BFT method (see page 562).

Basic bun dough – sponging method

strong flour	600g
milk powder	15g
salt	5g
fresh yeast	40g
tepid water	approx. 300ml
caster sugar	75g
soft butter	60g
egg	1 medium

Video presentation
Prepare bun dough shows you an alternative method of making this product. Which do you prefer?

Method

1 Sift the flour, milk powder and salt into a bowl.
2 Put the yeast into a smaller bowl. Dissolve the yeast with half the amount of tepid water and half the amount of sugar.
3 Make a well in the centre of the flour and pour in the diluted yeast mixture. Use a wooden spoon to draw some of the flour from the sides and mix it with the yeast water. The mixture should resemble a thick pancake batter.
4 Dust the surface with some flour from the sides of the bowl and cover with a cloth or a tray.
5 Put in a warm place until the yeast starts to bubble. This will take approximately 10–15 minutes.
6 Add the egg, soft butter, remaining sugar and water and mix. Gradually draw in all the rest of the flour, until a soft pliable dough is achieved.
7 Place onto a lightly floured surface and knead until smooth and free from stickiness.
8 Cover and prove, then knock back and use as required.

Basic bun dough – BFT method

strong flour	600g
salt	5g
soft butter	60g
milk	300ml
caster sugar	75g
egg	1 medium
fresh yeast	40g

Method

1 Sift the flour and salt into a bowl.
2 Rub the butter into the flour.
3 Place the milk in a pan, warm to blood temperature. Add the yeast and dissolve it. Add half the sugar to this mixture.
4 Make a well in the centre of the flour. Add the remaining sugar. Crack the egg onto the sugar and mix to dissolve the sugar.
5 Add the yeast mixture and mix, making sure the sugar has dissolved. Mix in the flour from the sides until a soft pliable dough is achieved.
6 Knead and prove. Use as required.

Did you know?

The egg used in these recipes has two functions. First to help moisten and enrich the dough, secondly to give the dough a slight yellow colour. This colour helps to turn the dough to a nice golden brown during cooking.

Chelsea buns

basic bun dough recipe	
butter, melted	to brush dough
dark soft brown sugar	30g
mixed spice	4g
sultanas	120g
currants	120g
mixed peel	30g
Oven temperature	200°C
Makes	10

Method

1. Follow the basic bun dough recipe.
2. Roll into a rectangle approximately 30cm × 20cm.
3. Brush with melted butter.
4. Sprinkle with the sugar.
5. Sprinkle with the mixed spice.
6. Sprinkle with sultanas, currants and mixed peel.
7. Roll up along the short end like a Swiss roll. Brush with melted butter on the outside.
8. Cut into 10cm × 3cm pieces.
9. Turn the cut pieces so you can see the filling when put onto the table. Put into individual moulds which have been buttered and floured or a large cake ring, allowing space in between to prove.
10. Prove until doubled in size.
11. Bake until golden brown.
12. Allow to cool slightly before turning out the moulds onto a cooling rack.
13. While still warm glaze with bun wash.

Bun wash

caster sugar	100g
milk or water	100ml

Method

1. Put the ingredients in a pan and boil for about five minutes on a medium heat.
2. Glaze the warm buns with the hot bun wash.

Swiss buns

basic bun dough

Oven temperature	200°C
Makes	20

Method

1 Follow the recipe for the basic bun dough.
2 Scale the dough into 60g pieces and roll into finger shapes.
3 Place onto a greased baking tray.
4 Prove in a warm place until doubled in size.
5 Bake until golden brown.
6 Allow to cool slightly before placing onto a cooling rack.
7 When cooled, glaze with fondant icing or water icing.

Water icing

icing sugar	200g
water	30ml

Method

1 Sift the icing sugar into a bowl.
2 Add the water and beat using a wooden spoon.

Jam doughnuts

basic bun dough

caster sugar	to roll
red jam	

Method

1 Prepare the basic bun dough.
2 Scale 60g pieces and roll into round rolls.
3 Place onto an oiled tray.
4 Prove in a warm place until doubled in size.
5 To deep-fry the doughnuts, heat the oil to 180°C.
6 Coat a wide spatula in the hot oil. Place it under the doughnuts and lift them into the oil.
7 Turn over with a spider, and remove using a spider when golden brown on both sides.
8 Place onto a cooling rack to allow excess to drip off.

Did you know?
Swiss buns can be filled with fresh whipped cream and/or fruit to make cream buns.

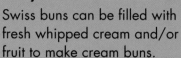

Video presentation
Follow these goodies being made step-by-step and learn more about fondant in *Make iced Swiss buns*.

Chef's tip
Add 20g cocoa powder to make chocolate icing.

Chef's tip
As an alternative, you can glaze doughnuts with water icing or chocolate icing and fill them with whipped cream.

Healthy eating
Replace the sugar coating on doughnuts with icing sugar.

A machine can be used to inject doughnuts with jam. The machine has a hopper that contains the jam and two injection points that insert the jam into the centre of the doughnut.

If no machine is available use a piping bag. Fill the piping bag with softened jam and make a hole into the doughnut with something like the end of a spatula. Give the spatula a wiggle to open the inside of the doughnut a little. Remove the spatula and push the piping bag into the space. Squeeze the jam using an even pressure to fill the gap. Remove the piping bag slowly.

Healthy eating
Use a vegetable-based cream instead of double cream.

Test yourself!

1. Why should strong flour be used to make bread and bun products?

2. What gives flour its strength?

3. Describe the sponging method used for proving.

4. What chemical is used to make soda bread rise?

5. List three different bun dough products that are deep-fried.

6. What are bread rolls glazed with before cooking?

7. What temperature should the liquid be to enable the yeast to start producing carbon dioxide?

8. How many proving steps are there when using the BFT proving method?

9. List three toppings that could be used to give bread loaves a pleasing look.

10. What is meant by the term 'scaling'?

Practice assignment task

Prepare and cook bakery products

Task

Prepare a report covering different types of:
○ flour
○ bread
○ additional commodities used in the production of bread.

Investigate different types of bread from other countries. Choose three to describe in more depth.

Index